Psychoanalytic Intersections

Psychoanalytic Intersections examines the influence and legacy of the Austen Riggs Center, one of the oldest psychoanalytically oriented psychiatric hospitals in America, and home of the Erikson Institute for Education and Research.

Former Erikson scholar Elise Miller brings together the work of a wide range of clinicians and scholars who have participated in the Erikson Institute's Visiting Scholars Program. Representing a variety of disciplines, departments, and methodologies, the contributors exemplify the cutting edge of interdisciplinary work at the intersections of psychoanalysis and academia, psychiatry, psychology, psychoanalysis, and hospital and private practice settings. For this unique collection, each contributor has selected a piece of their published work to be presented with a new afterword reflecting on how time spent in a clinical setting shaped their thinking and writing. These personal narratives also offer a unique opportunity to consider how this kind of scholarship was produced, and what it can teach us about the disciplinary crossings and migrations of applied psychoanalysis, especially as it continues to extend its insights and influences out into the world around us.

Psychoanalytic Intersections will be of great interest to psychoanalytic clinicians, psychiatrists, and psychologists engaged in cross-disciplinary work, and to academics and scholars of interdisciplinary psychoanalytic studies.

Elise Miller is Adjunct Associate Professor at Saint Mary's College of California and a clinician in private practice. She has published articles in literary journals and in the *Journal of the American Psychoanalytic Association*, winning the American Psychoanalytic Association Peter Loewenberg Essay Prize in Psychoanalysis and Culture two years in a row for her work on the writing process.

Psychoanalytic Intersections

Selected Writing of the Austen Riggs
Center Erikson Institute Visiting
Scholar Program

Edited by Elise Miller

Routledge
Taylor & Francis Group

LONDON AND NEW YORK

Designed cover image: Elise Miller

First published 2024
by Routledge
4 Park Square, Milton Park, Abingdon, Oxon OX14 4RN

and by Routledge
605 Third Avenue, New York, NY 10158

Routledge is an imprint of the Taylor & Francis Group, an informa business

British Library Cataloguing-in-Publication Data
A catalogue record for this book is available from the British Library

ISBN: 9781032345291 (hbk)
ISBN: 9781032345284 (pbk)
ISBN: 9781003322627 (ebk)

DOI: 10.4324/9781003322627

Typeset in Times New Roman
by codeMantra

For Madeleine and Isabel

Contents

99999999

Contributors

Daniel Burston, **PhD,** Associate Professor of Psychology at Duquesne University, is the author of numerous books and articles on psychoanalysis and society, including *The Legacy of Erich Fromm* (1991), *The Wing of Madness: The Life and Work of R.D. Laing* (1996), *Erik Erikson and the American Psyche: Ego, Ethics and Evolution* (2007), *A Forgotten Freudian: The Passion of Karl Stern* (2016), and *Anti-Semitism and Analytical Psychology: Jung, Politics and Culture* (2021).

Anne C. Dailey, **PhD,** is Evangeline Starr Professor of Law at the University of Connecticut School of Law. She teaches and writes in the areas of constitutional law, children and law, and psychoanalysis and the law. Her book, *Law and the Unconscious: A Psychoanalytic Perspective* (Yale Univ. Press 2017), won several awards.

Françoise Davoine, **PhD,** is a psychoanalyst in private practice in Paris who specializes in trauma and psychosis. A retired faculty member of the *Ecole des Hautes Etudes en Sciences Sociales*, Dr. Davoine presents internationally and is the author of many books and articles, including *Pandemics, Wars, Traumas and Literature,* a study of frontline medical workers during the Covid pandemic.

Dr. Stacey Dearing, **PhD,** is currently Teaching Assistant Professor of English at Siena College. Her essay on Dorothy May Bradford was awarded the 2021 Richard Beale Davis Prize for the best essay published in *Early American Literature.* Her work has also appeared in the *Journal of Medical Humanities.*

M. Gerard Fromm, **PhD,** is Fellow of the American Board and Academy of Psychoanalysis and Distinguished Faculty member and former Director of the Erikson Institute of the Austen Riggs Center. Fromm is the author of numerous publications, including the forthcoming co-edited volume, *We Don't Speak of Fear: Large Group Identity, Societal Conflict and Collective Trauma.*

Jean-Max Gaudillière was a psychoanalyst in Paris for 30 years and a professor at the *Ecole Des Hautes Etudes en Sciences Sociales* until his death in 2015.

Lewis Hyde, PhD, now retired, taught English for many years at Kenyon College. His published work includes *The Gift*, a defense of the non-commercial portion of artistic practice, and *Trickster Makes This World,* an argument for the disruptive intelligence that keeps any culture lively and open to change.

Mark Lipton, PhD, is Professor Emeritus of Management at Parsons School of Design and The New School in New York City. Mark Lipton has advised Fortune 500 corporations, think tanks, philanthropies, not-for-profits, and start-ups. His work has been published in books and journals like *Harvard Business Review*, *MIT Sloan Management Review*, and *Journal of Management Consulting.*

Nancy McWilliams, PhD, teaches at Rutgers University's Graduate School of Applied & Professional Psychology and practices in Lambertville, New Jersey. She is the author of *Psychoanalytic Diagnosis* (1994, rev. ed. 2011); *Psychoanalytic Case Formulation* (1999); *Psychoanalytic Psychotherapy* (2004); and *Psychoanalytic Supervision* (2021).

Elise Miller, PhD, is Adjunct Associate Professor at Saint Mary's College of California and a clinician in private practice. She has published articles in literary journals and in the *Journal of the American Psychoanalytic Association,* winning the American Psychoanalytic Association Peter Loewenberg Essay Prize in Psychoanalysis and Culture two years in a row for her work on the writing process.

Diane O'Donoghue, PhD, is the Director of the Program for Public Humanities at the Jonathan M. Tisch College of Civic Life at Tufts University, where she has chaired the Department of Visual and Material Studies. She is the current chair of the Division for Interdisciplinary Psychoanalysis at the Boston Psychoanalytic Society and Institute and also directs the Ecker Fellows Program there.

Ann Marie Plane, PhD, is Professor Emerita of History at the University of California, Santa Barbara. An expert in North American colonialism, she holds a PsyD and was a training analyst at the Institute of Contemporary Psychoanalysis (Los Angeles). The author of two books and an anthology, she was in clinical practice from 2001 to 2014.

Annie G. Rogers, PhD, is Professor Emerita of Psychoanalysis and Clinical Psychology at Hampshire College and has a private practice in Amherst, Massachusetts. She is a supervising and teaching Analyst at the Lacanian School of Psychoanalysis in San Francisco, California, and has published internationally in her field.

Ellen Handler Spitz, PhD, is Senior Lecturer in Humanities at Yale University and Honors Professor Emerita at the University of Maryland (UMBC). Her books on art, literature, psychology, and the aesthetic lives of children include *Art and Psyche, Image and Insight, Museums of the Mind, Inside Picture Books, The Brightening Glance, Illuminating Childhood,* and *Magritte's Labyrinth.*

Jane G. Tillman, PhD, ABPP is the Evelyn Stefansson Nef Director of the Erikson Institute for Education, Research, and Advocacy of the Austen Riggs Center. An Assistant Clinical Professor at the Yale Child Study Center, and a Teaching Associate in the Department of Psychiatry at the Harvard Medical School, Dr. Tillman is also Associate Editor for the *Psychoanalytic Quarterly.*

Acknowledgments

The story of Austen Riggs and its Erikson Institute is a big one to tell. Only part of it is contained in this book, which is dedicated to everyone I met during my time as a visiting scholar in 2018: the patients who chose to share their lives, their clinicians who talked with me about their work and also their writing, and the staff who took my writing seminar, including Greg Farr, whose archival assistance throughout my time as a visiting scholar was invaluable. I am grateful to Jane Tillman, Director of the Erikson Institute, who offered me a much needed place to assimilate everything I was learning at Riggs. (How many scholars interested in psychoanalysis get to have weekly meetings to discuss their work with a psychoanalyst?) This book was born in those conversations. Special thanks also goes to Jerry Fromm, who warmly welcomed me and this project, and whose writing has helped me think more deeply about applied psychoanalysis, and about how intergenerational legacies influence writers and writing.

There would be no book without my fellow Erikson scholars, those included in this edited volume and those waiting for its future iterations. What a rare interdisciplinary education it has been getting to know them. I first met them on the shelves of the Austen Riggs Library, in encounters with their papers and books that made me curious about their time in Stockbridge, what they saw and heard and learned and wrote. Their gracious support of this project, several years in the making, has been a testament to what it means to be embedded in the life of a psychiatric hospital like Austen Riggs. Reading their scholarship, emails, and personal reflections confirmed early on that there was an important story—about psychoanalytic influences and intersections—to tell.

And for saying the right thing at just the right time, I am grateful to Robin Deutsch, Lee Watroba, Jim Anderson, Wendy Martin, Jean Kirsch, Claire Kahane, Peter Rudnytsky, and especially Mimi Sprengnether, who played a key role in getting this book launched.

How many iterations and drafts of a writing project can someone read? Ask my husband, John Gray, who took time out of his own writing to help me at every stage of this consuming project. And ask the members of my longtime writing group, a place where clinicians collaborate with academics in ways that first taught me about the interdisciplinary intersections of applied psychoanalysis.

I've been working in these intersections since I was a graduate student. It isn't always easy to think and write in these spaces that can sometimes feel neither here nor there. A special acknowledgment of Dr. Steven Joseph – for helping me contain and understand disparate worlds over the years.

I have spent my academic career as an adjunct professor, a member of a class of faculty who do not get sabbaticals or research funds from their academic institutions. This book would not have been written without the Erikson Institute for Education, Research and Advocacy, a setting that has been providing an intellectual home for interdisciplinary collaboration, research, and writing since 1985.

Permissions

This is a book about what happens when clinicians collaborate with academics; it is also about the influence of context or setting on thinking and writing. To that end, I asked my fellow visiting scholars to choose a book or journal article that they worked on with the support of the Erikson Institute, and that illuminated how their time in Stockbridge shaped or changed them.

Permission to reprint and/or excerpt their previously published scholarship has been graciously granted for the following:

Françoise Davoine's and Jean-Max Gaudillière's selections (pp. xvii–xxix, 144–150) from *History Beyond Trauma: Whereof One Cannot Speak, Thereof One Cannot Stay Silent.* Copyright © 2004 Françoise Davoine and Jean-Max Gaudillière. Reprinted by permission by Other Press, New York, 2004.

Diane O'Donoghue's "Introduction," "Conclusion: Object Lessons," and "Afterword" from *On Dangerous Ground: Freud's Visual Culture of the Unconscious* (New York: Bloomsbury Academic, an imprint of Bloomsbury Publishing Plc., 2019).

Ellen Handler Spitz's "Too Young to Understand," Chapter 7 from *Illuminating Childhood: Portraits in Fiction, Film, and Drama* (Ann Arbor: University of Michigan Press, 2011).

Lewis Hyde's selections (pp. 3, 4, 13, 50, 63, 64, 131, 133, 136–139, 141–143, 155, 207–210, 218, 338, 339) from *A Primer for Forgetting: Getting Past the Past.* Reprinted with permission from Canongate Books Limited, United Kingdom; and Farrar, Strauss, Giroux, New York, 2019.

Ann Marie Plane's "Emotion, Embodiment, and Context," reprinted with permission of the University of Pennsylvania Press for material excerpted from chapter 5 of *Dreams and the Invisible World in Colonial New England* (2014).

Stacey Dearing's "Remembering Dorothy May Bradford's Death and Reframing 'Depression' in Colonial New England," a shortened version of the original, reprinted from *Early American Literature* (56/1, 2021), North Carolina Press.

Annie Rogers's "Encounters with a Ghastly, Enigmatic Other," Chapter 1 of *Incandescent Alphabets: Psychosis and the Enigma of Language,* Copyright 2016 by Annie Rogers and reproduced by permission of Taylor and Francis Group, LLC a division of Informa plc.

Mark Lipton's "The Hero's Personality," an edited version of chapter 2 from *Mean Men: The Perversion of America's Self-made Man* (New York: Voussoir Press, an independent publishing house, 2017).

Anne Dailey's "Guilty Minds," Chapter 4 of *Law and the Unconscious: A Psychoanalytic Perspective* (New Haven: Yale University Press, 2017).

Daniel Burston's "Wooden Ships: Cultural Cohesion and Continuity in Freud and Erikson," *Free Associations: Psychoanalysis and Culture, Media, Groups, Politics,* 17/2017, place of first publication.

Nancy McWilliams's "Psychoanalytic Reflections on Limitation: Aging, Dying, Generativity, and Renewal." *Psychoanalytic Psychology,* 34(1), 50–57. Copyright © 2016 by the American Psychological Association. Reproduced with permission.

Foreword

Jane Tillman

The Institute in the Twenty-first Century

Named for the psychoanalyst Erik Erikson, the Erikson Institute for Education, Research, and Advocacy of the Austen Riggs Center holds a place for scholars and clinicians to learn about "the individual in context," a perspective Erikson brought to his clinical work and writing long before this was accepted by American psychoanalysis. In his work, he was clear that the inner world is shaped not only in early life but throughout the lifespan by the various sociocultural and historical contexts in which an individual develops. Erikson was prescient, and now his wisdom about the importance of identity, culture, ethnicity, and human development throughout the lifespan is finally becoming central to both clinical and academic work in psychoanalysis. In 2021, the Erikson Institute was awarded the prestigious Sigourney Award recognizing our commitment to psychoanalytic education, research, and advocacy for the previous ten years. The selection committee recognized the important contribution of the Erikson Scholar-in-Residence program to the intellectual life of psychoanalysis and interdisciplinary studies.

Interdisciplinary conversation enriches our understanding of human experience and human development. Psychoanalysis in academic disciplines often rests on richness of theory but does not have the clinical engagement to see how theory does (or does not) come to life in the clinical setting. The Erikson Scholar-in-Residence program provides a place for mutually enriching learning to take place in the context of a psychoanalytic hospital and residential treatment setting where staff, patients, and visiting scholars come together to speak about what matters to them and how they understand human suffering and human flourishing. The stories that are told by patients and staff about family, institutions, psychiatric treatment, the little history of the individual within the big history of time and culture, and the different ideas about the role of each of these has in creating and treating mental suffering provide a rich source of learning for all involved.

We aim to have two visiting scholars come to the center each year, each for a 3.5 month term. Scholars come from academic disciplines of history, comparative literature, philosophy, law, poetry, clinical research, and of course from psychoanalysis and allied clinical disciplines. A committee of Austen Riggs staff and former Erikson Scholars reviews applications and selects Erikson Scholars who can articulate how the specific project they are working on (often a book) will benefit from interacting with clinicians and staff at Riggs, along with the use of our library and/or archives. In turn, these scholars enrich our intellectual life by teaching, presenting talks to patients and staff, and bringing a unique perspective to clinical data through their own expertise. Immersion in the community of Austen Riggs allows the scholar to engage in formal and informal conversations throughout the institution in ways that contribute to their own ideas and projects.

The Erikson Institute's Erikson Scholar-in-Residence program seems increasingly relevant in our current context as we seek to understand more about mental illness; the weight of history in terms of white supremacy, racism, genocide, and escalating violence; climate change; artificial intelligence; gender and sexuality; and the awareness of the fragility of law and democracy. All these forces are changing and shaping our world in ways that require interdisciplinary collaboration and study to better understand the issues and how to address the legacies of injustice and harm that burden us and cause suffering at the level of both the individual and society. Learning to listen across differences, to learn from multiple perspectives, and to think together about complex problems remains a central task of the Erikson Institute.

The Erikson Institute carries out its mission through numerous other programs as well. We have a four-year fellowship in Adult Psychoanalysis open to post-doctoral psychologists and post-residency psychiatrists. Erikson Scholars often teach a seminar to our fellows or offer a study group. Conferences and teaching that promote a psychoanalytic point of view and training for psychiatric residents, psychologists, social workers, and the larger professional community of clinicians address a wide range of topics such as suicide, moral injury, psychotherapy for psychosis, advocacy, and access to care, among others. Our Friday Night Guest Lecture series, with its over 50-year history, and our newer Grand Rounds series, are open to the public, and are now offered virtually, which allows for greater access to these free-of-charge continuing education events. Our specialty library with notable historical collections and archives is available to researchers and Erikson Scholars. Research both qualitative and quantitative on questions of clinical significance is a growing presence within the Institute as we learn about loneliness during the pandemic, suicidal thinking and behavior, personality assessment, treatment of psychosis, and clinical outcomes. Our research department is increasingly active and has formed collaborative projects with other researchers and institutions. Locally, the Erikson Institute engages in our local community supporting an award-winning model of collaborative care among schools, pediatricians, and the behavioral health system. Access to mental health care is an ongoing challenge in this country, which is worsening with the pandemic and the awareness of mental health needs that exceed available resources. Advocating for access to care through legislative and judicial channels, educating clinicians about mental health policy, and using our clinical expertise to promote the benefit of intermediate levels of psychiatric care are also a part of today's Erikson Institute.

Elise Miller, the editor of this book and one of its contributing scholars, came to Riggs in 2018 as an Erikson Scholar-in-Residence to study the conscious and unconscious dimensions of scholarly writing and publishing, research that expanded to include her fellow visiting scholars. *Psychoanalytic Intersections* compiles the selected work of former Erikson Scholars across several decades, demonstrating the interdisciplinary breadth and depth of the scholarship that has been nurtured during the brief period each Scholar spends at the Austen Riggs Center while they pursue their academic project. Each prospective Erikson Scholar-in-Residence proposes a writing project they will focus on during their time at Riggs, outlining in their proposal how encountering the psychoanalytic clinic will benefit their work. Of course, no Scholar knows exactly how that will unfold or what they might encounter once they join the Center's community. Dr. Miller has invited each Scholar to reflect on how the experience of being at Austen Riggs shaped their writing and their thinking. Her own interest in the psychology of writing and writers allows Dr. Miller to examine the writer's experience through a uniquely psychoanalytic lens. The learning in this book is two-fold: (1) how the intellectual project of the scholar taking place within the context of a psychoanalytic hospital may inform a scholar's project in unexpected ways; and (2) how a scholar's process and experience of writing unfolds when given the time and space to reflect on this unique context. This has been a major undertaking, several years in the making, and a testament to Dr. Miller's vision, persistence, and confidence that this community of academic and clinical writers could tell us something about their experiences thinking and writing in the intersections of clinical and academic knowledge.

Preface

M. Gerard Fromm

The Erikson Institute: A Personal History

The Erikson Institute, as its formal name indicates, is *of* the Austen Riggs Center, that "of" signifying that the interdisciplinary learning of the former is intrinsically linked to the clinical work of the latter. The Center's treatment program is unusual in today's world; quite troubled patients are seen in intensive psychotherapy in an open therapeutic setting. The very personal data from such intensive work, and from the breadth of activities patients and staff engage in together, is quite rare these days.

It is this rare and precious data that led Austen Riggs to create the Erikson Institute, the job of which is to bring this data into dialogue with others, to see what all of us can learn in the overlap of our interests. Over the years, we have done this in many different ways: fall conferences on subjects like moral injury and the psychological effects of social media, an annual creativity seminar, a pro bono consultation service for local human service organizations, an annual conference for college counseling centers, a prize for media reporting on mental health, a partnership with the Yale Child Study Center and, perhaps most importantly, a program of Erikson visiting scholars. We learn from these events and so do our partners-in-dialogue. In particular, academicians interested in psychoanalysis, who tend to be already knowledgeable about its concepts, find Riggs case conferences to be transformational learning experiences; as one Erikson Scholar put it, Riggs is a place "where the theoretical rubber meets the clinical road." And whatever learning we are able to offer is repaid by the learning we receive.

Through all of this, we hold, as our North Star, Erik Erikson himself, this restless, creative man who, with his own wounds from a complicated growing up and only a high school degree, became the pre-eminent developmental psychoanalyst of the mid-twentieth century. Erikson spent ten years on the staff of the Austen Riggs Center as a full-time clinician, but also as an intellectual wanderer. In a sense, while keeping one foot in the psychoanalytic consulting room, he put the other into a different discipline – history, anthropology, sociology – to see what could be learned at those intersections. His first major psycho-historical work, *Young Man Luther* (1958), was to some degree inspired and informed by his treatment of a patient at Riggs, whose breakdown, like Luther's four centuries before, occurred in the seminary.

As he famously put it in his masterwork, *Childhood and Society*, "I have nothing to offer except a way of looking at things" (1950, 403) – a perspective we might now call "applied psychoanalysis." Erikson's insight was that not only is a child's development profoundly influenced by the family context, but that family context is also profoundly influenced by its historical and sociocultural context (Erikson, 1950). And, that a young person's struggle toward identity may also include influencing the next phase of that larger context, for better or worse. Witness his work on Gandhi (1969) but also on Hitler (1950), both of whose lives were shaped by the traumatic conditions – the brutality, humiliations, and pervasive losses – of their societies. Erikson expanded the theory of human development to the whole life cycle; he made it inter-generational as well.

When I first came to Riggs, Erik had just retired from his University Professorship at Harvard. He and his wife, Joan, spent the fall and spring seasons in Stockbridge, and Erik attended the Wednesday case conferences. At the end of the day, the Fellows were invited to his home across the street for a glass of sherry and further discussion of the case. Erik, it seemed to me, had his theory in his bones. He would "read" the patient's development as though looking into a clear mountain stream, directly to the bottom. And he seemed able to read the therapist too and to help us see how these two people were coming together, or not, at this moment in time. The advice I most remember was both simple and profound: that as a therapist, "You need a history and you need a theory. Then you must forget them both, and let each session stand for itself."

A few years before these case discussions, Erik had lost his close friend and mentor, Robert Knight, the first Medical Director of Riggs' psychoanalytic era and the person who had brought Erik to Riggs. He and Joan soon moved back to California; our clinical discussions over sherry did not last long. But Mary Carswell, the new, young Board President, in her genteel yet tenacious way, was not about to let Erik go, and when Dan Schwartz became Medical Director, the two of them worked to create the Erikson visiting scholar program. Erik was very pleased with the idea, and pleased with Mary's insistence that "You are part of the deal!" Mary wanted him to visit Riggs annually for a week of teaching, and Erik and Joan were happy to oblige. A number of lovely and fascinating September visits followed.

And so, the dream of an Erikson Scholar Program became a reality, as did, ten years later – with the family's support and through the vision of the next Medical Director, Ed Shapiro – the dream of an Erikson Institute. I was fortunate to have chaired the Erikson Scholar Search Committee, and even more fortunate to have directed the Institute, from 2002 to 2013. A year into my tenure, through the generosity of Evelyn Stefansson Nef, the Institute directorship became an endowed position.

As we were creating the Scholar Program, I made another appointment with Erik, this time to ask him what he hoped for from it. In that last conversation, a very old Erikson responded that he did not want the program to focus on his theory, but, between us, we did come to the importance of maintaining his stance, the interdisciplinary stance mentioned earlier. At the end of our meeting, Erik spoke poignantly – even, I thought, a bit nostalgically about the wandering young man he once had been – when he said that his main hope was that the program would "give a promising person a real chance, the chance I had when I came to Riggs." How moving, and how personal this program was to Erik! Riggs had been the place where this adopted son had found a home and had filled out as a clinician. But it also offered him the leeway – one of his favorite words – to embrace his restless creativity. It's exactly this kind of chance – this safe space for serious play – that the Erikson Institute offers its Scholars and those who attend its events.

We need a history, Erik taught us, and our Erikson Scholars have provided that for us, along with a window into culture and society and philosophy and any number of other critical topics. As clinicians, we sometimes fumble in the dark, but Erikson Scholars aim a searchlight onto the larger context, and, among other things, offer ways of seeing the interaction between context and family life. And, because Scholars come to Riggs for what the clinical program can offer their research, we ground ourselves there. Indeed, the War Trauma conference in 2012 came about not only because of its timeliness in our national history but also because I promised a patient that we would do it. She had come to realize through her treatment how profoundly her growing up had been shaped by her father's unspoken experiences in war, and she was determined to help others who had suffered similar trauma.

Actually, I had one more conversation with Erikson, in a dream more than 20 years after his death, in which he told me that he had been "teaching in the streets." I realized that Erikson Scholars help us do that: bring psychoanalysis outside the office and as much "into the world" as possible. And if we have been a haven – providing, as one Scholar put it, "the courage to work in the unfriendly environments" out there – Erikson Scholars have given us the courage to join them, just as Erikson did. Indeed, through the various programs the Institute has offered, we have built a network of people, passions, projects, and conversations that have sustained and enlivened Austen Riggs for almost four decades.

A number of years ago, quite by chance, the Erikson Institute inherited Anna Freud's drapes – luxuriant old-world material that must have traveled with the Freuds as they escaped Austria in the late 1930s. Anna Freud had directed the nursery school in which Erikson, the struggling artist, found his calling in the newly developing field of child psychoanalysis. Decades later, she visited the Eriksons at Riggs, and a wonderful photo of her leaving the front door of the Activities Department – which includes a nursery school – hangs in the Riggs library to this day. Eventually, her drapes became pillows, given as gifts to those who knew Erikson and those who would be taking up new leadership roles at the Center. One of them now rests on the couch of the library's reading room. Near Anna Freud's photograph. Near Erik's hand-drawn, illustrated-with-doodles timeline of Gandhi's life history. At the heart of the Erikson Institute.

References

Erikson, Erik, H. 1950. *Childhood and Society.* New York: W.W. Norton.

Prologue

Elise Miller

The Hospital as Setting

Let me set the scene. We are in Stockbridge, Massachusetts, a small, secluded town nestled in the Berkshires, home of Norman Rockwell, the Tanglewood Music Festival, and also the setting for the contributions assembled in this volume. Established in 1919, the Austen Riggs Center was one of the major psychoanalytically oriented hospitals (along with the Menninger Clinic, Chestnut Lodge, and others) that developed in the context of the post-war effort in America "to regularize psychoanalysis and foster its assimilation by psychiatry, medicine, and the universities" (Hale 1995, 124). Although the early years of Riggs were shaped by the flourishing of ego psychology during 1950s in America, its clinical staff eventually began to incorporate families, groups, and social systems into their approaches to treatment. The result, according to Otto Kernberg, is that Riggs has "defied the serious difficulties that have impinged on psychiatric hospital treatment in this country in the last 20 years" by avoiding an overemphasis on medication and restrictive, locked settings, and by specializing in "transgenerational and infantile trauma affecting the patient's early development and his or her unconscious adaptation to the family structure" (2011, x). One of the few remaining psychiatric settings today offering in-patient, intensive, and long-term care, Riggs provides interdisciplinary, collaborative, and team centered, care by psychoanalytically trained psychologists, family social workers, psychiatrists, medical doctors, psychiatric nurses, art therapists, and more.

Patients who come to Riggs for help struggle with mood and personality disorders, depression, and suicidality and are sometimes considered treatment resistant and distrustful of authority figures and clinicians.[1] However, rather than a collection of symptoms leading to diagnostic labels, Riggs patients are seen as having stories that need to be uncovered, heard, and understood. Whatever "human beings cannot contain of their experience – what has been traumatically overwhelmingly, unbearable, unthinkable – falls out of social discourse, but very often on to and into the next generation…" (Fromm 2012, xvi). These intergenerational narratives include personal and familial histories that often play out against a backdrop of war, immigration, genocide, poverty, discrimination, and more. Treating these patients requires interdisciplinary knowledge of their personal and familial histories as well as of the social, political, economic, and cultural contexts of their suffering, which is likely to include buried trauma. Riggs clinicians are skilled in understanding how history inhabits, haunts, and immobilizes the patients who come for help, an orientation difficult to find in this era of pharmacology and managed care that has forgotten that intense pain and dysfunction can signify that "patients are bearers of painful truths – for their families and for the larger society" (Shapiro 2011, 280).

As a voluntary hospital offering a continuum of care, Austen Riggs provides Erikson Institute visiting scholars many opportunities to get to know this patient population. Consider what exposure to intensive, psychoanalytic treatment might mean to these visiting scholars, who may be more familiar with psychoanalytic theory than they are with its practices. Long-term, intensive psychodynamic work usually occurs in the private practice setting, where what goes on between therapist and patient is private, confidential, protected – unless the analyst writes and publishes journal papers and books, and those are largely for clinical audiences. But because Austen Riggs conducts research and trains psychologists and psychiatrists, its clinical work is visible, public-facing, and thus knowable in ways that distinguish its treatment from that of other settings. The highly regarded case conferences, for example, are an important aspect of treatment, training, as well as of the visiting scholar experience. Twice a week, clinicians and also visiting scholars gather to hear a case presented by a team of psychiatrists, psychologists, nurses, art therapists, and the family social workers who conduct extensive interviews with a patient's family to provide broad and deep perspectives, a 360° view of pain that is usually not accessible to those interested in psychoanalysis. *Psychoanalytic Intersections* honors the interdisciplinary learning that comes out of these encounters.

Note

1 For more on how Austen Riggs approaches psychiatric treatment, see the excellent *Treatment Resistance and Patient Authority: The Austen Riggs Reader* edited by Eric M. Plakun, current medical director and C.E.O (Norton, 2011).

References

Fromm, M. Gerard. 2012. "Introduction." In *Lost in Transmission: Studies of Trauma Across Generations*, edited by M. Gerard Fromm, xv–xxi. London: Routledge.

Hale, Jr. Nathan G. 1995. *The Rise and Fall of Psychoanalysis in the United States: Freud and the Americans, 1917–1985*. New York: Oxford University Press.

Kernberg, Otto F. 2011. "Foreword." In *Treatment Resistance and Patient Authority: The Austen Riggs Reader*, edited by Eric M. Plakun, viii–xi. New York: Norton.

Shapiro, Edward, R. 2011. "Examined Living: A Psychodynamic Treatment System for Patients with Treatment-Resistant Disorders." In *Treatment Resistance and Patient Authority: The Austen Riggs Reader*, edited by Eric M. Plakun, 269–284. New York: Norton.

Introduction

Elise Miller

In a recent issue of *Psychoanalytic Perspectives* devoted to psychoanalytic writing, Alexander Stein asks a question that the contributors to this book have also taken up in different ways: what can psychoanalysis "do today and tomorrow to have a more significant impact on human affairs beyond the profoundly important work analysts do with their patients every day?" Stein is challenging his fellow analysts to write and publish in ways that "effectively present and demonstrate to the outside world what psychoanalysis is and what psychoanalysts do" (2020, 142). The result, Jill Gentile observes in her response to Stein's paper, is "a renaissance of the public psychoanalytic essay" (2020, 161) that is meeting "psychoanalysis's social calling" (163). In order to make sense of "a world that is reeling from its own devastating creations" (161), Gentile adds, psychoanalytic writing must "function psychoanalytically" (168), that is, it must be willing to disrupt, dislocate, and unsettle. A chorus of voices and methods is now occupying the public spaces of psychoanalysis and its many interdisciplinary applications:

> Our conversations with each other are no longer self-confining, penning us into inscrutable, elitist discipline, our fanciful silo of the stratified psyche. We find ourselves now at a crossroads, a junction where it is impossible to sustain mere futile repetition. If we take one path, we inevitably stumble onto one another; we are intersected, crisscrossed, entangled. We meet at the intersections, perhaps congested, between the psyche and the collective....
>
> (Gentile, 2020, 161)

You will encounter some of those conversations and collisions in this edited volume, which honors the considerable intellectual legacy of a unique visiting scholar program: the Erikson Institute for Education, Research, and Advocacy of the Austen Riggs psychiatric hospital.

The Erikson Institute has been supporting interdisciplinary research and scholarship at the crossroads of clinical theory and practice and the discourses of academic knowledge since 1985. In these decades, more than 50 visiting scholars – clinicians from around the world as well as academics representing a variety of disciplines, departments, and methodologies – have been invited to Stockbridge to spend time

DOI: 10.4324/9781003322627-1

researching, studying, observing, and writing in a setting especially suited to those working in the intersections of psychoanalysis and academia, of psychiatry, psychology, and psychoanalysis, and of hospital and private practice settings. Perhaps in part because so many Riggs clinicians are accomplished scholars and educators, the Erikson Institute appreciates how much time and attention is actually required to research, write, and publish journal papers or books. Thus, it offers its visiting scholars the best of both worlds: time for their researching and writing as well as countless opportunities to collaborate with seasoned psychiatrists, psychologists, psychoanalysts, family social workers, art therapists, and clinicians in training. Psychoanalytically informed scholars, former Director Fromm explains, "do not usually get to know the patient in such depth, don't usually learn about the sufferings of their parents and grandparents, don't see their artistic work in the local gallery or on the local stage, and don't get to discuss problems of living and working together in patient-led community meetings" (2022, xx). It is this kind of exposure to clinical work that distinguishes the Erikson Institute visiting scholar program from other fellowships and writing programs.

How to account for this unique program? We can begin by looking to Erik Erikson's interest in interdisciplinary collaboration and in the psychological foundations of meaningful work, which informed his vision for the Institute he helped develop. Along with his Riggs colleagues, Erikson knew that just as clinicians are enriched when they collaborate with experts from different fields so are academic specialists who come to Riggs for opportunities to observe clinical processes in ways that breathe life into the theorizing they have read. It's one thing to read theory, but deep psychoanalytic knowledge comes from observing theory in action as it informs the actual processes and challenges of clinical treatment. Featuring twelve examples of this thinking and writing completed in proximity to and also under the influence of acutely ill patients, *Psychoanalytic Intersections* exemplifies the reach and relevance of psychoanalysis in the twentieth and twenty-first centuries, as well as the "extension of psychoanalytic sensibilities to the fields of education, biography, sociology and history" (Schlein, 2016, 22).[1] Understanding how we do what we do as scholars is essential to being able to continue to do it in the future. This is especially true for those interested in applied psychoanalysis as a theory of knowledge and as an interdisciplinary practice. My hope is that this book will make a strong case for more programs like the Erikson Institute, a model of investing in scholars, scholarship, and also of interdisciplinary collaboration. To illustrate, I will share some of my experiences as an Erikson scholar, an intensely transformative interlude that changed me and my scholarship in ways that are relevant to understanding the other examples of applied psychoanalysis contained in this edited volume.

What Writers Need

As a licensed clinician, a college professor of literature and writing, and a psychoanalytic literary scholar, I came to Riggs to understand more deeply what scholars need in order to flourish as original writers and thinkers who contribute in creative ways to the cultural spaces of intellectual and artistic discourse. Because of what I came to research and how I chose to structure my time, I used this semester off in ways that many of my fellow scholars, who brought pressing projects and looming deadlines with them to Stockbridge, might find surprising. A story of what I learned about what happens when we get away from who and what we know, my time in Stockbridge is relevant not because it was typical of what other scholars did with their time but because it wasn't. Thus, though my experiences might be unique, I believe they have important applications for all scholars and writers – and also, or perhaps especially, for their research institutes, training settings, colleges, and universities – about what scholars need in order to develop new knowledge and share it in the public spaces of their professions.

"Generally material circumstances are against" writing, Virginia Woolf observed in *A Room of One's Own*. "Dogs will bark; people will interrupt; money must be made; health will break down" (1929, 51). And then there is "the world's notorious indifference," which "does not ask people to write poems and novels and histories" (52). Woolf is thinking about "the state of mind that is most propitious to the act of creation" (51) for female authors, but her recommendations – a private, quiet room of one's own, and enough money to free up time to write – are relevant to all writers, including the scholars in this book. Woolf's cure for what ails writers is quite specific. "There must be freedom and there must be peace," she advises. "Not a wheel must grate, not a light glimmer. The curtain must be close drawn" (104). Victoria Nelson, the author of a popular book about writer's block, concurs: "Getting away from the routines and setting of the ordinary can have a wonderfully vivifying effect on a writer's work – and spirits" (1993, 23). A "room or garage in someone else's house" or an invitation to a "writer's retreat" or "writer's colony" enables struggling writers to experience "an inviolable space in which to be alone with one's thoughts" (Nelson, 1993, 23, 22). Nelson cites Henry David Thoreau and his "cabin in the woods" (23) at Walden Pond, a setting free of "family, duty, business, and other distractions" that get in the way of the "uninterrupted concentration" conducive to "a great flood of creativity" (1993, 23). "For the slow labor of realizing a potential gift," former Erikson Scholar Lewis Hyde adds, "the artist must retreat to the Bohemias, halfway between the slums and the library, where life is not counted by the clock, and where the talented may be sure they will be ignored until that time, if it ever comes, when their gifts are viable enough to be set free and survive in the world" (1983, 53). For those engaged in the "task of setting free one's gifts" (Hyde, 1983, 55), being somewhere that is neither here nor there has many advantages.

Erikson would have appreciated the kind of environment Woolf and Hyde describe because he experienced it himself while working at Austen Riggs from 1951 to 1960, continuing for several decades as a consultant to the hospital, and eventually playing key roles in the development of the Erikson Institute. Thanks to Riggs's support, Erikson was invited to do "what is almost impossible in private practice": to engage in "intensive clinical observation and discussion while following wide ranging interests and to free large blocks of time for travel, studying, and writing" (1972b, 737). His years at Riggs enabled him to make the best of his clinical and scholarly gifts by providing him an ideal setting for thinking about identity, creativity, and meaningful work. As an early prototype of what Erikson later envisioned for visiting scholars, the Institute today continues this "Eriksonian" influence in its commitment to research and theorizing in the intersections of clinical and academic, and also in its recognition that everyone, including scholars, benefits from what he called "the opportunity to deploy special gifts under favorable circumstances" (1958, 8). Visiting scholars take full advantage of what Erikson termed an "extended intellectual 'moratorium'" from professional obligations, a retreat that combines the restorative spaces of "lonely discovery" (1958, 9) with the company of clinical experts who are willing to share what they do, and who welcome collaboration.

Erikson, who once wrote that he lived "in the Berkshire hills – Thoreaulike, on the western frontier of Massachusetts" (1970, 741), thought a great deal about the foundations of meaningful, creative work, As "a witness to the predicament of over-commitment" (1958, 43), he worried about "the danger of success without identity," when "things were going meaninglessly well" in ways that make us feel as if we are "being lived by them, rather than living them" (1958, 43, 44). In some of his writing, Erikson seems to be planting the seeds for the Erikson Scholar program. For example, in "Play and Actuality," a paper he presented at the Erikson Institute for Early Education, Erikson proposes that "in order to be truly adult," we must "renew some of the playfulness of childhood" (1972a, 332). According to Erikson, "man is never more human than when he plays," and for that he must "step outside of his most serious and most fateful concerns" (1972a, 331), as the Erikson scholars are invited to do during their time in Stockbridge. Did he have Stockbridge in mind when he wrote that a creative person must "transcend his everyday condition and be 'beside himself'" in a "twilight" region between self and other, imagined and real, play and work (1972a, 331)? Perhaps. "Strong individuals create their own 'psychosocial moratorium,'" Erikson writes in "Late Adolescence," which cites time in the military or other forms of public service, a college education, or, for the "young person with neglected gifts and a history of perverse guidance," a period of time in the "role of a patient" who has suffered a "'breakdown'" (1959, 639). "It is very important for some young people at a certain time to do 'something else' for a while," he concludes in the same essay (1959, 638). It is also important for researchers and scholars. "Potentially creative men," Erikson explains, citing the lives of Martin Luther, George Bernard Shaw, Freud, and Darwin as examples, often "build the personal fundament of their work during a self-decreed moratorium," an interlude for letting "the grosser weeds die out, make way for the growth of their inner garden" (1958, 44).

Psychoanalytic Intersections asks, and offers twelve answers to, an Eriksonian question. In what ways are the inner gardens of researchers and scholars being cultivated today? How many scholars have what Erikson considered enough opportunities to "make contact with a nutriment specific for their gifts" (1958, 44)?

According to Erikson, a misalignment between individual gifts or ambitions and the environment that should welcome and sustain them can result in "an acute state of ideological undernourishment" (1958, 103). He has in mind the challenges of adolescent development, but I believe this same diagnosis applies to clinicians and academics researching, writing, and publishing today. Lisa Ruddick would agree. Concerned about the current state of literary criticism, Ruddick interviewed some 70 graduate students in English, whom she refers to as "the canaries in the mine" (2015, 71). Ruddick's "When Nothing is Cool" is part of *The Future of Scholarly Writing,* a collection of essays that wonder whether scholarly writing has a future at all. Worried that "ivory tower academics are out of touch with the real world," and that they are "producing scholarship that only the most specialized audience of peers can understand, much less appreciate," editors Angelika Bammer and Ruth-Ellen Boetcher Joeres urge us "to expand our very idea of scholarship, what it is, what it does, and what it looks like" (2015, 1). "Academic cool is a cast of mind that disdains interpersonal kindness, I-thou connection," Ruddick agrees. "The problem is systematic" and has succeeded in creating "a corps of compliant professionals" who suffer from "a malaise without a name: socialization has left them with unaccountable feelings of confusion, inhibition, and loss" (Ruddick, 72, 71). Ruddick considers a number of causes of this disease of scholars: market pressures, to be sure, but also an overemphasis on using theory "to burn through whatever is small, tender, and worthy of protection and cultivation" (72). The scholars Ruddick interviewed are "benumbed," as if "his or her private self stands in the doorway, listening in," as if "their souls have gone into hiding, to await tenure or some other deliverance" (75).

I recognize the writers Ruddick is describing, because many of them have come to me for help with their writing impasses. Years of teaching undergraduates, consulting with scholarly authors, and also writing about what authors say about their writing processes have taught me that writers of all ages – novice and seasoned, prolific or stymied – struggle to express themselves and be recognized in the public spaces of intellectual life, sometimes during the earliest stages of creative thinking and reverie, and certainly when their writing is being reviewed, evaluated, and criticized during the fraught stages of revision, submission, and possible publication. Though research, thinking, and writing represent, in theory, opportunities for passionate, absorbing intellectual play, the working lives of busy academics and clinicians often fall short of the very ideals that inspired the wish to write and publish in the first place. Whether I am assisting discouraged undergraduates, overwhelmed graduate students, candidates in training at psychoanalytic institutes, or overcommitted colleagues whose time to write is confined to occasional evenings or weekends that rarely materialize, I have found that those who *must* write as part of their professional lives are often doing so under circumstances that are enervating, depleting, and sometimes disabling. Colleges and universities, analytic institutes, and research programs expect academics and clinicians to be prolific scholars, who have internalized systemic myths and fantasies about how much time it actually takes to research compose, revise, submit, and publish. How, Erikson might ask today, can gifted intellectuals cultivate their "inner gardens" when adequate time for writing and publishing is treated as if it happens in an imaginary dimension or parallel universe?

I applied for a position as an Erikson Institute visiting scholar to get away from the demands of my professional life, but I brought the voices of all of these struggling writers with me when I came to Stockbridge. I needed time to review years of interviews with these writers and their eyewitness accounts of the unconscious and social dimensions of thinking and writing, and I was curious what observing supervision and case conferences might reveal about the art of giving and receiving feedback. It had long been clear to me that writers need more support, more time off, more grants and fellowships, more sabbaticals, or other forms of moratorium and refreshment. (After all, the Latin root of "moratorium" refers to a pause or delay, but it's also worth remembering that the word originally was a legal term about extending time for a debtor to make a payment). I invite my readers to use this exploration of the ways that Austen Riggs and its Erikson Institute are getting it right as a way to think more deeply and more constructively about who in the world of research and scholarship owes what to whom, and how these debts might best be settled.

My time in Stockbridge as a visiting scholar gave me something priceless and rare: countless opportunities to lose track of time and become lost in thought, absorbed in and preoccupied with the contents of my own mind. As I will explore in "Writing and Reverie at Austen Riggs," I was able to listen to myself think with intense focus and productive attention to the flux of free associations, first-thoughts, and half-thoughts, as well as the kinds of connections and links that are the earliest iterations of original insight and new knowledge. Winnicott would have thought of this interlude as "a good-enough facilitating environment" (1971, 139), a state of self and mind I had known more in theory than in practice. There is no place I know that is more conducive to self-reflection and self-knowledge than Austen Riggs, a setting that urges turning inward to the landscapes of imagination, transformation, self-knowledge, and new knowledge. Introspection, creative insight, reverie, and new knowledge flourish in these transitional spaces between inside and outside, imagined and real, personal and social, play and work. It is as if there is nothing to do and nowhere to go but deep inside the self. This is as true for the patients seeking to know themselves more deeply and be themselves more fully as it is for the visiting clinicians and academics who come to learn and to work. Austen Riggs and its Erikson Institute not only provide a facilitating environment for patients who have lost their way but also one for scholars who may have lost sight of the very intellectual passions that originally inspired them to become academics and published authors.

Listening to Others

The Erikson Institute training, research, and education programs provide researchers and writers something even more important than relief from their busy lives as clinicians with full-time private practices or as academics managing the responsibilities of teaching and committee work while keeping up with pressures to publish or perish. Because Erikson Scholars are invited to spend their time in proximity to a psychiatric training and treatment center, away from what is known and familiar, they have room to think and breathe and stretch themselves, to create and play with new ideas, to share them with professionals from other fields to test, verify, adapt, and revitalize their thinking. The journal papers and book chapters assembled here were all influenced by a unique opportunity to study what happens when scholars interested in psychoanalysis have opportunities to listen, observe, and learn from the work of acute psychiatric care. Is there a better place to learn about intense listening and introspection than a psychiatric hospital devoted to acute care? Perhaps not, but I'd like to emphasize another essential aspect of being embedded in a setting like Rigg: the chance to listen to others . I have a question for my readers: how many opportunities do you have to share your scholarship with specialists from other fields? And another question for scholars invested in applying the insights of psychoanalysis to other disciplines: do you get enough chances to learn from and collaborate with practicing clinicians and their patients?

In order to appreciate what distinguishes its visiting scholar program from other writing fellowships, it's important to keep in mind that Austen Riggs is a sanctuary of the care and insight that privileges listening. Austen Riggs and its Erikson Institute is an intensely interpersonal environment of accidental intersections (over lunch, in the hallways, and after meetings or hospital events), informal conversations, and active collaborations. Listening to and learning from others is at the heart of these collaborations and interdisciplinary encounters. Let me share an example of my daily routine. After mornings spent immersing myself in books and articles about creativity, free association, and reverie, I would venture out of the cocoon of the Scholar Cottage onto the wider hospital campus. Walking across the grounds, past the hospital building where the patients lived, I entered the administrative building to have lunch with Riggs social workers, art therapists, psychiatrists, and psychologists. We talked a lot about their writing, and sometimes conversations started during a quick lunch would continue in one-on-one meetings that taught me a great deal about what it's like to have ambitions to research, write, and publish – while also honoring serious responsibilities to help patients in an acute care setting whose small size complicates questions of privacy and confidentiality. *Psychoanalytic Intersections* grew out of these discussions: my weekly meetings with Jane Tillman, who helped me assimilate what I was learning, the research help from librarian Greg Farr tracking, the course I taught to staff about clinical writing, the case conferences I was invited to observe, and more. I left Stockbridge with a deeper understanding of the ideal conditions for and unconscious obstacles to thinking and writing. And as I will take up in more detail in the next chapter, my time listening, thinking, and writing in the spaces where clinicians and academics encounter one another, confirmed what psychoanalysis has to teach writers who are willing to listen.

In her 2019 keynote address honoring the centennial of Austen Riggs, Carol Gilligan cited the life and work of Erikson, especially his "ability to listen" in ways that help us "recognize our common humanity." Gilligan, a founding member of the Erikson Council of Scholars who teaches a seminar on listening at New York University, believes that individual, social, and systemic change depend upon what she calls a "method of radical listening," a mode of intense curiosity and attention that is essential to "our human capacity and desire to live in connection with ourselves and with others" (2019, 8, 10). Riggs patients, their clinicians, and the researcher–scholars who spend time in their presence, know a great deal about this kind of deep listening, which thrives on connections and also cultivates them. Riggs and its Erikson Institute are places of "radical listening," where patients and their clinicians, as well as visiting scholars, come to talk and listen, moved by the kind of intense curiosity that the drive to know inspires. Exposure to that intensive clinical work influenced me in ways that only a setting that specializes in the art and practices of careful listening and attention could have. It also taught me a great deal about the foundations of intellectual work. Radical listening – the act of listening *to* – is what we do when we read experts in our field, or case histories, or when we turn to colleagues, teachers, and consultants for fresh perspectives. Radical listening is also essential to the free-floating attention of clinical work that entails listening *for* covert communications, accidental slips, and evidence of buried voices from a patient's past. Because visiting scholars are embedded in the day-to-day life of a hospital that provides psychoanalytically informed care, they are able to observe and learn from devout listeners: psychiatrists completing intakes, psychologists treating patients, social workers interviewing their families, and many others. The diverse scholarship gathered here was produced under the influence of the art and science of all this listening.

The Erikson Institute Visiting Scholars

In a recent collection of essays about his years working at Riggs, M. Gerard Fromm writes that the Erikson Institute brings "many travelers from other disciplines" into contact with Riggs staff in ways that live up to Erikson's own life as "a traveler, both intellectually and physically" (2022, xxiii). I hope readers will consider *Psychoanalytic Intersections* a kind of scholarly travelogue, a record of inward-looking, introspective wandering and wondering, and also of outward-facing disciplinary crossings and encounters. Scholarship, especially when it represents the kinds of intersections of clinical and academic knowledge you're about to read, is a form of migration entailing encounters with new places, people, practices, languages, and ways of thinking. We see this throughout Erikson's career and also in his scholarship, which is always reminding us that the Latin root of "research" signifies exploring, circling, moving outward, and then returning. How often do specialists with advanced degrees and training have time for such broad, far-ranging reading and research that moves freely across topics, questions, inquiries, and disciplinary divisions of methods and styles? It was this kind of intellectual travel that first led me to my fellow Erikson Scholars, whose publications I encountered in the Austen Riggs Library on the bookshelves of its stacks.

Since I had come to Stockbridge to study the social, intellectual, and psychological conditions of scholarship, reading the Erikson Institute's legacy of journal articles and books seemed to be a good place to begin to consider whether and how a psychiatric hospital could become a facilitating environment for this impressive archive. The result of all this reading was a true interdisciplinary education – in psychology, psychoanalysis, art history, children's literature, film, history, law, business and management, early colonial America, music, and much more. These journal articles and books made me curious to learn more about their authors. Had my fellow Erikson Scholars sat at this same desk in the same scholar office, looking out at this same tree, perusing a similar pile of journals and books? Had this hybrid setting exerted an influence their thinking as well? This education continued once I left Stockbridge and began reaching out to former scholars. Out of this initial curiosity about the work my fellow Erikson Scholars did and the experiences they had in Stockbridge came the idea for this edited volume – an interdisciplinary collection of papers and book chapters by scholars who had all spent time in the same clinical setting – and whose experiences you'll hear more about in the Afterwords I invited them to compose.

I soon realized that a complete archive of the journal papers and books sponsored by the Institute would require several volumes, so I decided to start small, beginning with clinicians and academics whose work had something to say about what it means to apply psychoanalytic concepts to other fields. (An additional edited volume is being developed.) The scholars included in this volume came to Stockbridge from France and from many regions in the United States, including California, New Jersey, Connecticut, Ohio, and Massachusetts. They came from big cities like Boston, Pittsburgh, New York City and from smaller college towns like Santa Barbara, Berkeley, College Park, Maryland, and Loudonville, New York. Most of the contributors in this volume are teachers – professors from large land-grant state universities as well as from small Catholic liberal arts colleges. Affiliated with varied academic departments, these scholars teach courses, to undergraduates and graduate students, in psychology, history, art, literature, film, psychoanalysis, psychotherapy, and business administration. And though everyone came to research and write, many of them also taught classes and gave lectures to Riggs staff and patients during their time as scholars. Like the patients who come to Riggs for insight and healing, Erikson Scholars bring a variety of complicated, pressing questions, and inquiries that test the limits of what they have known and assumed to be true in the past. As you will see in more detail in the Afterwords, each scholar brought a research project informed by an interest in psychoanalysis, and more importantly, an intuition that their own disciplinary lens and methods could only take them so far.

Though most of these scholars are affiliated with traditional academic departments, such as history, literature, or psychology, their research projects often challenged discipline-based divisions. For example, an interest in the psychology of

CEOs in America moved Mark Lipton, the author of *Mean Men: The Perversion of America's Self-made Man*, to deepen his research into the "dark side to entrepreneurship" by spending time as a scholar at Riggs, "a singular opportunity to learn about psychopathology" and the "collateral damage to employees" (2017, 8, 15,) and to their families, including, Lipton learned one day, fathers of some of the patients who seek help at Riggs.[2] Nancy McWilliams and Annie Rogers, both clinicians in private practice as well as professors of psychology, spent their time in Stockbridge as students of the hospital's approach to treatment and also as teachers. McWilliams gave talks to patients on the history of diagnosis, co-taught a seminar on paranoia, and consulted with staff on their research projects. Rogers's book, *Incandescent Alphabets: Psychosis and the Enigma of Language* (2016), seeks to "translate and open up the subjective interior of psychosis" by examining the lived experiences of patients as shared in their "first-person accounts, books, letters, art, and interviews" (2016, 20, 1). Rogers, a psychoanalyst with interests in art, poetry, and printmaking, gave a seminar on psychosis to trainees and also led poetry workshops for patients, who have while at Riggs opportunities to learn ceramics, weaving, woodworking, painting, and theater.

Some scholars came to Riggs to take advantage of the considerable archives of the Austen Riggs Library, which contains the correspondence, publications, and manuscripts created by Erikson while he was on the staff of the Austen Riggs Center, the papers and letters of a number of former Directors, a special collection of primary works in the fields of psychoanalysis, philosophy, literature, drama, and poetry, and the contents of the Chestnut Lodge Library in Maryland. Daniel Burston, an historian of psychology who came to study the Library's Erikson Collection, used his time as a scholar to uncover important chapters of clinical treatment and theory in America. However, his background (with doctorates in psychology and also in social and political thought) bends disciplinary boundaries in a number of ways. *Erik Erikson and the American Psyche: Ego, Ethics, and Evolution* (2007), the book he worked on during his time as a Scholar, examines the social and cultural contexts of Erikson's clinical and scholarly work. Its insights are extended in, "Wooden Ships: Cultural Cohesion and Continuity in Freud and Erikson." Burston's paper, which wonders what "holds cultural communities together, especially in time of crisis" (2017, electronic), explores intergenerational connections and antipathies in ways that illustrate the social and cultural applications of psychoanalytic thinking. Like Burston's work, which reaches into dimensions of society, politics, and culture, McWilliams's contribution, "Psychoanalytic Reflections on Limitation, Aging, Dying, Generativity, and Renewal," applies the insights of Erikson and other psychanalytic theorists to the challenges of aging and mortality faced by clinicians. Acknowledging the deaths of "many of our cherished elders" in Division 39 of the American Psychological Association, and concerned about "the time-honored task for elders to pass on their wisdom to their successors," McWilliams worries that the clinical profession "has failed the next generation": "We have not sufficiently preserved a psychoanalytic presence in academia, agency practice, counseling centers, hospitals" (2017, 56). I agree, and I hope that by assembling examples of the legacy of the Erikson Institute, *Psychoanalytic Intersections* can address these concerns about generativity, influence, and continued relevance.

How, some of the contributing scholars here have asked, do we go about preserving and transmitting chapters of history that have almost been lost and then found, and then are collected in ways that argue for their ongoing significance? Are personal, familial, and broader intergenerational histories always worth remembering? Yes, Lacanian analysts Françoise Davoine and her late husband, Jean-Max Gaudillière, would say, given their thesis about psychosis as an attack on social discourses that convey personal and world histories. Beginning in 1979, their visits to Riggs and their collaborations with staff helped the hospital to synthesize its ego psychology roots with an appreciation for the ways that social structures are "invested in cutting that history out of the sanctioned social narrative" (Fromm, 2004, xii). "Educated Europeans know and live in history much more fully than we Americans do" (2004, xiv), Fromm explains in his Foreword to their *History Beyond Trauma: Whereof One Cannot Speak, Thereof One Cannot Stay Silent*, whose authors "are listening to history" with the help of experts "from different fields of specializations" (2004, xiv). Historical excavation – in treatment or for scholarly purposes –pushes past conventional divisions of discipline and methodology. This would come as no surprise to Diane O'Donoghue, who researched some of these historical landscapes, including Freud's "engagement with his physical and material surroundings" (2019, tbd 319), in *On Dangerous Ground: Freud's Visual Culture of the Unconscious* (2019). If French psychoanalysis is thick with references to history, literature, and philosophy, O'Donoghue's research uses the methods of an art historian to investigate how Freud's collections of paintings, architecture, books, and other artifacts not only decorated his treatment room but also informed the origins of his psychoanalytic thinking. A "city's buildings, a cathedral's paintings, and a dealer's treasure trove," O'Donoghue suggests, signify in ways that "extend the reach of the disciplinary fields in which these objects are most commonly situated" (2019, 322). "Freud leads his readers to connect" the paintings of Luca Signorelli and Botticelli to Catholic theology, and O'Donoghue follows as she reconstructs these "crucial participants in this scene of Freud's writing of the first workings of his unconscious" (2019, 236, 237).

Psychoanalysis also intersects with the methods of an historian in Ann Marie Plane's chapter from *Dreams and the Invisible World in Colonial New England: Indians, Colonists and the Seventeenth Century*, which asks "how much weight to give to knowledge gained from" (2014, 127) the dreams of early American colonists? A specialist in early American history who also completed psychoanalytic training in southern California, Plane peers into the dark recesses of American history in search of expressions of the unconscious and "all sorts of wondrous experiences" (2014, 127), including the emotional, psychological, social, and cultural functions of dreams and dream reports. How does a modern reader and dreamer, Plane asks, listen to the dreams and dream interpretations of early Americans living in the 1700s – without reducing them to mirrors of our own experiences of the psyche? These methodological concerns also inform Stacey Dearing's contribution, "Remembering Dorothy May Bradford's Death and Reframing 'Depression' in Colonial New England," which employs, and also critiques, "a psychodynamic methodology that draws on aspects of psychobiography and psychohistory" (2021, 79). Like Plane's analyses of the cultural meanings of dreaming, Dearing's reconsideration of key elements in Bradford's biography complicates questions about depression and possible suicide and concludes that "attempts to retroactively analyze or diagnose historical figures with any kind of mental illness can be difficult to substantiate" (2021, 79).

As Dearing explains her interest in depicting early American settlers "as emotional complex, whole people" was enhanced by frequent collaborations with Riggs clinicians who helped her to see her historical sources in new ways (2021, 81). Riggs staff, Dearing continues, "helped me grapple with 400 years of theories, myths and, and legends around female mental health and suicide" (2024, 144). The work of scholars like Dearing and Plane is truly Eriksonian in the strong case it makes for the essential role psychoanalysis – as a method, a set of theories, and also an epistemological discourse with the capacity to question itself and to think about what it knows and cannot know– can play in uncovering historically distant experiences of other psyches and lives. As many of these contributing scholars teach us, looking back into the recesses of American history with the aid of a psychoanalytic lens can help scholars ask different questions and think in new ways. Developing a nuanced history of mental health offers a way to think more deeply about the myths of America's founding, the traumas of the colonial period, and the ongoing psychological effects of settler colonialism, slavery, and the challenges of immigration.

Exposure to the intensive work at a psychiatric hospital also influenced legal specialist Anne Dailey, who recalls her time in Stockbridge as "central to my identity as an interdisciplinary scholar" (2024, 190). Dailey's unexpected immersion in clinically centered ways of understanding "why people behave the way they do" challenged "the legal fiction of rationality" responsible for "law's failure to take human subjectivity seriously" (2017, 3). "Psychoanalysis and law are natural allies" (2017, 10), Dailey suggests in *Law and the Unconscious: A Psychoanalytic Perspective*, the book she worked on during her time as a visiting scholar. Consider the subject of her contribution, "Guilty Minds," a reminder of the "messy, disruptive reality of unconscious guilt and self-punitive forces behind a veil of free will and voluntary choice" (2017, 116) that informs our legal systems in America. And let's not forget what psychoanalysis understands about the complex nature of memory, for example, the central distinction between "absolute historical accuracy," which comes up so often in law, and "the meaning of these memories in the mind of a patient" who seeks out "psychic truth" (Dailey, 2017, 9). For Dailey, psychoanalysis speaks to the very limits of the law, which can exclude the accused and the guilty from storytelling. Survivors of trauma – resulting from war, genocide, or other social catastrophes in the immediate or distant past – "are no longer part of the world of the living," Davoine also cautions; their memories and stories, "the lessons of history remain buried" (*History,* 115, 110). Citing the experiences of war veterans Cervantes, Faulkner, and Bion, Davoine believes that psychotic patients "need to speak of the real disasters of space and time" (116). Sometimes, only the interdisciplinary eye can detect these burials and obfuscations.

And yet. *Psychoanalytic Intersections* complicates what it means to preserve and understand the past. Consider, for example, the questions Lewis Hyde asks in his analysis of memory and forgetting in *A Primer for Forgetting: Getting Past the Past*: what are "the virtues of forgetfulness" (2024, 102) Can a case ever be made in favor of forgetting history, of keeping its secrets from being transmitted, in order to move past them? "Once a grave has been marked, you can visit it, but you do not have to" (2019, 141), Hyde adds. With Lacan, Bion, Nietzsche, Homer, Plato, Nabokov, Borges, and others as his travel companions, Hyde examines "cases in which letting go of the past proves to be at least as useful as preserving it" (2019, 4). Ellen Handler Spitz also takes up this hypothesis in "Too Young to Understand," a chapter from *Illuminating Childhood: Portraits in Fiction, Film, and Drama*. Spitz uses *Mendel*, a Norwegian film about a child of Holocaust survivors, to examine dilemmas "of knowing but not telling," that is, when parents find themselves "keeping secrets from children" in order to protect them from "the brutalities that ravaged their families and deformed their lives" (2012, 77). Those buried secrets, Davoine might warn, eventually fall, sometimes several generations later, onto patients, whose illness keeps "trying to make a story out of what has not been received by any form of speech" (2004, xxviii). Spitz's empathy, however, is intergenerational. She appreciates how parents who have "endured torture, shame, confusion, and far worse" cannot "find the words to tell" (2012, 91) at the same time that she warns that "being in the dark does not lead to a child's peace of mind" (2012, 85).

A psychoanalytic psychiatric hospital like Austen Riggs presumes something Spitz proposes at the end of her contribution: "Yet what matters must be communicated and passed on. Moreover, what matters *will,* in some form, be passed on" (2012, 96). Erikson Institute visiting scholars observe clinicians who are specialists in the art of intense listening to and for the debilitating burdens and unexpected inspirations of history. These scholars also learn from patients and experts with first-hand knowledge of what is gained and what is lost in the struggle to excavate the kinds of historical horrors that lay waste to lives and psyches. By preserving the interdisciplinary scholarship that has come out of these encounters, this book ultimately aligns itself with preservation, with the wish to remember, collect, collate, and explain legacies in order to transmit them in ways that are generative not only for patients but also for future clinicians and academics. Thus, the scholarship contained in this collection demonstrates the intellectual advantages – as well as the potential perils – of spending time researching, thinking, learning, and writing at the intersections of clinical knowledge and academic discourse. "If one truly takes up the task of learning in the area between disciplines," Fromm notes, "the risk is of leaving one's own home, so to speak – which also means leaving one's area of expertise – and being a guest – or worse – in another" (2022, xxvi).

What does it mean to be a guest inside of an entirely different discipline with its own rigorous education, training, and credentialing requirements? Is an interest in or curiosity about psychoanalysis, the next chapter will wonder, a legitimate passport into the fundamentally private world of clinical treatment? Clinicians interested in becoming psychoanalysts must pursue rigorous and time-consuming training in order to help their patients navigate the unconscious. But what about scholars? Who or what authorizes the border-crossings of applied psychoanalysis, its importing and exporting of intellectual sources of knowledge? What qualifies visitors and travelers from other disciplines to seek access into the intensely confidential processes of the analytic relationship? Does observing clinical treatment ever slip into intellectual eavesdropping? Should we worry, as Freud, Erikson, and other theorists of applied psychoanalysis did, that the diverse applications of psychoanalytic knowledge are in danger of becoming casual appropriations from specialists without sufficient training and knowledge? In the opening chapter of this book, I offer some answers to these questions by drawing upon the insights of psychoanalytic theorists interested in thinking about thinking, about the writing process, and about creativity and also free association and reverie as ways of assimilating new methods, languages, and insights, and applying what was learned in the process. I will also invite readers to keep in mind the potential hazards of listening to, or should we say, and listening in on, the work of a private psychiatric hospital.

Notes

1 In the decades since the establishment of the Erikson Institute and its visiting scholar program, psychoanalysis been stretching its insights to address questions beyond the consulting room. To illustrate the reach of the Erikson Institute for Training and Research, whose trainings went virtual during the pandemic of 2020/2021, consider some of the Zoom seminars, lectures, and public offerings serving western Massachusetts communities as well as clinicians and academics from all over the world: "Mental Health in Times of Challenge: From Vietnam to Covid"; "Finding a Place to Connect: The Connection Between Institutional Membership and Citizenship"; "Suicide, Culture and Community"; "When Social Privilege Favors the Patient"; "Social and Psychic Lives of Asian Americans." Other topics included a discussion of large-group psychology in the context of the Capital insurrection; a study of loneliness during the Covid crisis; perfectionism; the psychology of online groups and communities; mental health challenges of college students; a conference on Moral Injury by experts in military, medical and racial research.
2 Page numbers for quotations from scholar-contributions in this Introduction refer to the original, and sometimes longer, previously published version as listed in the References —unless I am quoting the scholar's Afterword, as it appears in this edited volume, *Psychoanalytic Intersections* (2024).

References

Bammer, Angelika and Ruth-Ellen Boetcher Joeres. 2015. "Introduction." *The Future of Scholarly Writing: Critical Interventions*, edited by Angelika Bammer and Ruth-Ellen Joeres, 1–27. New York: Palgrave Macmillan.

Burston, Daniel. 2007. *Erik Erikson and the American Psyche: Ego, Ethics, and Evolution.* Lanham, Boulder, New York, Toronto, Plymouth: Jason Aronson.

———. 2017. "Wooden Ships: Cultural Cohesion and Continuity in Freud and Erikson." *Free Associations: Psychoanalysis and Culture, Media, Groups, Politics.* 71: Dec. 2017.

Dailey, Anne C. 2017. *Law and the Unconscious: A Psychoanalytic Perspective.* New Haven, CT: Yale UP.

———. 2024. "Afterword." In *Psychoanalytic Intersections: Selected Writing of the Austen Riggs Center Erikson Institute Visiting Scholar Program,* edited by Elise Miller, 189–190. Abingdon and New York: Routledge.

Davoine, Françoise and Jean-Max Gaudillière. 2004. *History Beyond Trauma: Where of One Cannot Speak, There of One Cannot Stay Silent.* New York: Other Press.

Dearing, Stacey. 2021. "Remembering Dorothy May Bradford's Death and Reframing 'Depression' in Colonial New England," *Early American Literature* 56, no. 1: 74–104.

———. 2024. "Afterword." In *Psychoanalytic Intersections: Selected Writing of the Austen Riggs Center Erikson Institute Visiting Scholar Program,* edited by Elise Miller, 144–145. Abingdon and New York: Routledge.

Erikson, Erik. [1958]1962. *Young Man Luther: A Study of Psychoanalysis and History.* New York: W.W. Norton.

———. [1959]1987. "Late Adolescence." In. *A Way of Looking at Things: Selected Papers from 1930–1980, Erik H. Erikson,* edited by Stephen Schlein, 631–643. New York: W. W. Norton & Co.

———. [1970]1987. "Acceptance of the National Book Award for *Gandhi's Truth.*" In *A Way of Looking at Things: Selected Papers from 1930–1980, Erik H. Erikson,* edited by Stephen Schlein, 741–742. New York: W. W. Norton & Co.

———. [1972a]1987. "Play and Actuality." In *A Way of Looking at Things: Selected Papers from 1930–1980, Erik H. Erikson,* edited by Stephen Schlein, 311–338. New York: W. W. Norton & Co.

———. [1972b]1987. "Robert P. Knight: by Way of a Memoir." In *A Way of Looking at Things: Selected Papers from 1930–1980, Erik H. Erikson, edited by* Stephen Schlein, 733–738. New York: W. W. Norton & Co.

Fromm, M. Gerard. 2004. "Foreword." *History Beyond Trauma: Whereof One Cannot Speak, Thereof One Cannot Stay Silent,* edited by Françoise Davoine and Jean-Max Gaudillière, xi–xv. New York: Other Press.

———. 2022. *Traveling through Time: How Trauma Plays Itself Out in Families, Organizations and Society.* Oxfordshire: Phoenix Publishing House.

Gentile, Jill. 2020. "On Psychoanalytic Writing (and Writing Psychoanalysis) as Migratory Action and Postcolonial Revolt: A Response to Alexander Stein." *Psychoanalytic Perspectives* 17, no. 2: 61–172.

Gilligan, Carol. 2019. "Responding to the Crisis of Connection: Remembering Erik Erikson." Unpublished Talk in Stockbridge, MA, October 31.

Hyde, Lewis. 1983. *The Gift: Imagination and the Erotic Life of Property.* New York: Vintage.

———. 2019. *A Primer for Forgetting: Getting Past the Past.* New York: Farrar, Straus & Giroux.

———. 2024. "Afterword." In *Psychoanalytic Intersections: Selected Writing of the Austen Riggs Center Erikson Institute Visiting Scholar Program,* edited by Elise Miller, 102–103. Abingdon and New York: Routledge.

Lipton, Mark. 2017. *Mean Men: The Perversion of America's Self-made Man.* New York: Voussoir.

McWilliams, Nancy. 2017. "Psychoanalytic Reflections on Limitation, Aging, Dying, Generativity, and Renewal." *Psychoanalytic Psychology* 34, no. 1: 50–57.

Nelson, Victoria. 1993. *On Writer's Block: A New Approach to Creativity.* Boston: Houghton Mifflin Co.

O'Donoghue, Diane. 2019. *On Dangerous Ground: Freud's Visual Culture of the Unconscious.* New York: Bloomsbury Academic.

Plane, Ann Marie. 2014. *Dreams and the Invisible World in Colonial New England: Indians, Colonists and the Seventeenth Century.* Philadelphia: U of Pennsylvania Press.

Rogers, Annie G. 2016. *Incandescent Alphabets: Psychosis and the Enigma of Language.* Boca Raton: Routledge.

Ruddick, Lisa. 2015. "When Nothing is Cool." In *The Future of Scholarly Writing: Critical Interventions*, edited by Angelika Bammer and Ruth-Ellen Boetcher Joeres, 71–85. New York: Palgrave Macmillan.

Schlein, Stephen. 2016. *The Clinical Erik Erikson: A Psychoanalytic Method of Engagement and Activation.* London and New York: Routledge.

Stein, Alexander. 2020. "Psychoanalysis in the Public Sphere: A Call for Taking Analytic Thinking, Writing and Action into the Broader World." *Psychoanalytic Perspectives* 17, no. 2: 141–160.

Winnicott, D. W. 1971. *Playing and Reality.* London: Routledge.

Woolf, Virginia. [1929]1981. *A Room of One's Own.* San Diego, Harcourt Brace & Co.

Memory and Forgetting

Chapter 1

Writing and Reverie at Austen Riggs

Elise Miller

In his preface to *Psychoanalysis and the Question of the Text,* Geoffrey Hartman asks "what kind of event in the history of interpretation psychoanalysis is proving to be" (1978, vii). I believe we are still figuring out the answer to that question today, and I hope this opening chapter contributes something relevant to this effort. When Hartman surveys "thinking and writing at the Freudian boundary" (xix), he sees literature, history, philosophy, and many other disciplines congregating and colliding with American and French iterations of psychoanalysis. In order to keep updating the "changing vocabularies and modified models of applied analysis" (vii), Hartman suggests we must be wary of disciplinary distinctions and methodological differences. This still applies today, which is why I will foreground Hartman's claim that psychoanalytic writers are neither here nor there, but rather, "*en voyage*, passing through psychoanalysis, which seems to be passing through itself, and no destination is assured" (xii-xiii). I embarked on such a journey during my time in Stockbridge, and so did my fellow Erikson Scholars, whose articles and book chapters have passed through or passed time in proximity to a psychoanalytic psychiatric hospital. This chapter will consider what can be learned from these intellectual, theoretical, sometimes intensely psychological encounters with the often-hidden world of acute hospital care of patients grappling with loss, depression, suicide, trauma, and intergenerational suffering. You won't hear about these patients directly, but I think you will feel their presence, sense their lessons, and register what they teach us about the relationship between psychoanalytic theory, practice, and application. The patient, my own intellectual excursions as a visiting scholar confirmed, is both the epistemological foundation of psychoanalytic theorizing and writing and also often a resident of its shadows. Programs like the Erikson Institute, and scholarly projects like this book, bring clinical work out of the dimensions of what is often inferred, assumed, and posited. This means that those of us whose thinking and writing are informed by patients like the ones who seek help at Austen Riggs, and who theorize on the basis of these patients, can better understand how we come to know what we know.

I came to Stockbridge to research the unconscious dimensions of writing and knowledge-making; I ended up learning a great deal about how psychoanalytic knowledge gets made at these interdisciplinary crossroads and intersections. To

DOI: 10.4324/9781003322627-3

tell that story, this chapter will begin with my experiences as a visiting scholar, an education that included Austen Riggs patients, their clinicians, and a number of psychoanalytic theorists. Because I am interested in what it means to be *en voyage*, en route, in the process of linking, connecting, and applying clinical knowledge, I'll focus on the means of my intellectual travels – "reverie." A psychoanalytic concept with a great deal of relevance to scholarly research and writing, reverie privileges thinking as a process, a voyage, a form of travel to unknown places, people, and points of view. Ways of taking notice of someone else, of something other than or otherwise, reverie, and the listening it processes, enable us to assimilate new information and experiences, and also to identify our biases and assumptions in ways that make us receptive to new influences. Because listening and reverie function both in and as potential spaces within which the language and ideas of others float and mingle with our own, they also, I will contend here, are an essential aspect of the process of applying psychoanalysis to other disciplines.

In the final sections of this chapter, I will offer some reflections on what programs like the ones sponsored by the Erikson Institute can teach those who are invested in the ongoing relevance of psychoanalytic knowledge and its many interdisciplinary expressions and applications. The invitation the Institute extends to scholars and researchers to observe clinical treatment is invaluable, but it also raises questions about what it means to expose those with an interest in psychoanalytic theory to the very real, sometimes overwhelming world of actual patients and clinical work. The etymology of "influence," we should keep in mind, suggests a flowing into, an openness or receptivity to being filled or changed in some way. This receptivity, a willingness to question what we think we know, to change our minds, and perhaps also to transform our disciplines, reinvigorates scholars as well as the intellectual discourses of their fields. It also has its hazards. Thus, I will conclude this chapter by inviting you to join me in thinking about containment and assimilation, problems or predicaments with intellectual, methodological, and also moral, dimensions.

Lost in Thought at Austen Riggs

I arrived in Stockbridge late in the evening of January 17, 2018. The Erikson Institute had provided me not just a room of my own but an entire cottage as well as an office in the Riggs Library and access to its extensive catalogue. An urban dweller for most of my life, I had never been somewhere so remote, and with so few distractions. Inured to the overcommitted, multitasking life of an academic and part-time clinician, I was feeling both eager and anxious. Would the pressures to produce, to publish or perish that were part of my socialization as an academic, be of use to me here? The quiet setting of my temporary home offered answers to these questions. A recent snowstorm had blanketed the landscape, and when I stepped outside of the Scholar Cottage, the silence was almost deafening. A wintry landscape signifying blank spaces, not yet filled pages, and open schedules reminded me that my time indeed was my own. With snowdrifts and icy walkways outside my windows encouraging me to stay indoors and sink deep inside myself and my writing, I came to feel as if I were inhabiting a kind of transitional space, where the boundaries between inner and outer dissolved, the emptiness and silence alternately disorienting, calming, and refreshing. I didn't know a soul in the Berkshires, though this initial feeling of intense solitude abated when I looked across the lawn and saw lights in the windows of the residential building that housed the hospital patients. Would I get to know my neighbors? Had they also upon their arrival felt disoriented, apprehensive, homesick, and filled with questions? Did they sometimes wonder whether and how spending time at Austen Riggs would help? What would I learn from them? And how would the intensive clinical work taking place all around me illuminate what I had come to study?

For years, my scholarship had focused on the writing processes and impasses of authors of fiction and also of academic writers, including clinical scholars. It didn't take me long to realize that there was no better way to study creativity, free association, and free writing than by engaging in them myself. I would take all the time I needed for my associations and mental meanderings to emerge in the margins of my lecture notes or in my annotations of the reading and research I was completing. Christopher Bollas advises analysts to help the patient become "an attentive and dispassionate self-observer" by eschewing "conscious expectations," and so I sought a scholarly version of the clinician's "state of evenly suspended attention" (2002, 7, 12). Determined to listen deeply, attentively, and receptively to whatever was going on inside of my own mind, I was emulating, I now see, the clinical processes taking place all around me, letting my mind and attention wander from Bollas, to Thomas Ogden, to Thoreau's mediation on "Solitude" in *Walden Pond*, and to Virginia Woolf's celebrations of the advantages of surrendering to free-floating states of mind and self. "Follow your genius close enough, and it will not fail to show you a fresh prospect every hour" (1854, 76), Thoreau seemed to promise me and anyone seeking new ideas and novel perspectives. Thoreau found the perfect setting for his intellectual project at Walden Pond, a landscape uniquely suited to a meditative state of listening to one's own mind and mental processes.[1] Would I make a Walden, a place where thoughts have sufficient "time to take root and unfold themselves" (1854, 1966, 89), from my time in Stockbridge? Though I took courage from my associations to Thoreau's narrative and its reminders of an essential conviction of psychoanalysis – that there is much to be gained from taking full advantage of process, procedure, and journey-- I had misgivings. I wondered whether I could engage in this experiment in being *en route* without becoming self-absorbed or lost in reveries that would take me too far afield from the rigors of producing original and publishable scholarship I had come to research.

I found a kind of itinerary for the intellectual travel I had in mind in Bollas's discussion of what we owe Freud's insights into free association,

You are riding on a train, absorbed by the sights flying by. It passes an airport, crosses a canal. Traverses a meadow, climbs a long, low hill graced by rows of vineyards, descends into a valley choked with industrial parks, winds its way through dark forests, and finally comes to the outskirts of the small city where you are to disembark. Each location evokes sets of associations.

(2002, 3)

Thoreau plots a similar course for his readers: "You want room for your thoughts to get into sailing trim and run a course or two before they make their port" (1854, 94). As a restorative environment for patients who have lost their way, and also for scholars who sometimes fear they have lost their souls, Austen Riggs and its Erikson Institute set me free to do something different as a scholar. I had left my home in northern California, and also my professional obligations and routines, and had arrived in the transitional worlds described by D. W. Winnicott and Marion Milner. These potential spaces of play, experiment, and creativity, states of self and mind, Winnicott teaches, are experienced at the beginning of life, in the therapeutic relationship, and also in the "intense experiencing that belongs to the arts and to religion and to imaginative living, and to creative scientific work" (1971, 14). The way I chose to spend my time in Stockbridge soon confirmed that the improvisations, experiments, and trial-and-error procedures of serious intellectual play are essential to the work of scholars seeking to discover or construct new knowledge in their fields.

Did I have to be in Stockbridge to take advantage of this state of mind? Winnicott had an answer to this question. The capacity for creativity, he writes, originates in the "*potential space* between the mother and baby," which he thought of as a "playground" (1971, 47), a term not usually associated with a psychiatric hospital, or with scholarly writing. To better understand the connection between the work I was doing and the setting that was facilitating it, I re-read Milner's account of creative awakening, *On Not Being Able to Paint*. Her psychoanalytic autobiography is not only relevant to the work of scholars mandated to develop new knowledge and original ideas, but it also helped me to identify the inspiration I was finding in the clinical work taking place around me. Like Winnicott and Erikson, whose writing I'll consider later, Milner recognizes the parallels between the conditions for intellectual creativity and for psychoanalytic treatment. "Both ventures, the analytic and the creative seem to demand similar external and internal conditions" (1950, xiii), Anna Freud explains in her "Foreword" to Milner's narrative. Because of the "all too common and distressing restrictions by which the creativity of the average adult individual is held in check" (Freud, 1950, xiii), Milner recommends "absent-mindedness," which flourishes in an environment in which it is "safe to indulge in reverie" (191, 193). According to Anna Freud, Milner's "fight for freedom of artistic expression" has a lot in common with the "battle for free association and the uncovering of the unconscious mind" (xiii) of psychoanalytic treatment. My time at Austen Riggs confirmed this. I was in the right place, at the right time, engaging in the right project – a psychoanalytic study of mental processes, some conscious, others unconscious, at the heart of thinking and writing – even when scholars are too busy to take note of them. As a tool of clinicians and scholars, reverie was emerging as the means and the destination of being *en voyage* to insight and new knowledge.

Although my surrender to reverie and absentmindedness may seem a strange state for someone accustomed to the life and labors of the mind, I've never worked harder than I did during my months in Stockbridge. Eschewing self-imposed time-lines and to-do lists, I assigned myself one task: to do nothing but read, think, write, and sink deep inside myself and my mind. I became an avid student of rev-erie, receptive in ways that mirrored the analytic processes I was either observ-ing directly or hearing about in Riggs seminars and lectures. With ample time for mental wandering and free associations – and also room to *think about* these half-conscious states of attention, receptivity, and listening – I made sure to preserve this material in free writing at the end of every day, a practice I've recommended to the writers I teach and study. Bollas talks about the analyst's sensitivity to words and images "on the rim of consciousness" (2002, 16), an image that captures the qualities of informal, casual, free writing that preserves the flux and flow of mental processes – without fixating on premature conclusions. Bracketing ambition was turning out to be quite productive. "How glad I am to escape to my free page," Woolf proclaims in her *Diary,* a celebration of the "fertility and fluency" of free writing, and a record of whatever she might later learn from the streams of con-sciousness of her inner world (1953, 84, 308). I took her advice and made the most of the luxury of this kind of aimless, perhaps impractical, writing by producing a great deal of it during my time in Stockbridge.

I wrote about what I read, and what I thought about what I had read. I took note of case conferences, lectures, and meetings with Riggs clinicians. While I was pre-serving these annotations, notes, commentaries – that quick gathering up of free associations, intuitions, and hunches before they are judged or dismissed – I began to notice that all this free writing was constituting the first steps in linking and then applying the clinical material to the writing processes I had come to study. My longtime habit of free writing (a technique I teach to students and to writers who seek my help) seemed to inhabit the transitional spaces between my inner and outer worlds, between my mind and the minds of others, between primary and secondary processes, between conjecture or hypothesis and proven certainties, and between first thoughts and the formal journal papers and books of the intellectual spaces of public discourse. This writing served several purposes. By preserving everything I was learning and observing, I created a record of first thoughts and initial inspira-tions that eventually formed the basis of more formal scholarly writing, including this book.[2] As a conversation with myself and with others, this free writing also per-formed an important psychological function by helping me contain and metabolize everything I was experiencing at Austen Riggs. In an article on taking notes during treatment, Howard Levine recommends note-taking not for the purposes of remem-bering a session, but rather, as a "centering and self-regulating device employed to help maintain one's analytic composure and competence in the face of stressful or difficult situations" (2007, 982, 983). I found Levine's advice indispensable.

Riggs and its Erikson Institute offer visiting scholars countless opportunities to watch, emulate, and cultivate the capacity to listen deeply, to hear, feel, empathize, and connect. Like my fellow scholars, I listened to Grand Rounds presentations, and Friday Night Lectures, I listened to staff talk about their work and their writing, I listened to the social workers talk about researching family histories, I listened to the residential nurses, the art therapists, the fundraisers, and the publicists talk about their work. I listened to case conferences that consisted of presentations by the interdisciplinary treatment team, a live interview with the patient, deliberations by Riggs staff who had been briefed in advance with a lengthy case report containing relevant medical and educational information, and family histories so thick with detail that it was as if the patient's siblings, parents, and grandparents were in attendance. The material was confidential, and though the printed case reports had to be returned at the conclusion of the meeting, I retained a vivid impression of these collective efforts to understand a single psyche, its histories, stories, and suffering. I didn't so much take notes on as *take note of* everything that came to mind as I absorbed chilling stories and intensely painful feelings – associations, reveries, daydreams, and questions that set this book project in motion. Though I cannot reveal what I *heard* during those twice-weekly conferences, I can share what I *learned* about listening as a form of learning.[3] And though I cannot divulge identifying details, I can disclose what I learned by keeping what clinicians call process notes on the free associations and reveries prompted by being given access to dimensions of suffering only seen in a hospital setting. I came to see this kind of note-taking, which traced my associations to the clinical material I was observing, as the first step in applying clinical insights to academic knowledge.

However, and this is important to anyone interested in applying psychoanalysis to other fields, being embedded in a psychiatric hospital means that visitors witness and listen to a great deal, and much of it can be extremely intense, painful, and unsettling. Welcomed, within limits, into the life of a psychiatric hospital, visiting scholars spend a lot of time inside of the unconscious – their own and that of Riggs patients and their clinicians. (You will hear many of the scholars in this book speak of this). There is a great deal to assimilate and integrate at Austen Riggs. I spent many hours observing clinical treatment, in the mornings, reading psychoanalytic literature in the afternoons, and then attending seminars and lectures in the evenings. I was grateful for the invitation to get to know the work of many remarkable clinicians, role models in persistence and curiosity who showed me how to tolerate uncertainty and not knowing, and who came to seem like students or scholars of the unconscious. What a gift to watch these intelligent, seasoned psychologists, psychiatrists, and social workers engaged in their high-stakes work that involved thinking aloud, asking questions, and listening to conflicting answers in ways that were always pushing their impressive and eclectic knowledge of psychoanalytic theory toward insight and healing. In other words, in ways that *matter*. I came to feel as if I were witnessing psychoanalytic knowledge in the making, *en voyage,* as it passed from what might be true in theory to what actually helps acutely ill patients, that is, what applies to their disease in practice.

The Erikson Institute invites scholars to "stand on a boundary, with one foot in the daily, real, gut-level clinical experience of Riggs and one foot" (Fromm, 2002) in their other professional fields. Applied psychoanalysis flourishes where clinical wisdom and academic expertise intersect. Even though I am a psychotherapist, I did not anticipate that it would be the patients who would have the greatest influence on me and my scholarship, stretching, and pushing me in ways that both deepened and *grounded* me and my thinking. But what did these eye-opening, painful, and sometimes overwhelming encounters with patients have to do with my research into the writing process? This was a question I often asked myself, especially during my early days as a visiting scholar. Any initial reservations I had about the relevance of the psychiatric work I was invited to observe, however, disappeared in the middle of an early case conference I attended one morning. When it was over, my project on the unconscious dimensions of scholarly writing, including years interviewing stymied clinical and academic writers about their early family and education histories, came into focus for me in new ways. Before my time as a visiting scholar, I had heard a great deal about writers' efforts to express themselves and be recognized in the public spaces of intellectual life, but I had always suspected that these writers struggled with ghosts that haunted, sometimes disabled altogether, their efforts to speak up and be heard.[4] I certainly hadn't come to Riggs to study intergenerational transmissions of trauma, but I left with a new and deeper understanding of how family history casts wide shadows onto the ambitions and striving of subsequent generations, and their yearning to have a voice, a mind, and a capacity for thinking and insight. The patients featured in the case conferences had all been stopped dead in their tracks by illnesses that derailed them from the developmental tasks of education, individuation, and meaningful work. Many of them were college-age students whose struggles had disrupted their educational pursuits.[5] I had to wonder. Did the undergraduates I teach ever experience this kind of pain? Was their talk of writer's block, of not knowing the "right way" to go about an essay or a dissertation, or of not being "good enough," sometimes a cover story for the kind of dysfunction and despair out in the open at Riggs? The stories Riggs patients shared, I eventually came to understand, were different in degree, not kind, from those I hear from struggling writers of all ages and levels of experience.

I had many intuitions, inferences, and speculations about how the clinical work I was encountering applied to writing and its impasses, but could I make a case in peer-reviewed writing for linking patients and writers in these ways? My challenge – getting my thinking, logic, and writing from here to there --was both methodological and epistemological. Freud, who "used train travel as a model for his theory of free association," taught Bollas that "we create lines of thought, branching out in many differing directions," which eventually tell "a story revealed not between the lines, but in the chain of ideas within the lines" (2002, 4). I employed reverie as a way of reading between the lines of everything I was absorbing in order to discern the stories that emerge. And since Austen Riggs is a treatment and training setting devoted to the kind of introspective reflections and memories that lead to insight, my methods mirrored my environment. Patients engage in reverie, and its impasses, during sessions with their clinicians, who in turn are assimilating what is being said or shared, and then thinking about it later during lunch, after case conferences, or Friday night lectures. Everyone is lost in thought at a place like Austen Riggs. Any sight – of a patient walking across the grounds, someone waiting outside of the meeting room where the case conferences are held, a psychiatry fellow quietly returning his lunch tray before an afternoon session – became a site of my own associations and intellectual ruminations.

I look back on this time in Stockbridge as an education in the clinical phenomenon that Ogden characterizes as "the analyst's experience of his own reveries," which are sometimes dismissed as "forms of mental activity that often appear to be nothing more than narcissistic self-absorption, distractedness, compulsive rumination, daydreaming, and the like" (1994, 95). But there is value in these seemingly inconsequential mental contents for Ogden, who admits that his mind wanders during sessions, when something a patient says reminds him of a dream he had last week, which inspires him to make a mental note of an errand he should run at the end of the day. Minds will meander, Ogden reminds us, but there is much to be learned about the psychoanalytic experience of thinking *about* this form of thinking. A "way of being with myself and of hearing myself come into being," as Ogden describes it, reverie is a "heightened state of receptivity to unconscious experience while, at the same time, bringing to bear an ear" for what can be learned from it in the process (2005, 22, 23). Ogden is thinking about the deeper psychoanalytic meanings of the mundane minutiae of quotidian consciousness, our use of which "requires tolerance of the experience of being adrift" (1997, 569). He is addressing clinicians when he writes this, but I believe that his argument in favor of an open-minded approach to mental processes is also relevant to scholarly work, especially when it is informed by psychoanalysis. Pay attention, Ogden urges – and so I did, eventually learning that the reverie serves as a kind of mental net that gathers up, sorts, and categorizes whatever we encounter.

Writing in the Intersections: Erikson's Legacy

We develop a mind, Bollas learns from Bion, "because we have thoughts and eventually thoughts demand the arrival of a thinker to think them" (2011, 226). As a visiting scholar, I decided to show up as a thinker who happened to be thinking about the processes of thinking and writing. Reverie came to feel as a way to gather up, hold, and contain what I was reading, watching, and hearing – until I could put it into the kind of writing you're reading here. Psychoanalytic theorists, such as Bollas and Ogden, reminded me to take seriously my own associations – for instance, of an aspect of a patient's family history to something an 18-year-old flummoxed writer told me once about his inability to revise his prose. A habit of curiosity about the seemingly tangential helped me have faith in the connections and resemblances, the seeds of fully formulated insights, I was noting between something remembered by a patient's grandmother and a story told by an accomplished author who had just won a prize for her writing. A single phrase from Erikson's *Young Man Luther*, an early example of applied psychoanalysis that was written while he worked at Riggs, showed me I was on the right path. Erikson believed that psychoanalysis "often occupies a position on the borderline of what is demonstrably true and of what demonstrably *feels* true" (1958, 21). I suspect that he is drawing on his own mental journeys back and forth between and across different disciplines and discourses when he makes this claim. As an analyst and a scholar, Erikson knew that listening stimulates associations and reveries, creative states that relax logic and reveal unexpected connections. In "Play and Actuality," Erikson credits Freud for inventing "a method of playful communication called 'free association' which has taught man (way beyond the clinical setting) to play back and forth between" (1972, 335) what is known and what is not yet known.

Although Riggs's approach to psychiatric treatment today is theoretically eclectic, I felt Erikson's presence as a kind of shadow during my time at Riggs – in photos, painted portraits, on the website, and in the name of the Institute, whose interdisciplinary missions were already being mapped and modeled in his writing. *Young Man Luther* is not only a precursor of the kind of psychoanalytic writing included in this collection, but it also offers a kind of anatomy of interdisciplinary knowledge-making, and thus, of what it means to apply or *use* psychoanalysis as an explanatory lens. Erikson thinks a lot about "the hyphen of the psycho-historical as well as of all other hyphenated approaches" (1958, 16). Consider an epistemological claim he makes early in *Luther*, one that easily could serve as the epigraph of this edited volume: "Clinical as well as historical scholars have much to learn by going back and forth between these two kinds of recorded history," that is, between the "clinical encounter" and "recorded history" (1958, 16). Erikson is thinking and writing, and also theorizing *about,* the methodology of thinking within a kind of transitional space that seems to exert different pulls on him as he both discovers and constructs his insights. The image of the hyphen is key here, and not just because it is relevant to the scholarship contained in this edited volume. A hyphen implies the linking of two equal parts that are joined by means of, that is, as a result of the process of Erikson's thinking, which avoids segregating psychology and history into two static entities at the same time that it prevents them from collapsing in on one another.

Erikson's extensive clinical experiences are evident throughout his 1958 psychobiographical study of *Luther*, which continually marks the influence of acute psychiatric treatment on his insights into history and religion. Its subtitle, "A Study in Psychoanalysis and History," signals right away to readers that they are entering a transitional space somewhere *in between* psychology and history, patient and historical figure. Erikson invites readers into the "and," a space of listening where disciplines intersect, connections and links, and associations are made, and mutual influences flourish. The title of Chapter 1, "Case and Event," for example, coordinates rather than subordinates hospital and history by linking, and treating as co-equals, the individual with his or her historical context. Erikson is clear: "we clinicians have learned in recent years that we cannot lift a case history out of history." History can be a tool of psychoanalysis, he adds, which in turn is also "a tool of history" (1958, 9). For Erikson, scholars who apply psychoanalysis must have a "special awareness" (1958, 16) of the differences between a patient and an historical figure. Although Luther's conflicts mirrored those of the adolescent patients Erikson treated and studied, Luther was not his patient. Erikson's "awareness" marks a transitional space where clinical and academic expertise intersect, the mechanism of linking always in motion, in process, checking itself, suspicious of false conclusions, or misleading analogies. Tread lightly, be wary, think carefully about what you think you know, Erikson is always urging. He understood that psychoanalysis is dedicated to monitoring and interrogating itself, to examining its assumptions about what it does, who gets to do it, and how they are authorized and trained to do it.

Early in *Luther*, Erikson makes a prediction about the future of applied psychoanalysis that is relevant to the work I'm doing in this chapter and to the scholarship that follows it. At the conclusion of a truly interdisciplinary paragraph that covers St. Augustine, the *Psalms*, and Kierkegaard, Erikson offers an interesting meditation on method. Are either/or disciplinary allegiances, he wonders, just as dangerous as unexamined comingling of psychoanalysis with other academic fields? His answer is worth unpacking: "So we may have to risk that bit of impurity which is inherent in the hyphen of the psycho-historical as well as of all other hyphenated approaches" (1958, 16). For Erikson, the "hyphenated approaches" of interdisciplinary scholarship may break some rules, but they will ultimately nurture new growth: "They are the compost heap of today's interdisciplinary efforts, which may help to fertilize new fields, and to produce future flowers of new methodological clarity" (1958, 16). In Erikson's imagery, the scholar of applied psychoanalysis is a gardener or farmer, and also sometimes a wanderer, who travels from the hospital to the academic halls of learning, crossing borders of different settings and disciplines and methods of knowing. Psychoanalysis and history, held together by a hyphen in some of his sentences, can also in others be mixed and combined in ways that enrich the soil of a garden – especially in settings that find ways to expose interested scholars to the actual, serious, and often quite urgent work of clinicians. By facilitating transformative encounters among academics, patients and their treatment teams, the Erikson Institute for Education, Research, and Advocacy, and the considerable intellectual legacy of its visiting scholar program, has flourished in the garden Erikson imagined.

This kind of writing, interdisciplinary and collaborative, is distinguished because it is influenced by clinical processes of introspection, free association, and reverie. If psychoanalytic treatment is always *en voyage*, traveling into and out of the unconscious, so is psychoanalytic writing. Ogden confirms this when he compares his experiences of reverie as an analyst to his own writing process, which he characterizes as a form of "guided dreaming" that combines "hard work" with a feeling of "being passively entranced" (2005, 22). Fromm, a prolific author who cites free association as "one of Freud's greatest discoveries," is making a similar claim when he writes that "we all possess a second form of thinking—more imagistic and associative—which coexists alongside of more linear, logical, verbal thinking" (2022, xxiv). Erikson understood this kind of writing and its debt to the very clinical processes it seeks to explore and apply. He is a wonderful writer, who recognized that good writing gives readers "the tangible sense of an attempt a search, a wandering, a willingness and a desire to leave a prescribed path now and then" (Joeres, 2015, 115). Joeres praises writers who "acknowledge the process, the attempt, thereby underlining the fact that we cannot know everything, that we can only try things" (115). These authors are willing "to wander, to test things, maybe even to take false turns – to detour via details that actually are neither distracting nor misleading, that indeed may be fruitful" (Joeres, 115). I think Erikson knew this wandering as a writing style, and also as a way to construct new knowledge. Reading *Luther* reveals a method, an epistemology, an attempt to know, connect, or link that is at the heart of the enterprises of applied psychoanalysis. To wander, as Erikson does, back and forth from clinic to history, from what he knows best to what he wishes to know, is to privilege process, the swerves and detours and free associations of reverie as a route to insight.

Applying Psychoanalysis

For Fromm, "psychoanalytic thinking is now part of the culture" in part because of programs like the Erikson Institute, which brings experts from different fields together in "ways that could be called 'applied psychoanalysis.'" Fromm eschews the word "'applied,'" however, because it is "too one-directional and hints at too much expertise" (2022, xxiv). In contrast, the interdisciplinary collaborations at Riggs are "curious and consultative, rather than knowing and authoritative" (Fromm, 2022, xxiv). I agree. And though I employ the language of application, I seek to do so in a manner that interrogates it. This orientation, anticipated by Erikson's scholarship, is something I emulate in my own writing, and it is also an approach you will see in the contributions you're about to read, which presume that thinking psychoanalytically is an action that keeps the objects of thought in motion, tentative, fluid, changeable, and (this is important) adaptable, revisable, in other words, *applicable.* The etymology of "apply" confirms this, its meanings conveying the actions and motions of joining, connecting, attaching – not gluing in place, but rather, folding or braiding together. "What a relief to make a book whose free associations are happily foregrounded," Lewis Hyde says of *A Primer for Forgetting,* "a book that does not so much argue its point of departure as more simply sketch the territory I have been exploring, a book that I hope will both invite and provoke a reader's own free reflections" (2019, 4).[6] If insight is the destination, then the associative wandering of reverie is the journey, the way we move "from one idea to the next in an endless chain of associations," as Bollas describes (2002, 4).

You'll encounter a lot of this intellectual travel in this edited volume, in which American history, film, literature, and business management meet and mingle, linking what in one field is known or decided with psychoanalysis, the domain of what is unconscious, known but unthought (Bollas, 1987). "The unconscious leaves a trace, a trail through the effects of speaking" (2021, 4) Annie Rogers claims. Can we write psychoanalysis, she asks, in a way that reaches for words that "raise us out of habits of speaking and theorizing" and that "pushes language to a limit that makes the unconscious audible, if only for a moment" (Rogers, 2021, 7)? *Incandescent Alphabets,* the book she worked on during her time in Stockbridge, provides one answer by folding together her own personal history, her interactions with Riggs patients, memoirs about psychosis, "letters, works of art, texts written into and around intricate drawings, and interview excerpts," which provoke "wondering" (2016, 2) about how psychosis transforms language and thought. For Rogers, that wondering is "a place of desire" that carries us away, leaving us "surprised by the unconscious, surprised onto a new track" (2021, 6). O'Donoghue's *On Dangerous Ground* is one example of such a journey that "begins and concludes on Vienna's urban ground," with a book that is "indebted to encounters with objects, places, and texts, and the many individuals and institutions that made it possible for me to perceive connections among them" (2019, xii). Finding the connections between places, objects, and the "beginnings of the Freudian unconscious," O'Donoghue adds, "is a bit like grasping at the imagery of a dream as one awakens" (2019, 2), a feeling I often had during my time as a visiting scholar.

Reverie, an important aspect of listening, is essential to the capacity for empathy, a way we step outside of ourselves and our points of view to experience that of another. My fellow Erikson Scholars know this, and I think they would agree with me that spending time with Riggs patients cultivates the kind of empathy that moves us closer to others and also to new knowledge. As Rogers explains, the enigmatic world of psychosis is accessible only through empathy: "we can enter imaginatively; we can see it in our mind's eye as it unfolds. Any of us can imagine ourselves" (2016, 11) in the position of the acutely ill patient. Similarly, in her reading of Lorraine Hansberry's *A Raisin in the Sun,* Ellen Handler Spitz also highlights the role of empathy. Intergenerational divides create walls between parents and children, neither willing to "try to see from another side" (2012, 158). Overcoming these "walls of brick" depends upon the "imaginative action" of empathy that broadens perspectives and unsettles rooted projections and biases. In Spitz's analysis, the stakes are high, the suffering and dysfunction entrenched when parents, children (and perhaps also clinicians and scholars) behave "like the stationary artist who draws the model by positioning the easel in the same spot everyday" (2012, 158).

Empathy, Spitz urges, dislodges, unsettles, and opens minds and hearts by helping us escape a "unitary perspective" (2012, 159) in order to enter the mind and experiences of someone else, someone other. With insights that connect Hansberry's play to Tolstoy to William James and back again to the play, Spitz plays with analogies and parallels that perform the intellectual flexibility she advocates: "Our ability to change places with each other mentally—to move around the model's stand or scale the wall that divides us" (2012, 158) will save us, Spitz insists. If psychoanalytic treatment depends upon the capacities for listening and empathy, so perhaps do its many interdisciplinary applications. "To make this enquiry," Rogers claims, "I must enter the experiences of others living in another time—imaginatively, compassionately, and with fresh questions" (2016, 2). The case she makes for empathy as an emotional, psychological, and intellectual tool prefigures Lipton's research into toxic business practices, Plane's analyses of early colonial dreams, and also Dearing's invitations in her scholarship to approach Puritan experiences of suicide and depression by acknowledging that "mental illness has always been present in America" (2021, 94).

The Hazards of Listening

Thinking about the empathy in the research and writing supported by Riggs brings us back to the questions I raised at the beginning of this discussion. I have pointed to the many advantages of being *en voyage*, in between, navigating the potential spaces where clinical and academic discourse intersect. But what about the costs of traveling back and forth from erudite pursuits of academic research to sobering stories of the anguish and frailty that are part of the life of a hospital like Austen Riggs? Are scholars interested in the interdisciplinary applications of psychoanalysis engaging in hazardous work? Anyone who writes is likely familiar with its inescapable side effects. "Writing is a lonely vocation," Nelson notes, which is why "some writers risk turning Prospero's cell into a padded one" (1993, 23). The "wilderness is full of demons that feed on the souls of solitary human beings," she warns. If you are seeking an isolated interlude of a "cabin in the woods" with the "sole intent of tuning into your unconscious, you may be swallowed up by what comes out" (Nelson, 1993, 24). Nelson's research into writer's block echoes what some of my fellow scholars remember about their time at Riggs. The "cut out lessons of history are waiting for us around the corner of madness" (2004, 209), Davoine warns. What do the "demands of being fully immersed in the trauma of others" mean, Plane asks, for those "without the established structures that enabled staff to cope"? (2024, 123) Even scholars with clinical training (and that included several of us) need to brace themselves when facing the kind of human pain and paralysis found in a psychiatric hospital. Time spent in the company of clinicians and patients can lead to a serious reckoning with one's own unconscious.

Milner knew all about the relationship between creativity and regression. Learning how to paint taught her that creativity "requires a mental setting, an attitude, both in the people around and in oneself, a tolerance of something which may at moments look like madness" (1950, 192). "An artist does not go easily into this altered state of consciousness," Bollas also cautions. The "boundary between ordinary psychic life and the artistic workspace," he adds, "is difficult to cross, and sometimes unbearably so" (2011, 200). Once crossed, however, the differences between the work of the scholar and the work of the patient can dissolve, a slippage I experienced more than once during my time in Stockbridge, and even while working on this book. No wonder I often identified with the patients, especially late at night when I would look out of my cozy Scholar Cottage and see the lighted rooms of their residences. Were they feeling lonely, overwhelmed, wary, homesick, lost in space and time? Were they worried they spent too much time in their heads? Did they wonder what life would be like after they emerged from this intensive interlude in Stockbridge? Their willingness to reveal their psyches was profoundly instructive, but it also brought me into sometimes disorienting proximity to real pain and suffering, a response clinicians think of as counter transference or parallel process. Listening and learning, especially in the context of acute psychiatric care, require corrects verb-agreement problem open-mindedness, empathy, and sometimes a powerful identification with those seeking insight and relief. Those moments led me to wonder if familiarity with the theories of psychoanalysis is a sufficient container for academics without extensive clinical training.

"Wild" Psychoanalysis

Erikson's clinical training taught him that

> we learn from patients only to the extent that we realize (and the patient realizes) that what is said and done in treatment is based on a formal contract between healer and patient and must be carefully transposed before being applied to the general human condition.

> (1958, 20)

Let's consider for a moment this caveat, which privileges and also protects confidential clinical processes in ways that are relevant to those thinking and writing in the spaces and places where treatment and academic inquiry meet. "A future psychoanalyst," Erikson notes, "must undergo a personal psychoanalysis," which develops "the candidate's increasing ability to converse with his own unconscious well enough to recognize the unconscious motivations of others" (1958, 151, 152). Before a new analyst sees patients, he must complete his own analysis, Erikson continues, which "must overlap with years of practical and theoretical training in the new science" (1958, 152). Erikson was not alone in worrying about willy-nilly borrowing, transferring, outright appropriating, or misinterpreting psychoanalytic knowledge. These concerns have been part of psychoanalysis since its beginnings, when Freud was also wondering who is authorized to practice psychoanalysis and also to apply its principles in writing.

In his 1910 essay, "'Wild' Psycho-analysis," Freud takes up questions of training, education, and certification in ways I believe are relevant to understanding Erikson's concerns, and also the kind of scholarship Riggs and its Erikson Institute have made possible over the years. Who, Freud wonders in this paper, is qualified or authorized to treat patients psychoanalytically? What constitutes expertise in a field like psychoanalysis? Freud's position is clear; familiarity with psychoanalytic precepts that comes *only* from reading about them is inadequate: "If knowledge about the unconscious were as important for the patient as people inexperienced in psycho-analysis imagine, listening to lectures or reading books would be enough to cure him" (1910, 354). To illustrate, he compares reading theory to being offered a "menu-card in a time of famine" (1910, 354). Neither addresses "hunger" in any meaningful, substantial, effective way. Divorced from deep knowledge of the techniques and processes of psychoanalytic treatment, some interpretations offered by poorly trained clinicians may be correct in theory, but not in practice. A "psycho-analytic point of view" does not come from "listening to lectures or reading books," but rather, from long exposure to "those who are already proficient in it" (Freud 1910, 354), something an analytic institute provides. An inexperienced and insufficiently trained physician, Freud worries, "undoubtedly oversimplifies the problem greatly" when applying "psycho-analytic theses" wildly in ways that "leave no room for – psycho-analysis" (1910, 353, 354).

What about academically trained scholars interested in applied psychoanalysis? We find Freud's answer 16 years later in "The Question of Lay Analysis." Here, Freud continues to think about questions of expertise and accreditation, but in this paper, he concedes that training requirements can become too narrow. Freud has in mind an overemphasis on medical degrees in American analytic institutes, but his call for a broad knowledge of what we today think of as the liberal arts pertains to the scholarship that follows. "A scheme of training for analysts has yet still to be created," Freud insists. "It must include elements from the mental sciences, from psychology, the history of civilization and sociology" and from other biological sciences. Interdisciplinarity and intersectionality, in other words, offer the best "training for the intellect and for the powers of observation" (1927, 680). Freud could be describing the mission of the Erikson Institute, and the opportunities it provides, for both its own clinical staff and its visiting academic specialists, for interdisciplinary conversation, collaboration, and mutual education. One year after the Institute is formally created, Gerald J. Gargiulo revisits "The Question of Lay Analysis Sixty-Six Years Later" and builds a case for more interdisciplinary collaborations, mutual education, and influence. Echoing Freud, Gargiulo proposes that the

> skills needed by an analyst encompass the sensitivity of a poet, the intellectual range of a philosopher, the discipline of a researcher, the patience of a medieval cathedral builder…Thus psychoanalysts are, we could say, midwives of memory and as such they need to know man's cultural heritage, the language through which human beings organize experience…
>
> (1993, para. 10, 11)

Good analysts, in Gargiulo's view, should have interdisciplinary educations that expose them to the world that shapes patients' suffering, a conclusion that mirrors the clinical and scholarly missions of the Erikson Institute since its inception.

Similarly, psychoanalytic literary critic Meredith Skura reminds us that "data in psychoanalysis come ultimately from the clinical situation," which means that "all attempts to actually reproduce the psychoanalytic process must to some degree be makeshift ones" (1981, 5). As a clinician and psychoanalytic literary scholar, I share her concern that those who come to know psychoanalysis from their own individual treatment and by reading its theories may lack the empirical foundations of those theories that only come from experiencing actual treatment. Historian Thomas Kohut, an Erikson Institute board member, who also pursued analytic training, takes up these questions in "Psychohistory as History." He believes that scholars whose "familiarity with analysis is usually based almost exclusively on reading psychoanalytic theory," may have "little knowledge of analytic technique, clinical theory, and the nature of the psychoanalytic situation," that is, of "how analysts think when treating their patients" (1986, 342). This is why Vera Camden, a literary scholar who trained as an analyst, argues for the interconnectedness of academic and clinical expertise:

> Without diminishing the interest and utility of psychoanalytic theory as it is employed to interpret culture and society in all its dimensions, it can still be emphasized that psychoanalysis is founded in clinical practice as well as in literary and cultural knowledge. The two go together.
>
> (2011, 601, 602)

Research and writing by "scholars of the humanities and the social sciences," Camden proposes, "play a vital role in keeping the theory and practice of psychoanalysis alive, enriched, and transformative in its impact" (2011, 602, 603).[7]

Camden hopes that academics interested in the practice of psychoanalysis can find ways to "augment, intensify, or discover the roots of their psychoanalytic quest within clinical contexts" (601). Her argument for providing access to non-mental health professionals has its own practical limitations, however. Many psychoanalytic institutes around the country offer programs about psychoanalysis for an interested public. The American Psychoanalytic Association has an educator membership track for teachers and scholars interested in deepening their knowledge of psychoanalysis. Then there is the formidable Research Associate track Camden cites, a path toward formal training as an analyst that is, however, a time-consuming and expensive one for busy academics with full-time teaching and administrative responsibilities. So how much exposure to actual clinical treatment is enough for someone seeking to apply knowledge of psychoanalytic theory to his or her academic specialty? Who is qualified to use psychoanalytic theory? Should knowledge of clinical treatment be required? How much and what kind? I would say that generally it is editors of peer-reviewed journals who are in a position to answer these questions, since they determine whether clinicians or academics whose scholarship draws upon other disciplines have done so in rigorous, convincing ways. The training and visiting scholar programs of Riggs and its Institute have certainly gone far in addressing these persistent questions about the relationship between "wild psychoanalysis" and applied psychoanalysis.

Austen Riggs: Afterwards and Afterwords

As a psychoanalytic literary critic for most of my professional life, I have long believed that discipline-based knowledge refreshes, renews, and verifies its insights when it comes into contact with the thinking and methods of other fields. This conviction was confirmed by time as an Erikson scholar, and later, my work on this book. Because of its hybrid identity as a place of treatment, training, and research, Riggs and its Institute provide visiting scholars time to write and also unusual access to an intensive psychiatric setting that fosters the "application of psychoanalysis outside the office and as much in the world as possible" (Fromm, 2018). Academics "interested in psychoanalysis, who tended to be already extremely knowledgeable about its concepts" (*Traveling,* xxi) are given unique opportunities to see the theories they have been reading come to life. Thus, the Erikson Institute exposes scholars to ways of seeing and knowing that make it possible for them to learn how to think about what they think they know as well as *how* they came to know it. This is important information for those who believe in the ongoing relevance of psychoanalytic treatment and the value of its ways of seeing and knowing. You have heard about my own experiences of reverie, wondering, and writing in the intersections of clinical work and academic inquiry. However, any discussion of what I learned about being *en voyage*, about passing through a psychiatric hospital offering psychoanalytic treatment, would be incomplete without hearing from my fellow travelers, and my Erikson scholar colleagues. Therefore, in addition to the interdisciplinary scholarship gathered in this book, readers will also find the scholars who produced it. I invited all of them to look back upon how their time at Riggs shaped their thinking, learning, and writing.[8] In these brief Afterwords, my fellow visiting scholars reflect upon their time in Stockbridge. Each Afterword tells a unique story, an archeology of knowledge-making, an excavation in reverse of what it meant to think and write in close proximity to a psychiatric facility, and also what it was like to get to know patients during painful chapters of their lives, and to talk to and collaborate with the clinicians supporting them. These Afterwords make a strong case for the kinds of intersectional collaborations and mutual influences Riggs and its Institute makes possible. This kind of self-conscious, introspective, self-reflective writing is also very much in the spirit of the psychoanalytic enterprise. "Unlike novelists or poets, academic writers are rarely asked about their creative practices and endeavors," Hirsch and Spitzer claim in a paper about writing. Scholarship will continue to be seen as "cerebral, disembodied, produced within more-or-less-agreed-upon disciplinary conventions" – unless scholars choose to "make their presence as authors – and their role in the construction of the text – visible" (2015, 191, 192). Gentile applauds this transparency, confirming that the "borders are now fluid that formerly distinguished scholarly writing from personal writing or writing explicitly aimed for the public" (2020, 168). In "Critic, Define Thyself," Murray Schwartz, who believes that the "dynamics of the interpreter's personality" (1985, 12) are at the heart of every interpretive enterprise, asks scholars to come right out and introduce themselves. I have invited each contributing scholar to do just that in the Afterwords that follow each contribution, a hybrid genre of writing that combines autobiographical recollections with important insights into what stretches, confounds, revises, and deepens a scholar's search for new knowledge.

Notes

1 "There was pasture enough for my imagination" (1854, 59), Thoreau says of Walden Pond. By investing not money but rather "imagination" in the natural scenes he traversed and surveyed, Thoreau is in possession of priceless memories and words without the burden of a mortgage: "…I retained the landscape, and I have since annually carried off what it yielded without a wheelbarrow" (*Walden*, 55).

2 Two journal articles reflect the thinking and writing I completed as a visiting scholar. "Empty Minds and Blank Pages: The Scholarly Writer at Work" (*Women's Studies: An Interdisciplinary Journal.* 48/8, 2019) employs the lens of psychoanalysis to examine writing impasses at the beginning of a writing project. "Writing Under the Influence: The Scholarly Writer at Work" (*American Imago*, 76/4, 2019) is a psychoanalytic study of the unconscious dimensions of completing research and citing relevant authorities.

3 When I first arrived at Austen Riggs, I completed an orientation that covered many aspects of what it means to have access to the work of a psychiatric hospital. The Human Resources Director focused specifically on policies regarding confidentiality in general, and especially those related to any invitation extended to visiting scholars to attend the case conferences. If patients have agreed to have visitors in attendance, scholars will find a copy of the extensive case report in a private mailbox the night before a case presentation. We can refer to these reports during the actual meetings, but they must be returned to Riggs staff at the conclusion of the conference. I consider these written reports (which cover medical and school records and breathtaking historical and intergenerational research) along with the patients' willingness to share their lives, which often involved speaking at their own case conferences, a priceless gift.

4 For over 15 years, I have conducted IRB-approved interviews with writers (clinical authors, students, and scholars, that is, academic writers seeking to participate in the public spaces of their professions). Questions cover early educational experiences, familial memories of having a voice and being heard, and more. I ask about writing dreams and ambitions as well as about just how projects are executed. I invite these writers to share their experiences of the various stages of the writing process, including what goes well and where they can get stuck or stymied. I have also developed and taught interdisciplinary college classes on writer's block that invite students to think psychoanalytically about their ambitions for their college career and after.

5 See Fromm's "Unconscious Creative Activity and the Restoration of Reverie" in *Traveling* for a discussion of his treatment of a college student at Riggs (2022, 102–122).

6 Page numbers for quotations from scholar-contributions in this chapter refer to the original, and sometimes longer, previously published version as listed in the References —unless I am quoting the scholar's Afterword, as it appears in this edited volume, *Psychoanalytic Intersections* (2024).

7 See also Robert S. Wallerstein's "Psychoanalysis in the University: A Full-time Vision" (2009).

8 The Introduction and this chapter represent the scholarship I completed at Riggs as well as my later reflections upon my time in residence, so I will not add an Afterword to this discussion.

References

Bollas, Christopher. 1987. *The Shadow of the Object: Psychoanalysis of the Unthought Known.* New York: Columbia UP.

———. 2002. *Free Association.* Cambridge: Totem Books.

———. 2011. *The Christopher Bollas Reader.* New York: Routledge.

Camden, Vera J. 2011. "Psychoanalysis and the Academy: Practical Aspects and Philosophical Foundations." *American Imago* 67, no. 4 (Winter): 601–603.

Dearing, Stacey. 2021. "Remembering Dorothy May Bradford's Death and Reframing 'Depression' in Colonial New England," *Early American Literature* 56, no. 1: 74–104.

Erikson, Erik. [1958]1962. *Young Man Luther: A Study of Psychoanalysis and History.* New York: W.W. Norton.

———. [1972]1987. "Play and Actuality." In *A Way of Looking at Things: Selected Papers from 1930-1980, Erik H. Erikson,* edited by Stephen Schlein, 311–338. New York: W. W. Norton & Co.

Freud, Anna. [1950]2010. "Foreword." *On Not Being Able to Pain,* xiii–xv. London: Routledge.

Freud, Sigmund. [1910]1989. "'Wild' Psycho-Analysis." In *The Freud Reader,* edited by Peter Gay, 351–356. New York, London: W.W. Norton & Co.

———. [1927]1989. "The Question of Lay Analysis." In *The Freud Reader,* edited by Peter Gay, 679–685. New York, London: W. W. Norton & Co.

Fromm, M. Gerard. 2002. "Remarks at the Erikson Centennial Party." Unpublished talk, August 24.

———. 2018. "Remarks on the Erikson Scholar Reunion." Unpublished talk, July 22.

———. 2022. *Traveling through Time: How Trauma Plays Itself Out in Families, Organizations and Society.* Oxfordshire: Phoenix Publishing House.

Gargiulo, Gerald J. 1993. "The Question of Lay Analysis Sixty-Six Years Later." *International Forum of Psychoanalytic Education Newsletter* 11, no. 1: 4, 5.

Gentile, Jill. 2020. "On Psychoanalytic Writing (and Writing Psychoanalysis) as Migratory Action and Postcolonial Revolt: A Response to Alexander Stein." *Psychoanalytic Perspectives* 17, no. 2: 61–172.

Hartman, Geoffrey. [1978]1985. "Preface." *Psychoanalysis and the Question of the Text,* edited by Geoffrey Hartman, vii–xix. Baltimore: Johns Hopkins UP.

Hirsch, Marianne and Leo Spitzer. 2015."First Person Plural: Notes on Voice and Collaboration." In *The Future of Scholarly Writing: Critical Interventions,* edited by Angelika and Ruth-Ellen Boetcher Joeres, 191–204. New York: Palgrave Macmillan.

Hyde, Lewis. 2019. *A Primer for Forgetting: Getting Past the Past.* New York: Farrar, Straus & Giroux.

Joeres, Ruth-Ellen Boetcher. 2015."Found in the Details: Essaying the Particular." In *The Future of Scholarly Writing: Critical Interventions,* edited by Angelika and Ruth-Ellen Boetcher Joeres, 111–125. New York: Palgrave Macmillan.

Kohut, Thomas A. 1986. "Psychohistory as History." *The American Historical Review* 91, no. 2 (April): 336–354.

Levine, Howard B. 2007. "A Note on Notes: Note Taking and Containment." *The Psychoanalytic Quarterly* 76, no. 3: 981–990.

Milner, Marion. [1950]2010. *On Not Being Able to Pain.* London: Routledge.

Nelson, Victoria. 1993. *On Writer's Block: A New Approach to Creativity.* Boston, MA: Houghton Mifflin Co.

O'Donoghue, Diane. 2019. *On Dangerous Ground: Freud's Visual Culture of the Unconscious*. New York: Bloomsbury Academic.

Ogden, Thomas, H. 1994. *Subjects of Analysis*. Northvale NJ: Jason Aronson.

———. 1997. "Reverie and Interpretation." *The Psychoanalytic Quarterly* 66, no. 4: 567–595.

———. 2005. "On Psychoanalytic Writing." *International Journal of Psychoanalysis* 86: 15–29.

Plane, Ann Marie. 2024. "Afterword." In *Psychoanalytic Intersections: Selected Writing of the Austen Riggs Center Erikson Institute Visiting Scholar Program*, edited by Elise Miller, 122–123. Abingdon and New York: Routledge.

Rogers, Annie G. 2016. *Incandescent Alphabets: Psychosis and the Enigma of Language*. Boca Raton: Routledge.

———. 2021. "Writing Psychoanalysis?" *Psychoanalysis, Self, and Context* 16, no. 2: 163–170.

Schwartz, Murray M. 1985. "Critic, Define Thyself." In *The Question of the Text*, edited by Geoffrey Hartman, 1–17. Baltimore: Johns Hopkins UP.

Skura, Meredith. 1981. *The Literary Use of the Psychoanalytic Process*. New Haven, CT and London: Yale UP.

Spitz, Ellen Handler. 2012. *Illuminating Childhood: Portraits in Fiction, Film, and Drama*. Ann Arbor: U of Michigan P.

Thoreau, Henry David. [1854]1966. *Walden and Civil Disobedience*, edited by Owen Thomas. New York: W. W. Norton.

Wallerstein. Robert S. 2009. "Psychoanalysis in the University: A Full-time Vision." *International Journal of Psychoanalysis* 90, no. 5: 1107–1121.

Winnicott, D. W. 1971. *Playing and Reality*. London: Routledge.

Woolf, Virginia. [1953]1982. *A Writer's Diary*. San Diego, New York, London: Harcourt Brace.

Chapter 2

History Beyond Trauma[1]

Françoise Davoine and the late Jean-Max Gaudillière

The first draft of this book was completed in mid-August 2001. We had begun it in September 2000, and we brought it to the publisher in New York at the end of August 2001.

It was a very beautiful day. To show the horizon to some young people who were with us, we went up to the top of the World Trade Center. One week later, when we were back in Paris, we heard the news in the middle of the afternoon. Impossible to believe it; it wasn't true. All those people dead, all those missing. Suddenly, we realized that we were at war. War was right there. The collapse of the towers and lives made time stand still.

Several months later, life resumed its course. The war had apparently taken place far away from us. Others, in Afghanistan and in the Middle East, were undergoing those collapses of time. As they had so recently done in Rwanda and the Balkans. For a moment we thought we were living through World War II again, or even World War I. As in the last century, totalitarian slogans were chanted to a familiar tune, sounding hackneyed.

Within a few months' time, we had experienced concretely what we are talking about in this book:

Denial: what happened didn't happen.
Survivor guilt: "Why them and not us?"
Identification with the aggressor: "We had it coming."
Perversion of judgment: the victims were guilty and vice versa.

The fascination with criminals and mass destruction noted by Hannah Arendt in *The Origins of Totalitarianism.*[2]
The revival of the catastrophes: the old people were sounding the alarm to us; we're in 1938: Munich; we're in 1939: the *Blitzkrieg*; we're in 1941: Pearl Harbor. And, finally, trivialization: the proliferation of explanations going hand in hand with the anesthetization of feelings.

DOI: 10.4324/9781003322627-4

In all this, we recognized the scansions of our work as psychoanalysts: in the psychiatric hospital, in the clinic, and in our offices, with patients whose madness, transient, or ongoing, keeps on exploring these traumatic breaks in the social link and the political outcomes of such traumas. When psychoanalysis grapples with madness, it is essential that analyst and patient pass through these moments and not just denounce them.

Lacan, War, Madness

Jacques Lacan, whose seminars we attended during our years of training, went to England as early as 1945 to see Wilfred Bion. In his 1947 paper on "British psychiatry and the war," he gave an account of the field of research opened by the war—although he abandoned his practice during that time—and the importance of the social link in such circumstances. His theory of "The four discourses" structuring the social link was developed in the seminars following the events of 1968, especially in *L'envers de la psychanalyse* (1969–1970). This was exactly the time when we began attending Lacan's seminar.

Throughout his work, Lacan sets forth concepts for the psychoanalytic exploration of the field of madness. But in his seminar on the psychoses and the paper in *Écrits* that summarizes it (1957–1958), he deliberately stops short of the issue of handling the transference in psychosis.[3] As for psychiatry in France, after World War II, it was oriented toward reforms that were primarily institutional. The institution of imprisonment in all its forms, along with its historical critique, had also been the axis chosen by the philosopher Michel Foucault (1961).

This was just the right moment for the translation of the collected papers of Harold Searles (1965), describing his clinical work with madness, published in French under the title of one of his papers, "The effort to drive the other person crazy." We immediately recognized in this book one of the transferential modalities we had encountered in practice.

Madness without Borders

Reading Searles committed us to crossing the ocean separating the two traditions, Anglo-Saxon and French. In 1979, we were invited by Jim Gorney (2021), John Muller, and William Richardson (1982, 1995) to present our clinical work in the light of Lacanian concepts at the Austen Riggs Center, in Stockbridge, Massachusetts, which is dedicated to the analytic psychotherapy of the psychoses. This initial contact with clinicians coming from diverse theoretical horizons (Kleinian, Winnicottian, Anna Freudian, Sullivanian, etc.) was as beneficial as could be for us. After our talk, some elements of which are to be found in the present book, Dr. Ess White, director of admissions, asked us simply, "This is all well and good, but now tell us how you do it."

In our pidgin English, without thinking, we found ourselves telling stories of sessions to elders whose respective theoretical reference points we did not know. The work of Sullivan and Frieda Fromm-Reichmann was for the most part unknown to us at the time, among other reasons because there were no translations. We were amazed to find how pleasurable this impromptu exchange was. For what the Austen Riggs clinicians did was to offer their own clinical vignettes, their chief aim being to describe the impasses in which patients know how to drive their analysts into a corner—patients who came to see us, as they came to Riggs, drained, out of breath, after exhausting the theories and ideologies of their former therapists.

We rediscovered this form of clinical exchange several months later, with Sioux medicine men in South Dakota to whom we had been introduced by Gerald Mohatt (Mohatt and Eagle Elk 2000). Mohatt, who was also invited to give a paper at Austen Riggs the following summer, had found our Lacan to be a close kin of the Plains Indians. The puns and the theory of lack and loss as the basis of desire reminded him of "give away" rituals. And in fact, this notion was anchored, for Lacan, in Marcel Mauss's *The Gift* (1924), which was itself influenced by the Amerindians. So we transferred to one of the sources of Lacanian theory. Thus, for several consecutive summers, on the Rosebud Reservation, and then on Manitoulin Island in Ontario; we exchanged clinical stories with medicine men and analysts.

In the context of Sioux or Lakota ceremonies, a person is greeted not just as an individual but in the name of all those to whom he is related. The ritual formula is "all my relatives" (in Lakota, *mitakuye oyasim*). This relationship is conveyed through words and through pledging one's word. We were surprised, therefore, to find direct experience of a theory of speech and language that was familiar to us (Lacan 1953), right down to the comic use of jokes and double entendre during the meal following the ceremony. In the past, in medieval Europe, laughter had been part of the rite. Had we, then, come all this way to find the near and distant trace of language games that had been in use in our own part of the world? In any case, this is how Stanley Red Bird, one of the leaders of the Rosebud Reservation, put it during one of these meetings: "You're finding here what you also have at home."

But in France, at this time, the art of telling clinical stories was hardly in favor. As a rule, in the human sciences, seriousness of conceptualization relegated such stories to the rank of anecdotes. In retrospect, the pleasure of such an exchange—at Austen Riggs in Massachusetts, at the Sinte Gleska University on the Rosebud Reservation in South Dakota, on Manitoulin Island in Lake Huron, at the University of Alaska in Fairbanks—had to do with one detail that, though often forgotten, is fundamental: the therapists admitted that they did not always have it easy or offer the right interpretation but were working on the basis of their own flaws. This work was part of the path they had to walk in the transference to a chosen other, analyst or medicine man. Such a skill had not been gained once and for all in moving up through the stages of official training. Jacques Lacan had already been ironic about the "Lacan label" marking the boundaries of all the conformities and registered trademarks and, obviously, providing no definitive passport for clinical experience.

History's Stories

The stories we were beginning to tell then, with complete freedom, seemed from the outset to be the stories of history,* the history to which these patients never stopped bringing us back. Thirty years later, the title of the present book still emphasizes this point. As Lynn Hunt, a historian of the French Revolution (1992), has recently noted in juxtaposing history and psychoanalysis, the two disciplines were made to encounter one another. But the meeting has been a difficult one. According to Hunt, the trouble stems from the incommensurability between the historical approach, based on the analysis of social forces, and the clinical approach that is so quickly reduced to the individual scale. Between the "tyranny of the social and that of the individual" (Hunt 2002), the outcome, as always, cannot be found in dichotomy.

Where it occurs is in the gap opened up by those patients who rightly lament that they have no self, no "me," no individuality. They teach us that this absence of boundaries is the source of their ability to bear witness to the stories that have been erased from history, the history of breakdowns in the social link,[4] whose disaster they reveal at the price of their own identity. They enable us to see in a "decided simplification of the ordinary life situation [met with in our dealings with schizophrenics] manifestations of the subject matter of each of the social sciences" (Sullivan 1974, 223), as well as concrete examples of the encounter described by Lynn Hunt (2002). Indeed, in the very place where the analyst and the historian find it hard to connect with one another, analytic experience returns to another of its roots, one that is even more deeply buried: the epic function that confronts what has never before been said. In so doing, it once again discovers the rhythms and landmarks of the oral traditions, beginning with the *Iliad*, discussed by the Hellenist Gregory Nagy (1979).

Epics always relate stories of war and battles. In our experience as psychoanalysts, war and madness have an odd relation to one another. As Socrates says at the beginning of Plato's *Gorgias* (1952, 447a), analysts usually arrive after the fighting is over. And yet we always go back there. Is this just our "hobby horse," making us the heirs of Don Quixote or of the Uncle Toby of Sterne's *Tristram Shanty* in order to make contact with difficult patients?

In Extreme Conditions, a Social Link Outside the Norm

At any rate, it is hard to pinpoint such patients without discrediting them; euphemisms like that adjective "difficult" are hardly more illuminating. And so we shall speak of madness. Starting right now, we have to make it clear that we never use this word to describe the psychic structure of an individual but instead to characterize a form of social link in an extreme situation. Wars on whatever scale—worldwide, civil, or ethnic wars, wars of decolonization—are such extreme circumstances, in which the breakdown of all reference points gives rise to links outside the norm. People said to be crazy, in the ordinary sense of the term, show us what it was necessary to do in order to survive.

Thus, in our experience, the successive shocks that constitute the rhythm of an analysis of madness always lead us back to the same region, the field of historical and social traumas. During "the long week-end" between the two wars (Bion 1982), even patients who never directly experienced battlefield traumas show through their symptoms such as collapses of time and guarantees of speech.

But no sooner have these areas been acknowledged than they are reenacted here and now, in the work of the transference. It's war in the analysis, without metaphor. Analytic experience shows that long-ago wars form a precipitate in the sessions on the basis of resonances with the analyst's historical bearings. Such bizarre, uncanny interferences add dimension to these erased catastrophic areas and bring them back into awareness. Their historicization results in unarguable improvements on the individual level.

A Memory That Does Not Forget

What about people living today in countries or on continents that were not territorially affected by world wars? And what about their therapists, who are also too young to have been touched by these historic earthquakes? When someone like this from overseas asks us such questions, we simply reply, "How about your grandparents and your ancestors three or four generations back?" The same comments, the same questions, hold true for analysts' forebears.

To mention only the United States, which is entirely oriented toward the future to be constructed, these resistant symptoms keep on asking,

> Your families that immigrated: where did they come from, when did they leave their country of origin, under what catastrophic circumstances? And what about the frontier, and the Indian Wars, the Hispanic Wars, the Civil War? And the African, American, Canadian, Australian, English and other national cemeteries on French soil? And the wars in Asia and Africa, and social, economic, and natural disasters, on whatever scale?

It would take too much time to list all the countries from which refugees have fled in order to start a new life and forget.

Despite the understandable determination to forget the past, all we had to do is mention this connection between psychoanalysis and the madness of wars for the audiences at the seminars in which we set forth this experience to be reminded, hesitantly but so easily, of the ruined worlds from which their patients' ancestors had escaped. And the analysts' forebears as well: "My father was wounded in Italy and my grandfather was a prisoner for five years; when they came back they were never the same again," we were told at a lecture in Vermont.

At the invitation of the Appalachian Psychoanalytic Society,[5] we gave a talk in Knoxville, Tennessee on *Absalom, Absalom* (Faulkner 1936, 1990), which had been in the forefront of our seminar. That evening, one of the participants continued, over drinks, reconstituting for us in detail the battle of the War of Secession in which two of his ancestors had taken part on each side of the frontline: here was the escarpment, the steep slope (fascinated, we watched the great-nephew's hands), over there was a safe zone, but here one was sure to be killed. As though it were yesterday, and more intensely than in the movies, this analyst seemed to us to be stepping right out of the smoke and dust of battle with mustache, tunic, large hat, or peaked cap. Patients, too, speak in a temporality outside of time.

During these conferences, it happened that Americans, in turn, reminded us of a memory that does not forget. In a pow-wow on Manitoulin Island, in Canada, at a dance around the feather that falls for each warrior killed in combat, someone mentioned those who lie dead in France under wooden crosses. In Alaska, a former World War II pilot took us to task, mentioning his buddy killed in the sky over France.

In 1995, when, invited by The Washington School of Psychiatry, we began working on the relationship between war and the psychoanalysis of the psychoses, Nancy L. Bakalar, M.D., spoke to us at the end of our seminar about "forward psychiatry" and "the Salmon principles," about which we hadn't the slightest idea. We had seen the name Salmon 20 years earlier in Lacan's paper (1947) without realizing how important it was. Nancy Balakar sent us articles that we shall be citing in the course of this book.[6]

During a stay in Paris, Skip Meade, the descendant of an African-American fighter in World War II, offered our seminar excerpts from the writings of W. E. B. Dubois (Dubois 1921) on the role of black US soldiers during the first world war. He told us about how the Red Hand Division distinguished itself heroically under French command.[7] Had we too, then, forgotten, withdrawing into some sort of insensitivity?

Traumas without a Lesion

It is precisely with the critical question of insensitivity that we begin this book. In the first part, we discuss the arguments of the neurologist Antonio Damasio (1995, 1999). But, as it happens, the relationship between madness and neurology has a history that once again takes us back to the war of 1914. The English historian Ben Shephard gives a detailed account of this in *A War of Nerves: Soldiers and Psychiatrists in the Twentieth Century* (2000). To some extent, the psychoanalysis of the psychoses got its start on this front, exposing psychiatrists from the outset to the confusion between madness, psychic trauma, and cerebral lesions.

How, then, does the question present itself? Patients who are clearly afflicted with a cerebral lesion retain an intact intelligence. But, disconnected from their affects, that intelligence leads them to make incoherent and disastrous decisions. Yet a very specific transference joining the researcher to his patient, and attested by the neurologist himself, opens up a fertile area of contact between neurology and psychoanalysis. This prompts us, personally, to think about symptoms that are similar but that are not related to any lesion. Damasio goes as far as to extrapolate this paradox to a "sick culture" (1995, 178) and wonders about the brilliant and affectless intelligence that may constitute its breeding ground. For totalitarian systems and "scientifically programmed," mass exterminations are still in the news today.

Temporal Paradoxes of the Transference with Madness

For us, three factors have constantly brought us back to these war zones:

1 Our patients' crises open an investigation of the sociopolitical fault lines in which the self has exploded.
2 These crises resonate with our own situation during World War II. Both of us were born during this troubled period, and it is activated for us by analogous areas in the space-time of our patients, even if they are bringing us experiences from the other end of the planet with decades of intervening years.
3 The analysts who oriented our research and our clinical work were directly involved in these wars. We shall be describing this dialogue that has gone on for over 25 years, either face to face or through their books and papers.

In this way, the principles of war psychiatry gradually came to seem to us like a framework and a method that were familiar to us in practice even before we discovered their formalization by Thomas Salmon. Salmon had presented them on the basis of his reconnaissance mission in France in 1917. They underlie the presentation of our clinical and theoretical work in the second part of this book.

Still, we are not claiming to provide an extensive treatment of the field of trauma, war, or madness, already covered by an abundant literature,[8] nor to add to a semiology that is, to say the least, problematical when it comes to psychoanalysis. An objective presentation would classify mass or individual trauma on a quantitative basis. In a cultural relativism, it would differentiate what is normal here and what seems intolerable over there. It would make a chronological distinction between wars in past times and wars today.

We have made the opposite choice. We cannot, of course, support the fraudulent notion of an ahistorical and universal psychic reality. The constant changes of scale and the temporal paradoxes we encounter in the examples we give imply precisely that they are located with the greatest exactitude in history, space, and time. But we have emphasized the critical moments of the transference where the exactitude of these references gets blurred and becomes irrelevant. The crises of the planet are the objects of rigorous studies in each discipline charged with analyzing them. But these analyses change their frames of reference abruptly as soon as the event touches you personally.

At these times when he is somehow *touché*, as they say in fencing, the analyst is caught up in the catastrophic area of the investigation. Subject and object are confused: here and there, inside and outside. The past is present, the dead return. It is a child's voice that is speaking, in a session, through the mouth of the adult he has become, in the name of an entire society threatened with disappearance.

Killings on the far-off African shores take up residence in a massacre that occurred in the mountains where the analyst was born, at the same time or years earlier.

Our work brings into existence zones of non-existence wiped out by a powerful blow that actually took place. But whatever the measures chosen for erasing facts and people from memory, the erasures, even when perfectly programmed, only set in motion a memory that does not forget and that is seeking to be inscribed. In Greek, non-forgetting is, literally, *a-letheia*: this is the very name of truth, at stake in this specific memory as in the scientific approach. Hence we do not have to choose between the minute detail and the global fact. Sometimes a fit of madness tells us more than all the news dispatches about the left-over facts that have no right to existence.

Short Stories for a Micro-History

Our accounts of the ways in which these remnants make themselves felt will be intentionally short. In their straightforwardness, they correspond to the critical, heuristic moments of analysis, and to the moments of impasse as well, when the available ways of knowing are no longer effective. These pivotal episodes involve a small number of sessions. We wanted to capture them in their conciseness. In these accounts of when the analytic process founders, the findings and the interpretation always have to do with a piece of the story that escaped history. Actualized in the transference, it sometimes allows time to start moving forward again. These examples are not so much illustrations of a theoretical schema as they are instants of on-the-spot discovery, and so they do not call for an exhaustive case presentation. Nor can they be processed by a statistical treatment or measured against standard scales, forcing them into a pseudo-scientificity.

It is true that, today, psychoanalysis looks antiquated. Its vignettes seem outdated when everything comes down to averages. An almost picturesque vestige, it has left the Broadway footlights of conferences on mental health. Hence the idea of this book: off-Broadway, where psychoanalysis can be found in the company of Quixote-like veterans, a bit ridiculous, not very brilliant. But, in the case of madness, when the time is out of joint, hasn't offstage always been where rather foolish old warriors who keep on saying the same thing meet up with those—little children or therapists—who can't help listening to them, so that, in different ways according to the time and place, narratives emerge out of what has not been received by any form of speech?

One of the important tasks we have set ourselves in this book is describing how the coming into being of the subject of speech, in circumstances created for its destruction, is a matter of life or death. The destruction—this is no metaphor—of the guarantees of speech and the deconstruction of all reference points leave the subject who is confronted with them in a state of total estrangement, of absolute aloneness with regard to all the ties that, up to that point, were familiar (Shapiro and Carr 1991). This alienation from the world is transmitted to whichever of the person's descendants try, in some outburst of madness, to communicate and demonstrate the deafening screams that were left in a state of suspension, until they find someone to whom it has been given to accompany them to those places that no one wants to look at or hear about anymore, so that they can begin a transmission. In this way, a child's gaze can transmit the reflection of a people's disappearance or the vanishing of a social bond on whatever scale. Must we really try to subdue this hypersensitivity? And, most important, how is it to be described?

Martin Cooperman became a great teacher for us when we visited Riggs every summer. A veteran of the Battle of Guadalcanal, he awakened our child's gaze during the two first years of our life, spent, in my case, in a combat zone of the Resistance in the Alps. Like that of Ukrainian children right now.

What we shall be doing, then, is chronicling the battles to which our patients incited us. These critical moments are also moments of theoretical encounters that lead us, each time, to understand that the connection between madness and trauma is not a causal one. For there can be no transition from the past to the present when the impact of the disaster has immobilized time. Thus, the stories we shall tell are those of descendants whose task it was to transmit, from generation to generation, pieces of frozen time. The problem is to recognize that these moments excised from history are reenacted in the present of the analytic work.

A veteran of the Thirty Years War, René Descartes, says, in the *Discourse on the Method* (1637)—written in French to be read by women "who are half of the world":

> Those who little by little discover the truth in the science…can well be com-pared to commanders of armies who have need of more leadership to maintain themselves after the loss of a battle than they do after having won one. For to vanquish all the difficulties that prevent us from arriving to the knowledge of the truth, is truly to engage in battles…. And to accept some false opinion is to lose one of them.
>
> (1996, 93)

So it goes when we engage in battle with[9] these patients who literally fight with their backs to the wall in order to bring forth rejected truths. After all, according to Gregory Nagy (1979), the etymology of the word therapist,—*therapôn*—means, in the *Iliad* the second in combat, also in charge with funeral rites.

Children on the Firing Line

After the wars of the period of decolonization, military psychiatrists were struck by the proximity of symptoms affecting soldiers, civilians, and even children, who had had no direct contact with the fighting. Today, we have come full circle with child soldiers being sent to the front lines in a real and organized proximity with gunfire.[10]

In 1986, an investigation into the dramatic collision, 11 years earlier, between two American ships ascertained that not only the sailors but also their families had been affected in a major way. The wife of one of the crewmen consulted a pediatrician: her baby was not gaining weight. The doctor saw that the child was not being fed enough. Its mother, distressed about her husband, who had begun to drink after the collision, had her mind elsewhere. Six people had been killed and 46 wounded on his boat (McCaughey 1986).

In 1977, it had finally been admitted officially that such symptoms were similar to those found in soldiers, and it was decided to reactivate the Salmon principles[11] for traumatized patients and their relatives. For a long time, the magical belief in pharmacology as a panacea had rendered them obsolete.

For, even in children, the widespread use of psychotropic drugs leads to increased dosages in the face of resistance to treatment, to the point where a veritable chemical straitjacket is created—for whose protection? One wonders. The relevance of the allegedly serious studies that have multiplied since the 1980s, based on the illusion of objective observation and statistical curves, has finally been challenged, "for, in this regard, they in fact seem tautological, biased, at a time when neutrality is being questioned even in the basic sciences" (Bailly 1996, 13).

Children are the first to be pushed into proximity with strangeness, even if it is silent. From this interface, they bring back eloquent symptoms. As the child psychiatrist Lionel Bailly puts it, when "children hear the voices of the dead" these are most often the voices of those who died without burial, without a rite. This brief hallucination will cease as soon as it is heard by a therapist in whom the voices of the dead can resonate instead of remaining a dead letter. If the voice finds no echo, he says,

> we have the seed of psychosis... In the face of this call for symbolization, the causalist biologistic explanation in terms of the release of neurotransmitters deals with the vector and loses sight of the message being transmitted. There is no discontinuity between trauma and psychosis.
>
> (Bailly 1996, 32)

Frieda Fromm-Reichmann (1946, 1959) stated that emotionally traumatic experiences underlie all psychoses. The therapist's proximity consists of the exercise of tact to a superlative degree. For, in trauma, huge quantities of rage and resentment are expressed in response to this experience and expressed toward the therapist as well. Fromm-Reichmann goes on to explain that the meeting must take place on an egalitarian footing, not that of preordained authority, even if the psychiatrist is an officer. What is this equality like?

In the case of children, who sometimes demonstrate excitation—including sexual excitation—that they are unable to articulate in words, so as to feel alive, the only possible reply, Lionel Bailly writes, varies with the interference of the transference. Far from pushing the child to abreaction and arousing affects that quickly get out of control, the analyst must not give in to a fascination, intrusive or passive, that consists in wanting to know everything or wanting to know nothing.

His only resort is to begin by saying what he knows about the history, the situation, his impressions, and the therapeutic unconscious activated in him by the power of the images that have not yet entered a language game.

This renunciation of neutrality can be reassuring, in that it makes it possible not to deny death or the truth, however, painful: yes, it is normal to have nightmares in such a situation, and this can happen to anyone. But, at the same time, we are well aware that the analyst's words also give rise to a negative transference and attract the destructive force of the traumatic event. In both cases, haven or tinder, it is important "to exchange one's own knowledge of catastrophes for the child's terrible knowledge, so that the child is no longer the only one holding it" (Bailly 1996, 102).

They Are Right to Be Crazy[12]

We have been describing traumas that are identifiable in time and space. Even when the symptoms affect a descendant, the connection with the traumatic catastrophe is often clear. But sometimes it is impossible to rewind the film. At those times, if the elements that have been cut off from the world of the living are to be made visible, recognized, and inscribed, we need history to act as our compass. Investigating history in the making means getting one's bearings when the compass needles are spinning in the zones of the spasms of time. The search is for names lost, people betrayed, facts covered up on the border with the wild space in which the Erinyes of vengeance fill the air with their formless howling (Loraux 1990). John Ford's film *The Man Who Shot Liberty Valence* (1962) is a perfect representation of such a moment when time stops and official history is rewritten on the basis of betrayal, silence, and lies: the tone is on the level of classical tragedy, and the name of the sacrificed hero, Tom Doniphon, is a phonetic sign to those who understand Greek, since it means "the monster slayer."

There is no relativity when it comes to betrayal: whether the scale is that of a nation, a village, or a family, the lethal zone opened up by this catastrophe in the domain of giving one's word results in the same confusion. Where there is no trust, inscription—that is, transmission followed by forgetting—becomes impossible.

In Sophocles' (1954) *Antigone*,[13] Polynices, who betrayed the city, is killed in a fratricidal war. His body is rotting, given to the dogs on the order of the tyrant Creon. In his commentary on the play, Lacan (1959–1960, ch.21) defines the space into which the heroine enters in order to bury her brother as "the space in between two deaths."

Between real death, which belongs to the cycle of decomposition, and death inscribed in the register of the Symbolic, between the rotting of the body and the ritual inscription of the name, a space–time is inserted, that of the tragedy, where figures of the unspeakable make their appearance. All reference points are lost, all otherness, and hence the possibility of a subject, is banished. At the same time, the repetition compulsion is in fact reaching toward a tentative inscription. Antigone keeps on provoking the tyrant so as to assert the unwritten laws toward her dead brother, even if he is a traitor, even at the cost of her own death. And this is, of course, why she is crazy, as the increasingly exasperated Creon complains.

This is the madness of children who have seen too much. Whatever their age, to accompany them into the field of their rigorous action means leaving aside the fascination for horrors. Taking up this very question, Plato emphasized the connection between the Real, "that entity without color, form, or name, whose being is being" (*Phaedrus*, 1995, 247c), and madness, ultimately conceived as an implement of cure (244d). We offer here our own translation of this luminous passage, often obscured by inexact interpretations:

> But diseases, immense sufferings come from ancient rages and exist in certain members of a lineage. By occurring and doing the work of interpretation in those who need it, madness has found the way to remove them. By recourse to prayers and services to the gods, by carrying out purifications and ceremonies, madness frees those whom it possesses, for the present and afterward. Thus it finds a way to release whoever is caught in a just madness [who has reason to be crazy] from the present evils.
>
> [244a]

Thus, babies have direct access not only to domestic violence but to the rage of the Erinyes, which, charging down the course of several generations, can slip into a simple household quarrel. Suddenly, the validity of the child's perceptions is denied, and the official doctrine offers him deceptive gestures, words, and silences. As a result, the baby knows too much for his age.[14]

They Know Too Much for Their Age

Such a precocious and premature knowledge is not able to be remembered as past but occurs as an arousal without chronological perspective. At certain moments—birth, imminent death, becoming a father, childbirth—where the radical novelty calls for the giving of a name to inscribe what has happened into the process of exchange, there is a risk that "the tool with the name" called forth will break (Wittgenstein 1945, 41). Then the continuity of transmission is interrupted on this point in the "string of words" (Sullivan 1945, 214), and something that cannot be spoken erupts as uncanny sensorial images, seeking the doorway of language.

Hannah Arendt (1971, 100) contrasts this symbolic welcome of the novelty with the anonymous mechanism, still current nowadays, in which people are reduced to numbers: "The sheer naming of things, the creation of words, is the human way of appropriating and, as it were, disalienating the world into which, after all, each of us is born as a newcomer and a stranger." It is in the name of this radical newness and its potential that Arendt opposed the deliberate use of children for the purposes of war or to serve their parents' claims, however justified.

Now in the cut-out unconscious of a family line, this precocious knowledge may sometimes rush, with an incredible concentration, into a mind and a body too small to contain it. It is always the baby in the adult who knows too much for its age. Its irruption is a rupture of continuity in the world and in discourse that bursts the boundaries of the self and activates similar zones in the analyst. When that happens, interferences and coincidences become the sole referents of what has disappeared from the exchange between people. How do we spot this moment?

The irruption of the Real into a session is made apparent by the fact that everything becomes "as if" and begins to obey a pseudo-rule of free association or even the rules of etiquette. The analyst is suddenly deprived of his role as Other. The patient wants to stop right there: trust has been broken; the given speech does not hold anymore. This rupture may come back several times.

Analysts approach these phenomena, in terms of countertransference, and projective identification. But in that case, what can "to *project*" mean when the inside and outside of an oriented space as well as the past or future of the arrow of time are not constituted in this particular situation. On the other hand, the analyst's reactions are registered from the outset by such hyper vigilant patients, creating a breach in neutrality. The disclosure and formulation by the analyst of what happened in their interaction validates the premature knowledge at stake, instead of reducing the patients to the state of invalids implied by their psychotic structure.

In order to constitute an Other when it has been destroyed, the analyst puts together bits and pieces of these interferences, which are "imponderable evidence" (Wittgenstein 1954, 228) of the registering of the inaudible and the annulled. From my experience of supervision, I contend that we are never proud of sharing such particulars, but we offer them as tiny attempts to create a subject of speech for the unspeakable, corresponding to precise moments, that we would, however, never dare to boast of before our colleagues.

Supervision sessions teem with such anti-exploits, which some analysts relate shamefully even though they have been endowed, in fact since childhood, with the ability to work with madness and traumas. Acknowledged in the context of limited transmission to one's peers, and often condemned by scholastic doxa, such critical moments allow the birth of a political subject, a witness of events without a witness (Laub and Felman 1992).

Notes

1 This chapter includes selections from *History Beyond Trauma: Where of One Cannot Speak, Thereof One Cannot Stay Silent* (New York: Other Press, 2004).
2 Arendt 1951, pp. 326–340 (Chapter 10, "The Temporary Alliance between the Mob and the Elite").
3 As we go along, we shall be presenting the aspects of Lacan's teaching that have been of use to us.

 * Translator's note: in French, the same word, _histoire_, means both "story" and "history."
 4 For this term, which we shall be using throughout the book, see Book 4, Chapter 8 of Rousseau 1762.
 5 William MacGillivray, at that time president of the Appalachian Association, gave us the opportunity to get to know Pat Barker's **Trilogy** (1992, 1994, 1995).
 6 We presented them in 1996–1997 in our seminar entitled "The Madness of War," at the Ecole des Hautes Etudes en Sciences Sociales in Paris.
 7 DuBois cites the letter of December 15, 1918 from the French general Goybet, who led the Red Hand division for eight months, when he handed it over to American command. He praises the men for their performance in the battle of Champagne in September of that year: "The Red Hand Division has, during nine hard days of battle, been ahead in the victorious advance of the Fourth French Army ... and led us to victory. Soaked in the blood of the brave, those bonds will be indestructible" (p. 66).
 8 Cf. the recent works of the Erikson Institute first director Gerard Fromm (2022), and of its current director, Jane Tillman (2016).
 9 "With" in both senses: "alongside" and "against."
 10 Cf. Arendt 1959. No matter what ideologies seek to legitimate such engagements, Arendt warns us to recognize the signs of totalitarianism.
 11 "In January 1977, staff at the Portsmouth Naval Hospital Psychiatry Department observed that the kinds of psychological problems generated by military disasters were similar to those encountered by the battlefield soldier. It was hypothesized that the same early intervention techniques developed during World Wars I and II could also be used to treat disaster victims" (McCaughey 1987, 133).
 12 Cf. tô orthôs manenti (Plato, Phaedrus, 244a).
 13 Aeschylus, Sophocles, Socrates, and Thucydides were war veterans.
 14 Cf. the expression _parentified child._

References

Arendt, Hannah. 1951. _The Origins of Totalitarianism._ New York: Harvest, 1976.
———. 1959. "Reflections on Little Rock." _Dissent_ 6, no. 1: 45–56.
———. 1971. _The Life of the Mind._ New York: Harcourt Brace.
Barker, Pat. 1992–1995. _Regeneration Trilogy._ New York, Penguin.
Bion, Wilfred. 1982. _The Long Week-End, 1897-1919._ London: Karnac.
Bailly, Lionel. 1996. _Les Catastrophes et leurs conséquences psychotraumatiques chez l'enfant. Description cliniques et traitement._ Paris: ESF.
Damasio, Antonio. 1995. _Descartes' Error. Emotion, Reason, and the Human Brain._ New York: Avon.
———. 1999. _The Feeling of What Happens: Body and Emotion in the Making of Consciousness._ New York: Harvest.
Descartes, René. 1637. _Discourse on the Method,_ A Bilingual Edition, Ed, Trans, G. Heffernan, Saint Paul. Notre Dame, IN: Notre Dame University Press, 1994.
DuBois, W.E.B. 1921. _The Seventh Son. The Black Man in the Revolution (1914-1918.)_ New York: Random House, 1986.
Faulkner, William. 1936. _Absalom, Absalom!_ New York: Vintage International, 1990.
Ford, John (director). 1962. _The Man Who Shot Liberty Valence_ (film).
Fromm-Reichmann, Frieda. 1946. _Psychoanalysis and Psychotherapy._ Chicago, IL: The University of Chicago Press, 1959.

Foucault, Michel. 1965. *Madness and Civilization: A History of Insanity in the Age of Reason.* New York: Vintage, 1988.

Fromm, Gerard. 2022. *Traveling through Time. How Trauma Plays Itself Out in Families, Organizations and Society.* Oxfordshire: Phoenix Publishing House.

Gorney, James E. 2021. "Otto Will and the Art of Relationship, More Simply Human Than Otherwise." *Contemporary Psychoanalysis* 57, no. 1 (May): 85–114.

Hunt, Lynn. 1992. *The Family Romance of the French Revolution.* Berkeley: University of California Press.

———. 2002. "History and Psychoanalysis." Paper delivered at the colloquium "Why Psychoanalysis?" Radcliffe Center for Advanced Studies, Cambridge, MA, February.

Lacan, Jacques. 1947. La psychanalyse anglaise et la guerre. In *Autres écrits,* 101–120. Paris: Seuil, 2001.

———. 1953. "The Function and Field of Speech and Language in Psychoanalysis." In *Ecrits. A Selection,* trans. A. Sheridan, 30–113. New York: Norton, 1977.

———. 1957–1958. "On a Question Preliminary to any Possible Treatment of Psychosis." In *Ecrits. A Selection,* trans. A. Sheridan, 179–221. New York: Norton, 1977.

———. 1959–1960. *Le séminaire, livre VII. L'éthique de la psychanalyse.* Paris: Seuil, 1986.

———. 1969–1970. *Le séminaire, livre XVII. L'envers de la psychanalyse.* Paris: Seuil, 1991.

Laub, Dori and Felman, Shoshana. 1992. *Testimony: Crises of Witnessing in Literature, Psychoanalysis and History.* New York and London: Routledge.

Loraux, Nicole. 1990. "La métaphore sans métaphore. À Propos de l'Orestie." *Revue philosophique.* 2: 115–139.

McCaughey, Brian G. 1986. "The Psychological Symptomatology of a U. S. Naval Disaster." *Military Medicine* 151: 162–165.

———1987. U. S. Navy Special Psychiatric Rapid Intervention Team. (SPRINT). *Military Medicine* 152: 133–135.

Mauss, Marcel. 1924. *The Gift. The Form and Reason for Exchange in Archaic Societies.* trans. W. D. Halls. New York: Norton, 1990.

Mohatt, G. and Eagle Elk, J. 2000. *The Price of a Gift. A Lakota Healer's Story.* Lincoln: University of Nebraska Press.

Muller, John P. 1995. *Beyond the Psychoanalytic Dyad. Developmental Semiotics in Freud, Peirce, and Lacan.* New York and London: Routledge.

Muller, John P. and. Richardson William J. 1982. *Lacan and Language: A Reader's Guide to Ecrits.* New York: New York University Press.

Nagy, Gregory. 1979. *The Best of the Achaeans: Concepts of the Hero in Archaic Greek Society.* Baltimore, MD. Johns Hopkins University Press.

Plato. 1952. *Gorgias.* transl. W.H. Helmbold. New York: New York Press Hall.

———. 1995. *Phaedrus.* trans. A. Nehamas. New York: Hackett.

Rousseau, Jean J. 1762. *Du contrat social,* IV,8, § 20.

Searles, Harold. 1965. "The Effort to Drive the Other Person Crazy." In *Collected Papers on Schizophrenia and Related Subjects.* Madison, CT: International Universities Press.

Shapiro, Edward and Carr, A. Wesley. 1991. *Lost in Familiar Places. Creating New Connections between Individual and Society.* New Haven, CT: Yale University Press.

Shephard, Ben. 2000. *A War of Nerves: Soldiers and Psychiatrists in the Twentieth Century.* Cambridge, MA: Harvard University Press.

Sophocles. 1954. *Antigone.* In *Sophocles I. Four Tragedies,* trans. E. Wyckoff, 157–204. Chicago, IL: University of Chicago Press.

Sullivan, Henry Stack. 1945. *The Fusion of Psychiatry and Social Science.* New York: Norton.

———. 1974. *Schizophrenia as a Human Process.* New York: Norton.

Tillman, Jane. 2016. "The Intergenerational Transmission of Suicide: Moral Injury and The Mysterious Object in the Work of Walker Percy." *Journal of the American Psychoanalytic Association* 64, no. 3: 541–568.

Wittgenstein, Ludwig. [1945–1949] 1958. *Philosophical Investigations.* Oxford: Blackwell, 1954.

Afterword

Françoise Davoine

I came to Austen Riggs in 1979 with my late husband, Jean Max Gaudillière to learn about the psychoanalysis of psychoses, which we already practiced in a public psychiatric hospital in France, although we were neither psychologists nor psychiatrists. As faculty of a social science institute, the EHESS in Paris, we had started to research the relationship between madness and historical catastrophes—the topic of our mandatory weekly seminar, entitled "Madness and the Social Link," for 40 years.

Our arrival at Riggs opened a whole world of research and clinical experience. We heard there for the first time the names of Frieda Fromm-Reichmann and Harry Stack Sullivan, who, like us, had close links to social science researchers. For the first time, we could tell stories of how our practice put patients before theoretical issues. To our astonishment, we discovered at Riggs a new way to handle transference, especially through conversations with Dr. Martin Cooperman, then Medical Director of Austen Riggs.

Austen Riggs was for us the origin of other relationships throughout the United States, mainly with clinicians interested in the psychoanalysis of psychosis and trauma. In the Lacan forum, which was held regularly at Riggs, we met William Hurst, who translated my book *Wittgenstein's Folly,* which includes several chapters staged at Riggs.

The first summer we spent there, we met the late Gerald Mohatt, also a future Erikson scholar and a psychologist on the Rosebud Reservation, where he later invited us to talk with medicine men. So, each summer, over several years, we spent some weeks at Riggs, and then flew to South Dakota to participate in ceremonies and share clinical stories with the medicine man, as we did with our colleagues at Austen Riggs. In 1985, we met its former medical director, Dr. Otto Will, whose jubilee was celebrated there. Many important collaborations followed, thanks to Austen Riggs, a setting central to our research with patients who have gone through extreme experiences at the crossroads of personal stories and historical upheavals.

Jean Max Gaudillière and I were first invited as Erikson Scholars in October 2002, as we had completed the first draft of *History Beyond Trauma*, an excerpt from which is included here. In 2017, after Jean Max's death in 2015, I was invited again as an Erikson Scholar, in order to transcribe the notes I took during his

DOI: 10.4324/9781003322627-5

seminars at the EHESS, since he spoke without any written text. This dream came true thanks to the Erikson Institute's generosity and that of its successive directors Jerry Fromm and Jane Tillman. I spent the summer in a house on the grounds of the clinic, working in an office next to the library. I was warmly supported during weekly meetings with John Muller, and the kindness of all the staff. I returned to France with the two future volumes published by Routledge: *Madness and the Social Link* and *The Birth of a Political Subject.*

Needless to say, my gratitude toward the Erikson Institute is immense.

Chapter 3

On Dangerous Ground

Freud's Visual Cultures of the Unconscious[1]

Diane O'Donoghue

Introduction

Questions of materiality and meaning—matter and what matters—are compelling both as contemporary and as historical inquiries inseparable from the tangled, and at times tragic, determinations of who and what would merit value and worth. This book places these concerns at the fore of a series of narratives examining the relationships between visual culture and Sigmund Freud's construction of an "unconscious." Such a locus is not a common one, as material objects have tended to be the subject of psychical analysis; here their physical presences will be more vividly drawn, and drawn into, the making of psychoanalysis itself. To embark on such an endeavor, one must first determine when and how to enter into this dynamic, complex, and—as I will argue—exquisitely particular story. I locate my inquiries in the earlier half of Freud's long life, which spanned eight decades, from 1856 to 1939: the book's final chapter focuses on *The Interpretation of Dreams,* published just as the twentieth century was to begin. Much of what will be discussed occurred in the 1890s, when Freud first formulated ideas that would become foundational to the work to follow: fantasy, defense, repression, childhood sexual wishes given credence by the story of *Oedipus Rex,* and the functioning of dreams. My chapters introduce into this consequential and highly scrutinized period for psychoanalysis certain travelers who were also part of this journey yet whose roles have been largely unexamined. Some are individuals whose lives intersected with Freud's, but their experiences are all inextricably aligned here with other presences, not of flesh, but of stone, clay, pigment, or paper. These latter objects, and those persons associated with them, participated in what we might call, inspired by the title of one of Freud's well-known works, his "psycho-materiality of everyday life."[2] Specific buildings, "antiquities" (objects removed and transferred from various early cultural sites), paintings, and books are located here as constitutive, rather than illustrative, of Freud's early notion of an unconscious.

Attributes Freud would associate with psychical functioning—not infrequently described using a rhetoric of "discovery"—were often considered innovative and consequential because they were enunciated as operating autonomously, separate from both conscious awareness and investments in power located within

DOI: 10.4324/9781003322627-6

physical objects. Freud's origin narratives invariably gesture inward, recounted in the language of instincts and drives, of residual, phylogenic legacies from an often-colonialist creation of a "primitive" past. [3] To give the beginnings of the Freudian unconscious a cultural and visual history in their own moment, as discursive formations, opens a productive space for these seemingly intrapsychic mechanisms to "materialize;' and as a concurrent and coeval gesture, for certain buildings and objects, significant to Freud, to be reckoned as sites of affective experiences, albeit not among those he accorded much attention analytically. Peter Galison has described this as a "re-literalization" in his work identifying how synchronized clocks were really "at the heart" of the "more abstract reasoning" of Albert Einstein and Henri Poincare (Galison 2012, 237). [4] He has also applied this inquiry to Freud, considering the role of censorship in political practices, specifically by the Viennese press, in the shaping of psychical processes. Galison's (2012, 238) "abstract concreteness" and "concrete abstractions" find parallels here as I suggest aspects of visual culture whose practices and representational capacities may have animated—whether because embraced or disavowed—Freud's formulations.

One strategy for such an inquiry is to begin our investigation as certain of Freud's ideas are coming into being, before they appeared in published form and thus become productive of what is posited as *a priori* functioning. Much of this thinking is found in letters to Freud's intimate interlocutor during much of the 1890s, the Berlin otolaryngologist Wilhelm Fliess. [5] There are often disparities between what Freud expressed privately, especially in his earliest sharing of experiences later to become exemplars of psychical functioning, and in published work. Once iterated, these ideas quickly naturalized, and what began as descriptive speculation became descriptors of functions and mechanisms; as imagined constructions, following precedents of both European empiricism and empire, they were claimed to have been "found": Freud's thinking of course shifted over the ensuing decades, and to hold him to these originary musings would be untenable in a study of his psychoanalytic project as a whole. However, returning to the start is particularly relevant for considering the place and provocation of visual and cultural objects, as this is a time before their importance was subsumed within the mechanisms to which, as I argue, they significantly contributed. In the chapters to follow, I consider certain physical presences—built structures, paintings, illustrated books—as generative of affects and associations that preceded what Freud will "discover" as psychical attributes.

To hold the originary moments of Freud's ideas is a bit like grasping at the imagery of a dream as one awakens. In this case, the encompassing "reality" our eyes fix upon is what has become known as psychoanalysis. I attempt to hold open some space not made accessible solely by what we know will follow in Freud's oeuvre. If this is a challenging enterprise, then identifying the meaning we can grant particular objects and structures—those existing in the world, or as memories or dreams about them—within these nascent ideas is an even more elusive operation. For to suggest that visual culture was *productive* of psychical value contrasts sharply with how much of it came to be reckoned "psychoanalytically": this imagery frequently was cast as meaningless, made to not "matter" in both readings of the term. We can identify an instance in Freud's understanding of the visuality of dreams, where the imagery recalled from sleep is relegated to a hallucinatory function ("manifest content") in the service of repression, and thus mediated by the intention to disguise the dream's "latent meaning": Another form of "not mattering" involves physical objects themselves whose impact is rendered inconsequential within Freud's project. I argue that such disavowal was a way for Freud to contain experiences of vulnerability, betrayal, and danger, and the feelings they may have elicited in him. While Freud's pursuits have become known through John Kerr's (1993) descriptor of a "dangerous method,"[6] those foregrounded here are associated with objects and experiences whose perils lay upon the ground, and often in plain sight. We will encounter certain irreducible threats and disruptions that, as such, would be destined to remain beyond reach. But if we stand outside of analytic meaning, we are better able to see its borders. Readers of this book are asked to imagine what Freud considered inconsequential as defining yet another entity that only becomes visible when our attention shifts to it, as in viewing an illusionistic image, when mere background is revealed as itself formative of an often quite different picture. My hope is that by identifying how certain claims to value were established, we are able to resist the ontologizing tendencies around the discourse of the "unconscious"; and to see how the impact of exclusionary ideologies, to which Freud was both subjected and in which he participated, shaped the contours and mechanisms of his psychoanalytic project.

The book opens ("The Lost Language of Stones") on Vienna's urban ground, from which a vast architectural program arose in the course of Freud's youth and young adulthood as a striking array of buildings along the newly constructed Ringstrasse. His early visual and affective responses to the city's new structures are little known, although we consider ways in which these surroundings, into which he came as a three-year-old, may have been meaningful to him. It will be in another European city and in the unlikely surroundings of arguably its most notable church—Paris's Notre Dame—that Freud, now nearly 30, will leave evidence of the ways in which he could enter into a relationship with architecture. The Neogothic edifice served as a haven for him, an unexpected role, given that Freud, as a Viennese Jew, regarded his own city's medieval cathedral as an object of considerable scorn. Yet, while in Paris on a fellowship in the winter months of 1885–1886, Freud found in Notre Dame both an enclave and an extension of the lectures he attended at his sponsoring institution, a vast public hospital, the Salpetriere. Its director, Jean-Martin Charcot, focused much of his work at that time on the construction known as "hysteria," whose representations in clinical displays and photographs of patients—Charcot was very aware of the hysteric as a trope of medieval visualizations—Freud may have seen as akin to the statuary, the architect's fantasy of gargoyles, on his frequent visits to viewing platforms on the church's roof.[7] That Freud was so in thrall to this building suggests insights into meanings that he may have associated more widely with its architectural idiom. While one thinks of this nineteenth-century phantasm of a medieval edifice—most of what stood in Freud's time was a reconstruction—as melded to Paris, there was a very distinctive and important *Neugotik* presence in Vienna in the last decades of that century. I will introduce two buildings in this style, both the work of the Germanborn architect Friedrich von Schmidt, and chart Freud's relationship to them, their very specific meanings within Vienna's civic topography, and ways in which this architecture may have become, for Freud, the site of betrayal. One example will be an apartment building where he moved, setting up his residence and practice there, soon after returning from Paris and at the time of his marriage to Martha Bernays. Schmidt and his family would be the Freuds' neighbors, living in the building as well. The other is the architect's most notable edifice in the Habsburg capital: the Rathaus, Vienna's City Hall.

These buildings each held different narratives for Freud. Connected with his residence was the loss to suicide of Pauline Silberstein, a patient whose death was made possible by specific structural particularities of the building, itself a memorial to tragic deaths. The City Hall, with its assertions of a secular vision of a "free" polis, was occupied, by the mid-1890s, by a mayor whose reactionary ideologies turned the building's founding vision into a ruin, without damaging a stone. I read these experiences alongside two points in Freud's work during that period when architectural imagery enters, materializing aspects of his conceptualizations of "hysteria" and suggesting how betrayal, defense, and protection may have moved from stone to psyche in unexpected ways, and once naturalized as internal functions become difficult to re-trace.

The relationships between Freud and the structures introduced earlier have been largely overlooked; when he is associated with a building, the narrative has focused, with good reason, on the place that succeeded Schmidt's apartments as his home and working space for over four decades. This latter building did not in fact betray him until the very end of the family's residence there, when its owner displayed Nazi symbols on it, as Freud, now gravely ill and over 80, Martha Freud, and their youngest child, Anna, were forced to emigrate to London, in the spring of 1938, where Freud would die the following year. It is in this long-time residence that he would find an interiority both architecturally—his home at Berggasse 19 in the ninth district had little in the way of a distinctive façade or civic presence, unlike his previous dwelling—and in the increasing elaborations of the workings of an unconscious and its intrapsychic mechanisms. It is in certain rooms there that Freud's connection to visual culture is also most commonly located, in his vast collection of "antiquities": well over 2,000 objects from various early sites associated with Egypt, the Greek, and Roman empires, and areas in the eastern Mediterranean. They were gathered exclusively in his working spaces, filling every surface of his consulting room and study. Edmund Engelman would create his well-known photographs of these rooms just as the Freud family was forced to leave, with the merger of Austria and Germany *(Anschluss);* these images thus reveal the assemblage in its final moments as participants in the scene of Freud's psychoanalytic work. There has been a considerable body of scholarship on the collection as it was in these rooms, where the objects were a striking presence for patients and visitors. Once relocated to London, the contents have become the holdings of the Freud Museum and thus removed from the role they may have played in the therapeutic encounters and writing that they quite literally encircled.

But even while still in Vienna, Freud's "antiquities" are usually imagined as a somewhat static collection, and with no visual record to match that of Engelman, the assemblage of these objects is melded to the contours of these small spaces, to each other, and the work that Freud did among them in the first decades of the twentieth century. His deliberate choice to contain the objects exclusively within his psychoanalytically charged space certainly suggests their roles as companions and agents provocateurs, but little has been said about how these functions may have emerged, although their sheer number alone would make those claims highly credible. The collection's beginnings have remained obscure, linked frequently with a comment Freud made to Fliess in December of 1896, in the months after Freud's father, Jacob, had died: he mentioned placing plaster casts of Renaissance statuary in his office, and the comfort they afforded him. These were reproductions, and as such could gesture quite specifically back to well-known "originals" whose narratives, as notable "works of art," were an inextricable part of the copies.

But what Freud turned to collect was a different "matter": small objects whose meaning referred less to a specific moment or creator, but more to an amalgam of historicized sherds, the criterion for their acquisition being a discernment of their value; it has been suggested that Freud was able by this time to afford "authentic" objects, and this economic factor is not to be dismissed. But the earliest history of the collection, as we are able to reconstruct, suggests a genealogy considerably more specific and locates Freud's turn to such objects at a time of profound transition, in September 1897, in his thinking from the role of traumatic events in early life to the effects of repressed childhood sexual fantasies, directed primarily at parents. Prompted by this coincidence, I explore the very beginnings of the collection ("Phantasmal Fragments") and ask whether the inauguration of this assemblage can be associated with a change in Freud's understanding of the efficacy and value of singular evidential remains of an "ancient past." I focus on the circumstances under which Freud purchased among the first of his objects—an Etruscan storage container—from a dealer's shop in the Italian town of Orvieto, presenting his acquisition as the inaugural gesture validating performative acts of selection and the prerogatives of ownership. The object is examined not in relation to the rest of the collection that accrued at Berggasse 19, but as it was transformed into an "antiquity" by excavator/dealer Riccardo Mancini in Orvieto, and the role this process played in the period immediately following the acquisition, as Freud was amassing evidence in his self-analysis, picking, and choosing his psychical assemblage.

The phantasm of Freud's Etruscan vessel (falsely sold to him as a "cinerary urn") —it only survives as it appeared in a dream he had about it—will be read alongside a particular psychical fragment that Freud claims to have found in his cluttered storeroom, an image he does indeed use at this moment, of his recollections and dreams in the autumn of 1897. This recollection was a golden treasure indeed, as it provided Freud with evidence of the exact moment and place that he first experienced sexual desire, at age three, for his mother, at a time when he was speculating to Fliess about the universalized possibilities of familial desires he would associate with the story of *Oedipus Rex*. Freud mentions that this revelatory experience took place as he and his family were traveling to Vienna, when he supposedly had the opportunity to see his mother naked, in the final portion of a migratory experience that had begun in his Moravian birthplace and was punctuated by a brief and difficult residency in Leipzig. I reinvest this story of the activation and agency of childhood eroticism back into the circumstances of its original moment ("Libido Awakened: In Transit and Enframed"), before it entered into the specifics of meaning registered only in a psychical realm. By doing so, a different story is revealed, not of desiring, but instead of a vulnerable, dislocated child, experiencing multiple moves that at times must have felt interminable: by the age of ten Freud had lived in nine places in three different central European locations.[8] But by turning his story of arriving in Vienna into an Oedipal "antiquity," giving it much vaunted value, he leaves the remaining aspects of the narrative unspoken, just as the objects in his office, taken from their specific sites, lose memory of that violence done to them, and instead become exemplars of narratives created by those who traffic in and collect them.

Freud would extract much of the early life detailed in this chapter from visibility, making such omissions a condition of an unconscious forgetting that he imagined as universal and extending through nearly the first decade of childhood. He would come to call this "infantile amnesia"; whose first exemplar would be his own assessment of his first years in Vienna, when "nothing was worth remembering"; a statement that suggests intentionality and particularity. His psychical enactment of this, however, becomes a non-remembering bound up with a mechanism and singular motive, assuring the inaccessibility of repressed incestuous desires in childhood. Threading through this book is a tension between what is deemed "forgotten"—a repression identified with unconscious functioning—and a second form of omission of memory within Freud's work, crucial but unspoken, which allows his psychical model to function: the "forgettable." What was forgotten, as repression, is not irreparably lost; in fact, this kind of forgetting signaled the location of unconscious processes, and the repressed could, through psychoanalysis, potentially be made accessible; this was the currency of analytic work. The forgettable, by contrast, is not intended ever to return to view, much less scrutiny. Although Freud placed such extraordinary importance on the internal vicissitudes of childhood fantasies and sexual desires, he utterly detached them from the forces at work around him in his own early life.

We turn in the last two chapters to examples where Freud's mechanism of repression and its evidence in the workings of displacement, in speech and sleep, bring us back to visual culture and the makings of psychoanalytic "forgetability." Freud would have us turn away, both from the sight of an object holding certain childhood "sorrows" and from representations of antisemitism, by relegating their presence to the periphery of meaning. While the surface imagery was posited as being at the service of prediscursive operations of the psyche, the unconscious was far from ideologically innocent. I trace how Freud fueled the workings of repression in his first published exposition of a psychical mechanism through allusions to thoughts about the "peculiarity" of the "Bosnian Turks" in matters of sexuality and death, imagining his readers would find such stimulus credible to set these mechanisms in motion.

Although Bosnia is a crucial aspect of Freud's 1898 essay on the "psychical mechanism of forgetfulness"; the story begins a year earlier, in Orvieto, and on the same trip in which Freud purchased his Etruscan vessel. In Chapter 4 ("The Painting of Everyday Life"), I locate another aspect of visual culture—a series of Renaissance-period paintings—at the center of his inaugural publication on an example of a common occurrence—forgetting a name—that attested to the workings of repression. Freud recounts to Fliess a conversation he had while on holiday in the Balkans, when he was speaking about paintings, specifically those seen the year before in the Orvieto cathedral, and could not recall the artist's name, Luca Signorelli. It is significant that although the story is based on his experience of a very compelling series of frescoes of the Last Judgment, Freud takes great pains to resituate his memory lapse away from these objects. The psychical meaning is contained exclusively to the operation of the mechanism that he charts here, with the memory lapse cast as the result of a repression of thoughts he directs toward the "Moslem" communities of Bosnia. But by examining aspects of this story that have not mattered, I offer a quite different reading of this incident, suggesting that the paintings turned suddenly from an affirmation of Freud's enfranchisement as a cultured Viennese traveler to a source of vulnerability and threat. His vivid memory of the artist's self-portrait is recounted at the moment he loses the artist's name. This image stands as the hinge between two chapels, each with prominent examples of anti-Jewish imagery, referring to fabricated and horrific accusations against medieval Jews that had returned in the 1890s, after being dormant for centuries, to parts of Europe as accusations of ritual murders and host desecrations. Freud was, by this time, rather desperate to find evidence of normative examples of psychical functioning. This instance of a memory slip offered one, albeit only after he had extracted the most affectively powerful aspect of the story, the paintings themselves, turning attention as far away from them as possible, a deflection facilitated by a construction of Islamic alterity and exotification.

As we turn to Freud's last area of unconscious "revelation" appearing in the late 1890s—culminating in the publication of *The Interpretation of Dreams* at the very moment of the turn of the century—we encounter another attempt to manage uncontainable threats by again disavowing the importance of visual imagery. Freud would construct a binary structure within the "dream work": the remembered surface as manifest content that served to veil the far more consequential latent meaning. A psychical apparatus of repression was thus solely responsible for the dream's visuality, a hallucinated facade allowing unacceptable wishes to be shielded from "view." As an internal derivative, inseparable from the unconscious, any "day residues" that occur within the memory content of the dream are frequently dismissed as "indifferent" to its actual meaning, so it has been difficult to wrest the dream's surface free from its purported generative sources in the mechanisms of repression. But it *is* possible to extract the "manifest" and here I give it two genealogical strands: one within the dream in *The Interpretation* where the latent and manifest functioning was first articulated and then came to be emblemized; and contemporary, alternate understandings of the uses of dream imagery at the moment when Freud's dream book was just one among others in Vienna, a fact long forgotten (*"The Magic of the Manifest: Paper Dreams"*).

My analysis of the dream that Freud puts forth as typifying his latent/manifest bifurcation shows that the "surface" image—a book on plants—carries considerable significance from his childhood, being connected with experiences painful and poignant, and is very much part of the "meaning" here, although Freud makes it utterly invisible by locating the significance of the dream in a register far from any physical object. This distancing was intentional and protective, although the volition and motives that made it possible were erased when "indifferent" imagery was incorporated into the processes of dreaming. I extend this "genealogy of the manifest" to the political and cultural ramifications—and dangers—of investing in dream imagery in late nineteenth-century Vienna, when the "dream book" was a popular medium for the transmission of stereotypes, most prominent among them anti-Semitic ones, naturalizing such images through the "universal" act of sleep.

How Freud equated meaning with value was no ordinary empirical process, despite being presented as such. Because his extraction of phenomena from scrutiny—the psychical disguise, the utterly forgettable memories—was powerfully formative for what was retained, absence was necessary to create a presence: there could be no latent meaning to uncover without the indifferent "manifest content" attempting to obscure it. It is possible, in scrutinizing Freud's extractions, to identify how this process of removal was then made part of psychical mechanisms themselves. Because this assigning of worth then became part of the *a priori* working of the unconscious—obscuring its actual function as the originary gesture—its presence was absorbed into the configuration that it created, and thus lost from view.

This book is not an attempt to accord a new place of privilege to art historical objects within Freud's psychical project, although this story is being told by an art historian. These chapters are narratives intended to suggest the complexities that surrounded Freud's navigation of visual cultures. Such an inquiry required new material—and a new reading of materiality—to enter into the beginnings of psychoanalysis in a more robust way than in the past. Because much that is discussed here is outside the margins of histories of the Freudian unconscious or of Freud himself, it is fortunate indeed that we have no lack of scholarship on both of these topics, evidence being the many and diverse texts cited throughout this book, a small portion of a vast literature. Here, the relationship between surface and depth is up-ended, the often—dangerous ground beneath Freud's feet revealed as not inconsequential, but instead uncontainable. In constructing the psychoanalytic process, Freud decided what would not matter, but in fact what he conceptualized was often the wish that it would not matter.

Conclusion: Objects' Lessons

This book has offered accounts, as cultural and visual narratives, of certain ideas that would prove decisive for Freud's early formulations of psychoanalysis. Such an endeavor is predicated on the recognition that, in a construction intended to enframe an "inner life"—one that eludes conscious awareness and possesses its own distinctive mechanisms and functions—Freud actually reveals much about his engagement with his physical and material surroundings. We have accessed some of these experiences by returning to his origin stories of his psychical formulations, as he made them, returning to his term "credible," through much volitional effort in the service of making an unconscious. But the scaffolding of his edifice will disappear once the structure has been cast as a discovery, as if always standing beyond time and place, waiting to be revealed. There are many important reasons to turn Freud's project back to the moments of its emergence, among them the insight informing this book: that psychoanalysis, if viewed from another vantage point, can be as much a discourse on what Freud disavows, discards, and "forgets" as on what he reified. Granted, such an inquiry is not "psychoanalytic" as we know it—after all, that would defeat its purpose—but it provides important insights about Freud and his work, and helps chart, as part of a broader inquiry, how certain ideas come to matter and others, even though seemingly compelling and worthy, do not.

Here, the issues are addressed close to the ground. The topographies vary, extending from Vienna's Ringstrasse to the streets of Orvieto, a carriage in Bosnia, and a train car in Leipzig, but the focus is on details that grant vividness to objects, individuals, and experiences that have remained unexamined. Yet what Freud deemed dismissible was nevertheless generative of his structuring of psyche. I have offered here a preface to this one located not in prediscursive constituents of the unconscious—his Ur-history of a primordial territory, with all the Eurocentric tropes that entailed—but rather in what preceded them: Freud's volition, intention, and motives. By locating the inaugural stimulus for psychical functioning there, with the help of visual culture, I have given these attributes a material history that had been rendered invisible.

We saw how Freud seemed to leave traces of his own footprints in the "architecture of hysteria"; where he not only created the sketch but enacted, in piecing together the workings of "hysterical fantasies"; the mechanism of the removal of memory; he then announced this to Fliess as an intrinsic function. Several months later, in the autumn of 1897, as Freud turns away from a reconstructive model of traumatic "scenes"—whose fore-shadow was already being cast by the architectural image he had drawn—he must create another viable conduit through which the past, often from early life, can be reckoned as evidential. Like Mancini, who would determine what portions of a grave assemblage would be brought to the marketplace, the first gestures of what would be gleaned from Freud's thoughts of childhood in this period were carefully curated, and, also following a practice familiar in the antiquities trade, falsified when necessary to enhance them. This did not undermine their intrinsic value, for that was no longer dependent upon a particular "scene" of history—whether in the objects gathered for an Etruscan burial or the specificity of childhood details of an abuse victim.

The mechanism of repression, identifiable in the displacement and contiguity decisive for the workings of the Signorelli "parapraxis," was traced here as a secondary effect rather than, as Freud would say, a "primary process." His narrative and attendant diagram are themselves a transposition, made believable only after several replacements: imagery related to Bolsena, on the other side of the "crossing" in the main aisle, returns as the phantasmal "Bo-snia"; the source of his associative process featuring three artists' names displaces the originary sequence of paintings on a gallery wall; and a portion of the Signorelli narrative occurs in what follows it, in the second chapter of *Everyday Life*. In our discussion of "dreams," which I suggest was a fluid category for Freud, the presence of a wish, emergent from the unconscious and thus the latent meaning, was prefaced by an earlier wish making possible a construction by which the unwanted imagery of dreams and their associations could be extracted. In fact, the originary wish was to remove material from meaning, so "genuine" meaning could be enunciated.

Such doublings-back enables us to better understand where Freud's fault lines of analytic engagement lay and to illuminate why the model he espoused was so decidedly intrasubjective. In this book, I have posited that this "one person" construction—largely superseded by intersubjective models in psychoanalysis, but nevertheless a decisive factor in its creation—was an assertion of agency, appearing as the workings of one's sexual and aggressive impulses. We have considered Freud's privileging of these latter drives as reflecting something other than their seemingly irreducible—virtually ontological—stature within psychical life, and instead have regarded them to be a consciously crafted modality of self-protection. In viewing his project this way, the incontrovertible components of the unconscious are actually its manifest content, masking experiences of vulnerability and disenfranchisement, and Freud's attendant responses of dread, fright, and sorrow. These were accorded little significance in contrast to the extraordinary power Freud granted to factors exclusively generative of a psyche of one's own.

This may explain why Freud located his Oedipal awakening as he did. Since we can be quite sure its circumstances could not have occurred as he claimed, why did he locate it so specifically in that moment of disruption and transition? Perhaps because he could then contain it fully and exclusively as being about his own possession, *meine Libido,* something extractable from time and place. By doing so, he discursively obliterated the impact of those circumstances, removing them from meaning so that the coincidence of these two events would virtually escape notice, as indeed it has been the case. Thus, despite more than a century of florescence and critique within analytic theories and practices, there remain areas of genealogy that offer insights of both historical and contemporary relevance.

As we journey along the outer borders of Freud's psychical constructions, there is a change in language, as if we are entering a different gee-cultural territory. The early terminology of psychoanalysis, often of Freud's own making or appropriation, falls away at the edges, and the discourses can be articulated in terms and phrases whose resonances are found in our current moment: reactionary political regimes, dis-criminatory policies, both anti-Jewish and anti-Islamic representations, childhood instabilities and familial shifts, economic distress, insecurities around residency, lack of a "homeland," and the return of age-old, racist ideologies. But these issues inhabit an amnesic core rather than the periphery of the Freudian unconscious: their disavowal generates the capacity to designate a separable terrain, governed according to a rule of autonomy in profound, and at times poignant, contrast to the vulnerabilities and dangers residing just beyond the walls of Freud's fragment-filled rooms. But Freud's experiences, and the objects and people associated with them, inhabit, as its revenants, the psychical formulations that he espoused and, as such, continue to be part of its legacy. Certainly, the impact of these and related issues can be found in the scholarship and practice of many analysts today, but might it be possible to imagine an even more fully engaged involvement in civic as well as clinical discourses? The ramifications of all the endangerments cited above, for adults and especially children, are profound and multifaceted, with the threats to individual survival and agency reverberating through families and communities, nationally and transnationally. These concerns had a decisive presence within the earliest shaping of psychoanalysis; in the twenty-first century, the field might return to them as it looks to grow and expand its work in the world.

This book has been about the lives of individuals, most notably Freud, but also about the lives of objects, and they are given the concluding word here. We have privileged certain physical presences as a means to revisit the formation of psychical concepts and mechanisms—a strategy predicated upon affective and ideological constituents indivisible from the visual cultures introduced here, imbri-cated within the reception of their materiality. As such, they were able to elicit from Freud a considerable range of responses that, whether embraced or disavowed, became part of his construction of an unconscious. Although this is only a small part of their histories, it is nevertheless a site of their significance. The making of phantasms is not exclusive to psychical functioning: it is part of what generates the meaning of a city's buildings, a cathedral's paintings, and a dealer's treasure trove. Recognizing this co-creation can extend the disciplinary reach of the fields in which these objects are most commonly situated, for, as we have seen here, they indeed have mattered elsewhere.

Afterword

As Freud and members of his family struggled to make arrangements, at times under extreme duress, to leave Vienna in the spring of 1938, they were hardly alone in their plight. Under the same roof, other Jewish families that lived at Berggasse 19 were experiencing similar upheavals, as made visible by Lydia Marinelli's 2003 catalog-*Freuds verschwundene Nachbarn* ("Freud's vanished neighbors")-for an exhibition held in the rooms of the Freuds' apartment. One of the most horrifying revelations was that the family's departure did not leave these rooms empty for long: the Freud apartment served as a holding place for Viennese Jews after they were seized for deportation. In 1942, 17 people were living there, all of whom were forced on to camps or, as the record described, to "ghettos"; in either case, every one of those confined at Berggasse 19 was eventually murdered. On the other side of the city, in another of these so-called "collective apartments;" four of Freud's elderly sisters-Pauline Winternitz, Adolfine Freud, Marie Freud, and Rosa Graf, all of whom had remained in Vienna-were also held; they, too, all died in various camps after their deportations in 1942.

The destruction of Vienna's Jewish community was systematic and cruel, but not only the living were victims of inhumanity. Not far from Berggasse 19, and not long after some of the Freud family were able to escape to safety, the Wahringer Jewish Cemetery, a large burial ground dating to the eighteenth century, was subjected to extreme forms of destruction. Thirty thousand people were buried there, and Nazi desecration affected a stunning number of them: many of the 10,000 headstones were smashed, graves opened, and remains removed. Some of this carnage was thoughtless barbarity, but for the most part, it was carefully planned. A number of the remains were taken to the city's natural history museum to be studied for future installations on the imagined-to-be-exterminated Jewish "race." In 1942, a portion of the cemetery, with more than 2,000 graves, was seized for the putative creation of a large bomb shelter, which was never built. Members of the ever-dwindling Jewish community hastened to remove and rebury as many individuals as possible; we have records that about 120 graves were moved to the Zentralfriedhof ("central cemetery") before the bulldozing began. The headstones were cast aside and the remains, along with the earth in which they had rested, were dug up and carried to various sites nearby. There, the soil and those interred in it were used to "repair" damage done to the streets and train stations. Among those taken was the grave of Jacob Nathansohn, Freud's grandfather, who appeared several times in his book, providing, along with his wife Sara Wilenz Nathansohn (who eventually returned to Odessa and was buried there), what may have been Freud's most stable domestic space in the first years of his life in Vienna. It was seeing his grandfather on his deathbed, in 1865, that Freud recalled when he published the one dream belonging to his childhood.

Little has changed at the Währinger cemetery over the ensuing decades; it is still a site of numbing destruction today. Nearly a decade ago, I became involved in a descendants' advocacy group there, but it was only when finishing this book that I realized Jacob Nathansohn had been among those disinterred. Many tragic lessons can be learned from this place, but the fate of 2,000 individuals, whose remains are now incorporated namelessly into these streets, is particularly wrenching. It was as though the dead were not dead enough; they needed to disappear completely from what became a dangerous ground. These remains taken from the Währinger cemetery, even today, are not buried deeply; they are closer to the manifest than to the latent. What is hidden is not their materiality, as fragile as that is now, but the stark narrative of brutality; this is a repression, not one that forgets a name, but a far greater pathology: one that forgets any person ever answered to it.

Notes

1 Selections from *On Dangerous Ground: Freud's Visual Cultures of the Unconscious* (New York: Bloomsbury Academic, 2019).

2 My choice of phrase plays upon the title of Freud's *Zur Psychopathologie des Alltagslebens* (The Psychopathology of Everyday Life), first published in 1901. The English version appears as volume 6 of *The Standard Edition of the Complete Psychological Works of Sigmund Freud*, ed. James Strachey (London: Hogarth, 1953–1974).

3 An excellent analysis of the points of connection between psychoanalysis and ethnology is offered by Ranjana Khanna in *Dark Continents: Psychoanalysis and Colonialism* (Durham, NC and London: Duke University Press, 2003), particularly 66–83.

4 My thanks to Elizabeth Lunbeck for calling this article to my attention. For Galison's work on Einstein and Poincare, see his *Einstein's Clocks, Poincare's Maps: Empires of Time* (New York and London: W.W. Norton, 2003).

5 The complexities and eroticism of the Freud-Fliess relationship are best rendered in Daniel Boyarin's chapter, "Fliess's Baby, Freud's Maybe: Or, Male Hysteria, Homophobia, and the Invention of the Jewish Man" in his *Unheroic Conduct: The Rise of Heterosexuality and the Invention of the Jewish Man* (Berkeley: University of California Press, 1997), 189–220.

6 Kerr's book of this name was also the basis for the 2011 film *A Dangerous Method*, directed by David Cronenberg.

7 The vividness of Freud's engagement with Notre Dame, and especially its rooftop assemblage of statuary, is very much indebted to Michael Camille's posthumously published The *Gargoyles of Notre-Dame: Medievalism and the Monsters of Modernity* (Chicago, IL; London: University of Chicago Press, 2009).

8 An accounting of all of Freud's residences in childhood is provided by Georg Augusta in "'Dann kamen die langen, harten Jahre': zur Situation der Familie Freud nach ihrer Ankunft in Wien im Jahr 1859," *Luzifer-Amor: Zeitschrift zur Geschichte der Psychoanalyse* 56 (2015): 213–215.

References

Augusta, Georg. 2015. "'Dann kamen die langen, harten Jahre': zur Situation der Familie Freud nach ihrer Ankunft in Wien im Jahr 1859." *Luzifer-Amor: Zeitschrift zur Geschichte derPsychoanalyse* 56: 108–129.

Boyarin, Daniel. 1997. "Fliess's Baby, Freud's Maybe: Or, Male Hysteria, Homophobia, and the Invention of the Jewish Man." In *Unheroic Conduct: The Rise of Heterosexuality and theInvention of the Jewish Man*, 189–220. Berkeley: University of California Press.

Camille, Michael. 2009. *The Gargoyles of Notre-Dame: Medievalism and the Monsters of Modernity*. Chicago, IL and London: University of Chicago Press.

Galison, Peter. 2012. "Blacked-out Spaces: Freud, Censorship, and the Re-territorialization of Mind." *British Journal of the History of Science* 45, no. 2: 235–266.

Kerr, John. 1993. *A Most Dangerous Method: The Story of Freud, Jung, and Sabina Spielrein.* New York: Alfred A. Knopf.

Chapter 3

Afterword

Diane O'Donoghue

It was the book project whose beginning and ending have been included here that brought me to Stockbridge and the Erikson Institute at Austen Riggs in the winter of 2014. Coming with two chapters completed, I hoped to write several more while in residency. This aspiration was fulfilled, but not in the rather systematic, predictable manner I sketched out for myself before arriving. In fact, virtually nothing about this span of nearly six months in the Berkshires unfolded as I had imagined. I had mistaken months of quietude—a gift that I had never been given in quite this way—with a kind of benign, productive stasis. From home in Cambridge, I pictured those upcoming months as a spare composition, with lots of space between passages of thin lines and muted colors. I was, after all, a tired art historian, coming to do work after a long stint as department chair. Perhaps that is why I didn't recognize that I was being offered a chance to extend myself, not to pare down. I quickly realized that the time and surroundings were unexpectedly conducive to roaming, both around the hills behind Riggs and also within my own thinking and writing. The introduction and conclusion (and especially the afterword) to *On Dangerous Ground* were not selected because they were written during my time as an Erikson Scholar—they were to come later—but because many of the ideas that fill these pages were begun there. And beyond my office in the library and landscape outside of it, there were myriad opportunities to allow for memorable growth, expansions that could not be counted in manuscript pages. My attendance at case presentations offered moments that were unforgettable in their poignancy and depth, and working with a kind and wise "advisor," John Muller, with whom I met each week to read texts together, allowed the rare chance to be a student again. There were also occasions to remember the pleasures of being a teacher, something that my administrative responsibilities had very much curtailed. I was able to present a series of art history talks—taken from undergraduate courses I'd taught in the past—for the patients, whose enthusiasm and insights allowed a connection to them that I would not have otherwise known. This was a high point for me, and I will always remember being moved as they discussed images and sites that I knew very well, projected on a rather grand scale in the community center's meeting room.

There also were chances for me to share my work in progress; among these was a presentation as part of the Williams College–Riggs seminar series, given

DOI: 10.4324/9781003322627-7

on Freud's birthday and focusing on his collection of "antiquities." Jane Tillman, as the Institute's director, was an invaluable friend to me and my project and facilitated various opportunities such as this. The seminar room where that talk took place in early May had become familiar to me over the course of my stay. The presentations of patients' cases were held there, along with many meetings and programs, and at mid-day it also served as the staff's lunch room, with its tables providing chances for the visiting scholar to connect to colleagues who were otherwise much occupied in their clinical work. I focus on this room because it was here, even more than in the library above it, that some of the deepest and most abiding growth within my work took place. This was for me a space of revelations, those of others to whom I listened but then also for my own. When offered the chance to do a Saturday program, I opted to shift the lens from Freud's Vienna to my own, telling a story that until then I had held quite apart from my academic pursuits. I brought the audience to a vast, desecrated (from the Nazi period and later) Jewish cemetery for which I had become, by a remarkable stroke of circumstance, one of its descendant advocates. Titling the talk "A Cemetery's Lament," I spoke about the despair of confronting a recalcitrant bureaucracy and the pernicious anti-Semitism, past and present, whose ravages this destroyed burial ground so vividly represented. I wanted, in that room, to address the psychical implications of both our attempts to restore this place, and the encounters we had with the Viennese who came to help us, many with family histories tied to its destruction. The response of the audience was remarkable, and that program has had for me a very meaningful legacy, living on as a chapter in a work authored by the person who was the paper's discussant that day, the former director of the Institute, M. Gerard (Jerry) Fromm.[1]

A center of gravity in my work shifted after that: the art historical and archaeological pillars that had long supported it seemed able to carry more affective, analytic weight. That Freud had a direct connection to the cemetery was only revealed to me later. We discovered that his maternal grandfather had been interred there when Freud was a child; eight decades later, in the early 1940s, that grave was destroyed among many others in an act of extreme cruelty. I added this as an Afterword to my book. It is in this present volume because, without my time as an Erikson Scholar, I can say, in this Afterword, that it never would have been conceived and written.

Note

1 M. Gerard Fromm, *Traveling Through Time: How Trauma Plays Itself Out in Families, Organizations and Society* (Bicester: Phoenix, 2022): 173–183.

Chapter 4

Too Young to Understand[1]

Ellen Handler Spitz

What is the purpose of keeping secrets from children? And what are the effects? Adults conceal aspects of the past, so it seems, not only for reasons of privacy, prudence, and occasionally prudery but because we want to protect our young ones. We want to prolong their innocence and keep them safe by suppressing what we think might sully or unsettle them. We hide, therefore, what we deem unsuitable. But we also keep silent because we ourselves cannot brook suffering or an exposure that might cause shame. Something in the past may have stunned or wounded us. Doubtless, we have performed acts of which we cannot feel proud. We may need to flee the reexposure of our well-defended yet vulnerable hearts to former moments of helplessness or humiliation. Why revive them? Especially when they are not old but of relatively recent vintage? Moreover, if we refuse to talk about them, they might recede: as per the conceit in Moliere's *Tartuffe*, where the impostor—as he tries to seduce the beautiful wife of his host, Elmire—proposes that, unless something is talked about, it never actually takes place. In any case, how *should* we talk about the past? How *can* we explain? Where do we find the right words? Better to remain silent.

And what about children's images of us? As heroic? Shall we, like Freud's father, when Sigmund was a boy of 12, tell stories that might make our children ashamed and cause them to lose confidence in our ability to protect them? Freud's father said that, once when he was out walking, a Gentile knocked his new fur hat into the gutter and, pejoratively calling him a Jew, ordered him to get off the sidewalk. When the shocked boy asked his father what response he made to this gratuitous insult, Jakob Freud answered that he simply picked his hat up out of the mud and walked away, an answer that bitterly disappointed Sigmund and rankled with him for years. What the boy had wanted from his father was an openly angry and aggressive retort to the bigot. Thus, blended motives—altruism, self-protection, indolence, and pride—all beguile us into presuming that we can and should protect the next generation by covering them each night with a thick blanket of ignorance.

This strategy never works. Curious, sensitive, probing, and irrepressibly ingenious, children, vis-à-vis their concealing parents, are like Dostoevsky's Porfiry Petrovitch vis-à-vis Raskolnikov in the gripping drama of hide and seek that is *Crime and Punishment*. They want and *need* to make sense of what matters to

DOI: 10.4324/9781003322627-8

them: they *must* know what happened, and why, and how. Their powerful desire to uncover truth resists the silences that would annul their search and obscure its object. Not right away, not all at once, but eventually. And then, when they find out at last, they feel, not incomprehensibly, betrayed. A bitter question, sometimes left unvoiced, forms and echoes within them: "Why didn't you tell me?"

In the work of artists who have sought to represent this theme, a child's relentless drive to penetrate parental silence may prove both explosive and dangerous. Into gaps made by parents' refusal to talk and by their genuine inability in some cases to do so, an avalanche of fantasy, suspicion, misconception, and delusion may fall into a child's mind, as it were, along with other ruinous shards. We must remember, though, that exaggeration in the realm of the aesthetic serves an important purpose. It enables us to crystallize a problem and to bring issues into sharp focus. Characters in film and fiction, far from providing us with emulable models, often enact in hypertrophied forms the emotions we occasionally feel but manage under ordinary circumstances to temper, modulate, and deny.

We see all this clearly in *Mendel*, a 1997 film made in Norway by Alexander Rosler, a Jew born in postwar Dachau, in 1947, who foregrounds and explores the theme of knowing but not telling. His film, *Mendel*, explores and foregrounds the theme of knowing but not telling. Rosler reveals, little by little, the metastases of malignant symptomatology that proliferate when children are (as one character in the film puts it) "born too late" to have experienced firsthand the brutalities that ravaged their families and deformed their lives. *Mendel* tells its story almost exclusively from the vantage point of the child.

The omission in *Mendel* of any reflective rendering of the parents' perspective is my strongest critique of the film and has caused me considerable anguish as I have viewed it repeatedly and familiarized myself with other literature and artifacts and reviewed the history of the period. I have come to feel ever more wary of casting blame on Bela and Aron, the loving but severely traumatized couple who fail to explain anything about the past to their younger son. In the following pages, we shall both reflect on these parents, who say almost nothing, and glance at a mother who explains "everything." Both are extremes. By implication, they may teach us to grapple toward compromises that avoid the damaging results of either immoderate solution.

Lilting klezmer music fills our ears as the film begins, and an establishing image takes shape: a tangle of roots, gnarled, broken, and sprawling above ground, the partially destroyed foundations of a gargantuan unseen tree. Far below, in a valley blurred by distance, one tiny car speeds along. A pale Volkswagen. What comes next zooms in close: a crucified roadside Christ, its carved feet pierced by nails. The first words we hear are those of Mendel Trotzig, the title character, a nine-year-old boy who says in German: "I didn't have any bad memories from Germany." Thus, as in any finely wrought work of art, we have it all with us right from the start.

War, violence, and religious persecution produce noxious psychic matter in all children, but here we are dealing with the children of survivors of the Holocaust, the so-called "second generation." As in certain forms of illness, the survivors suffer a poison that pervades its victims, wastes them with its toxicity, and, despite occasional respites, pitilessly and relentlessly attacks them from within, inflicting cycles of post-traumatic malfunction that, in a significant number of cases, has led to tragic late life suicide. Even, moreover, when pathology abates and, as in many instances, a measure of health is restored, permanent cure remains elusive. For the parents of "the second generation," silence in the face of what they have witnessed and endured is not a choice (There are many distinguished authors, books, and articles that deal with the phenomenon of the "second generation": Dori Laub, Marianne Hirsch, Cathy Caruth, Saul Friedlander, etc.).

Little Mendel Trotzig has nothing to remember. His opening words are uttered as his family is leaving Germany in order to be resettled in Norway in the early 1950s when the Norwegian government imported a quota of Jews left homeless by the ravages of World War II. Mendel's older brother David, who *does* know what happened in Germany, roughly slams down the window of their train compartment moments later in the film, thus blocking out the view of what is to him still a terrifying country.

Mendel does not understand. His father Aron nervously chain-smokes and compulsively repeats ethnic self-mocking jokes at which other characters titter uneasily. Having survived the camps at the cost of his religious faith, he scorns the ritual practices of Judaism. He awakens at night soaked in his pajamas after terrifying dreams. In one recurring episode, his shoes are stolen.

"You can't trust anyone," he tells his little son.

Mendel's mother Bela hides photographs, constantly shoos Mendel away whenever he appears curious, and, at bedtime, she sings sadly in Yiddish to her older son David, who softly weeps. Bewildered by this theater of unintelligible behavior, Mendel poses a continual stream of questions. Invariably, he is put off with slogans: Be quiet. Go back to bed. You are too young to understand. This is not for children.

Little by little, the family—as a whole and individually—attempts to acclimate itself to its new surroundings in Lutheran Norway. Once there, however, it becomes quickly apparent, as can be deduced from the image of the crucified Christ at the start of the film and by the sign in Norwegian: "*Jesus verdens lys*" ("Jesus light of the world"), that their kindly but pious hosts have elected to welcome them not only with the aim of performing a charitable deed but also in order to proselytize and convert them—this tragic remnant of exiled Jews—to their own particular form of Christianity. To that end, the pious Norwegian characters prepare speeches that sound tactless to this tragic remnant of exiled Jews. They expose the immigrant children of Mendel's cohort to signs, symbols, and songs that seem harmless to the children themselves on account of their naïveté but that provoke understandable resentment on the part of the children's survivor parents.

At holiday time, for instance, a Norwegian dressed as Father Christmas offers gifts to the Jewish children, and when Mendel wants to accept one, he is admonished by his parents, who interpret the child's acquiescence as capitulation to a pernicious form of religious seduction, a brazen form of enticement on the part of the Lutherans. During this Christmas party scene, one of the Trotzigs' neighbors, a religious man who is the father of Mendel's friend Markus, remarks pointedly that the *goyim* may sing tenderly and with feeling about their little infant Jesus, but, without remorse, they murdered Jewish infants in cold blood. Later in the film, his wife repeats this charge with terrible anguish. She asks the pious Lutherans if Jesus can bring her dead children back. Mendel looks on. The words make no sense to him. When he asks what they mean, he is rebuffed. He is told to be quiet, and the mantra is intoned that he is too young to understand: what he seeks to know is "not for children."

Unable to speak Norwegian and still quite young, Mendel, unlike David, is not sent to school right away by his parents. In the cramped quarters of the decrepit building in which the family has been lodged after their requisite stay in a welcome shelter, the little boy feels trapped. Lonely and bored, he is ignored by his gentle disoriented mother who distracts herself obsessively with a ceaseless round of domestic chores. The Scandinavian climate proves too severe for daily outdoor play; Mendel is even forbidden to bounce his ball indoors on the stairwells. Complaints are made about this activity by a German-hating custodian who lurks about the building with her sharp-edged cleaning implements. Like a tarantula, she materializes spookily to menace and threaten the little boy. Because he and his family are German speakers, the bitter crone takes them for enemies and despises them accordingly. Who knows, however, what she herself has suffered? To Mendel, she is a veritable witch or *Hexe*.

Cast into this atmosphere of paranoia, claustrophobia, gloom, and chronic anxiety, the child—in his inchoate way—longs for a return to what he fantasizes as the benign *Deutschland* they have left behind. Thus, we can see how distortion follows fast upon the ignorance perpetrated by parental silence and how it fills gaps when explanations are not forthcoming.

Like Mendel, another child character named Momik (who is not in this film) was created by David Grossman (1989) in his novel, *See Under: LOVE*, exemplifies this phenomenon as well. I want to mention Momik, because he, too, exemplifies this phenomenon. Momik is an Israeli boy of similar age to Mendel who likewise struggles fiercely against the secrecy of his elders. Momik tries with every fiber of his being to decipher the meaning of what happened "Over There," in other words, in the European theater of war and death during World War II.

Returning to Rosler's film, on the eve of Yom Kippur, the most solum day of the Jewish year, Mendel watches his religious neighbor lay *tefillen* (as he prepares to pray), and he notices, on the man's bare arm, a row of numbers stamped into the flesh. Staring at these marks, the child surmises that they must have come from Germany along with the man himself, and he therefore asks wistfully:

"Can I have a number like that too?"

Needless to say, this innocent request meets with chilled horror and unbroken silence on the part of his parents. Mendel is left again with no understanding. Later on, in an imitation of these "desirable" marks from Germany, he actually paints a set of numbers on his friend Markus's arm, an act that scandalizes all the adults in both families. Yet even now, the mortified parents provide no explanation for their reaction and no guidance. The children remain ignorant. They learn nothing except that they have angered their parents.

In an analogous scene, in Grossman's novel, the little Israeli Momik, who gives daily care to a deranged survivor uncle, whom he calls "Grandfather" because his real grandfather is no longer alive, tries to wash the numbers off the old man's arm with soap, water, and spit. Momik rubs and scrubs with all his might, but to no avail. Once he realizes that he cannot succeed, he reflects that, whereas anything like dirt or ink, which comes to the body's surface from the outside *can* be removed by this method but that these numbers cannot, he begins to imagine that there must be some mystery about them. Puzzled and fascinated, Momik fantasizes about what the numbers are and where they might have come from. Could they have arisen somehow from *inside* Grandfather? And what could they mean? Momik guesses that the numbers might have letter equivalencies, as in *gematria*, the numerical system of Hebrew letters associated with the Kabbalah. Perhaps, he ponders, the numbers on the old man's arm possess some arcane, spiritual, or magical properties. He speculates whether, like the secret numerical combinations used to open a safe, they could, if deciphered, make his Grandfather split apart so that, instead of the demented old man he is, a saner, healthier, more responsive Grandfather might emerge. Thus, little Momik carries on his experiments, trying with all his might to understand. When his efforts fail, he feels "strangely sad." As Grossman knowingly writes, he goes over to embrace his Grandfather tenderly and hugs him tight. The numbers will not yield. Not even to love.

Let's return to the film. Mendel, in a state of mingled apathy, ennui, and pent-up energy, wishes to escape from the strictures of his caring but resolutely unresponsive family. He wanders off and climbs the stairs of the building where his family's apartment is located. Passing hanging laundry and exposed wires, he reaches the uppermost level under the eaves. There, to his surprise, he comes upon a solitary human being—an old man, a Norwegian, who seems to be living all by himself in a small open area with a humble pallet and a few rudimentary supplies. This unexpected apparition seems uncanny to Mendel, who watches stealthily from a safe distance in the attic half-light. He notices that the man is absorbed in carving a small horse out of wood. Mesmerized, standing perfectly still, he observes from his post at the edge of the living space, while the old man, who seems reminiscent of Ibsen's character Old Ekdal from *The Wild Duck* (1884)—similarly an attic denizen—becomes aware of his presence. Neither speaks. Some magnetic force draws the boy in closer, and, finally, the old man comments that it is good to have a place of one's own where one can have peace.

With that, he reaches out and hands Mendel a block of wood and a piece of sandpaper. This simple gesture is exactly what our lonely, displaced child needs. The wise stranger has performed an act of empathy. In one fell swoop, he has fulfilled two of Mendel's most pressing needs. He has offered the child a real task to perform, a small manageable one with a clear goal and thus a way to feel useful rather than superfluous. And he has included Mendel in his own endeavors rather than shunting the boy aside. Immediately, Mendel begins to work on sanding his block. After this fortuitous encounter, he mounts the stairs to the attic regularly and spends time with the old man.

Soon we learn that a young woman, apparently a grown daughter, visits on a regular basis with her baby in her arms; it is she who delivers meals and administers basic care. Mendel witnesses the old man's pleasure as he fondles the plump baby. In a natural, gracious way, whenever Mendel is present at these visits, the old man offers him a portion of food to share, and Mendel—with a growing boy's voracious appetite—partakes willingly, consuming cold potatoes and herring with relish. By watching, helping, and quietly communing, the immigrant child finds solace with this native-aged stranger, and it is clear that these visits afford them both mutual satisfaction.

Downstairs with his family, however, Mendel worries now about his *own* grandparents. Where, he asks, is *his* grandfather? Why does no one speak of him? He poses this question outright, but his parents fail to answer him. Mendel persists. He points out the discrepancy that, whereas grandfathers *do* exist here in Norway, he, Mendel, has none. Pressed, his mother finally responds by offering him a partial truth:

"Our old ones were the first to die," she says cryptically.

This statement, however, devoid of a modifying context, makes, as usual, no sense to Mendel; it fails to clarify or resolve his problem. He knows, after all, that there was war in Norway too; yet, in Norway, there are grandparents nonetheless. Throwing her hands up, his mother finally, in desperation, silences him and pronounces her dictum that he is not yet old enough to understand.

At last, one day, the old man finishes his carving, and he hands the wooden horse to Mendel. The little boy is overjoyed at this gift, all the more precious to him because it is given so spontaneously and unexpectedly and because it is an object whose genesis and evolution he has witnessed. In a gesture that mirrors the apparent impetuousness of the bestowal, he jumps into the old man's arms and embraces him with the special fervor of a truly happy child. Delicately holding his treasure, Mendel plays with it now downstairs in his family's apartment. He shows it proudly, but when asked where he got it, he slyly turns the tables and announces triumphantly that *this* is *his* secret.

His survivor parents cannot play games. Insecure, and mistrustful, they cannot—despite their own concealments—fathom the meaning of Mendel's joke. Instead of learning from it, or honoring it, they simply grow fearful. After all, the withholding of information could be dangerous. They *will* not allow Mendel to have any secrets from them. They question him persistently until he gives in and tells them about his visits to the elderly Norwegian grandfather who lives in solitude under the roof.

His revelation prompts a volley of vituperation, which erupts and crescendos from the mouths of both parents. They seem deeply shocked at their son's clandestine behavior and by his apparently close hidden friendship with a person they fear may prove a sinister foreigner: a *goy*. Verbally chastising him, they deny him further access to the old man and forbid him to go upstairs in the future. Mendel is likewise forbidden to accept any gifts from persons unknown to the family. Hearing this dictum, we hark back to the Christmas scene earlier in the film and to the parents' understandable fear that all gifts to Jewish children from non-Jews might be a means of seduction and persuasion, a design to lure them away from their gnarled roots.

Parenthetically, it may be worth recalling here that, among the most repugnant anti-Semitic Nazi picture books of the pre-war era made for German children and distributed by the propagandistic *Stürmer Verlag* of Nuremberg, a similar message was given in reverse. One such book, *Der Giftpilz* ("The Poisoned Mushroom") of 1934, features among its illustrations an obese, unshaven bulbous-nosed Jew offering bags of sweets in the street to blonde blue-eyed "Aryan" children. Thus, bigotry and fear recrudesce, betraying the xenophobia that motivates them. In such moments, we confront our own irrational, overwrought suspicion, and mistrust of others who appear different from ourselves.

Mendel protests until finally his father, in a fit of rage, grabs the little wooden horse and hurls it to the ground, thus breaking off one of its legs. Startled by this violent act, the boy cringes. His parents' behavior, as always, baffles him and fails to enlighten him. This time, however, it appears as cruel as it is unreasonable. We, on the other hand, watching the story unfold on screen, can assume a distance unavailable to the characters. We can sense the invisible terror that pervades Bela and Aron. We recognize the cracked lenses through which they must filter Mendel's surreptitious forays into the attic. Unlike them, locked as they are into their respective viewpoints, we, watching, can sympathize both with the child's pain at his loss and with the wellsprings of fear that motivate his exiled parents.

With power and clarity, the film goes on in this way to portray the practice and fallout of adult secrecy. Wishing to keep Mendel innocent of the Holocaust, his mother and father cannot step back to consider that being in the dark does not lead to a child's peace of mind. "Not telling," we are made to see, places its own inescapable burden on the one who is not told and its own heavy load of anxiety. At the milder end of the spectrum, Mendel is simply confused and bewildered. The inscrutability of his parents' reactions to daily life makes it impossible for him to feel at ease in the new world that surrounds him. At the more extreme end, he gradually starts to exhibit acute symptoms of his own. Yet, despite their occasional severity, these symptoms, partly physical and partly mental, bespeak the fact that, notwithstanding their occasional severity, Mendel is a child who knows he is securely loved; his parents are both affectionate and kind.

Like the four-year-old girl character Ponette, who loses her mother in a traumatic car accident, Mendel evinces a resiliency and an adaptive strength that carry him through. Never fully capitulating to the unnamed malaise that lurks below the surface of his parents' silence, he resists. Unlike Momik, he does not grow thin and pale from anxiety. Perhaps because of his innate toughness, his capacity to act and react, and because of the felt presence of his parents' love no matter how ill-expressed at times, he never crumbles passively. Eventually, like Ponette, he prevails. At least, to some extent. He prevails—unlike Momik—in his struggle against censorship and concealment. This comes, however, at a cost we cannot measure.

Meanwhile, pictures form in his mind which join and overlap in bizarre ways so that, like his father Aron, Mendel soon begins to awaken at night with bad dreams. He loses urinary control from time to time, and these bodily disturbances—the sleep dysfunction and lapses into incontinence—seem blatantly symptomatic of his chronic failure to exert cognitive control over his life and world. Snooping among his mother's private articles, Mendel casts about like a detective for the photographs she has sequestered, and, when he finds an album, he searches in it for pictures of his missing grandparents.

At one point, noting empty spaces on the pages, he surmises that these are spaces formerly occupied by photographs of people who have died. In an effort to be helpful and to honor these dead relatives, he takes a pen and begins to mark black crosses on every page where a space denotes that a photograph was removed. He does this because, as a child growing up in Norway now and attending, by this time, six months later, a local public school, he has learned that crosses are the conventional way Norwegians commemorate their dead both in graveyards and in newspapers. Coming suddenly upon him as he is defiling the family album in this way, Bela cannot believe her eyes. Snatching it away, she is beside herself at his innocent act.

"We are not Christians," she tells him: "We are Jews."

Once again, the sentence, all by itself, means little to Mendel who, shortly after-wards, is shown sitting in his class in school while a sanctimonious female teacher weeps in front of the children as she tells them, slowly and deliberately—and with full awareness of Mendel's presence—the poisonous story about how the Jews let Jesus die by choosing to free Barabbas instead: "The Jews killed Jesus." We can-not tell whether Mendel makes a connection between this teacher's story and his mother's horror at the crosses in the family album. The message, however, along with other fragments and images from a fire that actually takes place in their build-ing one night, as well as fantasies about the war in Germany which occurred before he could remember it, and his father's nightmares, images of the old man in the attic—all merge in his mind to produce nightmares and bed-wetting.

On Yom Kippur, one of the most wrenching scenes of the film takes place. It is so affecting, because here we enter momentarily into a parent's perspective as well as a child's. Spurning religion, Mendel's father Aron insists on eating and behaving as usual on this holy day of remembrance, but Markus's family next door are observ-ing with fasting and prayer. In imitation of them, Mendel puts on a hat and shawl and wants to participate in their rituals, but Aron becomes furious and shouts at him. Their neighbor opens the door between the two apartments and gently chastises him for threatening his son on such a holy day and for showing disrespect to the dead.

Bela turns pale. Disappearing into another room where she covers her head with a lace veil, she prepares to light candles. The boys gather near her, and we hear soft chanting from next door. Aron paces the floor, smoking. Suddenly, he walks over to the grandfather clock against the wall and begins striking his forehead with his fist, a movement that shifts so that soon he is striking his forehead against the hard surface of the clock itself. Each time he hits himself, he speaks a name and repeats it: "Benjamin, Elias, Benjamin." Watching this in horror, little Mendel runs to him begging:

"Papa, stop!" he pleads, "I'll never wear a hat again."

Rather than turn timid, self-conscious, and pathologically antisocial, as some children would and as many did (including the fictional Momik), Mendel veers in the opposite direction. Six months later, as the family has relocated to the countryside, he befriends a group of the blond Norwegian children at his neighborhood school, and he grows increasingly brash and reckless. In a dangerous, counterphobic effort to be and to feel heroic, to experience himself as other than the passive, helpless victim he confusedly associates with being a "Jew," he eventually performs a dangerous act of aggression that, fortunately, miscarries. He attempts, using live ammunition, to shoot a gun he has learned to handle, having been instructed by a local farmer, the father of one of his new friends, to kill someone.

The target of Mendel's misguided aggression is a masked man who gallops by on the road each day in a horse-drawn cart and who is chased and mocked by the gang of children to whom Mendel is now attached. This stranger's hands are covered by dark gloves, he never speaks, and he cracks his whip over the back of his horse. Referring to him as "the Mitten-Man," the children invent wild fantasies about him and speculate on the origins of his supposedly hideous deformities. They repeat descriptions of his alleged lewdness, depravity, and salacious practices. Mendel, with childish naiveté, decides he will become a hero by doing away with this fellow who, he concludes, must surely be an "anti-Semite." Not clear, however, exactly what this term means, Mendel prays:

"Dear God, Buddha, Allah, Jesus, let me meet a real anti-Semite so I can fight back."

His appeal reminds us of Ponette who, longing for her mother's return, likewise, when she seeks divine intervention, invokes every deity she can think of, so as to hedge her bets.

Mendel aims the farmer's gun, one day, at the so-called Mitten-Man as the fellow rides by, and when his horse shies and rears, Mendel falls to the ground; the startled driver halts in profound shock. Outraged that the boy has threatened him this way, he takes off his mask and points out that his horse might have been injured or killed. Mendel bravely claims responsibility, and he announces that he is a Jew. The man responds by pointing out, both to Mendel and to the other children who timorously reappear now to watch what happens, that, in fact, *they have no idea who he is.*

"Do you know who I am?" he asks them angrily. And then, he says with feeling:

"Maybe I am a Jew too, or a gypsy."

To this, there can be only silence.

Thus, the film raises its questions about the conditions for learning about matters that are all but impossible to teach. In part, this is because we have no answers to the hardest questions children broach. Even if adults would and could talk, how might they give satisfaction? In David Grossman's novel, a time comes when Momik begins to go to the library so as to read about what happened "Over There." He attempts *The Diary of Anne Frank* and other books but finds he cannot understand much of what he is encountering. At this point, he appeals to his family's kindly neighbor, Bella Marcus, who tries to respond to his questions:

> What was the death train, Bella? Why did they kill little children? What do people feel when they have to dig their own graves? Did Hitler have a mother? Did they really use soap they made out of human beings? Where do they kill people nowadays? What's a Jude? What are experiments with human beings? What and how and why and how and what?
>
> (Grossman, 1989, p. 67)

We do not learn Bella's answers, but we see that Momik grows increasingly worried and distraught. As his mental state and physical condition deteriorate, Bella stops answering him. By this time, he has secretly caught and caged several small animals in the cellar of the building where he lives because he has conceived the bizarre idea that, through them, he can somehow vanquish the terrible "Nazi Beast," which he thinks of in literal terms; hence, the live animals. To bait, coax, trick, and foil this so-called "Nazi Beast," Momik cuts yellow stars out of cardboard and glues them to his father's old overcoat, which he dons in the basement. He covers his arms with numbers from discarded lottery tickets. Disguised this way so as to impersonate what he conceives of as "the Jew," he sits motionless for hours in the dark after school with the caged animals, waiting (like Ponette for her dead mother) for the Nazi Beast to appear. In unconscious imitation of the secrets that circulate in the air he breathes, Momik tells no one of these occult activities. Meanwhile, Bella notices his pallor and sees that he has grown thinner and more abstracted and estranged with each passing day. She starts to feel terribly guilty. She is overcome with remorse and believes that, by answering his questions, she has harmed him and driven him insane.

What, after all, we may wonder, as we reflect on these scenes, *can* children gain from adult answers and explanations? Especially when we try to explain to them what is beyond our own comprehension.

One day in Paris, while browsing in the FNAC, I came upon a small book entitled *Auschwitz expliqué a ma fille* (*Auschwitz Explained to My Daughter*) by the French historian Annette Wieviorka (1999). I was curious. I acquired it and found that it consists of a well-crafted dialogue between the author and her young daughter, in which the daughter's urgent questions (mostly about what actually took place vis-à-vis the Jews during the war) are clearly and accurately answered by her highly knowledgeable mother. Initially, I deemed the book worthy, a model of good parenting. It made me think of a claim by the American psychologist Jerome Bruner, who has written: "There is no reason to believe that any subject cannot be taught to any child at virtually any age in some form" (1960, p. 47). Wieviorka, in this modest French text, apparently exemplifies that audacious claim.

Yet, as I reread the book more closely, my assessment changed. This is because in it we hear in it only one voice: we hear the calm rational sentences of the historian mother as she reveals the most inhuman facts about the Holocaust to her child and does not palliate its painful details. In response to each of her statements, the "child," like a mechanical puppet, poses a follow-up question. Indeed, there is no child at all in this book! There is merely an automaton with a child's name, a robotic question-generating sham. Even if the book merely adopts its structure for rhetorical purposes and only pretends to be a realistic representation of an actual parent–child interaction, it falls short. Never mind that the Socratic dialogue is turned on its head; what matters far more is that, as my finest students have noted over the years, a Socratic dialogue possesses, in addition to its logical step-by-step inquiry, an important vein of *feeling*.

In this case, we find an impassive child character who—hearing, whether for the first, tenth, or hundredth time from her own mother's lips, sentences about what went on, about what was perpetrated on women and small children—fails to evince any emotion. Is there a child who would simply move on to pose the next question? Yet, surely, a child's emotional responses to what she is hearing from her mother need to be an integral part of such a text. *The reason for this is that the child's emotional reactions is itself a crucial part of the story that needs to be passed on.* It should never be blanched out. Without it, the project rings hollow.

I would go further. Insofar as this parent–child dialogue has been sanitized and purged of feeling, it uncannily repeats—*in this sense*—a species of "cleansing." Children who learn about the Holocaust in terms of statistics and gruesome facts tend to treat this history as if it were a fictional horror show. Or, just as they might memorize baseball statistics—the number of home runs and so on—they learn to recount the number of victims gassed or Jewish soap bars. They comprehend nothing. Thus, the "dialogue," with its dispassionate rendition and dry tone, fosters distortion. I see it no longer as a worthy parenting tool but rather as a foil for the richly honest, imaginative works of art under discussion here.

Children, Bruner implies, can grasp some part of such truths if what is offered to them matches and builds on their present level of understanding. In Wieviorka's case, her daughter Mathilde is meant to be 13, thus capable of formal operational thought in a Piagetian sense. In other words, she could be expected to be able to grasp potential relationships and hypotheticals, which would not be the case vis-à-vis the fictional Mendel and Momik who, because they are younger, are still operating quite literally and concretely. Mathilde, moreover, would be further removed from the Holocaust than either of the boys; her mother, born in 1948, would be of Mendel's and Momik's generation. Yet this fact should have little bearing on a child's capacity to understand and to be moved by what happened.

To accept Bruner's premise, as I do, is to locate the problem of secrecy and silence not in children's own supposed inability to comprehend but in adults' incapacity to tell. Yet, as we have seen, in the post-traumatic situations portrayed by Rosler and Grossman, parents—because of what they have endured—may be rendered incapable of telling. When they are the victims of split consciousness, when they have suffered torture, shame, confusion, and repression, they often cannot find the words, and this goes way beyond wanting to protect their children. Yet, neither Grossman, within his literary genre, nor Rosler, in his visual format, probes the situation of, or elicits sympathy for, his respective set of parents.

Notwithstanding this, both works of art, remind us that parenting calls for more than affection and care. Being a parent remands uneasy efforts at learning and teaching. It calls for awkward, halting efforts to share with our children what we have suffered, what has happened and not happened, what might have happened, what may yet happen, and what we hope will or will never happen. It calls for attention to *their* silences and for valiant forays, whenever possible, into "the no-man's land between parents and children," a phrase coined by another Israeli writer, Nava Semel (quoted in Y.S. Feldman, 2004). Semel's novel, *And the Rat Laughed*, recounts the almost unbearable story of a small Jewish girl given for safety by her parents to farmers and hidden during the war "Over There" in an underground pit with a rat. It is a story finally coming out for the first time when the girl has become old and is with her granddaughter. Children, as we have seen, when they are not told, will try to find out for themselves. And for Mendel, as for Momik, such learning may come with maximum risk.

Returning now to the film, it is not—in the end—Mendel's parents but his older brother David who helps him learn and face at last some of the unbearable truths of the Holocaust. This happens in a way that involves several moments of abject horror for both boys, and I want to underline the point here that it is the absence of parental guidance that propels the sibling intervention. The scene I am about to describe, while including no parental figures on screen, includes them implicitly. It is largely their incapacity to teach Mendel what he needs to try to understand that causes a penultimate confrontation between the two brothers.

In the vacuum created by Mendel's traumatized parents, the following scene occurs. Playing daily with his Norwegian friends after the resettlement, Mendel hears incessantly about *their* fathers' bravery against the Germans during the war. He finds and peruses photographs that depict emaciated Jews in prison garb in the camps with hostile German guards watching, their weapons trained ready to fire. He knows that none of his own grandparents is alive. He has been told he is a Jew but grasps very little about what that means and still less about what actually happened to Jews during the war and why *they* did not have guns, like the Germans, or fight back bravely, as did the Norwegians, or so he thinks.

One afternoon, while David is studying at his desk presumably doing homework, Mendel comes along and confronts him with a typical barrage of questions.

"Why don't you tell me about the war?" the younger boy asks. Why (he wants to know) weren't the Jews brave? Why didn't they resist? Why didn't they snatch the guns from their enemies' hands and fight back? Nobody is ever going to be allowed to do that to me! Why did they stand around like sheep? They just prayed.

Disturbing as these questions are and motivated persuasively by Mendel's contact with the contrasting stories of his new Norwegian friends, there may be a certain feeling when we hear them uttered by this child character on screen that, in another sense, they have been planted by the filmmaker, Rossler, and are an imposition on Mendel of a later militaristic ideology espoused by certain Israeli Zionists whose aggression was and is fueled by the cry in their hearts of "Never again." If so, however, the imposition is not gratuitous. It makes psychological sense. For the etiology of such feelings, both for the child and for the adult political ideologue, remains the same. In any case, Mendel repeats it all and mimicks the davening (swaying) motions of a pious Jew at prayer while insolently making the sound, "Baaa-aaa."

"Why didn't they do something?" he asks again. He, Mendel, would not have been so cowardly. He would have grabbed a gun from the firing squad and died resisting bravely.

David squirms at his desk. He tries gallantly to shoo his little brother away and continue studying. He makes several efforts to deflect Mendel's onslaught.

"You haven't experienced anything," he tells him: "You were born too late to die."

Mendel, who does not understand this, persists in his davening and sheep imitation.

Finally, exasperated beyond the limits of his adolescent, far-from-perfect self control, David rises silently from his chair. Infuriated now by Mendel's taunts, he attacks his brother. He pins Mendel to the ground. Once again, there is no clarification. Holding him down and breathing heavily with exertion and emotion, David demands an apology. Mendel, however, who still understands nothing about the Holocaust, insolently repeats his "Baa-aaaa."

At this point, David loses his composure entirely. He picks Mendel up, and, with a flash of sadistic inspiration, he commences a brutal moment of instruction. He takes his struggling younger brother to the open window of the apartment. They are several stories up in the building with the ground far below. Holding the boy by his ankles so that he is upside-down outside the high window, David demands:

Say you're sorry or I'll let you go.

Mendel shakes his head, and we watch in horrified fascination as David shakes him by his feet over the window ledge and warns:

This is no game, you little Satan.

Finally, Mendel murmurs "Mercy," and David pulls him back inside. Standing him back on the floor, he looks down at him and says, contemptuously that he had his chance but his pride ran out.

Both boys notice at once that Mendel has wet his pants from fear.

There is no need to point out a moral, no need to say that no one has the right to predict his own bravery in the face of death. Mendel, after his brother's lesson, seems chastened and momentarily subdued. But he is unvanquished and still as ignorant about what happened in Germany as he was before. Suddenly, he turns and runs away from his brother. He dashes into the bathroom, where he locks the door defiantly.

In a split-frame screen, we see the faces of both brothers on either side of the door. Mendel opens it just a crack, and, at that, David instantly grabs him and squeezes him into a second deadly headlock. As Mendel winces, we watch, horrified again. But very slowly, this time, the aggression melts into an embrace. The two brothers hug each other, and David, with genuine affection, admits:

You're awfully irritating, but you're brave.
"Then," begs Mendel, "Tell me..."

Only now, after learning with life and limb at stake that no one can stand in the place of another, the boys finally begin to talk. For the first time, truths about the war are spoken. Secrets are shared. The *Shoah* and the concealed photographs are openly discussed. As they are, David reveals to Mendel that his own birth father died in Germany while resisting the Nazis and that Aron is, therefore, Mendel's own true father but not his. Thus, the past and present finally begin to clarify and to make more sense. Puzzle pieces start fitting together, and blurred shapes come forward gradually into sharper focus. Images that were superimposed slowly separate and therefore become more intelligible.

In the very end of the film, we watch as Mendel performs an act of derring-do: he climbs a rickety ladder set to a dizzying height against the building, his mother watching askance from the window, and, with an umbrella in his hand, he jumps down to the grass below in slow motion while his family, friends, and neighbors stand by, and he lands, at last, safely. We realize in this penultimate scene of mingled fantasy and reality that the child's entire way of being in the world, his personality itself, his recurring (and probably future) needs to reexpose himself to danger and to master it, have been molded by what we have witnessed—by the pulling down of shades on the train from Germany, by the sequestering of photographs, by the smashing of the little wooden horse, by the ankle hold outside an open window, and by the perpetual refrain: "You are too young to understand."

Reflecting on the film, we may doubt that, whereas it may have initially seemed clear that breaking through silence, divulging secrets, and answering a child's questions on a level best suited to his or her cognitive development would constitute the most auspicious parenting strategy, this viewpoint may now seem less convincing. After having living through the art, we may find ourselves reluctant to subscribe to a doctrine that advocates for the supervalent efficacy of adult verbal explanations. We might return once again to *Ponette*, to her confusing conversations with her well-meaning aunt, her father, her teacher, her peers; to her experiments—inside the garbage can, for instance; to her make-believe shooting on the playground.

We might turn back to Mendel's drawings of numbers and crosses, and to David's terrible, inexorable lesson, which was physical and dangerous. Each stressful sequence of trial and error occurs and fails before the words that are finally spoken make sense to the respective child. In both films, the protagonists, "too young to understand," undergo a process of co-constructing meaning with others and for themselves across a variety of experiential modalities. In the end, some of what the parents have kept silent remains so. The children learn what *they* need to learn, and this is always something a little different.

In the mind of David Grossman's Momik—unlike Mendel—there is a downward spiral. Words float like flakes of confetti in the air he breathes; chameleon-like, they morph into signifiers whose referents have come unraveled from public discourse. Spinning off toward meanings of their own, they enmesh him in a maze of whirling, disjointed, undecipherable signs. The harder he tries to understand, the more isolated he becomes until, ultimately, his world devolves uncannily into a veritable simulacrum of "Over There." In fantasy, in darkness, Momik reenacts the unassimilated trauma from which his family has suffered—the unpredictable chaos and loss of meaning in the camps. He is, at last, sent away from home to recover.

Because each child, parent, and situation differ, we have no formula to help us find a way to forestall the obliteration of what matters. Yet what matters must be communicated and passed on. Moreover, what matters *will*, in some form, be passed on. Even in defiance of all the taboos. Children find out: something. No one is too young to understand.

As to shaping and saving, how much are we up for? To live briefly with Mendel and again with Momik is to be sure there is no right way and no avoidance of risk. Conscious secrets and silences can, on the part of parents, even constitute a species of truth. For a while. They can be non-expedient and respectful, as Ibsen tries to show us in an earlier Norwegian setting, that is, in his tragic play *The Wild Duck*. We learn this, there, through the protective secrets of a character called Gina Ekdal, who is the mother of a daughter who—as another character suddenly reveals –may be and probably is illegitimate. We are asked to confront the fact that truth alone can never constitute the highest value in human affairs. Ibsen shows us that Gina's daughter, little Hedvig, loses her father's love when the uncertainty of his paternity is made known. Coldly, this father rejects his formerly beloved child because she no longer seems to belong to him and because he assumes that his wife, whom he associates with her, has betrayed him. Hedvig understands nothing at all except that her adored father has abandoned her. Stealthily takes her grandfather's pistol, climbs up into the attic, and shoots herself.

Silence, ultimately, proves lethal. With or without words, we must keep the lines of communication open. Parental mutism and withdrawal into abysses of the self beget the annihilation of children. Hedwig's father forsakes her, Momik's parents retreat into the sealed confinement of their lottery booth, Mendel's parents—mum and fearful—stand by.

Children need what may best be conveyed only piecemeal. In fragments. By means of zigzags, with stops, coughs, clumsy interruptions, and by means of approximations. With awkward gestures, reenactments, blurred imagery, by displacement, and metaphor. They need chances to be together with us in ways that foster the cocreation of mutual understanding on whatever levels that understanding can take place. We see this at the end of *Ponette* in the fantasy scene when the little girl's dead mother reappears and plays with her. Such methods may work well for us too. Perhaps this is why we crave the arts. What matters needs to be retold a hundred times in different ways, with kisses and with flowing tears, or with blank or stony faces, or with dry eyes that no longer have the wherewithal to weep.

Note

1 Excerpted from *Illuminating Childhood: Portraits in Fiction, Film, and Drama* (Ann Arbor: University of Michigan Press, 2012).

References

Bruner, Jerome. [1960]2003. *The Process of Education*. Cambridge, MA: Harvard University Press.

Feldman, Yael S. 2004. "Nava Semel." In *Dictionary of Literary Biography: Holocaust Novelists*, 310–315. New York: Gale Publishing.

Grossman, David. 1989. *See Under: LOVE*. Tr. Betsy Rosenberg. New York: Farrar, Straus, and Giroux.

Ibsen, Henrik. 1961. The Wild Duck. In *Hedda Gabler and Other Plays*. Tr. Una Ellis-Fermor. London: Penguin. (Originally published in Norwegian in 1884)

Rosler, Alexander. 1997. *Mendel*. Film. Released by First Run Features.

Wieviorka, Annette. 1999. *Auschwitz expliqué à ma fille*. Paris: Editions du Seuil.

Chapter 4

Afterword

Ellen Handler Spitz

Ever since my childhood in New York, my life has been shaped by the arts: literature, music, dance, theater, and the visual arts. These include subsets of poetry, opera, modern dance and ballet, as well as painting, graphic media, and the history of these arts. I've practiced (published, exhibited, and performed) as well as participated (as listener, viewer, and reader) in several of these arts and served for all my life as a teacher of the arts, their histories, and theories. Currently, as a Senior Lecturer in Humanities, I teach at Yale.

A semester at Riggs appealed to me because psychoanalysis has long figured in my thinking, and because I believe that, within academia, psychoanalysis is often abstracted, far removed from the consulting room. My initial recommender was Otto Kernberg, M.D. of New York. At Riggs, I hoped to inch closer to actual practice so as to observe psychoanalytic ideas *in situ* rather than as purely theoretical. Previously, in addition to several years of non-clinical training at the Columbia University Center for Psychoanalytic Training and Research, I worked with children diagnosed schizophrenic at the Ittleson Center in Riverdale, N.Y., a residential and day treatment center, an experience I captured in one of my books. Riggs promised to augment that firsthand exposure.

While on site, I read and wrote, attended all staff lunches, and dined with trainees. I attended the All-Community meetings and conferences. Led by Director Ed Shapiro, the All-Community assembly astonished me by its unstructured format: I struggled to navigate its free-flowing conversation, which arose spontaneously among staff, patients, clinicians, and trainees.

My weekly seminar on "Psychoanalysis and Greek Tragedy" delighted me when I saw my clinician students rediscovering their own patients' problems enacted by characters in the ancient dramas. I took long meditative walks. I "made friends" with several large brown cows who grazed in the meadow. They raised their gentle eyes to gaze in wonder at this odd city person, who seemed as curious about them as they were about me.

Jerry Fromm headed the Erikson Institute. Administrator Lee Watroba deserves special mention—so kind, responsive, and caring despite being extremely busy. From the start, Jerry tapped me for his annual Creativity Workshops, one of which, under Jane Tillman's aegis, I got to plan and lead—a perfect joy. My fellowship book,

DOI: 10.4324/9781003322627-9

which warmly acknowledges Riggs, came out in 2011: *Illuminating Childhood: Portraits in Fiction, Film, and Drama.*

I cannot rightly claim my thinking and work were dramatically changed by my time as Erikson Scholar. The experience was nevertheless incredibly valuable. I had never observed from the inside, except for Ittleson, the actual workings of a mental institution. It surprised me that clinicians and trainees took only a half-hour for lunch, as I could see the toll taken on them by the work they do. Every person I met, without exception, was dedicated. Ever since my fellowship at Riggs, my respect for them has grown to unwavering admiration. I found the clinicians and trainees and staff at Riggs unexpectedly intellectual. They were serious about connecting to larger social themes and cultural trends. This enabled me to listen with profit and contribute my own perspectives to conversations that were often far ranging but based in and oriented toward their patients.

In sum, although I cannot identify a dramatic change in my work that resulted from the Erikson fellowship, I believe the "Erikson effect" is a matter of subtle aura. In the Riggs community, I found my own psychological perspectives shared, valued, implemented. This constituted a great source of inspiration and filled me with energy. It gave me the desire to do and learn more, to bring psychoanalytic ideas out more expansively into the public sphere through writing, teaching, and lecturing. Subsequent to my sojourn at Riggs, I began to do more public writing, for example, for *The New Republic*, occasionally the *NY Times Book Review*, the *LA Book Review*, and to give non-academic lectures. Most recently, I have submitted two invited essays for publication: "Psychoanalysis and Children's Literature: Spotlighting the Dialogue" (forthcoming, *Cambridge Companion to Literature and Psychoanalysis*, 2022) and "On Children's Books, Home, and the Beginnings of Self" (*Psychoanalytic Inquiry*, forthcoming, special issue). A psychoanalytic reading of love in *Swann's Way* called "How Marcel Proust Can Change Your Life for Better or for Worse" (co-authored with my husband Howard Bloch, Sterling Professor of French at Yale) was published this year in the *Romantic Review*, 2021.

So, I unqualifiedly report a positive result, which continues. I am immensely grateful for my ongoing ties to this unique and amazing place.

A Primer for Forgetting

Getting Past the Past[1]

Lewis Hyde

From the Introduction

Many years ago, reading about the old oral cultures where wisdom and history lived not in books but on the tongue, I found my curiosity aroused by one brief remark. "Oral societies," I read, keep themselves "in equilibrium...by sloughing off memories which no longer have present relevance" (Ong 2002, 46). My interest at the time was in memory itself, in the valuable ways that persons and cultures keep the past in mind, but here was a contrary note, one that clearly stirred my own contrary spirit, for I began to keep scrapbooks of other cases in which letting go of the past proves to be at least as useful as preserving it.

My book, the late fruit of those gleanings, turned out to be an experiment in both thought and form. The thought experiment seeks to test the proposition that forgetfulness can be more useful than memory or, at the very least, that memory functions best in tandem with forgetting.

As for the form, I decided to build on my scrapbooks rather than mine their content for a more conventional narrative. I have written three long books—*The Gift*, *Trickster Makes This World*, and *Common as Air*—each of which spends over 300 pages defending its central proposition. Having done that kind of work for years, I found myself weary of argument, tired of striving for mastery, of marshaling the evidence, of drilling down to bedrock to anchor every claim, of inventing transitions to mask the native jumpiness of my mind, of defending myself against imaginary swarms of critics... What a relief to make a book whose free associations are happily foregrounded, a book that does not so much argue its point of departure as more simply sketch the territory I have been exploring, a book that I hope will both invite and provoke a reader's own free reflections.

From Notebook I: Myth

I MANUMIT. I HIDE. Let us imagine forgetting by way of two etymologies. The roots of the English "forget" go back to Old High German where the *for-* prefix indicates abstaining from or neglecting and the Germanic **getan* means "to hold" or "to grasp." To remember is to latch on to something, to hold it in mind; to forget

DOI: 10.4324/9781003322627-10

is to let it slip from consciousness, to drop it... To forget is to stop holding on, to open the hand of thought.

Greek terms present a different set of images, not letting go, but erasing, covering up, or hiding. Forgetfulness in Greek is *lethe*, in turn, related to *letho*, λήθω (I escape notice, I am hidden), ultimately from Proto-Indo-European **leh₂-* (to hide). The privative or negative form of this word, *a-lethe* or *aletheia*, is the Greek word usually translated as "truth," the truth than being a thing uncovered or taken out of hiding. In terms of mental life, all that is available to the mind is *aletheia*; what is not available is for some reason covered, concealed, hidden.

TWO BURIALS. Given that the etymological root of the Greek *lethe* suggests that forgetting is the covering up or hiding of something, we could extend the image and say that to forget is to bury. And to differentiate some kinds of forgetting—especially in regard to trauma, both individual and collective—let us say that there are two kinds of burials: in one, something is hidden because we can't stand to look at it; in the other, it is buried because we are done with it. It has been revealed and examined, and now it may be covered up or dropped for good. This latter is proper burial, burial after attention has been paid and funeral rites observed.

THE UNFORGETTABLE. Some emotions grip us, then fall away. A great happiness can bring sleepless nights when first it blooms, but the possession eventually fades. Two years out, no one says, "I cannot shake my joy!"

Grief and rage, however, these can go on and on. Decades go by and still a loss or wound from childhood colors our days. Two decades have passed since Odysseus left for war, and still, the old swineherd Eumaeus grieves "unforgettingly" for his absent master (*Odyssey* 14.174).

Rage may be the more troubling of the unforgettables, and especially rage knit together with grief because these don't just persist; they call for action, and in action taken, they reseed themselves generation after generation. All the years of the Trojan War have passed, and still, Clytemnestra cannot forget how Agamemnon sacrificed their daughter to put a wind in his sails, and so she takes her revenge, a revenge that plants the seed in turn for their children, Orestes and Electra, to seek vengeance against her.

In Sophocles's play that bears her name, Electra speaks of her father's murder as a sorrow (or evil) that cannot be forgotten and describes her own passion (or anger) in similar terms, though in this case, the Greek for "not forgetting" (*our láthei*) might better be translated from its root meaning—"it does not escape notice," "it is not hidden" (*Electra* 221–224, 1246–50). The image is of anger as a thing that the mind cannot bury and cannot help being aware of. Electra's passion won't let her alone. It's intrusive. It bugs her. We do not control the unforgettable; it controls us.

The spirits of such unforgetting are called the Furies, the Erinyes. They cling to the memory of hurt and harm, injury and insult. Their names are Grievance, Ceaseless, and Bloodlust. Their names are Grudge, Relentless, and Payback. They bloat the present with the undigested past. Most dreaded of the forces of insomnia, they harry the mind, demanding for its release a ransom paid in blood (Loraux 2006, 163).

From Notebook II: Self

Man does not die in a ditch like a dog—but at home in history.

Boris Pasternak (1991, 10)

Living in history without living in the past
Is what the task is.

—Charles Wright (2000, 13)

OTHER BODIES (A MURDER STORY). When I began my book, I thought to include a short section examining my own fragmentary recollections of a season of political engagement from my college days. As it turned out, there was no way to tell the story briefly, for my personal point of entry into that history soon led me to another man's much more complicated and traumatizing experience. Thomas Moore, an African American man a few years older than I, had a brother who was murdered by the Ku Klux Klan in the early 1960s. Moore's struggles with the legacy of that violence eventually led him to participate in the conviction and incarceration of one of the killers, to engage with and offer forgiveness to another one of them, and finally to give his murdered brother what I think of as a proper burial...[2]

As for my own connection to this history, I spent the summer of 1964 as a civil rights worker in the state of Mississippi, one of a thousand or so volunteers who traveled south that summer to register black voters and to help organize the Mississippi Freedom Democratic Party in hopes of unseating the all white delegation that the state's Democrats would inevitably be sending to the party's August nominating convention in Atlantic City.

Of all my scattered and fragmented memories from that summer, one in particular stands out: when Lyndon Johnson sent 400 sailors into the state to walk the swamps and drag the rivers searching for the bodies of three volunteers—Mickey Schwerner, James Chaney, and Andrew Goodman—murdered by the Klan on June 21, these sailors found other bodies, dead men no one had been looking for, no one had reported missing. "So this is Mississippi," I thought, a place where a walk through any swamp might uncover the invisible dead, unnamed, unsought.

SAMBO AMUSEMENT. In Mississippi in those days, the White Knights of the Ku Klux Klan believed that they were Christian soldiers opposing the forces of Satan on this earth and that the civil rights workers invading their state were the newly fashioned betrayers of Jesus the Galilean. The Imperial Wizard of the Mississippi Ku Klux Klan, Sam Bowers of Laurel, part owner of a jukebox and vending machine company called Sambo Amusement, had devised a secret code to tell his crusaders when to burn a cross or to whip a man or to firebomb a church or to eliminate a heretic, eliminate him without malice, in complete silence, and in the manner of a Christian act. In Mississippi in those days, the White Knights of the

Ku Klux Klan believed that young Negro men had signed agreements promising to rape, weekly, one white woman, that there was an impending Negro insurrection, that the Black Muslims in Chicago had smuggled 5,000 automatic weapons, "and maybe a machine gun," into the state and had hidden them in churches and graveyards. In Greenville, Mississippi, the Klan convinced Washington County deputies that by the act of "felony grave tampering" these guns had been hidden in the cemetery of a black church. "Working in the dark, foggy graveyard, heavily armed police pried the lid from a wooden vault," finding no guns but disturbing the rest of one James Turner, only recently buried.[3]

"What divides the dead?" Aeneas asks the Sibyl, his guide; she replies that those denied passage are the "helpless and graveless." Charon will not carry them across the waters "until their bones have found a resting place. A hundred years they roam and flit about these shores; then only are they admitted and revisit the longed-for pools."

(Virgil, Aeneid 6: 317–330)

ON SATURDAY, MAY 2, 1964. Charles Moore and Henry Dee, both 19 years old, were hitchhiking across from the Tastee-Freez on the outskirts of Meadville, Mississippi. Moore was a student at nearby Alcorn College, at the time suspended for joining a protest about the lack of social life on the campus. Dee worked at a local sawmill. Neither had any involvement in the civil rights movement.

James Ford Seale of the Bunkley Klavern of the Ku Klux Klan picked the boys up and took them into the nearby Homochitto National Forest, where he and four other Klansmen tied them to a tree and beat them savagely with sapling branches. Dee had recently returned from a trip to Chicago; he wore a black bandanna: surely he knew where the guns being smuggled into the state were hidden. One of the Klansmen, Charles Marcus Edwards, asked if the boys were "right with the Lord," the implication being that they were about to die. In desperation, one of them invented a story: yes, there were guns; they were hidden in Pastor Clyde Briggs's church, over in Roxie.

The Klansmen split up, one group going to the courthouse in Meadville to get Sheriff Wayne Hutto to go with them to Briggs's church (where they found no guns). The others took the beaten boys to a nearby farm. They were bleeding so profusely that the Klansmen spread a tarp in the trunk of a Ford sedan before stuffing the boys into it and driving them 90 miles north to Parker's Island, a backwater bend of the Mississippi River.

When they opened the trunk, they were surprised to find the boys alive. One of the men asked if they knew what was going to happen. They nodded. James Ford Seale taped their mouths shut and their hands together. He bound their legs with rope and wire. He and another man chained Henry Dee to a Jeep engine block, loaded him into a boat, rowed him out onto the river, and rolled him into the water, alive. Charles Moore watched from the shore. The men returned, chained Moore to another weight, rowed him out onto the river, and rolled him into the water, alive.

Later they were to say that they dumped Dee and Moore alive rather than shoot them because they did not want to get blood all over the boat.

It is an ancient theme, the consequences of denying the dead a proper burial. In Sophocles's play *Antigone*, the prophet Tiresias speaks to the stubborn king Creon, he who will not bury the body of Polyneices, now lying outside the gates of Thebes, picked at by carrion birds and dogs:

> As I took my place on my ancient seat for observing birds…I heard a strange sound among them, since they were screeching with dire, incoherent frenzy; and I knew that they were tearing each other with bloody claws, for there was a whirring of wings that made it clear. At once I was alarmed, and attempted burnt sacrifice at the altar where I kindled fire; but the fire god raised no flame from my offerings. Over the ashes a dank slime oozed from the thigh bones, smoked and sputtered; the gall was sprayed high into the air, and the thighs, streaming with liquid, lay bare of the fat that had concealed them.
>
> Such was the ruin of the prophetic rites.
>
> (Sophocles, *Antigone*, 998–1022)

The Klansman who owned the boat used in the murders of Dee and Moore had a brother who knew nothing about their drowning. But this Klansman felt he should tell his brother what had happened because at the point where the brother frequently crossed the river, he had the habit of dipping up water to drink and he should be warned that he was "drinking water off a dead Negro."

In the Dee–Moore murder case, historical memory—the contemporary written record—is almost as shabby as my personal memory. To take but one key example, the newspapers at the time reported that the Franklin County sheriff, Wayne Hutto, made some phone calls and located the boys in Louisiana. "I can't figure it out," Hutto is quoted as saying. "If these boys had been in any trouble around here I think I would have known about it."

But Mississippi in 1964 was a police state, meaning simply that the police were complicit with the Klan terrorists, Hutto in this case having helped the Klan search for weapons in the church in Roxie.

We know all these details because the Dee–Moore murder case was in fact solved by the FBI within months of the discovery of the bodies. The FBI had a paid informant in the Klan, a man to whom the killers told the whole story of what happened on May 2, 1964.[4]

That is why in late October of that year, the FBI was able to send navy divers into the muddy waters around Parker's Island and find the skeletal remains of the victims, along with the Jeep engine block. Charles Moore's skull was found—identified because he had lost some teeth playing football. Henry Dee's skull has never been found.

THE SECOND DEATH. They say that one way to lay a traumatic memory to rest is to create a particular kind of symbol: a grave marker. Once a grave has been marked, you can visit it, but you do not have to. Once a trauma has been properly buried, you can call it to mind, but you do not have to. It's available but not intrusive, not haunting.

"The first symbol in which we recognize humanity...is the burial," writes Jacques Lacan. "It is man who invented the sepulcher... One cannot finish off someone who is a man as if he were a dog...[His] register of being...has to be preserved by funeral rites" (Lacan 1992, 279).

This is from Lacan's seminar on *Antigone*, a play in which we find no proper burial. *Antigone* ends with three suicides, and suicide can be thought of as an attempt to signify through action what ought to be named through inscription. Lacan calls naming through inscription "the second death." "The symbol... [is] the killing of the thing," he writes, drawing on Hegel, whose idea was that conceptual understanding is a kind of erasure of the particular (Lacan 2002, 262, 263).

Take a living dog that runs and barks and eats and shits. As soon as that dog passes into the word "dog," its particular embodiment disappears: the word "dog" doesn't run and bark and so forth.

Let us put this in terms of trauma. A very particular, horrifying thing happens to someone—as happened to the families of Dee and Moore. How to recover from (or at least work with) such horror? The advice is to erase (or liquefy) the particular by putting it into symbols. If the story cannot be fully told, then the trauma persists. Time stops. Twenty years later, the dead still appear in dreams.

The grave marker is the symbol that makes it clear that whatever has happened need not live forever. The symbol lives on, but the real, once properly inscribed, is temporal and can be buried.

Forgetting is the erasing angel that murders particularity so that concepts can be born, so that time can flow again.

COLD CASE. In January 1965, for various reasons (the local DA stalling for "additional time," the FBI refusing to reveal its informant), the murder charges against James Ford Seale and Charles Marcus Edwards were dismissed for "lack of evidence," and law enforcement at every level—county, state, and federal—abandoned the case. Several journalists showed some interest in it during the 1990s, but nothing began to move until the summer of 2005, when the Canadian filmmaker David Ridgen got in touch with Charles's older brother, Thomas Moore.

Thomas Moore is the central character in the rest of this tale.

He was in the army when his brother was killed, and though he came home for the funeral, his mother told him that there was nothing he could do and that he had to forget about it and go on with his life. The army sent him to Vietnam, and he later served in the First Gulf War. He retired to Colorado Springs in the 1990s. During all his years in the military, Moore had nightmares about his brother's death. He would hear Charles calling out for help, asking, "Why?" The killing left him feeling trapped, he has said, "chained by pain, guilt, hate, and shame."

Ridgen persuaded Moore to go back to Mississippi and work on the case. Within weeks they had remarkable success: they found James Ford Seale (who had been reported dead), and they found what were supposedly lost FBI files. Soon they confronted Seale's conspirator, Charles Marcus Edwards, directly, approaching him one morning as he and his wife came to open the church where he was a deacon.

In Ridgen's film, *Mississippi Cold Case*, we see Moore hand Edwards a manila envelope of FBI files, and we hear him ask Edwards why the files contain his name. Edwards protests, "I'm not on the FBI report." (He had in fact never seen the files.) "I did not kill your brother," he says. "The FBI dropped all this case and you know that. They dropped the case because there wasn't any evidence. I've never been on that Mississippi River in my life," he says, shooing Moore and Ridgen away. "You all get off this church ground and quit stirring up trouble here on the church."

Not long after this encounter, Moore and Ridgen persuaded a US attorney in Jackson to give Edwards immunity in exchange for his testimony and to indict Seale for conspiracy in the murders. In 2007, Seale was convicted and sent to jail, where he died four years later.

[Omitted here: the full story of Thomas Moore's reconciliation with Charles Marcus Edwards. At the Seale trial, Edwards asked the victims' families if they could forgive him. Moore then worked toward that end.]

THE WORK. The story of Thomas Moore's journey from vengeance to forgiveness has two kinds of memory and thus two kinds of forgetting. Some things can be called to mind at will, and some intrude upon the mind no matter what we will. It is one thing to get angry when thinking back on an injury; it is quite another to be invaded by nightmares whenever sleep lowers the threshold of consciousness.

The Furies are embodiments of unforgettable grief and rage. *Their names are Grievance, Ceaseless, and Bloodlust. Their names are Grudge, Relentless, and Payback. They bloat the present with the undigested past.* They harry the sleepless mind, demanding blood for its release.

There are certain parasitic fungi that invade the brains of tropical ants, making them climb to the top of trees and die there so the fungus can grow from their bodies and widely spread its spores. In the same way, the Unforgettables control their hosts and seed themselves anew. The curse of the house of Atreus descends generation to generation. The story has no easy closure, each of its bearers being compelled to add another chapter and act it out in the incarnate world.

In the case at hand, the U.S. Army put weapons in Moore's hands and taught him how to kill; add to that his brother's restless, nightmare ghost, and before long you have a man plotting to murder white men in Meadville, Mississippi.

Of the many forces that combined to alter and close that plot, three stand out. First, there was the truth: in 2005, after 41 years, Moore got access to the FBI files and knew for the first time what had actually happened to his brother. Then there was "some justice": the government indicted James Ford Seale, a Mississippi jury convicted him, and a federal judge sent him to prison. Only after all of that did forgiveness enter the picture, and forgiveness turned out to be an object of study for Moore. "Research, research, research. Get an understanding," he told me.

To enter the work of forgiveness, it may not be necessary for the truth to come out and justice to be done, but it helps. It helps because it then becomes easier for the traumatized man to see the degree to which the wound has become part of his identity, his sense of self. If he is to change, he will first of all have to study that self and become intimate with it. ("Who is it really hurting?" Moore asked himself.) That doesn't mean a literal forgetting of the crime, but it does mean letting go of the person the crime brought into being. "Why drag about this corpse of your memory?" asks Emerson in one of his great odes to American self-renewal. Said Moore, "As hard and as brutal as it was…this was something that I was destined…to go *through* in my life in order to be who I am today." Who he is today is a man who has laid the ghost to rest ("my brother's got peace," he told me), freed himself from servitude to the Unforgettable, and become the agent of his own recollections.

From the point of view of the parasitic fungus, seizing the ant's brain is a wonderful thing. The fungus community endures and spreads. From the point of view of the ant, it's a disaster. In the human community, the spirit of the Unforgettable is useful when it comes to asserting self against others. The desire for revenge can be an expression of basic self-respect, and as the legal scholar Martha Minow writes, "Vengeance is also the wellspring of a notion of equivalence that animates justice" (Minow 1998, 10). But revenge without justice too easily descends into unending violence, blacks and whites killing one another year after year as each race claims and defends an identity rooted in *not* being the other.

For those whose goal is an end to conflict, then, better to become intimate with the self that clings to difference. And better then to forget about it.

From Notebook III: Nation

KOSOVO AND CHOSEN TRAUMA. For hundreds of years, beginning in the late twelfth century, Eastern Orthodox Christian Serbs dominated a huge part of southeastern Europe. In the summer of 1389, however, at the Field of Blackbirds in Kosovo, an army of Muslim Turks defeated Serbian forces led by the feudal lord Lazar Hrebeljanović. Within decades, the Ottoman Empire had fully absorbed its conquered foe. Its rule would continue for 400 years.

For the Serbs, Lazar's death and the date of the Battle of Kosovo—June 28— have ever since stood for what has been called a "chosen trauma," that is to say, an identity-informing ancestral calamity whose memory mixes actual history with passionate feeling and fantasized grievance and hope (Volkan 1998, 48).

Lazar's body and severed head—central emblems of that trauma and of all later Serbian resistance—were interred after the battle, at the Serbian monastery of Ravanica. The monks there canonized their hero and, as Ottoman rule expanded in later years, carried his remains into exile to a monastery on Mount Fruška Gora, northwest of Belgrade. As for the symbolically charged date of the battle, it was no accident that the precipitating event of World War I, the 1914 assassination of Archduke Francis Ferdinand, was carried out on June 28. That was, after all, the 525th anniversary of the Battle of Kosovo, and what an insult, then, that a representative of Austria-Hungary, the very heir of Ottoman oppression, dared to enter Serbian Sarajevo.

And flash forward to the late twentieth century, when Yugoslavia began to break into its constituent territories, thereby surfacing long-dormant ethnic conflicts, especially in Bosnia–Herzegovina, whose primary ethnic groups—Muslim Bosniaks, Roman Catholic Croats, and Eastern Orthodox Serbs—were soon at odds. During the Communist era, these groups had lived in relative, if imposed, harmony (marriages were often mixed; few Muslims attended prayers), but as Bosnia moved toward statehood, the Serbian population—about a third of the whole—feared it would become a second class minority, and in the spring of 1992, Serbian armed forces began to massacre their Muslim neighbors.

The seeds of that exercise in ethnic cleansing had been planted several years earlier, when Slobodan Milošević, Serbian politician and skilled apologist for the memory of difference, helped organize a series of celebrations in honor of the 600th anniversary of the Battle of Kosovo. On June 28, 1988, a year prior to the actual anniversary, Milošević arranged for Lazar's "exiled" body to be returned to the monastery in Ravanica, the relic case containing his bones being paraded through every Serbian village and town, mourned along the way by black-clad throngs of wailing Serbs.

The speech that Milošević gave a year later on the actual 600th anniversary included calls for tolerance ("Long live peace and brotherhood among peoples!"), but more often it recalled the ancient conflict ("Let the memory of Kosovo heroism live forever!"), a theme strongly reinforced by the stage-craft of the event: the celebratory crowd had gathered on the very Field of Blackbirds where the original battle had been waged, Milošević himself descending on the site in a helicopter as if the sainted prince Lazar were at last returning from on high. All of that, plus the podium's backdrop prominently displaying the dates 1389 and 1989, called to mind not so much brotherhood as the ancient animosity between Christians and Muslims, one whose time-collapsed modern iteration was highlighted by Milošević's constant references to dignity and humiliation, freedom and vassalage, motherland and treason, bravery and suffering, pride and shame. "The Kosovo heroism has been inspiring our creativity for six centuries," he declared, "and has been feeding our pride and does not allow us to forget that at one time we were an army great, brave, and proud, one of the few that remained undefeated when losing."[5]

I assume that odd last phrase is not a mistranslation but rather Milošević's invocation of the remarkable way in which the Serbs have imagined Lazar's defeat as a victory. Legend has it that before the Battle of Kosovo a gray falcon brought Lazar a message from the Virgin Mary giving him a choice: either win the battle and have a kingdom on earth or lose it and have one in heaven. A Serbian ballad has Lazar explaining why he chose death: "The earthly kingdom is of short duration/And the Heavenly is from now to eternity." Thus does a lost cause's apparent humiliation get turned on its head and become proof of the highest of ideals. "Even though we have lost our kingdom," sing the Serbs, "let us not lose our souls" (Volkan 1998, 63–65).

Positing that eternal kingdom has the imaginative effect of collapsing durational time. If an atemporal ideal lies hidden in Lazar's defeat, then 1389 and 1914 and 1989 are all one and the same, and the chosen trauma may work its magic at any time, its bound-up energy always available to fuel a present fire.

Vamik Volkan, the psychiatrist who gave us the term "chosen trauma," has noted that "the idea that [the Serbs] could change their minds and choose a kingdom on earth was not articulated until the awakening of nationalism in Europe in the nineteenth century" (Volkan 1998, 64, 65). Prompted by that awakening, Ernest Renan's 1882 "What Is a Nation?" warned against the very confusion of nationality and ethnicity that brought civil war to Bosnia: "Ethnographic politics is anything but certain... For everyone, it is better to forget" (Renan 1990, 11).

Or not, if a chosen trauma's wound is given over to the task of preserving identity by way of mourning without end. Mourning that *does* end, by contrast, promises to convert what has been lost into a memory, and given 600 years, most memories fade. "Fixed ideas" is what Pierre Janet once called those memories impervious to time; such atemporal artifacts are like blood clots lodged in the flow of time, something the years can neither expel nor dissolve.

In the 1990s, the Serbian genocidal campaign drove hundreds of thousands of Muslims and ethnic Croats from their villages, looting their homes and demolishing mosques and churches. Serbian fighters raped thousands upon thousands of women and, in the town of Srebrenica, massacred more than 8,000 Muslim men and boys.

The Unforgotten, destroyer of nations.

SUCCESSFUL MONUMENTS BECOME INVISIBLE. I once worked at a hospital in Stockbridge, Massachusetts. At the center of town stands a tall brownstone obelisk dedicated to those "who died for their country in the great war of the rebellion." A bronze eagle sits on top, a small cannon at the base. On the sides are inscribed the names of the dead and of the Civil War battlefields where they fought: Gettysburg, Wilderness, Spotsylvania, Antietam, etc.

I once asked my colleagues at the hospital if they knew what the monument stood for. Only one man did, and he knew because his brother-in-law from the South had pointed it out to him. For everyone else, and for northerners in general, the Civil War belongs to time out of mind.

"It is possible that there is no other memory than the memory of wounds," wrote Czesław Miłosz (Nobel lecture). In the South, the wounds of the Civil War are still felt; in the North, less so.

From Notebook IV: Creation

THE FORGETTABLE LIFE. Plato's "Myth of Er" has it that the souls of the dead get to choose the life they will lead when next reborn. Er witnesses several famous souls making their choices, the last of these being Odysseus:

> Now the memory of former sufferings having cured him of all ambition, he looked around for a long time to find the uneventful life of an ordinary man.

He had some difficulty in finding this, which was lying about and had been neglected by everybody else; and when he saw it...he chose it with joy.

(Plato *Republic*, 620)

We have no story of this "ordinary man," for his is a life that brings no glory, no *kleos*. It is a forgettable life, not a memorable one. Perhaps the reborn Odysseus, the happily uncelebrated man, still walks among us, living in a manner that leaves no mark on memory.

Forgetfulness...is a great aid to interpretation.

—Frank Kermode (1979, 14)

TO THE READER. I claim no strong connection between forgetfulness and this book's episodic form, but if there is one, it most likely lies in the way that juxtaposition encourages not just free association but free forgetting. Jumping from one thing to another, the entries decline to declare a train of thought. I realize that putting macho Nietzsche next to Hitler's abandoned bunker, for example, may be thought provoking and that some readers will bridge the gap with their own transitional abstraction. Myself, I leave it alone. Interpretation too readily declared dims the lights of things; holding off allows the elements to glow.

Readers then, as they cross the divide between any two entries, will enjoy or suffer their own level of state-transition amnesia. Some entries will fade immediately, others linger in the mind, and some disappear, only to later return unbidden, involuntary memory having drawn upon its treasure chest of oblivion. The spaces between entries foreground what happens with any book we read: we retain some things as we go along, while others drop away until, finally, out of the keepers and the discards, we extract the unique book of our own engagement. Unless we kill a book by committing it to memory, active imagination ("memory and oblivion, we call that imagination," wrote Borges) will make for us the book that is our book. The episodic form acknowledges the collaged afterlife of anything we read—or of any life, for that matter, for we too are discontinuous creatures, scattered in time, the meaning of our existence something we can only imagine.

Notes

1 Selections from *A Primer for Forgetting: Getting Past the Past* (New York: Farrar, Straus and Giroux, 2019).
2 David Ridgen's films, videos, and podcasts constitute the primary source materials for the Dee and Moore murder case. His multipart podcast can be found on the Canadian Broadcast Corporation website as season 3 of a series called *Someone Knows Something*, cbc.ca/radio/sks/season3. A link on that webpage ("Watch key moments from Dee & Moore") leads to a number of online videos, including that of the 2007 meeting between Thomas Moore and Charles Marcus Edwards, *Reconciliation in Mississippi*. See also Harry N. MacLean, *The Past Is Never Dead: The Trial of James Ford Seale and Mississippi's Struggle for Redemption* (New York: Basic Civitas Books 2009).

3 See *Activities of Ku Klux Klan Organizations in the United States*, part 4 of the *Hearings Before the Committee on Un-American Activities* (Washington, D.C.: U.S. Government Printing Office, 1966), 2945, "Ernest Gilbert Exhibit No. 1," reproducing an article in the *Jackson* (Miss.) *Clarion-Ledger*, Nov. 16, 1965, titled "Report of Arms Cache False; Officials Begin Probe of Klan."

4 Ernest Gilbert was the Klansman who became an FBI informant and, in August 1964, testified in secret as to the details of the murders. The FBI documents recording his testimony can be found at abcnews.go.com/2020/story?id=2826491.

5 "Slobodan Milosevic's 1989 St. Vitus Day Speech," slobodanmilosevic.org/spchkosovo1989.htm (a translation "Compiled by the National Technical Information Service of the Department of Commerce of the U.S"; another translation is available at www.hirhome.com/yugo/bbc_milosevic.htm).

References

Kermode, Frank. 1979. *The Genesis of Secrecy*. Cambridge, MA: Harvard University Press.

Lacan, Jacques. 1992. *The Ethics of Psychoanalysis, 1959–1960*. London: Routledge.

———. 2002. *Écrits* New York: W. W. Norton.

Loraux, Nicole. 2006. *The Divided City: On Memory and Forgetting in Ancient Athens*. New York: Zone Books.

Miłosz, Czesław. Nobel lecture. nobelprize.org/nobel prizes/literature/laureates/1980/miloszlecture.html.

Minow, Martha. 1998. *Between Vengeance and Forgiveness*. Boston, MA: Beacon Press.

Ong, Walter J. 2002. *Orality and Literacy*. New York: Routledge.

Pasternak, Boris. 1991. *Doctor Zhivago*, trans. Max Hayward and Manya Harari. New York: Random House.

Renan, Ernest. 1990. "What Is a Nation?" In *Nation and Narration*, 8–22, edited by Homi K. Bhabha. London: Routledge.

Volkan, Vamik. 1998. *Bloodlines: From Ethnic Pride to Ethnic Terrorism*. Boulder, CO: Westview Press.

Wright, Charles. 2000. *Negative Blue: Selected Later Poems*. New York: Farrar, Straus and Giroux.

Chapter 5

Afterword

Lewis Hyde

One fine bonus of being an Erikson Scholar is that the scholar's office sits smack inside the Austen Riggs library. For the months I was in residence, whenever I found my mind wandering I'd let my feet stroll as well, browsing the shelves to see what wisdom was on offer that day. My research topic was the virtues of forgetfulness, and there was Wilfred Bion suggesting that the analyst should "deliberately divest himself of memory and desire," and there was Pierre Janet counseling "the liquefaction if the fixed idea," and there was Vamik Vokan wondering how the symbols of "chosen trauma" could be left behind.

Better still, of course, was all that lay beyond the library, the Riggs staff especially. By some good fortune John Muller made himself available to introduce me to the Center and answer my questions. Early on he suggested I read his article considering "the phenomenon of treatment resistance as primarily resulting from the eclipse of the 'Third.'" I came to understand this "Third" as a thing that allows two people to step beyond themselves into something other than opposition, and I found in it a useful way to imagine what goes on in successful reconciliation work. The term appears several times in my subsequent book.

Then there was Jacques Lacan. Apparently a few Lacanians had blazed through Austen Riggs a few years back and the scorch marks they left had not faded. I confess that reading Lacan himself could sometimes send me into Stockbridge looking for ice cream but Lacan, skillfully translated into the Riggs vernacular, was useful nonetheless, especially what I take to be his idea of "the second burial" (look it up!) and what became one of my aphorisms, "You may visit a grave but you do not have to."

While at Austen Riggs I organized a discussion group around the topic of memory and forgetting. In one of our meetings, I presented the story of a racially motivated murder committed in Mississippi in 1964 (the year I myself had worked in that state registering voters). What was of real interest to me in that case was the reconciliation work that Thomas Moore, the brother of one of the murdered men, had undertaken. I tell Moore's full story in the excerpt reproduce in this anthology so I won't repeat it here except to say that during the course of a group discussion one of the psychotherapists remarked that Moore's ability to forgive meant he was no longer a captive of the past but "free to think about it."

DOI: 10.4324/9781003322627-11

I immediately appropriated that insight and use it toward the end of my account of the murders, noting that when Moore spoke to me about his trauma he had said, "as hard and as brutal as it was ... this was something that I was destined ... to go *through* in my life in order to be who I am today." That given, I conclude: "Who he is today is a man who has laid [his brother's] ghost to rest ... , freed himself from servitude to the Unforgettable, and become the agent of his own recollections."

There are many kinds of forgetting, one of which I call "free forgetting": it isn't that one cannot remember the past but one can remember or forget it at will. Maybe I would eventually have come across that point on my own—but I didn't have to. I was happily embedded in the Austen Riggs community whose library, hallways, and meeting rooms are so rich in therapeutic wisdom.

Lost Histories

Chapter 6

Emotion, Embodiment, and Context[1]

Ann Marie Plane

Despite formal opposition in radical Protestant ("Puritan") circles, New England's colonists at the end of the seventeenth century still embraced all sorts of wondrous experiences, from visits by specters and apparitions to dreams in which they communed with the dead or with relatives far from home. One problem they faced lay in how to discriminate a dream visitation from a material apparition, and another lay in how much weight to give to knowledge gained from their dreams. Because seventeenth-century magistrates allowed testimony about ghosts and apparitions to be offered as evidence in court, determinations about what had been a true visitation (either in sleep or in a waking state) and what had been a deluding dream sometimes became crucial.

Events that modern observers would class as dreams or sleep disturbances were often defined differently by colonists, and this usually depended greatly on the surrounding context, including the dream's manifest content, and most important, the feelings embedded in the dream. Whether dreams brought useable insight, vain hopes, or authentic connection to divine power remained very much in question during the latter decades of the seventeenth century and throughout much of the next. What was classed as dream experience, what was understood as waking experience, and which of these were seen as "real" was also deeply dependent on context.

Therefore, we might say that New England's puritans could never fully colonize dreams, at least not in the sense of either being able to contain them or to render them completely powerless. But certain forms of experience—apparitions, spectral visits, or conversations with the dead—might be classed as dreams (and therefore as something subject to question), or they could be determined to have really occurred. How wondrous experiences were defined depended on many factors, including who had experienced them and the nature of the feeling embedded within them. For some on the margins of colonial society—women suspected of witchcraft, for example—a neighbor's scary night-time experience could have consequences that were only too real. A great deal hinged on the sleeper's emotional experience on awakening: being soothed, enlivened, or happily "amazed" was a sign of a wondrous dream, worthy of scrutiny or even some active fulfillment, but

DOI: 10.4324/9781003322627-13

not a cause for criminal action. Terrifying experience was another matter and might result in legal action or scrutiny by the community. Whether happy or fear-inducing, such startling experience remained worthy of examination and reflection.

Above all, the emotional tone of the visitation seems to have determined its fate. Extended discussion of dreams reported by the important diarist, Samuel Sewall, suggests that happy or amazing experience could satisfy significant emotional needs. Modern interpreters would term these *self-object* experiences. Since they were usually not frightening, these sorts of positive experiences rarely became sources of controversy or conflict. Terrifying, assaultive, or otherwise troubling experience sometimes demanded further investigation. Context was therefore key in discriminating wondrous dreams from diabolical activity. Other dreamt wonders—visits from the dead, from angels, or other providential occurrences—occurred in less charged contexts. These sorts of dream visitations might arouse the dreamer and his intimates to action or, alternately, soothe, instruct, and inspire. Colonists depended on the dreamer's identity and circumstances as well as the content of the night vision to make these crucial distinctions. But powerful—even wondrous—experiences (a visit from a dead friend, relative, or mentor, for example) were taken as positive signs and worthy of reflection, while a frightening apparition (of a neighbor or even of a stranger) might be cast as a dreadful and only too real visitation by a witch, a ghost, or the Devil himself. Social stress resulted in scapegoating of various "others." In the increasingly stratified world of the late seventeenth century, naïve belief in dreams was now identified with indigenous peoples, witches, and the weak-minded or spiritually vulnerable—while those who cautiously hoped for spiritually enriching visitations through dreams might get exactly what they wished for.

This chapter considers dreaming as an embodied emotional practice, and it includes examination of the ways that dreams helped experience of the self to take form. The discrimination of dreams from other sorts of spectral events hinged largely on the social status and social context of the individuals involved. In this way, dreaming and dream reporting is intimately linked to other processes of social stratification at work in late seventeenth-century New England.

As David D. Hall suggested a generation ago, New England men and women who had been nurtured on so-called wonder tales would shape their own experiences according to this template (Hall 1989). This shaping process applies to dreams as well—which in turn became part of this fabric of wonders. The wondrous, therefore, helped colonists explain some of the mysterious aspects of dreams, both in how they took shape and what they might signify. Take, as an example, a dream of Thomas Minor, who emigrated very early to New England, possibly on the *Arbella* with John Winthrop, and who moved into Connecticut in 1645 as part of John Winthrop Jr.'s New London venture, eventually settling in Stonington by 1652 (Miner 1915, 11, 12). In 1662, Minor recorded a curious coincidence in which he and his wife dreamed at the same time, two dreams with almost the same content. The full report is challenging because of the lack of punctuation, but I include it in full here to allow readers to parse it for themselves:

> I & my wife dreamed at one time my wife dreamed that I struck her & said that I strucke at a dogg & I dreamed that I was going by a red bich [*sic*] which had a puppie and shee bit at me & I struck her & struck my wife in the face either with my hand or fist which waked my wife & shee waked me & asked me what I did doe.
>
> ([Thomas Minor [1662] 1899, 192)[2]

It is perhaps not too far-fetched to note that while Minor offered a culturally acceptable act of violence toward the "red bitch" in his dream, this dream experience resulted in an inadvisable (if not entirely unacceptable) act of violence and loss of control toward his wife (perhaps, sometimes, herself another sort of "bitch"?), which she duly protested ("& she waked me & asked me what I did doe").[3] The repetition of the phrases "I struck her" in the dream report, first when Grace Minor dreamed "that I struck her" and later when Thomas Minor says that the bitch bit at him "& I struck her" further entwines these two female figures (dog, wife). Minor makes no other comment about this dream, a circumstance that leaves modern readers almost in the dark. We know that it was important enough to him to write it down and to note the startling coincidence between the two dreams. This was enough to make it a wondrous event.

What historians have not recognized to date is that such wondrous dreams also functioned as elegant means to emotional containment. In a society where anger was conceived as a dangerous and divisive force and was often repressed and redirected outside of the household (Demos 1970; or, we might add, displaced onto the person of the vengeful witch or implacable Indian), Minor's sleeping mind seems to have redirected his anger (at his wife?) at the snarling "red bitch." This word had the same double meaning then as it does today. Note that two figures in this dream are angry—first the dog, and then Minor himself—a narrative doubling that would seem to reinforce the central affect of this brief dream report. Anger among intimates was tricky, and, as explored elsewhere, recorded dreams often presented dreamers with a challenging array of feelings, feelings likely to disrupt attempts at mastery and control. Subordinates (like a dog or a wife) were supposed to submit quietly to male authority, but male authority was also supposed to stay its hand from excessive violence. And thus, this brief and unelaborated report still offers a snapshot of Minor's emotional life, perhaps related to his wife, or other females protective of their pups. The evidence is only suggestive, however, more tantalizing than revealing. It is interesting, though, that while he records that he literally struck his wife, awakening her, and provoking her to ask, "what he did do," that his only feeling on awakening appears to have been "wonder," not anger. It is also noteworthy that he expresses no remorse, either to her, or, more privately, in his record of the incident. This gives us a sense of an early modern household in which the wife literally became "one flesh" with the husband—*feme covert* in a cultural and emotional as well as legal sense. Grace Minor's feelings, other than her indignation or amazement at being struck by her sleeping husband, were not important enough to her husband to be recorded as well. We do, in the end, though, have the sense that the couple did awaken and, perhaps, they marveled together at the strange event and its possible meaning.

One other couple is recorded to have worked together on a wondrous dream, a dream that once again involved an apparition, this time of an angelic nature. In October 1702, amid a health crisis that would prove fatal, Abigail Mather, who had been sick ever since a miscarriage in May, had a notable dream ([C. Mather, 1911, v. 7: 444, 445).[4] The dream occurred the very first night after a late-night fast and vigil that her husband Cotton had kept, during which he lighted on a particular psalm that encouraged him to "resign the Condition of my Consort, at last, unto what shall be done in the future State [i.e., to focus more on her spiritual estate rather than on whether she lived or died in this visible world]" (v. 7: 444). Closing his fast with the simple invocation, "Lord, Thy Will be done!" he continued: "Behold a strange Thing! On the Night after the Fast, my Consort had appearing to her, (she supposes, in her sleep) a grave Person, who brought with him, a Woman in the most meager and wretched Circumstances imaginable." In this dream, he continued, "My Consort fell into the Praises of God, in that her Condition was not yet so miserably Circumstanced as that woman's now before her. The grave Person then told her, that inasmuch as there were at this Time, a Couple of Symptoms become insupportable to her, he would propose a Way, wherein she should obtain some Help for them." What followed was a very specific recipe: "First, for her intolerable Pain in her Breast" (perhaps she had a breast infection, mastitis, or cancer), "said he, let them cut the warm Wool from a living Sheep, and apply it warm unto the grieved Pain. Next, for her Salivation, which hitherto nothing had relieved, said he, take a Tankard of Spring-Water, and therein over the Fire dissolve an agreeable Quantity of Mastic's, and of Gum Icinglass: Drink of this Liquor now and then, to strengthen the Glands, which ought to have been done a great while ago." Abigail reported the dream, presumably first to Cotton and then later ("on Friday"), "She told this to her principal Physician; who mightily encouraged our trying the Experiments (v. 7: 444)."

Cotton Mather first reports this all as if it were only his wife's fascination with her own dream vision. But now he joined her in the experiment:

> We did it [followed the instructions]; and unto our Astonishment, my Consort revived at a most unexpected Rate; insomuch, that she came twice on Saturday out of her sick Chamber, unto me in my Study; and there she asked me to give Thanks unto God with her, and for her, on the Account of the Recovery in so surprising a Degree begun unto her.
>
> (v. 7: 444, 445).[5]

In a sad turn of events, however, Abigail Mather would sicken again, and, continuing unwell, she would die on December 1 (v. 7: 448, 449).

This dream's significance lies in the ways in which the couple interpreted and acted on its message, but it is also noteworthy for the fact that no diabolical inspiration was suspected. Though "no credit nor regard" was to be given to dreams, Mather and his wife sought to implement a special cure brought to her through the medium of this "grave Person." Abigail actually reports the dream twice: once to Cotton, once to the physician, seemingly in that order. But the dream had a potent effect. Illness, suffering and death were excruciatingly painful passages, then as now. This dream and its enactment took a situation in which the Mathers were largely helpless and gave them something specific to do, perhaps a psychological relief if not a lasting physical one. This is one explanation for the dream's prominent reception in this otherwise devoutly orthodox household.

Another explanation, and one more closely grounded in period understandings, has to do with the motif of the "grave Person" who appears suddenly, offers advice, and then disappears again. Cotton and Abigail Mather would have been familiar with this personage. Indeed, Increase Mather's collection *Illustrious Providences* contains two relevant cases that might well have been familiar to his son and daughter-in-law. The first was the story of Innocentia's breast cancer (taken from Augustine's writings): "In her sleep she was admonished to repair unto the Font where she had been Baptized, and there to sign that place with the sign of the Cross, which she did, and was immediately healed of her Cancer" (I. Mather 1684: 272).

The second story, reprinted from a compendium of wonder tales, Clarke's *Examples*, is remarkably similar to Abigail Mather's reported dream, all of which suggests that this was a common folkloric motif of the day. In the story, as Cotton's father, Increase Mather, retold it, one Samuel Wallas of Stamford in Lincolnshire, who suffered from consumption, was reading a religious book on a rainy day when there was a knock on the door. He opened it, and "a comely and grave old Man of a fresh complexion, with white curled Hair, entred; and after walking several times about the room, said to him, Friend, I perceive you are not well." Wallas told the man that he had been ill for many years, and was quite "past cure, and that he was a poor Man, and not able to follow their [the Doctors'] costly presecriptions, only he committed himself and life into the hands of God, to dispose of as he pleased" (I. Mather 1684, 205, 206).

This pious answer pleased the visitor, who said,

> *Thou sayest very well, be sure to fear God, and serve him; and remember to observe what now I say to thee*; Tomorrow morning go into the Garden, and there take two leaves of red Sage, and one of Blood-wort; and put those three Leaves into a cup of small Beer, and drink thereof as oft as need requires; the fourth Morning, cast away those Leaves, and put in fresh ones, thus do for twelve dayes together; and thou shalt find e're these twelve dayes be expired, through the help of God they Disease will be cured, and the frame of they body altered.
>
> (206, 207)

"....Wishing the Lord of Heaven to be with him he [the grave man] departed." Wallas, who must have run to the window to look, could see the Man "passing in the Street, but none else observed him, though some were then standing in the doors opposite to Wallas his House." There was another strange detail, indicative of the grave man's otherworldly origins: "Although it Rained when this Grave Person came into the House, and had done so all that day, yet he had not one spot of wet or dirt upon him" (207, 208). Wallas tried the cure and found himself much improved.

The nature of his strange visitor remained to be determined. Mather (or, rather, Clarke) tells us that some ministers met at Stamford to discuss the nature of this man, and "concluded that this cure was wrought by a good Angel, sent from Heaven upon that Errand" (208). Mather *père* noted that it was "not impossible, but that Holy angels may appear, and visibly converse with some." Yet he added a strong note of caution: "For any to desire such a thing is unwarrantable, and exceeding dangerous. For thereby some have been imposed upon by wicked Daemons, who know how to transform themselves into Angels of Light" (208, 210).

Context seems to have been the only determinant as to whether these tricky figures would prove to be angelic or demonic in origin. For the younger Mathers, a consultation with their physician was an essential step before taking any action related to the dream. Of course, consultation with a physician was also necessary in witchcraft cases, in which a natural cause was ruled out before a demonic origin could be determined. This couple's mutual search to implement the knowledge that arrived in a dream vision also offered them a shared way of approaching what was already a horrific illness—for the sufferer, it was something to do despite her fears and sense of helplessness about illness and impending death.[6] The period pun seems significant too: these "grave" personages usually appeared just as the person had resigned themselves to their future "grave"—the tomb awaiting them at their death.

Samuel Sewall's recorded dreams offer a counterweight to such strange visitations suggesting another route by which extraordinary experience might be incorporated into daily life and shape emotional regulation (Sewall 1973). Indeed, when compared with examples from Cotton Mather's 1702 history of New England, *Magnalia Christi Americana*, we see that authentic dream visitations and the knowledge gained from dreams were commonly respected by the dreamers, and sometimes retold in ways echoed in Sewall's own reported dreams. As Hall notes, dreams played a central part in the lives of many pious New England men throughout the seventeenth century, despite their stated suspicions about them.

> Condemned in the case of Anabaptists, dreams [and prophesying] returned to center stage in the pages of the *Magnalia* as authentic promptings from the supernatural....Thus he (Cotton Mather) dared report that John Cotton and John Wilson learned in dreams who would be selected by the Boston church to succeed them.
>
> (Hall 1989, quotation 108–109, and 277, n. 112)[7]

Mather also noted that prophetic dreams had come to Thomas Parker, the minister of Newbury; his friend's son recorded, "I have heard him tell ... that the great changes of his life had been signified to him before-hand by *dreams*" (C. Mather, [1702] 1853, v. 1: 486). And John Eliot, "the great preacher to the Indians, 'often had strange forebodings of things that were to come'" (Hall 1989, 108–9 and 277, n. 112).[8] As these many examples suggest, wonders generally appeared through dreams.

Sewall's diary contains an especially rich trove of examples. Although there is no way that the prolific diarist can be anything other than exceptional because of his amazingly detailed record keeping, Sewall may nevertheless, in this case, represent the norm, as he seems to have taken his dreams in stride, even though they occasionally included remarkable or startling visitations. Sewall's dreams were often emotionally powerful; in modern terms, they seem to have served trans-forming *selfobject* functions, satisfying needs for archaic merger states, and—in the case of visitations from mentors, fellows, or alter egos—providing gratifying and crucial psychological experiences of twinship (Kohut 1984).[9] Sewall recorded, pondered over, and wondered at such visitations as spiritual messages with strong meaning. To write them down was another way to keep this desired experience near at hand.

Of seventeen dreams that Sewall had over the years from 1676 to 1728, three were wonders [that I have] discussed elsewhere: a 1675 dream about climbing stairs to Heaven; a 1686 dream about Jesus living in Boston; and a 1728 dream about a boy stealing his watch. These, along with a 1705 dream that he was judged and condemned and a 1706/7 dream that he had been chosen Lord Mayor of London (also described elsewhere [in the book]) played on themes of being chosen—elected, in the spiritual sense—or, at the least, were focused on position, status, and rank. His dream in February 1710/11, "Now I dream'd of being at the Commencement and seeing Mr. Leverett [the President of Harvard] in Scarlet," came on the heels of a hard loss, just after he noted the death of a trusted Council colleague and offered prayer: "The good Lord prepare the rest, and me especially to follow after" (Sewall 1973, v. 2: 653–54 [February 9, 1710/11]).[10] In short, Sewall seemed to be of two minds at least, dreaming of a "commencement" (a beginning), just after he had dutifully prayed for a sober and dignified ending.

Many of the remaining twelve dream reports had to do with loss, death of a loved one, or guilt over neglect of duty. These tended to be "heavy" in feeling (Sewall's own term) and somber or frightening in tone. Thus, in June 1685 Sewall recorded a lengthy and troubling dream in Latin, presumably to keep its shameful contents private from other family members, particularly his wife, whom it con-cerned. Translated, Sewall wrote: "I had dreamt that I returned to Newbury or some other town, and that during my absence, my wife died at Roxbury or Dorchester. I took the tidings very hard, and repeatedly called her name out." He was sur-prised that his father-in-law was gone from home; "they said that he had started for England: since his daughter had died he was free to travel as he wished." Then another daughter, Sewall's own Elizabeth (also known as Betty), then four years old, "whispered that the death had occurred in part because of my neglect and want of love. When I shook off sleep, I embraced my wife for joy as if I had newly mar-ried her" (Sewall 1973, v. 1: 65 [June 3, 1685]).

While it is impossible at this remove to speculate about the cause or the full meanings of this particular dream, nevertheless, a few things are notable about the report. One aspect that jumps out is the varying volumes in which the dream "speaks." First, Sewall's dream presents Hannah as dead, but then the dreamer calls out her name "repeatedly." When guilty feelings surface in Elizabeth's message ("my neglect and want of love"), they are only "whispered," a puzzling, and incongruous detail. Add to that the fact that he recorded it in Latin, and the dream, whatever its other meanings, seems to talk about a conflictual set of feelings—a Sewall who shouts out his attachment to his wife, but who, in the figure of Betty and the mode of recording, "whispers" his guilt and hides it in Latin. Could Sewall, like Father Hull, have felt tied down by his family obligations, and could he too wish to be "free to travel as he wished"?

This was not the only dream of Sewall in which his wife had died. Indeed, this dream pattern appears again four years later, nearly word for word the same. In June 1689—when Sewall was already six months into a journey to England—he had dreams on two successive nights, back-to-back, which betokened his wife's death. On June 16, the Sabbath, he wrote, "Last night I dreamed of my Wife, and of Father Hull, that he had buried somebody, and was presently intending to goe to Salem" (Sewall 1973, 1:219 [June 16, 1689]). In the other, recorded on Thursday, June 20, but dreamed on Sunday, June 16, he noted, "Last Sabbath day night dreamed of the death of my dear Wife, which made me very heavy" (Sewall 1973, v. 1:219 [June 20, 1689]). Sewall may have subscribed to the belief, discussed elsewhere in the full work, that dreams of loved ones far distant might, through some sympathetic connection or divine intercession, carry actual news of them.[11] These dreams appeared on the heels of having signed a petition "for leave to goe home." Sewall had also dreamed about a dead friend, "Mr. Adams" (William Adams, Sewall's classmate from Harvard College, who twice appeared in Sewall's dreams), and had busied himself with preparations to return (Sewall 1973, v. 1:219 [June 13, 1689] and v. 2: 1131). It would seem the return to New England, and to Hannah, was very much on Sewall's mind.[12]

Sewall again may have been of two minds about his return to Massachusetts. Accompanying the sad scenes of death, Sewall the dreamer had imagined that Father Hull, already dead for five years, "had buried somebody" and then was planning another trip ("presently intending to goe to Salem"). The very next night, Sewall himself killed off his wife (at least figuratively), though he did feel "very heavy" at the prospect. An ambivalent message keeps pressing for our attention: did Sewall feel "heavy" (sad, depressed, worried) about losing his wife? Yes, ostensibly. But might he not also have felt heavy about heading back to family and responsibilities after the exciting and important work in England?[13] And, more complex still, could separation have caused the continued travel to feel heavy, occasioning a desire to return home? Ambivalence seems to saturate these dream reports, and what predominates is the recurring heaviness of mood.

For all these dreams, Sewall might have proffered a spiritual interpretation regarding a central challenge in a pious puritan's life. Where the modern analyst might emphasize the emotions of sadness, loss (both past and anticipated), hidden aggression, and ambivalence, the early modern interpreter would likely stress instead the spiritual dilemma encoded in these dreams of family: the spiritual obligation of all puritan believers to never place things of this world above those of the next. In this view, the journeys to be undertaken and separations to be endured were spiritual ones. The deaths and the guilt stemmed from one's "neglect" of a spiritual duty and one's "want of love" for God. While Sewall might not have recognized the emotional panoply presented by these dreams, I like to think that he would have embraced this second reading as containing a central dilemma of his life that he articulated directly on many occasions: the puritan principle that one should never be more attached to things of this world than to God.

Two additional dreams circle around this theme. One, the dream of March 1695, is well known: "Last night I dream'd that all of my Children were dead except Sarah; which did distress me sorely with Reflexions on my Omission of Duty towards them, as well as Breaking oft the Hopes I had of them" (Sewall 1973, v. 1: 328 [March 18, 1695]). The other, rarely cited, involved Sewall's grown daughter, Betty Hirst:

> Last night I dream'd that I had my daughter Hirst in a little Closet to pray with her, and of a sudden she was gon[e], I could not tell how; although the Closet was so small, and not Cumber'd with Chairs or Shelves. I was much affected with it when I waked.
>
> (Sewall 1973, v. 1: 592 [April 2, 1708])

The first stresses feelings of loss and guilt, while the second carried a feeling of sadness and intensity even after Sewall woke up. One wonders if Sewall noticed a message in the second—that even when you have your loved one close (in a "little Closet," a space "so small") and even when you are knitted together in devoted prayer, even then you cannot safeguard against sudden and inexplicable loss. Perhaps it was feelings such as these that lingered on into the daytime, perhaps intertwining with worry about the actual fate of Betty Hirst or of all the paternal hopes she represented.

In addition to the culturally sanctioned belief about the significance of visitations from the dead, additional themes hint that Sewall may have been wrestling with growing older, maturing as a father (at, respectively, 33 and 42 years old), both for his family and in his duties to his community. In December 1685, just after the wrenching final illness and burial of his young son Henry, he wrote: "Dreamed last night of Mr. Chauncy, the President, and of Sam. Danforth" (Sewall 1973, v. 1: 90 [Dec. 26, 1685]; cf. entries 89–90). Danforth was a classmate from Harvard who had died in London in 1676, nearly nine years before to the day (Sewall 1973, v. 2: 1057, n. 9). Chauncy was Charles Chauncy, the president of Harvard College, who had died in office a few months after Sewall's graduation, eulogized by Increase Mather as "['a venerable old man, most accomplished ... most expert in the art of instruction, who devoted himself with exemplary and unfailing diligence to the instruction of the sons of the prophets.[']" Cotton Mather added, "The death of so great a man left the college crippled and well nigh crushed" (Harvard University 2013, *Charles Chauncy*; quotations, cf. C. Mather [1702] 1853, v. 2 14, and 14n).[14] On another occasion, in 1695, Sewall dreamed of Harvard again and his dead friend, William Adams, this time the dream focused on disturbances in the proper order between fathers and sons:

> Was somewhat exercis'd about my dream the last night, which was that Mr. Edward Oakes, the Father [of Urian Oakes, minister at Cambridge and president of Harvard College], was chosen Pastor of Cambridge Church. Mr. Adams and I had discourse about the Oddness of the matter, that the father should succeed his Son so long after the Son's death [Urian Oakes had died in 1681].

Sewall "excus'd my not voting, as not pertaining to me, though I had other reasons besides. Thus I was conversing among the dead" (Sewall 1973, v. 1: 326 [Jan. 5, 1695]; Harvard University 2013, *Urian Oakes*). It seems notable that each dream involves a pair of men: one junior, one senior. Each involves a Harvard classmate (Danforth and Adams, either of whom, as age-mates, could be a figurative representation of Sewall himself), along with a president of Harvard as the senior member (Charles Chauncy and Urian Oakes). In the second dream, there is the additional father–son pair of Edward and Urian Oakes.[15] It thus seems not too far a leap to suggest that Sewall's dreams—in addition to bringing him close to the honored dead—were also wrestling with issues of succession and seniority, all potent issues in the male life cycle and particularly relevant to Sewall, who buried a son just prior to the first of these dreams and who reported a visit to his "Unkle Quinsey" just before the record of the second (Sewall 1973, v. 1: 326 [Jan. 5, 1695]).

The last dream we shall discuss here also plays with issues of seniority and succession, or achievement and aspiration, in potent ways. Perhaps the closest thing to an apparition that Sewall ever saw happened in a dream he had while at sea, bound for England, and just after hearing of the Glorious Revolution staged by William, Prince of Orange. In the flush of excitement that must have followed hearing the news at sea from a passing ship, Sewall reported this lively dream:

> Last night I dreamed of military matters, Arms and Captains, and, of a sudden, Major Gookin, very well clad from head to foot, and of a very fresh lively countenance—his Coat and Breeches of blood-red silk, beckoned me out of the room where I was to speak to me [*sic*] I think 'twas the Town-house.

Sewall notes that in the evening (following the dream) he read "the Eleventh of the Hebrews [on faith], and sung the 46th Psalm [on God as refuge and strength]." He also notes, "When I waked from my Dream I thought of Mr. Oakes's Dream about Mr. Shepard and Mitchell beckening him up the Garret-Stairs in Harvard College" (Sewall 1973, v.1: 187 [Dec. 30, 1688]).

This dream offers a clear invitation to the ambitious Sewall, who was going to England hoping "to uphold the interests of the colony, now without a charter or a settled government, and to secure, if possible, a restoration of its privileges (Sewall 1973, v.1: 184, ed. note)." Not only did the auspicious news seem a hopeful sign, but now Major Gookin appeared, who, at his death in 1687 had been a vigorous defender of Massachusetts liberties (Thompson 2004). Auspiciously, he was "well clad," "of a very fresh, lively countenance" and arrayed from head to foot in "blood-red silk," a lively color if ever there was, and beckoned to Sewall. Still more fascinating is Sewall's waking reference to "Mr. Oakes' Dream," a suggestion of some prior dream sharing, that Sewall should know what Oakes had dreamed. Though its details are lost to us now, it seems to have been a similar dream of being invited in to take the place of a deceased predecessor (Shepard had been pastor of the Cambridge Church, where Oakes succeeded him), which has the effect of doubling (and thereby intensifying) the dream's message (C. Mather [1702] 1853, v. 2: 16).

Sewall's dreams—when read in context but with an eye to possible emotional meanings—give us a chance to explore more deeply the range of dream experience found among colonists in a maturing New England. While Sewall marked these sad dreams and visitations from the dead as nothing more than dreams, other members of this society sometimes experienced such events as literal visitations: from a neighbor or a sister or even an angel. The emotional experience embedded in these dream events and apparitions varied from terrifying to tantalizing. New England colonists embedded strong emotion within accepted frames or culturally sanctioned idioms and knitted expressions of the wondrous into a fabric of accepted spiritual experience.

This maturing colonial society thus had a range of approaches to dreams and dreamlike visitations. Meaning was assigned largely based on the context: a dream might be just that,—or it might be something much darker, and only the surrounding social fabric would determine its significance. Who dreamed it? Was there an ongoing crisis? Did it demand public expression? Was it part of a criminal action? Did it seem better suited to private reflection? The answers to these questions helped to shape responses to dreams, and the dreamer's approach to acting on dreamt experience, or not. In an increasingly complex, expansive, and segmented society, however, decisions about dream experience could have profound outcomes. In some cases—such as during the Salem Witchcraft Crisis—they might even lead to capital punishments.

Specters, familiars, apparitions, wonders, and angels remained relatively frequent occurrences in late seventeenth-century New England, along with emotionally powerful, spiritually awakening dream experiences. The invisible world remained a frighteningly vibrant potentiality, and two major Indian wars had left colonists keenly attuned to their own vulnerability. When witches walked abroad as at Salem, they made their neighbors painfully aware of this vulnerability and, as historian Mary Beth Norton and others have argued, they provoked a murderous response. Eager to kill off an external enemy—the threat of their Native neighbors—English men and women contented themselves with internal ones instead. As Sarah Osborne, one of the first women charged in the Salem crisis, had averred: "Shee was more like to be bewitched then that she was a witch." When asked by Justice Hathorne "what made her say so," Osborne responded:

> She was frighted one time in her sleep and either saw or dreamed that shee saw a thing like an indian all black which did pinch her in her neck and pulled her by the back part of her [head] to the dore of the house.
>
> (Rosenthal 2009, 127)

As Norton remarked in relation to this, "That nightmare would have been hardly unusual for a woman in northern New England familiar with reports of scalping and the recent raid on York, and Hathorne did not explore it further" (Norton 2002, 27). But now, spectators in the meetinghouse complained that Osborne had told them, "Shee would never believe that lying spirit any more." Asked what spirit she meant, and whether it had been the Devil, Osborne said that while she did not know the Devil and "I never did see him," she had been troubled by "a voice that I thought I heard" that said "I should go no more to meeting (Rosenthal 2009, 128)." Hathorne immediately pressed Osborne for an explanation as to why she had not been to meeting "thes yeare and two months (Rosenthal 2009, 128)." It is perhaps surprising that more New England colonists did not record troubling dreams about encounters with Indians on the order of Osborne's nightmare. The sources, however, are mute on this point. The closest we can come, besides Osborne's dream, is a nightmare that troubled Samuel Sewall in 1706, after several years of serious Indian disturbance during Queen Anne's War (the North American version of the War of the Spanish Succession, also known in New England as the Third Indian War). Sewall wrote on April 4:

> Last night I dream'd I saw a vast number of French coming towards us, for multitude and Huddle like a great Flock of Sheep. It put me into a great Consternation, and made me think of Hiding in some thicket. The Impression remain'd upon me after my Waking. GOD defend!
>
> (Sewall 1973, 1: 544)

The links of this dream to the wartime context are plain: several diarists of the period make it clear that many in New England were anxiously tracking news from the northern front, where every major twist and turn was recorded ([Marshall] 1884–1885, 157–161; [Green] 1866, 222, 223; and [Green] 1870, 74–101).

But the religious references fairly leap off Sewall's page as well: the Catholic French, who "huddle like a great Flock of Sheep," would have been a familiar image for the puritan Sewall, who was trained in the idea that Catholic adversaries and their Indian allies lived under the thumb of their priests. And yet, despite the incongruity, Sewall was scared by the dream—the "vast number" and "multitude" of enemies, "coming towards us"—which made him "think of Hiding in some thicket." It is hard, once again, not to think of the religious "thickets" (sinful retreats) that might have to be overcome on a regular basis in Sewall's demanding Protestant piety. There could be no retreat, no refuge, from God's enemies. Indeed, as diarist John Marshall of Braintree noted in 1707 of difficulties among the English militia at Casco, "I shall only remark that the disappointment of that design [attacking the French] speaks much of divine anger of which we are generally too insensible" ([Marshall] 1884–1885, 159 [July 1707]).

Doubtless, the English would have liked to reassure themselves that the Native threat was a thing of the past. But while they could hang convicted witches, they could do little about the Native peoples and their French allies that ringed the region, and who, from 1676 to 1713, regularly descended on towns in the various border regions, wreaking havoc on English communities (cf. Demos 1994, 134, 137). In the meantime, the English were left with apparitions and angels—frightening specters and helpful guides—whose role was to warn and to chasten, as well as to reassure and protect. The impact of colonialism was wide reaching, affecting not only its ostensible target—the Indians—but penetrating as well in the lives of English colonists, and even unto their dreams.

Try as they might, however, the English could not completely colonize their dream lives. As the dream reports of Thomas Minor, Samuel Sewall, or many others suggest, dreams would continue to startle, "exercise," and awaken dreamers, airing knotty feelings, raising surprising juxtapositions, and bringing uncomfortable knowledge. For many, dreams and dreamlike experience remained deadly serious and, in the right circumstances, might lead to deadly action. As this chapter has argued, dreams from the seventeenth century can also be read as sources suggestive of some of the emotional dilemmas, conflicts, and preoccupations of New England colonists, in a way that has not before been explored by historians. A psychoanalytic sensibility, held lightly and informed by sensitivity to the ways dreams were interpreted by the colonists themselves, helps to deepen our understanding of this colonial culture.

Notes

1 This is excerpted from Chapter 5 of *Dreams and the Invisible World in Colonial New England: Indians, Colonists and the Seventeenth Century* (Philadelphia: University of Penn Press, 2014).

2 The instance is recorded twice, in the body of the diary in chronological order: Wednesday August 20, 1662: "I & my wife both dreamed." (51), and again in random notes at the end, where the fuller report of content begins, "Agust [sic] 1662. I & my wife dreamed at one time" (192). I am grateful to Donald Larson for sharing his transcription from the original held in the Connecticut State Library, and for his thoughtful commentary that refined and corrected my initial reading of the source.

3 The *Oxford English Dictionary* indicates that the word had the same double meaning in Minor's period as it does in our own (accessed May 15, 2009).

4 For the timeline of her illness: ([C. Mather] 1911, v. 7: 430, 437).

5 The anxious husband continued, "After this, my dear Consort continued much refresh'd and yet feeble. We had great Hopes of her becoming a strong Person again, and yet great Fears, lest some further latent Mischief within her, prove after all too hard for her."

6 Cotton Mather continued to wrestle with the impact of these losses. He composed an epigram for his wife; he preached on the death of Ezekiel's wife; members of the congregation and other friends helped to build a tomb for his six lost family members; he meditated on the "benefits" of his wife's death, which included preserving him from disease and her from the painful knowledge of a sibling's death (C. Mather, 1911: v. 7: 450 (epigram, sermon, tomb); 7: 452, 453 (benefits); 7: 456 (publication of *Meat out of the Eater*).

7 In note 112, Hall is citing Cotton Mather's *Magnalia Christi Americana* (v. 1: 295). Mather's report of John Cotton's deathbed goes out of its way to preserve Cotton's reputation as a strict Puritan who gave no credit to dreams, saying that when his church asked him to recommend a successor, he named Mr. Norton: "That which gave encouragement unto this business, *was not a dream of Mr. Cotton's*, though it was indeed a strange thing, that Mr. Cotton in his illness, being solicitous what counsel to give unto his church, he dreamed that he saw Mr. Norton riding unto Boston, to succeed him, upon a white horse, in circumstances that were exactly afterwards accomplished." (1: 294, 295) [emphasis mine].

8 In note 112, Hall cites Mather; the full incident is in the *Magnalia* ([1702] 1853, 1: 544).

9 Kohut spoke about the lifelong "needs of man for sustenance of his self in … three areas (i.e., his need to experience mirroring and acceptance; his need to experience merger with greatness, strength, and calmness; and his need to experience the presence of essential alikeness) from the moment of birth to the moment of death." Such needs could be met not by real people, but through "cultural selfobject"—activities, creativity, music, and art and other "hallucinatory creations" (76). If deprived of access to such sustaining selfobject experience, the individual would experience rupture and a sense of disequilibrium (Kohut 1984, ch. 10, 76, quotation 194).

10 John Leverett was a judge of the Superior Court and became the first secular president of Harvard in 1708, serving until 1724 (Harvard University. 2013. *John Leverett*).

11 Sewall was already dreaming of his wife shortly after his departure and of having trouble reaching her, when he "dream'd much of my wife last night. She gave me a piece of Cake for Hannah Hett, was in plain dress and white Apron. Methoughts [she] was brought to bed [had given birth], and through inadvertency was got up into the uppermost Gallery, so that I knew not how to get down to hold up the Child (Sewall 1973, v. 1:186 [December 18, 1688])."

12 Preparations included obtaining a power of attorney to be able to conduct business in New England. Additional information about William Adams, who lived in Dedham and died August 16, 1685, can be found: (Sewall 1973, v. 2: 1057 n. 9). Sewall outlived all his classmates from 1671.

13 Hull had died October 1, 1683 (Sewall 1973, v 1: xxiv).

14 Sewall took his degree in August 1671, and Chauncy died February 29, 1671/2 (Sewall 1973, v. 1: xxiii).

15 Mather remembered Oakes as "the excellent Pastor of the Church at Cambridge" and made a play on his name (as an oak tree) to conjure up an image of students gathered round, "as a rendezvous of happy Druids, under the influences of so rare a President: But alas! Our joy must be short lived; for, on July 25, 1681, the stroak of a sudden death fell'd the tree (C. Mather [1702] 1853, v. 2: 16)."

References

Demos, John. 1970. *A Little Commonwealth: Family Life in Plymouth Colony*. New York: Oxford University Press.

———. 1994. *The Unredeemed Captive: A Family Story from Early America*. New York: Alfred A. Knopf.

[Green, Joseph]. 1866. "Diary of Rev. Joseph Green, of Salem Village," ed. S. P. Fowler, *Essex Institute Historical Collections* 8, no. 1: 215–224.

[————], 1870. "Diary of Rev. Joseph Green, of Salem Village," In *Essex Institute Historical Collections,* 10, edited by S. P. Fowler (2nd ser., no. 2: 73–104).

Hall, David D. 1989. *Worlds of Wonder, Days of Judgment: Popular Religious Belief in Early New England.* Cambridge, MA: Harvard University Press.

Harvard University. 2013. "History of the Presidency." *Charles Chauncy; John Leverett, Urian Oakes.* Harvard University Website, http://www.harvard.edu/history/presidents/ (accessed July 7, 2013).

Kohut, Heinz. 1984. *How Does Analysis Cure?* rpt. ed. Chicago, IL: University of Chicago Press.

[Marshall, John]. 1884–1885. "John Marshall's Diary," ed. Charles F. Adams Jr., *Proceedings of the Massachusetts Historical Society.,* 2nd ser., 1: 148–164.

[Mather, Cotton]. 1911. "Diary of Cotton Mather." ed. and intro. Worthington Chauncy Ford. *Massachusetts Historical Society Collections,* 7th ser., vol. 7.

Mather, Cotton. [1702] 1853. *Magnalia Christi Americana.* London; rpt. Hartford, CT: Silas Andrus and Son), vol. 1.

Mather, Increase. 1684. *An Essay for the Recording of Illustrious Providences: Wherein an Account is Given of Many Remarkable and Very Memorable Events, Which have Hapned This Last Age; Especially in New-England.* Boston, MA: Samuel Green for Joseph Browning.

Miner, Frank Denison, ed., with Hannah Miner. 1915. "Introduction." In *The Diary of Manasseh Minor, Stonington, Connecticut, 1696–1720.* n.p.: privately published.

[Minor, Thomas]. 1899. *The Diary of Thomas Minor, Stonington, Connecticut, 1653–1684,* edited by Sidney H. Miner and George D. Stanton Jr. New London, Conn.: Day Publishing Co.

Norton, Mary Beth. 2002. *In the Devil's Snare: The Salem Witchcraft Crisis of 1692.* New York: Alfred A. Knopf.

Oxford English Dictionary Online, 2009. Entry: "bitch." http://dictionary.oed.com, accessed May 15, 2009.

Plane, Ann Marie. 2014. *Dreams and the Invisible World in Colonial New England: Colonists, Indians, the Seventeenth* Century. Philadelphia: University of Pennsylvania Press.

Rosenthal, Bernard. 2009. "Sarah Good, Sarah Osburn, & Tituba, Examinations (Cheever), doc. 3 [March 1, 1692]." *Records of the Salem Witch-Hunt.* New York: Cambridge University Press.

Sewall, Samuel. 1973. *The Diary of Samuel Sewall, 1674–1729,* edited by M. Halsey Thomas. 2 vols. New York: Farrar, Straus and Giroux.

Thompson, Roger. 2004. "Daniel Gookin (bap. 1612, d. 1687)." *Oxford Dictionary of National Biography.* Oxford: Oxford University Press. online ed., http://www.oxforddnb.com/view/article/11005

Chapter 6

Afterword

Ann Marie Plane

Arriving at Austen Riggs in August 2010, I looked up at the Norman Rockwell portraits of the staff in the main reception area and felt optimistic. I hoped my work there might create a deeper *rapprochement* between the very different disciplines of history and psychoanalysis. I was also looking for a more fulfilling interchange between my interior and exterior lives, along the lines suggested by a mentor, Judith E. Vida, in her collaborative works with Gershon J. Molad on the need to bridge personal, clinical, and conference spaces. Perhaps Riggs would be the place.

Historians identify large structures—social stratification; racial, ethnic, or gender identities; political affiliations; changing economic orders—and look for change over time, applying models drawn from many disciplines. Psychoanalytic approaches are rarely used, especially in U.S. History, though history of the emotions has been a growing field of late. In the chapter excerpted above, I engaged colonial-era dream reports as windows on the emotional worlds of their authors. Some historians argue that such past domains are unknowable. In this view, cross-cultural psychoanalytic approaches inevitably lead to anachronistic interpretation, the historian's bugbear. But, as the historian and analyst Peter Gay pointed out long ago, many historians eschew psychoanalytic theorizing about human motivation only to adopt under-theorized "common sense" explanations of motivation. And, as another historian and analyst, Thomas A. Kohut, argued in his influential 1986 article in the *American Historical Review*, historians share a common method with the psychoanalyst. As developed there, and in a 2020 book, each discipline inevitably relies on the practitioner's empathy and introspection. For me, professional history's disinterest in feelings echoed painful invalidations and emotional distancing in my childhood; psychoanalysis offered a pathway toward a more nuanced historical truth. I was determined to find a voice in my writing that would make sense to both scholarly communities, and I hoped my time at Riggs would facilitate that.

Of course, psychoanalysis has long been critiqued for its reluctance to theorize societal structures as meaningful contributors to psychological life. Although the social "third" now plays a key role in some theory and the psychoanalyst has abandoned the method requiring faceless clinical neutrality, the traditional consulting

DOI: 10.4324/9781003322627-14

room retains its sequestration, elitism, and privilege, embodying the inequities of our society. As a historian attuned to structures, I hoped to temper the limitations of clinical analysis through rigorous inclusion of the social, while, at the same time, creating a more satisfying interrogation of the past. I was already well along the road, having completed my training in 2008 in Los Angeles, and maintaining a private practice under supervision, in accordance with California state law. For me, then, appointment as the Erikson Scholar at Riggs offered a further opportunity to explore connections between the disciplines of history and psychoanalysis.

In addition to a writing sabbatical, I hoped to diversify my experience as a clinician through direct observation. Therefore, I threw myself into the life of the community. I attended case conferences, reading groups, and seminars; I got permission to observe both community meetings and a clinical team. I even attended most of the psychological testing seminar meetings, relishing the conversation with the fellows in residence.

Since each Erikson Scholar arrives at a particular moment from a particular place, one person's Riggs is never exactly the same as anyone else's. I arrived at an institution steeped in melancholy and self-reflection, as the hospital was about to undergo a required post-mortem review. The community also sat on the cusp of major structural changes, as leading (male) figures approached retirement. When the CEO and director, Edward Shapiro, welcomed me to the community, he explained that the Erikson scholar could be useful to Riggs, observing the community as an outsider and then reporting what I saw. In the end, my experience was one of profound learning, but also some alienation. My final report described the demands of being fully immersed in the trauma of others—both patients and staff, without the established structures that enabled staff to cope. I also found it challenging to live as a female of ambiguous status within an institution headed by an established cadre of senior males. Even compared to my university, which is no feminist utopia, the Riggs of 2010 seemed to mute female voices that should have commanded more attention, especially those of the incredibly talented and dedicated women analysts then in the mid-level ranks, as well as the tremendously skilled social workers, addiction counselors, and residence staff. And so I reflected that, in writing, to management on my departure.

Still and all, my Riggs was an immensely generative place to be. Getting to know Thomas A. Kohut (then chair of the board for the Erikson Institute) and meeting the future Erikson Scholar, Annie E. Rogers, after admiring the writing of each, were high points for me. It has taken years to digest the experiences I had there, and I remain deeply grateful for my time with the committed professional staff. Their devotion to supporting my productivity and growth, as well as the chance to work unobstructed, made this a truly memorable and important fellowship, and one that left an indelible stamp on my work and my life.

Chapter 7

Remembering Dorothy May Bradford's Death and Reframing "Depression" in Colonial New England[1]

Stacey Dearing

On December 17, 1620, after traveling across the Atlantic on the *Mayflower*, Dorothy May Bradford (1597–1620) died while the ship was anchored off Cape Cod.[2] The first known record of her death was written 30 years later by her husband, William Bradford (1590–1657). In an appendix to *Of Plymouth Plantation* listing the passengers of the *Mayflower*, he writes one sentence about the death of his first wife: "William Bradford his wife died soon after their arrival, and he married again and hath four children, three whereof are married" (Bradford 2016, 444). The next record appears 82 years after her death in Cotton Mather's (1663–1728) *Magnalia Christi Americana*: "At their first landing, his dearest consort accidentally falling overboard, was drowned in the harbor" (1702, n.p.). Though these statements constitute the only semi-contemporaneous documentation of Dorothy May Bradford's death, in the late nineteenth century a story emerged alleging that her death was not an accident, but a suicide. Despite the absence of any concrete evidence, the notion that Bradford died by suicide stuck.[3] By the late twentieth century, Francis Murphy argued that "most historians do not think it was an accident; she probably preferred to take her own life rather than face the certain rigors of the future" (1981, xiii).

This essay seeks to understand why, regardless of all the evidence, the idea that Bradford took her own life persists. I have identified five major iterations of the myth over the past 400 years. The first iteration focuses on just the basic facts of Bradford's disappearance and primarily consists of William Bradford and Cotton Mather's brief accounts. The second adds elements of both gothic literature and historical romance and is the first time the possibility of suicide is formally introduced to the narrative. The third iteration prioritizes Bradford's identity as a wife and mother and argues that she most likely suicided because of her grief at being separated from her son or because she was overwhelmed by the New England wilderness. The most influential narrative in this iteration comes from Samuel Eliot Morison. The fourth incarnation of the Bradford myth takes on elements of a Hollywood romance in *The Plymouth Adventure* (1950/2). In this version, Bradford is depicted as a romantic, melancholic loner who nevertheless finds herself in multiple love triangles on board the *Mayflower*. Finally, the last iteration adopts the language of clinical depression, describing (without evidence) Bradford's last days of mental anguish, isolation, and despair prior to her assumed suicide. In my

DOI: 10.4324/9781003322627-15

analysis of the various iterations of the myth, I argue that these stories continue to resonate in part because they attempt to give Bradford interiority and agency in her own death. Instead of depicting her as a fully realized historical figure, however, these accounts rely on fictional tropes, stereotypes of depression, and a regressive female essentialism that limits early modern English women to the roles of wife and mother. Using the methods of psychoanalytic literary theory and psychobiography, this essay argues that rather than recovering Bradford's voice or agency, many of the narratives surrounding her death instead project our own feelings onto Bradford—arguing that she must feel similarly to how we imagine we might feel in her position—and as such suppress her voice. Instead of becoming a fully realized historical figure, Bradford's voice is further obscured. In conclusion, this essay considers the value of applying a psychoanalytic approach to colonial American literature and suggests ways scholars might ask better questions and engage in more productive arguments about mental health in early America.

The notion that Bradford killed herself first appears in a work of fiction written nearly 250 years after her death. In 1869, Jane Goodwin Austin (1831–1894), a Massachusetts author and *Mayflower* descendant, wrote the short story "William Bradford's Love Life" for *Harper's New Monthly Magazine*. In the story, Austin draws on a family legend that suggests the Bradfords were involved in a love triangle—the first of many love triangles invented to explain Dorothy Bradford's death.[4] The myth was ostensibly passed down by *Mayflower* descendants who, in the words of W. Sears Nickerson, "knew, or thought they did, that [William Bradford's] first wife committed suicide and why" (1995, 88). In Austin's version, William is in love with another woman—Alice Carpenter Southworth—whom the story claims had coquettishly rejected his proposal prior to his marriage to Dorothy in 1613. Though Alice did become William Bradford's second wife, the belief that she was his first choice has been thoroughly debunked.[5] Nevertheless, Austin develops the myth, employing conventional elements of both sentimental and gothic fiction to weave a story in which Bradford suicides so that William can marry his true love, Alice.

As proof, Austin claims to possess previously unpublished documents, "some precious letters, and a few leaves of a private diary in the faint and timid manuscript of a woman," that verify that the story is based on the "saddest and most undoubted fact" (1869, 139). For this reason, some readers seem to have interpreted the text as history rather than historical fiction. Later, Austin clarified that her account was fictional by adding an explanatory preface when the story was reprinted. Claiming to have been inspired by the rediscovery and printing of William Bradford's *Of Plymouth Plantation* and by her passion for Pilgrim stories, Austin admits she was carried away by "a youthful imagination and untried powers," which "may have induced a certain fermentation of fancy" (1893, v). She goes on to note:

> Certainly, the author recalls with rather rueful mirth the reproof received from an aged relative who, after vainly inquiring for "the documents in the case" of William Bradford, remarked:—"You have no right to defraud people by pretending

to have what you have not." The reproof bore fruit, as righteous reproofs always should, and in later and more extended narratives of the same events nothing is set down as fact that has not been carefully determined to be such.

(v–vi)

Despite her claim to stick more closely to the historical record, the story is reprinted exactly as it had appeared in 1869, with only the preface to amend the record.

Not only does Austin acknowledge that the story was invented, historians like George Ernest Bowman and Austin's own brother, John Goodwin, have discredited various aspects of her tale. Yet, as Kari Holloway Miller observes, "Austin's imaginative myth had power and was increasingly seen as fact" (2015, 43). Bowman, frustrated at the lingering impact of the story, protested that it "has many times been quoted as the authority, and the only authority, for saying that Dorothy Bradford died a suicide" (1931, 101). Indeed, no supporting documents "prove" Bradford took her own life. Yet despite the fact that Austin's story was debunked repeatedly and thoroughly, subsequent scholars continued to speculate or report Bradford's suicide as likely fact. Most notably, Samuel Eliot Morison repeatedly claimed that Bradford died a suicide. Speculation about her death is even printed on the back cover of Morison's edition of William Bradford's *Of Plymouth Plantation*, drawing attention to his salacious interpretation of her death. Of William Bradford, Morison writes that "it may be that he suspected (as we do) that Dorothy Bradford took her own life after gazing for six weeks at the barren sand dunes of Cape Cod" (2016, xxiv). Morison repeats this claim almost verbatim in at least three texts from 1930 to 1956: *Builders of the Bay Colony* (1930); *Of Plymouth Plantation* (1952); and *The Story of the "Old Colony" of New Plymouth* (1956). Though Morison does not cite Austin's story, James Deetz and Patricia Scott Deetz persuasively argue that Austin's interpretation of Bradford's death "cannot be unconnected to Morison's theory" (2000, 305). Eugene Aubrey Stratton also suggests as much, noting "[e]ven such a careful historian as Samuel Eliot Morison seems to have been taken in by [Austin's] hoax" (1986, 325).

Though Austin's story is not cited directly by historians speculating on Bradford's cause of death, all arguments that Bradford suicided either rely on speculation or on the assertion of scholars who draw on the same family legends that John Goodwin debunked in 1888 and Bowman further repudiated in 1931.[6] Not only has the myth that Bradford took her own life permeated historical accounts, it has also taken hold in the popular imagination. Novels such as Ernest Gébler's *The Plymouth Adventure* (1950) and TaraShea Nesbit's *Beheld* (2020), films including the cinematic adaptation of *The Plymouth Adventure* (1952) and National Geographic's *Saints & Strangers* (2015), and even Sophie Cabot Black's award-winning persona poems *The Arguments* (1994), all explore the circumstances surrounding Bradford's death and seek to explain if or why she may have suicided. Because many of these iterations draw on psychological or pseudo-psychological rationales to explain Bradford's behavior, I am approaching this topic through a psychological frame.

In analyzing Bradford's cause of death, I am cognizant of the need to be cautious in my methodology. By applying a psychoanalytic frame to Bradford's life, I am employing a psychodynamic methodology that draws on aspects of psychobiography and psychohistory.[7] It is important to note the limitations of this approach: attempts to retroactively analyze or diagnose historical figures with any kind of mental illness can be difficult to substantiate, as "We run enormous risks of misconstruing history when we project contemporary diagnostic categories and psychiatric understandings back on to the past" (Scull 2015, 15). In addition, Freudian psychobiography has been criticized for being overly reliant on speculation in the absence of facts.[8] Though post-Freudian psychobiographers such as Alan Elms, William N. Runyan, and William T. Schultz have developed more effective methods, even Erik H. Erikson—regarded by many as one of the premier psychobiographers of the twentieth century—acknowledges that "psychoanalysis for historical reasons often occupies a position on the borderline of what is demonstrably true and of what demonstrably feels true" (1993, 21).[9] Many of the accounts declaring Bradford's death to be a suicide, I suggest, reside in this latter category. Simply too little is known about Bradford's life or her death to form a cogent psychoanalysis, much less to clinically diagnose depression or suicidal tendencies.

In addition, many of the histories of Bradford's death do not follow the guidelines for ethical or effective psychobiography (Schultz 2005b, 7). Instead, when many scholars speculate on Bradford's mental state or cause of death, they rely on what Schultz identifies as markers of "bad psychobiography," particularly single cues and reconstruction (10). For the last 20–30 years, scholars have focused on one primary unsubstantiated point: that Bradford must have been distraught after the journey. The proposed reasons for her alleged anguish vary, including because she missed her son, because she was unable to cope with the New England wilderness, or because she was distressed at the death of young Jasper More (1612–1620). For instance, Darcy Lee reflects with empathy that "[o]ne can only imagine that Dorothy May Bradford believed her future to be tenuous at best in this new and unforgiving land" (2017, n.p.); Martha Finch suggests Bradford fell or "jumped in despair" (2010, 69); and Nathaniel Philbrick argues that "Dorothy certainly had ample reason to despair" without her son, a feeling that he suggests might have been exacerbated by William's temporary absence (2006, 76). Even Kathleen Donegan's scrupulously ethical exploration of misery in New England probes the silence around Bradford's death, speculating at one point that the authors of *Mourt's Relation* (1622) "could not speak of what may have driven Dorothy Bradford over the side of the *Mayflower* and into the icy water" (2014, 136).

Further, many ostensibly factual accounts of Bradford's final days rely heavily on what Schultz terms reconstruction, a sort of speculation about the mental state of a historical figure, one often employing what Jacques Barzun calls "Weasel words," which indicate that a historical figure must have or probably felt a certain way (Barzun 1989, 45). For example, Nickerson embellishes Bradford's story, painting a vivid if unsubstantiated picture of a weak, melancholy woman experiencing "taut nerves" from the close quarters and cumulative stress of the journey (1995, 92).

"Is it any wonder that the spirit of one poor woman should break under the strain, when the souls of such strong men as William Bradford were nigh overwhelmed?" he speculates, "Here, with every tie cut which ever moored her to normal living, in this desolate wilderness from which even God, Himself, whose spirit of grace she now so sorely needed, seemed absent, the utter hopelessness of it all may have become greater than she could bear" (91, 92). In a more recent account, Rebecca Fraser similarly portrays Bradford as exhibiting an "increasingly desperate mood" throughout the voyage, perhaps because of the separation from her husband and son (2017, 49). Fraser goes on to describe Bradford as "sinking into a depression under the cold snowy light and the mysterious backdrop of the new continent. She could not find a way back from her despair and she could not talk about it. In all the anxiety about landing and organizing arrangements, no one noticed William Bradford's wife Dorothy was becoming unreachable" (60). Though this account employs the language of clinical depression, there is in fact no evidence that Bradford displayed any of these behaviors. For Barzun and Schultz, reconstruction creates logical fallacies, because first the author interprets behaviors and events and then they manufacture proof to support what they want to be true. Thus, we should be skeptical of arguments that Bradford took her own life and, therefore, must have been depressed.

None of the arguments that Bradford took her life employ Pilgrim's understandings of melancholy or suicide, which largely presented self-murder as the result of sin or satanic temptation.[10] This lacuna indicates that the theories regarding Bradford's alleged suicide are largely anachronistic and, therefore, reveal more about how later readers understand mental illness and suicide than they do about Bradford's mental health. Whether they intend to or not, many scholars apply the language of mental health in their interpretations of Bradford's death. My methodology, then, is to reframe analyses of Bradford so that they fall more in line with ethical psychoanalytic principles and draw more deliberately on one of the most valuable aspects of psychobiography: the impetus to put the subject "front and center" in her own story (Schultz 2005b, 3). My approach thus both reframes the arguments being made about Bradford's cause of death and provides historical and cultural context about mental health and views on voluntary death in the seventeenth century.

Because of the dearth of archival evidence, it is unlikely that anyone will be able to offer a definitive conclusion about what happened to Bradford on December 17, 1620. There are apparently no extant letters or diaries that can substantially illuminate Bradford's life or death. Even basic biographical facts have been long disputed.[11] Nevertheless, as Ava Chamberlain argues, "the lack of a complete explanation does not mean that all explanations are equally valid. Likely stories must be measured against what can be known to suggest the shape of the unknown" (2012, 6). Though we may not resolve the mystery of Bradford's death, there is nevertheless value in analyzing the evolution of this myth because doing so forces us to interrogate our own assumptions about gender, melancholy, and voluntary death in the colonial period.

In many ways, efforts to uncover the truth about Bradford's death align with modern historical recovery work, in which scholars examine silences and mediated narratives to access historically marginalized voices. Scholars of early American literature and history have spent the last several decades developing effective recovery methods for colonial texts. However, in Bradford's case, these efforts have had the opposite of the intended effect: instead of recovering her voice, she has come to be portrayed as a stereotypical Pilgrim wife and mother.

With that in mind, let us reconsider the facts of Bradford's death. As I have stated, there is no evidence to prove suicide. The first iterations of the story are very brief, consisting solely of two succinct notes by William Bradford and Cotton Mather. Though short, these accounts are worthy of close examination, particularly because many subsequent histories argue that the brevity of William Bradford's and Cotton Mather's reports proves that Bradford suicided. The question, then, becomes: Are the records brief because her suicide was covered up? Despite its apparent simplicity, this question does not have an easy answer.

First, claims by scholars such as Morison and Kieran Doherty that suggest a cover up because William Bradford writes so little about his wife's death overlook how infrequently he writes about women in the colony, much less about their deaths. Doherty observes: "Because of Bradford's silence, it is thought likely—though not certain—that Dorothy had committed suicide" (1999, 73). However, I contend that this silence tells us very little about Dorothy Bradford's death because it is not an aberration in his text. William Bradford rarely writes about himself or about women in the colony. Though often described as a journal, William Bradford's *Of Plymouth Plantation* (*OPP*) was not a personal diary but a public document. When he references actions he undertook as governor, he often does so in the third person. Morison argues that William Bradford's tendency to exclude references to himself reflects his "modest reticence about his own role of leadership in the colony" (2016, xxiv). In addition to leaving out his first wife's death, William Bradford does not record his second marriage, the births of his children, or the arrival of his son John. The omission of Bradford's death, therefore, fits within a larger pattern of excluding his own experiences.

Furthermore, while his notation in the appendix is brief, William Bradford does not actually write significantly less about his wife's death than about any of the other passengers who perished in the first six months.[12] Brevity alone does not mean that her death was not significant to him. Perhaps, when he wrote the appendix 30 years after her death in 1650, he no longer had a strong affective response to the event. Perhaps he wrote about it in letters that did not survive.[13] All we know for sure is that he chose not to write about it in this particular text. We cannot assume, however, that William Bradford did not mourn his first wife's death merely because no extant record documents his bereavement. Not writing about his loss does not mean he did not talk about it. Nor does silence in the record indicates that someone does not mourn or has not mourned deeply. Perhaps, instead of indicating that he was ashamed of his wife's death, William Bradford's silence shows that his grief was beyond words.

Thus, there are many potential and logical reasons for William Bradford's silence about his wife's death, reasons that do not relate to suicide. In addition to those discussed above, we know that the pilgrims expected to lose lives at sea. Prior to their departure from Holland, the separatists extensively debated the decision to migrate; one serious consideration was that there would likely be "casualties of the sea (which none can be freed from)" (Bradford 2016, 26). Indeed, as Deetz and Deetz argue, "All of the adults who sailed on the *Mayflower* knew the risks that they were taking, and were as prepared for them as any immigrant can be" but that they ultimately concluded "that the risks were worth the gains of planting a new colony on the shores of the New World" (2000, 38). It is probable, then, that William Bradford had prepared himself to lose people he cared about while on the voyage.

There are a variety of ways to cope with death and we simply do not have enough detail to discern how William Bradford reacted to his wife's passing. That does not, however, mean that he did not have any feelings on the subject. Further, a lack of written evidence does not prove Doherty's claim that William Bradford apparently "never wrote or spoke [Dorothy's] name again" (1999, 72). If we cannot adequately interpret the absence of feelings, we certainly cannot argue for the presence of feelings such as shame. Further, William's affective response to his wife's death does not tell us about the cause of her death. How family or friends react after someone passes does not necessarily have a logical connection to the cause of death.

Similarly, there is little reason to doubt the veracity of Cotton Mather's 1702 record of Dorothy Bradford's death. As Bowman points out, Mather not only had access to 15 living *Mayflower* passengers, but he could also contact numerous *Mayflower* descendants while researching and writing the book (1931, 99). Consulting friends, neighbors, colleagues, and as many written sources as possible certainly corresponds with Mather's typical research methodology. We may not be convinced, as Bowman, that "[i]f it had been a case of suicide Mather would certainly have mentioned the fact, and would not have used the word 'accidentally,'" but we also should not discount Mather's word choice without reason (99). Additionally, we cannot assume that Mather would have lied about Bradford's death if it had been a suicide.

One reason we cannot assume that Mather would have covered up Bradford's suicide is that self-murders were documented and discussed in colonial Massachusetts. Both Cotton Mather and his father, Increase Mather, wrote or preached about self-murders, including accounts of people they knew who attempted to or took their own lives.[14] At this point, "self-destruction" was understood in colonial America "as a sign of diabolical possession or a sin against God" (Bell 2012, 12). This was true both theologically and legally, as seventeenth-century British legal theory "expressed the almost universal belief that suicide was literally diabolical" (MacDonald 1986, 55). As a result, describing Bradford's death as a self-murder, if that were the case, would have fit into Mather's providentialist framework. Both Mathers compiled providences, including self-murders, in their works, suggesting that such "sinful" events in the colony would not be obscured, but instead needed to be addressed so that the community could be right with God. Yet Bradford's death is stated as a simple fact, without any hint of sinfulness or diabolical intervention.

Similarly, the idea that Bradford's alleged suicide is shrouded in silence to protect her family from shame or stigma also relies on an anachronistic understanding of why family members in the period hid suicides. Most people trying to cover up self-murder in the seventeenth and eighteenth centuries were not avoiding shame as we might understand it today. Rather, since *felo de se* was a crime, self-murders were often hidden to avoid criminal penalties, including fines, desecration of the body, and/or burial restrictions. However, while such punishments were handed down in colonial Massachusetts in later years, it is unlikely that they could have been applied in this case. First, the Bradfords had sold their property in Holland and had essentially no money or goods to confiscate. Second, there was no coroner to rule on Bradford's death, nor was there a body to examine for evidence to prove the crime.[15] Even if there had been an inquest, under both English and later Massachusetts laws (1724) to prove *felo de se*: "[B]oth intention and motive had to be demonstrated. Without intention there could be no felony. If there were no felony, there was no suicide" (Minois 1999, 14). Without Bradford's body or a suicide note, it would be challenging to determine motive or intention. In fact, it is still difficult to parse accidental versus voluntary deaths, as intentions are extremely challenging to establish postmortem. Further, suicide is often impulsive. Studies estimate that 24–48 percent of suicide attempts are undertaken within five to ten minutes of suicidal ideation, leaving very little time to communicate intent or to establish a pattern of behavior for subsequent analysis (Lester 2015, 45). If Bradford had taken her own life, there is no guarantee that she would have communicated her intent to anyone. Attempting to establish intention is difficult days after a suicide, much less after 400 years, making it unlikely that William Bradford's or Cotton Mather's accounts were intentionally vague in order to cover up felony self-murder.

Furthermore, in the seventeenth century, it was exceptionally hard to determine whether a drowning was intentional or accidental. Drowning was especially common for women because so few could swim (Gunn and Gromelski 2011, n.p.). Nick Cook estimates that as many as 40 percent of accidental deaths in the Tudor period were attributed to drowning (2017, 9). Another pertinent factor was wool clothing, which "can absorb more water than any other fibre. As a result, if you fall in a river your woollen [sic] clothes soon become up to one and a half times heavier, making it difficult to struggle to safety" (Cook 11). If Bradford could not swim and fell into the cold waters of Cape Cod wearing woolen clothes, she would likely have drowned regardless of her intention. However, the fact that drownings were common does not preclude the possibility of suicide; according to Mario Barbagli, drowning was one of the most frequent methods women in the period used to take their lives (2015, 66). Thus, there are multiple factors that could support either interpretation, but none provide definitive proof for or against suicide.

There is an additional heretofore overlooked point undermining the argument that William Bradford attempted to cover up his wife's death: the timing. William was one of the last people to learn about his wife's death. Because he was away from the ship when Dorothy died, the rest of the passengers and crew would have known what happened several days before he did. We do not even know who told William of his wife's tragic death. From whom, then, was he keeping it a secret? It is unclear how he could have orchestrated a cover up under these circumstances. Writing his own record 30 years later would not have stopped gossip in Plymouth, nor would it have prevented a crew member from reporting a suicide when the *Mayflower* returned to England. It is unlikely that William could have controlled the story.

What, then, fuels the speculation about Bradford's death? In part, it's the appeal of a compelling mystery. Providing some sense of resolution is more narratively satisfying than concluding her death was an inexplicable accident. But determining her death to be a suicide would also allow scholars to uncover Bradford's voice by restoring her agency, if only by suggesting she chose the time and manner of her death. Bradford's case, however, strains the limits of existing methodologies because there is an extremely limited archive to analyze, as so few of the texts documenting the *Mayflower*'s voyage and the first years of Plymouth colony reference her life or death. Suggesting that Bradford took her own life is nevertheless an appealing narrative because it restores a sense of interiority, as we can imagine Bradford having a rich inner life and deep feelings for her family, son, and home in Holland. Such an interpretation relies on a false sense of historical empathy—in other words, it is easy for modern readers to believe that Bradford was depressed in these circumstances because we believe *we would feel sad* if we were in her place. This kind of anachronistic empathy projects our feelings onto Bradford, replacing her actual, lived experience with our imagined interpretation. Despite this, however, the stories are too often reliant on speculation or a single data point rather than on proof. In particular, many explanations for Bradford's death rely on stereotypes or extrapolate from the experiences of women entirely unconnected to Bradford. Such arguments suppress her voice by dubbing in an appealing, if unfounded, narrative to explain her death.

Along those lines, two main arguments develop in early twentieth-century scholarship to suggest that Bradford was depressed and thus suicided: the first contends that, as a woman, Bradford was utterly "overwhelmed" by the wilderness; the second posits that separation from her son caused Bradford to be depressed. Both rationales, however, were developed centuries after Bradford's death and are not supported by concrete evidence from her lifetime. The "proof" typically cited, however, does provide insight into historians' understanding of the intersections between mental health and gender, and, in some cases, illuminates the possible feelings of other colonial women. In the case of Bradford, though, both claims create a caricature. Rather than recovering her voice, these theories draw on an essentialized notion of motherhood and generalize from attitudes about the wilderness attributed to other colonial women. As a result, such theories depict Bradford as a generic "Pilgrim woman."

To start, despite the limitations of current approaches to analyzing Bradford's death—which as we will see tend to obscure her lived experience in favor of generalizations or stereotypes—there are reasons to consider the psychological impact of migration and settler colonialism in Plymouth. Indeed, recognizing the psychological stressors present in colonial contact zones, when done ethically, can offer an interesting frame for viewing European colonization. Migration is always psychologically intense and often involves "painful experiences of unbelonging, non-recognition, struggle, alienation, and trauma" (Beltsiou 2016, 1). Consciously or unconsciously, many of the separatists on the *Mayflower* may have feared migration to the colonies. In one of the first serious psychological studies of migration, Rebeca Grinberg and León Grinberg argue that, even in the best of circumstances, "migration is a potentially traumatic experience" and can cause "a crisis situation" (1989, 15). How the experience manifests in an individual depends, in large part, on their overall psychological health and on the presence of stabilizing factors. In many cases, migrants have "sufficient capacity for working through" the crisis and can overcome it and adapt, at least psychologically, to their new home (Grinberg and Grinberg 15). In other cases, however, "the emigrant's ego is too severely damaged by the traumatic experience or the past or present crisis … and he may suffer any one of the many forms of mental or physical illness" (Grinberg and Grinberg 15).[16]

However, for a psychologically healthy person with a stabilizing support structure, migration need not cause pathology. Certain factors of the Pilgrims' migration could mitigate most stressors—including not having to learn a new language, coming with a group, and, at least on paper, being on "English" land, so that the separatists, in theory, would not have to assimilate to a new culture as they had in Holland. Salman Akhtar might describe these as circumstances that could provide any of the separatists with "intramural refueling, or the anaclitic support offered him by family members who have emigrated along with him and by the larger network of a homoethnic community (e.g., friends, merchants, or physicians who are co-nationals)" (1999, 10). In addition to traveling with an anaclitic support network, it should also be noted that, unlike many other immigrants, the Pilgrims were not migrating from a cherished place. They were choosing to leave Holland, where they had previously experienced the pains of emigration, and where they were increasingly dissatisfied with their situation. Despite any potential fears about the wilderness, they looked forward to establishing their new home in Virginia where they could live according to their religious tenets without sacrificing their identity as English citizens. Yet these factors are seldom incorporated into analyses of Bradford's death. Instead, historical and fictional accounts focus on her inability to face the New England environment and/or her destabilized identity as a mother.

The first explanation for Bradford's alleged suicide—that she was overwhelmed by the wilderness—is typically supported by referencing the experiences of three other Puritan women: Anne Bradstreet, Anne Hutchinson, and Lady Arabella Johnson. In large part, this argument continues to resonate because of Morison's influence. Morison repeatedly asserts that Bradford suicided because she was "disheartened by gazing on the barren sand dunes of Cape Cod" (1956, 56). In his edition of *OPP*, Morison argues that

> we have it from other tenderhearted women who came to New England among the pioneers, that their hearts grew faint and sick when they first beheld that wild-looking northern land, so different from the green and cultivated England they had left.
>
> (2016, xxiv)

The problem with Morison's argument is that it assumes all women felt the same about New England's landscape.

The only colonial woman Morison cites whom we can prove found the wilderness unpleasant is Anne Bradstreet (1612–1672). We know that Bradstreet did feel disheartened by her new home, at least at first. Of her arrival in New England, she wrote: I "came into this country, where I found a new world and new manners, at which my heart rose. But after I was convinced it was the way of God, I submitted to it and joined the church at Boston" (Bradstreet 2019, n.p.). The expression "at which my heart rose" is generally understood to mean she felt sick or full of fear. Her hesitation seems entirely explicable considering everything the Bradstreets left behind. Yet she notably submits to the will of God and accepts her new home. Despite her initial feelings of uncertainty or unpleasantness, Bradstreet lived in Massachusetts for more than 40 years.

Another resident of Massachusetts Bay Colony, Anne Hutchinson, is also commonly invoked as an example of how Pilgrim or Puritan women reacted to New England's landscape. Yet Hutchinson is an interesting case because, during her 1637 trial for heresy, she denied having ever expressed anxiety about the wilderness. Taking some liberties with the trial transcript, Morison writes,

> Anne Hutchinson, a stouter-hearted woman than Anne Bradstreet, 'when she came within sight of Boston and looking on the meanness of the place ... uttered these words, if she had not a sure word that England would be destroyed, her heart would shake.' The man who reported those words said it seemed to him 'very strange that she should say so'— of course a man would!
>
> (1964, 322)

Morison's misogynist interpretation suggests that only brave, strong men can enter the wilderness unafraid and that men could never understand women's irrational fears. We should rightly be skeptical of such a frame. According to the actual transcript, Hutchinson rebuts the accusation in court, declaring "I do not remember that I looked upon the meanness of the place nor did it discourage me, because I knew the bounds of my habitation were determined" (qtd. in Hall 1968, 338). If Hutchinson denied in court that she ever made such a statement, why is Morison citing it as fact 293 years later? And why is it connected to Bradstreet's reflections on her own migration? They were, after all, different women coming to New England under unique circumstances. The primary thing the two have in common is their gender, which seems to be enough for Morison to assume they reacted similarly.

The final woman who allegedly provides "evidence" that English women feared the wilderness is Lady Arabella Johnson (1595–1630), wife of Isaac Johnson (1601–1630) and namesake of the *Arabella*, which came to Massachusetts Bay Colony with John Winthrop's (1588–1649) fleet in 1630. Lady Arabella and her husband both died shortly after their arrival and subsequent stories suggested that her death resulted from her incompatibility with the wilderness. Yet, much like the myth of Bradford's suicide, this story derives not from historical documents but from nineteenth-century fiction. In this case, the author is Nathaniel Hawthorne. In his children's novel, *Grandfather's Chair*, Hawthorne describes Lady Arabella as despondent and overwhelmed by the dark, foreboding forests—a situation directly attributed to her gender (11, 1841, 2017).

Morison pushes the connection further, arguing in 1930 that "Hawthorne inferred that the horror of wilderness life brought the Lady Arbella [sic] Johnson to an early grave; and I suspect some such thing behind the silence of Governor Bradford on the death of his young wife Dorothy" (1964, 322). Morison may suspect a connection, but it's odd to use a fictional tale about a different woman, composed two centuries after Bradford's death, to infer a motive for a suicide that may or may not have happened. After all, as Erikson's work shows, the way one person responds to a particular event does not, necessarily, tell us anything about how another individual will respond to the same or similar events (1993, 63, 64). Arguing about how Bradford "must have felt" in 1620 based on the alleged feelings of three women who all arrived in different parts of New England, with different groups of people, sometimes a decade or more after Bradford died, is tenuous. Even if all of the women had come at the same time, it is unlikely that they would have had identical responses to New England's landscapes.

The second theory, that Bradford was depressed because she had left her son behind in Holland, apparently has its roots in Austin's short story. In "William Bradford's Love Life," Dorothy Bradford's separation from her son, while important, is cast as a minor issue compared to her husband's emotional infidelity, and, therefore, primarily functions to reveal her psychological state. In particular, Bradford experiences recurring nightmares about her son's death that illuminate her feelings of betrayal and despair. In one such nightmare, she reflects, "my mother came to me with my baby dead in her arms—my baby, my one child. Ah! Child, you never loved another better than me, and yet I left you—for him" (Austin 1869, 139). The dream highlights Dorothy's desire to be a primary object of affection—indicated by her recognition that her son loved none better than her—and her realization that she may have lost that status forever by leaving him in Holland. The em-dash accentuates her disappointment, further separating her husband from her and their son. Her refusal to say William's name suggests an air of disdain for the man she married. In addition, the dreams themselves, rather than the actual distance from her child, push the already miserable (fictional) Dorothy to consider self-murder. She writes "They do not dream when they are dead, I think. I hope not, surely, for I would not be haunted with that dead baby, nor yet with his father, whispering in his sleep: 'Alice! Sweetest, dearest!'" (139). Dreams reveal truth in this story. William's confessions cause Dorothy to long for the untainted affection of her child. She continues to dwell on the idea that her son may already be dead, subconsciously manifesting her anxiety about losing him and of losing her status as a worthy love object.

While the separation from her son may have been a traumatic factor in Bradford's final months, historians did not endorse this as a rationale for her alleged suicide until the late twentieth century. In part, that may be because this argument does not acknowledge two points: that the separatists were emigrating in part for the good of their children, and that many children in the period did not live with their parents. First, the separatists saw emigration as ultimately good for their kids. Joseph Illick notes that

> William Bradford justified the Pilgrim movement to New England by observing that parents, now in exile in Holland, were obliged to become the too heavy taskmasters of their children, who were sometimes 'drawn away by evil examples into extravagant and dangerous courses' by Dutch youth.
>
> (Illick 2002, 23)

Even though Bradford's own son would not arrive for several years, ensuring that their children could one day live and worship as English citizens was a primary motivating factor for emigration. Second, children at the time were often "put out" or sent away to live with relatives or tutors in order to learn a trade or finish their education (Illick 20–23). Such separations were not necessarily seen as traumatic; indeed, many parents paid host families for the valuable experiences their children received. While leaving John may have been a difficult decision, there is no evidence that it was traumatic.

Nevertheless, in the twentieth century, the notion that Bradford despaired at being separated from her son took hold. Even when histories do not necessarily suggest Bradford's death was suicide, they often emphasize the separation from her son as one of the only known facts about Bradford's life. For instance, Annie Russel Marble notes that "there was a long tradition that she mourned grievously at the separation" from her son (1920, 54). Others, such as Nickerson, take this point further, contending that Bradford's misery at being separated from her child was exacerbated by the presence of the other children on the ship. In particular, he speculates that "[t]he whimpering moans of little Jasper More, sinking into his last sleep, tore at the mother's heart of her, lying lonely in her bunk" (Nickerson 1995,

92). Philbrick also emphasizes the significance of the four More children, claiming that "[f]or Dorothy, whose own young son was on the other side of the Atlantic, the plight of these and the other children may have been especially difficult to witness" (2006, 76). Yet the notion that she was depressed and/or suicidal because of the destabilization of her identity as a mother cannot be substantiated.

Indeed, the argument that Jasper More's death was the catalyst that pushed her over the edge imagines Bradford as such an essentialized mother figure that she takes on the role of mother not just to her own child, but to any distressed child. There is, however, no evidence that she had a particular bond with the children on the ship. That Jasper More's death happened shortly before her own is the only tenuous correlation offered as causation. Such arguments limit Bradford exclusively to this one role, mother, while ignoring the other roles in her life—including wife, member of the separatist community, migrant traveling with a group of close family and friends, and English woman—all of which might have been stabilizing factors. Further, her separations from both husband and son were intended to be temporary. Thus, while the theories that she missed her son are not unreasonable, they lack evidence. They also do not align with how female suicide was understood in the period. The belief that women are most likely to take their own lives on losing their positions as wives and mothers did not become a dominant theory of female suicide until the nineteenth century—around the time Goodwin wrote her story.[17]

In addition, the only concrete evidence we have to suggest that Dorothy Bradford was distressed by the separation from her son actually comes from William Bradford himself. As a result, based on the extant historical documents, it would be more appropriate to dig into William Bradford's psychological state. In just over a year, he underwent multiple, potentially destabilizing experiences that required intense shifts in his identity: he undertook his second migration, left his son behind, was widowed, narrowly survived the illness that claimed half of his compatriots, and ultimately became governor of the Plymouth colony. Of the separatists' emotional departure from Holland in July 1620, he reflects on "what tears did gush from every eye," at the "sad and mournful parting" (Bradford 2016, 48). By prioritizing Dorothy Bradford's feelings about John, we both overemphasize her role as mother and underemphasize William's role as a father. The tears gushing from every eye, after all, presumably include his own.

Unless additional documents are discovered, we cannot say for certain what happened to Dorothy May Bradford. Instead of speculating about her death, a more productive avenue for inquiry would be to reconsider the conversations about mental health in early America. It is valuable, for instance, to consider both Dorothy and William Bradford as emotionally complex, whole people in order to complicate the stereotyped depictions that flatten them into Pilgrim caricatures. By considering the psychological rationales for the many silences surrounding death in *Of Plymouth Plantation* and other texts offers the possibility of engaging with the layers of trauma, as well as with the coping mechanisms employed by all of the people inhabiting colonial contact zones. There is ample room for additional research into how the Pilgrims understood and cared for individuals experiencing melancholy and suicidal ideation; on the psychological impact of the separatists' first migration to Holland; on possible stabilizing factors present in their community; as well as for analysis of William Bradford, Tisquantum (Patuxet), and other prominent figures in the history of Plymouth plantation.

More importantly, it is vital to realize that mental illness has always been present in America. Whether Bradford suicided or not, depression and suicide are a central part of the national origin story and deserve critical attention. Studying the Pilgrim and Puritan approach to care and recovery can help us ask better questions about mental illness. How might mental health be treated differently in our society if we reduced stigma by recognizing it as a normal part of any society? How can we inspire an attitude of compassion and empathy, recognizing each other as equal regardless of any illness we might have in our lifetime? Resituating mental health in history—the good and the bad—humanizes the issue of mental health, making it something to which we can all connect.

The value of a psychological approach is not to solve the mystery of Bradford's death, but to explore the passengers of the *Mayflower* as dynamic, whole people, experiencing psychological stressors and emotional traumas. Applying a psychological frame, therefore, can help scholars ask different questions and think in new ways not only about Bradford's death but about the myths and legacy of the colonial period as well. Mental health issues, as with all health issues, would have been one of many factors of the Pilgrims' experience, but they did not necessarily result in suicide. The question then becomes, what happens if we ask questions about mental health focused on those who lived and thrived in the colonies over the coming decades? Or about those who were displaced by European settler colonialism? Further, focusing on the psychological stressors of colonial-era immigration could also help contemporary readers develop empathy for immigrants struggling with the traumas of migration today. Developing a nuanced history of mental health offers a way to think more deeply about the myths of America's founding, the traumas of the colonial period, and the ongoing psychological effects of settler colonialism and slavery.[18]

Notes

1 An earlier version of this essay was originally printed in: *Early American Literature*, Volume 56, Number 1, 2021, pp. 75–104, DOI: https://doi.org/10.1353/eal.2021.0004. The present version has been revised for length, with a few additional minor edits made for clarity. This project was funded by the Erik H. Erikson Institute at the Austen Riggs Center. I am particularly grateful for the insights and support of Dr. Jane G. Tillman, Dr. Katie Lewis, Alison Lotto, Dr. Kathryn Gallagher, Dr. Elizabeth Weinberg, Lee Watroba, Barbara Keegan, Dr. Jeremy M. Ridenour, and Dr. Eric M. Plakun. I would like to thank everyone at Riggs for their generosity and enthusiasm, without which this project would not have been possible. My thanks also to Arielle McKee, John Raymond, Sarah C. Symans, and Kari Holloway Miller. Thank you, especially, to Elise Miller for your encouragement, guidance, and leadership in publishing this collection.

2 Two notes on the text: First, I will refer to Dorothy May Bradford as "Bradford" throughout the essay when I am referring to her as a historical figure, as she is the primary subject. Her husband, William, will be referred to as William Bradford. I will only refer to her as Dorothy when needed for clarity. Second, for simplicity, I have updated all dates to the Gregorian calendar.

3 In this essay, I will not be using the phrase committed suicide as per the American Association of Suicidology guidelines. The phrase is no longer widely used "because of its strong association with moral failing or criminality'" (Ackerman et al. 2018, n.p.).

4 The first love triangle suggests that William Bradford is in love with Alice Carpenter Southworth. The second, in *The Plymouth Adventure* (1950), suggests Dorothy Bradford is in love with Gilbert Winslow. And in the third, in the movie *The Plymouth Adventure* (1952), Dorothy Bradford is allegedly in love with the *Mayflower*'s captain, Christopher Jones.

5 The legend that William and Alice had a failed match prior to William's marriage to Dorothy does predate Austin's writing, though her story seems to be the first to suggest suicide. In Charles Deane's introduction to *Of Plymouth Plantation*, he observes that "[t]here is a tradition that an early attachment existed between this lady and Governor Bradford, which was not favored by her parents" (1856, xix). Austin's story modifies the myth slightly, incorporating the nuances of sentimental fiction rather than histor-ical truth. Most notably, in his history *The Pilgrim Republic,* Austin's brother, John Goodwin rejects the family legend, and his sister's story, as simply that — an unsubstan-tiated myth that is contradicted by the known facts which he declares are "groundless and absurd" (1888, 248). In 1931 George Ernest Bowman thoroughly debunked the legend and Austin's story; he published a follow-up two years later when he discovered the "Preface" to Austin's later edition of the story acknowledging it was made up.

6 Many family legends, including Goodwin's, were proved to be inaccurate once primary sources from the founding of Plymouth colony were recovered and published in the nineteenth century. In addition to *Of Plymouth Plantation*'s publication in 1856, *Mourt's Relation* was published in 1841 (Miller 2015, 97).

7 To clarify my terminology: psychohistory is "the science of historical motivations, [and] combines the insights of psychotherapy with the research methodology of the social sci-ences to understand the emotional origin of the social and political behavior of groups and nations, past and present" (Association for Psychohistory 2019). Psychobiography is the practice of applying psychoanalytic methods to the study of one person's life. As Andrew McCarron puts it, psycho- biography examines "the salient themes of a life and the psycho-dynamics behind them in hopes of capturing the psychological 'fingerprint' of a person" (2017, n.p.).

8 See, for instance, David E. Stannard's *Shrinking History* (1980) and William T. Schultz's "Introducing Psychobiography" (2005b).

9 See the *Handbook of Psychobiography* (2005a), edited by William T. Schultz, for a primer on modern psychobiography, including chapters by Alan Elms and William N. Runyan.

10 See Marzio Barbagli (2015), Richard Bell (2012), David Lester (2015), Michael MacDonald (1986), or Georges Minois (1999) for more on the history of suicide.

11 Historians currently believe that Dorothy May was born to Henry and Katherine May of Wisbech, Cambridgeshire, ca. 1597. Caleb Johnson, Sue Allen, and Simon Neal (2017) have recently uncovered what seems to be the most accurate genealogy for Dorothy May Bradford.

12 Again, the rhetorical purpose of the text is pertinent for unpacking why this is the case: the appendix documents "the decreasings and increasings of" the original 102 passen-gers on the *Mayflower* (Bradford 2016, 443). To that end, each entry gives a very brief precis of whether the individuals lived, died, married, and/or had children. Overall, none of the records are particularly emotional, again perhaps because he was writing 30 years

after most of the deaths took place. The account of Dorothy Bradford's death seems to corroborate Kathleen Donegan's observation that "Many bodies disappear into the rhetorical shadows in *Of Plymouth Plantation*: the piled up dead; the pantomime of English sentinels; the decapitated fierce opponent; the emaciated figures of would-be traders. None is visible in Bradford's account" (2014, 151). The only reason the record of Dorothy Bradford's death seems like a major silence, when considered in context, is because she was the author's wife.

13 We know that some of William Bradford's documents have been lost. His letter book, for instance, recovered from "a grocer's shop in Halifax, Nova Scotia" sometime before 1792, only includes letters from 1624 to 1630, and begins on page 339, suggesting "that what was recovered was but a small part of what was lost" (Bradford 2018, v).

14 See, for instance, Cotton Mather "from Memorable Providences Relating to Witchcrafts and Possessions," (1689); Increase Mather, "A Call to the Tempted: A Sermon on the Horrid Crime of Self-Murder," (1723); and Cotton Mather, "De Tristibus. Or, The Cure of Melancholy," (1724).

15 Another common reason survivors cover up self-murders was to avoid burial restrictions or punishments to the individuals' body. Considering that Bradford's body probably was not recovered from the floor of the Cape, and because there was no cemetery yet established, it is unlikely that this was a major factor. For more on death ways and burial practices in Plymouth, see Erik R. Seeman's *Death in the New World* (2011) and Kathleen Donegan's *Seasons of Misery* (2014).

16 There is an increasing body of research on the psychological effects of migration. For instance, a recent study of immigrants in the Hague found higher rates of schizophrenia among immigrants "who lived in neighborhoods where their own ethnic group comprised a smaller proportion of the population" (Veling et al. 2008, 69). In this case, Wim Veling et al. posit that "a social network may have a normalizing function, thus preventing transition into psychosis" (72). See also Salman Akhtar's *Immigration and Identity: Turmoil, Treatment, and Transformation* (1999).

17 According to Howard I. Kushner, in the nineteenth century, portrayals of suicides in the newspapers "translated into the dictum that suicide rates among women reflected individual emotional acts, while male suicide rates were taken as a barometer of national economic and social well-being. Self-proclaimed nineteenth-century suicide experts, citing federal census returns, tied suicide by a woman to her social role as wife and mother" (Kushner 1991, 99).

References

Ackerman, John, et al. 2018. *Suicide Reporting Recommendations: Media as Partners in Suicide Prevention*. Washington, DC: American Association of Suicidology.

Akhtar, Salman. 1999. *Immigration and Identity: Turmoil, Treatment, and Transformation*. Lanham, MD: Rowman and Littlefield.

Association for Psychohistory. 2019. "Psychohistory." https://psychohistory.com/.

Austin, Jane Goodwin. 1869. "William Bradford's Love Life." *Harper's New Monthly Magazine* 39, no. 229: 135–40.

———. 1893. "Preface." *David Alden's Daughter and Other Stories of Colonial Times*, v–viii. Chicago, IL: Riverside Press.

Barbagli, Marzio. 2015. *Farewell to the World: A History of Suicide*. Translated by Lucinda Byatt. Cambridge: Polity Press.

Barzun, Jacques. 1989. *Clio and the Doctors: Psycho-History, Quanto-History, and History*. Chicago, IL: University of Chicago Press.

Bell, Richard. 2012. *We Shall Be No More: Suicide and Self-Government in the Newly United States*. Cambridge, MA: Harvard University Press.

Beltsiou, Julia. 2016. "Introduction." In *Immigration in Psychoanalysis: Locating Ourselves*, edited by Julia Beltsiou, 1–11. London: Routledge.

Black, Sophie Cabot. 1994. "The Arguments." In *The Misunderstanding of Nature*, 55–84. Minneapolis, MN: Graywolf Press.

Bowman, George Ernest. 1931. "Governor William Bradford's First Wife Dorothy (May) Bradford Did Not Commit Suicide." *Mayflower Descendant* 29, no. 3: 97–102.

Bradford, William. 2016. *Of Plymouth Plantation, 1620–1647* (1952). Edited by Samuel Eliot Morison. New York: Knopf.

———. 2018. *Governor William Bradford's Letter Book*. London: Forgotten Books.

Bradstreet, Anne. 2019. "To My Dear Children." *Early Americas Digital Archive*, http://eada.lib.umd.edu/text-entries/to-my-dear-children/.

Chamberlain, Ava. 2012. *The Notorious Elizabeth Tuttle: Marriage, Murder, and Madness in the Family of Jonathan Edwards*. New York: New York University Press.

Cook, Nick. 2017. "Tudor Hazards." *RoSPA OS&H Journal* 47, no. 12: 9–11.

Deane, Charles. 1856. "Editorial Preface." *History of Plymouth Plantation by William Bradford*, edited by Charles Deane, iii–xix. Boston.

Deetz, James and Patricia Scott Deetz. 2000. *The Times of Their Lives: Life, Love, and Death in Plymouth Colony*. New York: Anchor Books.

Doherty, Kieran. 1999. *William Bradford: Rock of Plymouth*. Patiala: Twenty-First Century Books.

Donegan, Kathleen. 2014. *Seasons of Misery: Catastrophe and Colonial Settlement in Early America*. Philadelphia: University of Pennsylvania Press.

Erikson, Erik H. 1993. *Young Man Luther: A Study in Psychoanalysis and History*. New York: W. W. Norton and Co.

Finch, Martha L. 2010. *Dissenting Bodies: Corporealities in Early New England*. New York: Columbia University Press.

Fraser, Rebecca. 2017. *The Mayflower: The Families, the Voyage, and the Founding of America*. New York: St. Martin's.

Gébler, Ernest. 1950. *The Plymouth Adventure: A Chronicle Novel of the Voyage of the Mayflower*. New York: Doubleday & Company.

Goodwin, John A. 1888. *The Pilgrim Republic; An Historical Review of the Colony of New Plymouth, with Sketches of the Rise of Other New England Settlements, the History of Congregationalism, and the Creeds of the Period*. Boston, MA: Ticknor and Company.

Grinberg, León and Rebeca Grinberg. 1989. *Psychoanalytic Perspectives on Migration and Exile*. New Haven, CT: Yale University Press.

Gunn, Steven and Tomasz Gromelski. 2011. "Drowning in Tudor England: Why Was Water So Dangerous?" *History Extra*, https://www.historyextra.com/period/tudor/drowning-in-tudor-england-why-was-water-so-dangerous/.

Hall, David, ed. 1968. *The Antinomian Controversy, 1636–1638: A Documentary History*. Middletown, CT: Wesleyan University Press.

Hawthorne, Nathaniel. 2017. *Grandfather's Chair: or, True Stories from New England History, 1620–1808*. 1841; CreateSpace Independent Publishing Platform.

Illick, Joseph E. 2002. *American Childhoods*. Philadelphia: University of Pennsylvania Press.

Johnson, Caleb, Sue Allen, and Simon Neal. 2017. "The English Origin and Kinship of *Mayflower* Passengers William White and Dorothy (May) Bradford of Wisbech, Cambridgeshire." *American Genealogist* 89, no. 2: 81–94.

Kushner, Howard I. 1991. *American Suicide: A Psychocultural Exploration*. New Brunswick, NJ: Rutgers University Press.

Lee, Darcy H. 2017. *Ghosts of Plymouth, Massachusetts.* Haunted America.

Lester, David. 2015. "The Body as a Suicide Note." In *Suicide as a Dramatic Performance,* edited by David Lester and Steven Stack, 41–50. Piscataway, NJ: Transaction.

MacDonald, Michael. 1986. "The Secularization of Suicide in England 1660–1800." *Past and Present* 111: 50–100.

Marble, Annie Russell. 1920. *The Women Who Came in the Mayflower.* Cleveland, OH: Pilgrim Press.

Mather, Cotton. 1702. "Life of William Bradford, ESQ., Governor of Plymouth Colony." *Magnalia Christi Americana.* https://www.pilgrimhall.org/pdf/William_Bradford_Mathers_Magnalia_Christi.pdf.

———. 1972. "De Tristibus. Or, The Cure of Melancholy." In *The Angel of Bethesda: An Essay upon the Common Maladies of Mankind* (1724), edited by Gordon W. Jones, 132–137. Barre.

———. 2015. "From Memorable Providences Relating to Witchcrafts and Possessions." 1689. *The Ethics of Suicide Digital Archive.* Oxford: Oxford University Press. https://ethicsofsuicide.lib.utah.edu/selections/cotton-mather/.

Mather, Increase. 2015. "A Call to the Tempted: A Sermon on the Horrid Crime of Self-Murder" (1723). In *The Ethics of Suicide Digital Archive.* Oxford: Oxford University Press. https:// ethicsofsuicide.lib.utah.edu/selections/increase-mather/.

McCarron, Andrew. 2017. "A Case for Psychobiography in 2017: A Holistic Approach to Studying Human Persons." *Psychology Today,* https://www.psychology today.com/us/blog/light-come-shining/201701/case-psychobiography-in-2017.

Miller, Kari Holloway. 2015. "'So Long as the Work Is Done': Recovering Jane Goodwin Austin." PhD diss., Georgia State University.

Minois, Georges. 1999. *History of Suicide: Voluntary Death in Western Culture.* Translated by Lydia G. Cochrane. Baltimore, MD: Johns Hopkins University Press.

Morison, Samuel Eliot. 1956. *The Story of the "Old Colony" of New Plymouth.* New York: Knopf.

———. 1964. *Builders of the Bay Colony* (1930). Houghton Mifflin.

———. 2016. "Introduction." *Of Plymouth Plantation 1620–1647,* xxiii– xliii. New York: Knopf.

Murphy, Francis. 1981. "Introduction." In *Of Plymouth Plantation 1620–1647,* edited by Francis Murphy, vii–xxiv. New York: Modern Library.

Nesbit, TaraShea. 2020. *Beheld.* London: Bloomsbury.

Nickerson, W. Sears. 1995. "William Bradford's First Wife: A Suicide." In *Early Encounters: Native Americans and Europeans in New England. From the Papers of W. Sears Nickerson,* edited by Delores Bird Carpenter, 88–98. East Lansing: Michigan State University Press.

Philbrick, Nathaniel. 2006. *Mayflower: A Story of Courage, Community, and War.* New York: Viking.

Plymouth Adventure. 1952. Directed by Clarence Brown. Starring Spencer Tracy, Gene Tierney, Van Johnson, and Leo Genn. Metro-Goldwyn-Mayer Studios.

Saints & Strangers. 2015. Directed by Paul A. Edwards. Starring Anna Camp, Vincent Kartheiser, Ron Livingstone, and Kalani Queypo. National Geographic.

Schultz, William Todd, ed. 2005a. *Handbook of Psychobiography.* Oxford: Oxford University Press.

————. 2005b. "Introducing Psychobiography." In *Handbook of Psychobiography,* edited by William Todd Schultz, 3–18. Oxford: Oxford University Press.

Scull, Andrew. 2015. *Madness in Civilization: A Cultural History of Insanity from the Bible to Freud, from the Madhouse to Modern Medicine.* Princeton, NJ: Princeton University Press.

Seeman, Erik R. 2011. *Death in the New World: Cross-Cultural Encounters, 1492–1800.* Philadelphia: University of Pennsylvania Press.

Stratton, Eugene Aubrey. 1986. *Plymouth Colony: Its History and People, 1620–1691.* Lehi, UT: Ancestry.

Veling, Wim, et al. 2008. "Ethnic Density of Neighborhoods and Incidence of Psychotic Disorders among Immigrants." *American Journal of Psychiatry* 165, no. 1: 66–73.

Afterword

Stacey Dearing

I came to Riggs in the summer of 2019 for three months to work on what I thought would be a new chapter for my dissertation/soon-to-be-book project. My previous research had focused on somatic health in early America, but I had always intended to include a chapter on mental health. Using the alleged suicide of Dorothy May Bradford as a launching point, I expected to explore pilgrim and puritan epistemologies of mental health. What I quickly discovered, however, was that all of the stories of Bradford's alleged suicide were entirely fictional. Each iteration of the story, I came to find, revealed far more about what the people writing that story thought about mental health and suicide than they did about Bradford. The folks at Riggs helped me grapple with 400 years of theories, myths, and legends around female mental health and suicide.

While at Riggs, I was particularly struck by the interdisciplinary framework that is used to approach each individual case. I want to highlight two particularly productive conversations I had that helped me re-frame my research on Bradford. First, I met with Jeremy Ridenour who helped me unpack why people might be persuaded that Bradford suicided: misplaced historical empathy. I was already arguing that part of why people are so easily convinced that Bradford took her own life is because we, as twenty-first-century readers, believe that *we* would be depressed if we were in her situation. Jeremy pointed out that this is an illogical line of thought, however, because the "we" in this example—a generic, twenty-first-century person—incorrectly applies twenty-first-century life expectations onto seventeenth-century people. Jeremy introduced me to the idea that we need to think about the psychological expectations of people in the time period in addition to their physical or material conditions.

A second example results from my experience attending case conferences. About two months into my residency, I worked up profiles of some of the major figures in my research, including Dorothy May Bradford, William Bradford, Alice Bradford, and Tisquantum (Patuxet), and invited colleagues to review them. Both Katie Lewis and Kathryn Gallagher met with me over coffee to work through the profiles. Though these were not intended to be full case conferences, it was incredibly valuable to hear what trained clinical psychologists thought was important in the profiles. Too often, early American scholars focus on specific moments in the lives of

DOI: 10.4324/9781003322627-16

the pilgrims, rather than considering the totality of their lived experiences. My goal with these profiles was not to diagnose any specific conditions, but to humanize the historical figures and to push back on the all-too-common caricatures of "pilgrims" or "puritans" in popular culture. Considering all the known details of specific pilgrims' lives—including childhood experiences, previous migrations, significant relationships, and religious beliefs—results in a far more complex picture than the pious figures often depicted in popular histories, stories, and movies.

As a result of my time as an Erikson scholar in residence, my project changed dramatically. About halfway through the summer, I realized that it was too big to be a single chapter. It was, in fact, its own book. In addition to drafting the article-length version of the project that is reprinted in this collection, I wrote approximately 100 pages of the first draft of my manuscript, tentatively titled *The Many Deaths of Dorothy May Bradford: Mental Health, Suicide, and American Myth-Making*. I have also given multiple public presentations on the project since leaving Riggs, including at Siena College, Albany Medical College's Alden March Bioethics Institute, the Society for the Study of American Women Writers, and a joint webinar with Kari Miller for the Pilgrim Hall Museum and Plymouth Antiquarian Society. Currently, my article about film adaptations of Bradford's death has been accepted for a forthcoming edited collection.

Overall, I learned a great deal about the history of mental health and suicide while at Riggs, all of which have helped me be a better scholar, but also a better teacher and presenter. For instance, whenever I teach or give presentations on Bradford's death, I am sure to include an AAS notice about suicide and to provide information about free resources. When I teach early American literature, I challenge my students to adopt a more psychodynamic frame so that they can think about early American figures as real people, rather than one-dimensional caricatures. To conclude, I am incredibly grateful for my time at Riggs; it has irrevocably changed the trajectory of my research.

Chapter 8

Encounters with a Ghastly, Enigmatic Other[1]

Annie G. Rogers

It is a crisp, cool morning in Stockbridge, and with a cup of tea on my desk, I enter another time, another space, another realm of experience: psychosis, as it has been lived through first-person accounts, books, letters, art, and interviews. Intrigued by the inventive language of psychosis, I think of how alphabets were first made by humans, drawn by hand, and then subjected to new forms through printing practices. I consider the paraphernalia of printers: composing sticks, in which one inserted letters as "sorts." "I am out of sorts" meant that I have run out of letters needed for the line I was composing. And I think of how language changes when one is "out of sorts" in psychosis; it may become difficult to follow one's own thoughts. Of necessity, the psychotic makes new words, and his language carries the sheer inventiveness of his quest to speak, to say what is happening to him.

I am at Austen Riggs, a private psychiatric hospital in the Berkshires, in Western Massachusetts, as the Erikson Scholar. This position affords me time to write, an office at the corner of the psychoanalytic library, an apartment, and a stipend. Austen Riggs is one of the very few hospitals left where psychoanalysis is the primary means of treatment, where patients do not live on locked wards, but wander a beautiful campus with wide lawns, trees, flowers. There is a working greenhouse and a community garden. When a young man (one of the patients) gives me a tour of the buildings, I learn that he and others participate in governance structures here, and everyone has access to psychoanalytic psychotherapy four days a week. The patients choose activities they have proposed, outlined on a white board in a spacious first-floor hallway of the main building called "The Inn" in which they live, work, and take their meals. There is a library with comfy reading chairs, run by patients. We walk into the town and find "The Lavender Door," a designated space for the arts that is "interpretation free" as the young man explains. Here, one might learn ceramics, weaving, woodworking, and painting, or engage in theatre productions—all facilitated by professional artists. In short, alongside their personal anguish and struggles, for the patients there is life, a real life to be lived.

In my office, I have collected memoirs written recently and written over a century ago, in the early 1900s. Some of these were composed while the writer was resident in a hospital or asylum, but most were composed later, in retrospect. I also have assembled letters, works of art, texts written into and around intricate drawings,

DOI: 10.4324/9781003322627-17

and interview excerpts. Each day I read and immerse myself in wondering about the transformations of language, thought, and experience in psychosis. This is my project: to explore how psychosis changes one's experience of language, what language is and how it works.

To make this inquiry, I must enter the experiences of others living in another time—imaginatively, compassionately, and with fresh questions. Entering into subjective experiences of living in psychosis (that in our present day have been attributed solely to genetics and biology gone awry), I hope to discover a logic and a language that carries truths we would otherwise not consider as meaningful or worthy of our time.

Who am I to take on such a project? I must say that I am utterly daunted by its scope and its demands. On a round table behind my desk, there is a scattering of books, notes in pencil on legal pads, printed articles, pens, a notebook open for more organized notes, and art materials, for those moments when I am beyond any comprehension, any words to convey what I am discovering. To enter this project fully, I not only have to read and immerse myself in the experiences of others I have never met but also have to keep company with my own past. As a young person of 16, I was a patient in a private psychiatric hospital where I encountered locked wards. I was treated as mentally incompetent, spoken about as if not present, and medicated (Thorazine and Haldol were the anti-psychotics of the time). I had been a charity case, and the generosity of the hospital ran out when my diagnosis was finalized: Schizophrenia. Much of my experience that year remains incoherent and therefore nearly impossible to narrate, yet unforgettable.

I lived in psychosis for the greater part of two decades of my youth, and then, following four years with a gifted psychoanalyst who worked with psychotic patients, I was free. I took up a life in the world, became a psychologist, and moved to Cambridge, Massachusetts, where I joined research on girls' psychological development, and later became a member of the Harvard faculty. This was a long time ago, and in the intervening decades I saw children and adolescents in a private practice, undertook training as a Lacanian Psychoanalyst, wrote books, wrote articles, wrote poems, painted and made prints, kept sketchbooks, and wondered, wondered, wondered—how did I escape, when others have not? I married a fiery, intelligent lovely Irish woman, and built a life in two places, two nations. I sang, danced, traveled, and experienced that great adventure of loving someone deeply, intimately, and over a long time. I moved to Western Massachusetts 12 years ago, to Hampshire College in Amherst, a unique place where young people are responsible for their own questions and learning, and became a Professor of Psychoanalysis and Clinical Psychology, then a Dean of the School of Critical Social Inquiry. Yet, for all of that, as I begin my project on psychosis, I am reminded of how fortunate I am to live this life.

Many people lost in psychosis (for a short time or over a very long time) experience things that cannot be symbolized, spoken, or received by others. I hear their efforts to write and to speak, sometimes eloquently, sometimes in words and forms that seem impenetrable, as both meaningful and compelling. What are their experiences? Is it possible to discern in delusion, knowledge in a new form? Is it possible to translate "incoherence" and discover a new language in the making, made of incandescent alphabets? I use this phrase to refer to elements of language that are creatively adopted when one must find a new way in language with respect to a strange world one has entered and cannot exit.

The heart of this book is an inquiry about language and its transformations in psychosis, particularly changes in language that accompany the experience as a subjective encounter with voices. Contrary to many clinical psychologists and psychiatrists, I consider language in psychosis not as language deficit, nor dysfunction, nor a brain-based and driven phenomenon. Rather, the individual's relationship to language is uniquely subjective, meaningful, and connected to experiences that have never been named, and lie outside discourse in the family and society.

For a long time, clinicians have remarked on the strange language of psychosis, particularly schizophrenia, characterizing speech as "gibberish" or "word salad." Often clinicians listen to language in psychosis to make a diagnosis of a "thought disorder" or to regulate medication, as though language has lost all subjective meaning. To be sure, a central and well-known characteristic of psychotic language is the use of peculiar words and phrases, sometimes in a context of disorganized, confused speaking (McGhie and Chapman, 1969). Linguists focus on the structural properties of language. They have discovered very particular qualities of psychotic speech, such as failure to find the right word and substitution of another word; distraction by the sound sense of words; a breakdown of discourse in associative trains; and the speaker's lack of awareness of strange language use. Yet, many characteristics of speech remain intact, such as the stress patterns and pronunciation rules of the original language, as well as syntax, even when phrases and sentences are disconnected (Covington et al., 2005). In other words, there is nothing ungrammatical in psychotic speech.

I begin my work from the premise that language is central to human subjectivity, and that all of us are subjects in relation to our own and others' interpretations of our speech and writing. We seek meaning through language, whether or not we have ever experienced psychosis. The psychotic, I will show, bears enigmatic traces of questions and experiences beyond a shared language, beyond what can be known or spoken in any social link. In psychosis, the subject takes the position of witness to a ghastly Other in social isolation.

As an adolescent boy the poet, Tomas Tranströmer (who would become a Nobel Laureate), had an encounter with "dread" that left him as a witness in language, both memoir and poetry, to this experience. In his memoir, *Memories Look at Me* (1995), he writes,

During the winter I was fifteen I was afflicted by a severe form of anxiety. I was trapped by a searchlight that radiated not light but darkness.... As I lay down to sleep suddenly the atmosphere in the room was tense with dread. Suddenly my body started shaking, especially my legs. I was a clockwork toy that had been wound up and now rattled and jumped helplessly. The cramps were quite beyond the control of my will. I had never experienced anything like this.

(pp. 43, 44)

He describes a time of elemental illness in vivid detail:

The world was a vast hospital. I saw before me human beings deformed in body and in soul…. It all happened in silence, yet within the silence voices were endlessly busy. The wallpaper pattern made faces. Now and then the silence would be broken by a ticking in the walls. Produced by what? By whom? By me? ….I was afraid… as in a film where an innocuous apartment interior changes its character entirely when ominous music is heard, I now experienced the outer world quite differently. A few years earlier I had wanted to be an explorer. Now I had pushed my way into an unknown country where I had never wanted to be. I had discovered an evil power. Or rather, the evil power had discovered me…. Mother had witnessed the cramps I suffered that evening in late autumn as my crisis began. But after that she had to be held outside it all. Everyone had to be excluded, what was going on was just too terrible to talk about. I was surrounded by ghosts. I was myself a ghost…. No prayers, but attempts at exorcism by way of music. It was during that period that I began to hammer at the piano in earnest.

(pp. 44, 45)

What had happened to this adolescent boy? And how do we understand his trajectory to becoming a musician, a psychologist, and a poet, an extraordinary, internationally recognized poet? Tranströmer, as far as I know, was never hospitalized. Later, I will talk about psychosis as a structure through the work of psychoanalyst Jacques Lacan, and the way that writing can serve to prevent living a life in psychosis as an experience that is utterly overwhelming.

What of others, also young, who were diagnosed as "schizophrenic"? I turn now to five writers (Ken Steele, Carol North, Whitney Robinson, Barbara O'Brien, Edith Weisskopf-Joelson), of first-person accounts of the initial invasion by an alien, enigmatic Other, and the effects of this initial experience at the beginning of a process that will be far-reaching in its consequences. I chose these five because in these books I found compelling and rich stories, and, importantly, none of the authors had a particular theory or angle they wanted to uphold as a filter for the narrative.

Ken Steele began quite suddenly to hear voices when he was unusually young, at age 14. He became chronically psychotic for several decades. Here, he writes about his early encounters in *The Day the Voices Stopped* (2001).

Whenever I was near a television set or radio, the voices grew louder and more intense, and there seemed to be more of them. It was as if they were writing and directing the story of my life, telling me what I could and could not do, leaving little room for improvisation. That evening, the voices won out. As my father quizzed me about what we had seen on TV, I did as the voices directed: I put my hands over my ears and turned my back to him. Dad became enraged. "Go to bed without dinner," he ordered me, stalking out of the living room. It was a punishment he rarely imposed. *Ungrateful boy.* Now see what you have done," said my voices. You have disappointed your father one more time. Your parents *deserve a better son than you.*

(p. 6)

Ken hears commands in his voices, which he follows, sometimes dangerously. He experiences these voices, intensified and multiplied by other voices and sounds, as imposed on him in a continuous commentary. Despite the fact that they sound utterly coherent and grammatical (and do not need to be deciphered), they introduce a contradiction. After they tell Ken to block out his father, they taunt him for the consequence. They also seem to be able to say know things that Ken can't quite imagine or articulate for himself.

Some time after the voices first visited me, my mother and father told me they were expecting a baby. They had tried for several years, but without success.... I did not share their joy. An only child for close to fifteen years, I wasn't eager to welcome a rival for their attention and affections. If I have to have a sibling, I prayed, let it be a sister. But the voices knew better. They had decided it would be a boy, and on several terrifying occasions, they made it seem as if "he" were speaking to me. *I am coming, I'm going to be born,* my soon-to-be brother would whisper from inside my mother's swollen stomach. *You have to leave.* Soon other voices would join in—in a deafening chorus that dictated ways in which I might manage my leave-taking: *Take a radio into the bathtub and electrocute yourself...Jump in front of a car on Route 69...Pour charcoal lighter fluid over your body and set yourself afire...Hang yourself in the forest....*My brother, Joseph Robert Steele, was born on May 10, 1964. The fact that the voices had correctly determined his sex gave them a lot of credibility. *He's here now,* they said, laughing maniacally, *Joey is the good son...he's the one they wanted.*

(pp. 6, 7)

Ken's fears, transmitted by external voices, are borne out in reality; his parents walked out of his life while he was still a teenager. Ken's voices comment on his experience, yet they come from outside, as alien, invasive, all-knowing presences. He discovers that he can work hard and to some degree, tune them out, especially at the beginning.

Only two things, reading and writing, could tone the voices down. When I read I entered the world of David Copperfield or Huckleberry Finn; I'd suffer the growing pains of Holden Caulfield or the agonies of Oliver Twist. The voices would then become muffled, like a radio playing in the background. As so I read voraciously. I read everything I could get my hands on, while the voices waited in the wings, ready to surge onto the stage as soon as I turned the last page.... Amazingly, I graduated from Junior High with honors. By graduation, however, I had separated myself from most of my friends.

(pp. 7, 8)

Ken's capacity to study, to tune out the voices to some extent, allows him to go to school and carry on, and yes, be quite successful at academics. But he is isolated within a short time. His experiences set him apart from both family and peers. The voices comment on his life, predict his fate, and call out to him to leave his family and to end his life. Throughout his account, these voices remain coherent as they command, direct, and comment. Not all his voices were threatening or demeaning; some offered good company to a young man who was quite alone.

Carol North, who would later become a psychiatrist, began having vivid and terrifying visual perceptions and hearing voices as a six-year-old child, but she manages to navigate the world until she reaches college. The voices do not surprise her. They come and go; some have names and they are familiar. The Other that is terrifying and enigmatic is the Other world, a place that can leak into this world. In her book *Welcome, Silence* (1987/2002), she recalls an early hospitalization as a college student:

A nurse breezed into the dayroom on her way down another hallway. "There goes the nurse," said a voice. A flash of light zoomed across the dayroom, burning out and disappearing into thin air. Had I really seen that? "There goes another comet," said a voice. Okay, I did see it. This could only mean one thing: further leakage of the Other Worlds into this world. The comet had been a sign. "It's alright," Hal reassured me with his sugary voice. "We're here with you." Interference Patterns began to materialize in the air. I stared at their colorful swirls. When the voices spoke, the patterns shifted... Frightening. I didn't know if existence in the Other world would be divinely magnificent, beyond human description, like heaven, or whether it would be like the worst imaginable hell.... I froze, not wanting to produce further patterns from my bodily movement. I did not want to be responsible for encouraging such change in the world. Live your life as a prayer, I reminded myself. I heard a news announcer on TV parrot my words: "Live your life as a prayer."

(pp. 101, 102)

Visual patterns and voices work in concert in this passage to point to another realm. Carol believes that Other Worlds can leak into the world she knows. She is not able to control what is happening but thinks she can stop the process by not moving her body. But suddenly her thoughts are no longer private; they can be broadcast to the world, another kind of leakage. What is this strangeness she is now entering? How will she manage it, endure it, and be changed by it?

Whitney Robinson also experiences something very strange when she is in her first year of college. The voice (singular) came after striking changes in perception. In her book, *Demons in the Age of Light: A Memoir of Psychosis and Recovery* (2011), she writes about her first experience that something is terribly awry.

> When I turn off the television at 2 a.m., the house vibrates with silence. Already, I have trouble remembering the resonance of the words in my mind, the sensory flashes combining to form an illusion of meaning. But something's wrong. I feel like a cat in the moments before an electric storm. My mind is a stranger to itself, and its sudden anonymity is malicious, like a photograph that's been scribbled on and the eyes crosses out. I... the pronoun rings hollow in my head, the way every other word does when repeated nonsensically.
>
> (p. 66)

This experience captures two trends in language: words dissolving into sound and nonsense, and an impression of "meaning." I will return to this duality later as I explain how and why it is that one's very thoughts can suddenly vanish, while at the same time, the smallest detail implodes with meaning. In this short paragraph, we also see a foreshadowing of the erosion of the sense of "I" as viable, alive and in control, a process that will continue and will have far-reaching consequences.

Here is Whitney again, writing about her first encounter with an alien Other:

> The strangeness is that I'm not alone, here in my bed. I will never be alone again. I feel it slithering out of the darkness for the first time, a presence that's been whispering its sinister enigmas. A living, breathing thing—cold stars and glittering mathematics with the inhale, hot copper and rotten fruit with the exhale. Foreign from everything I have ever known. Other. *Shhh*, it says, though I have made no sound. A rattling snake noise that brings no comfort. What is happening? *Awakening. Awakening from a deep sleep in the dark...* Who are you? *Lucifer, Legion, Machiavelli, Moriarty, Mephistopheles, I am the serpent, the shadow, the swan.* The voice is almost giddy...I feel a moment of nausea. *We are* whispers the Other from inside my prefrontal cortex. *I am Eudaimon. We are together.* My body stages a violent rebellion again the ephemeral parasite. Every substance that can be released is released. The surge of epinephrine produces panic so pure it is like white light in my veins, bursting behind my eyes. My muscles freeze and seize and I cease to breathe, and something hot trickles down my leg. *Don't fight it. Surrender.*
>
> (pp. 72, 73)

Whitney's terror is palpable, and her experience real, as real and indelible as any truly frightening encounter can be for any one of us. The Other she encounters is also enigmatic and alien, both there and "ephemeral." She asks (herself or the Other, it's hard to know) "What is happening?" And the explanation comes *through the voice*, not through her own voluntary, free-of-the-voice thinking process. This is important to note, because she, like so many others who have been through psychosis, will find in time that she cannot distinguish her thoughts from this invasive Other. But I am getting far ahead of myself here. I will return to this point when I explain how the speech of psychotic persons can and does slide among various pronouns and speaking positions.

Let's look now at a very different first encounter with an alien and enigmatic Other. In her book *Operators and Things: The Inner Life of a Schizophrenic* (2011 [1958]), Barbara O'Brien (her chosen pseudonym) writes about the moment she encounters an alien Other as multiple, distinct presences.

> When I awoke they were standing at the foot of my bed looking like soft, fuzzy ghosts. I tried feeling the bedclothes. The sensation of feeling was sharp. I was awake and this was real. The boy was about twelve years old, handsome, and with a pleasant, relaxed smile. The elderly man was impressive: solid, conservative, a reliable man with built-in rules. The third was a real weirdo with hair three inches too long, black, straight and limp, and with a body that was also long and limp. The face didn't belong with the body or the hair; the features were fine and sensitive, the expression, arrogant and unbending. The elderly man suddenly cleared his throat. "It is necessary for the good of all concerned that you get to know Hinton better." He turned and looked at the weirdo.
>
> (p. 55)

Barbara presents her experience as having veracity—because she can feel her bedclothes, yet she acknowledges that her visitors look like "soft, fuzzy ghosts." At first, they do not seem to be as menacing as the figure that Whitney encountered. They read almost like characters in a novel, well observed and sketched for the reader.

> "I am Burt," said the elder man. He seemed concerned but in a dead, resigned sort of way, a man who had lived long with order and system and who was having difficulty adjusting to the role of master of ceremonies at a holocaust. "And this is Nicky." The boy smiled a wide, sunny smile. Burt explained. I could see why he was chosen as spokesman. What he had to say he said clearly and in a few words. I had been selected for participation in an experiment. He hoped I would be cooperative; lack of cooperation on my part would make matters difficult for them and for myself. There were Operators everywhere in the world although they were rarely seen or heard. My seeing and hearing them was, unfortunately, part of the experiment. I thought: I have come upon a knowledge that is obviously dangerous to have; others would be in equal danger if I revealed it to them. "Yes," said Burt, and he looked pleased. But I had not spoken. I considered this for a moment.
>
> (pp. 55, 56)

Barbara can distinguish her own thoughts from the others in the room with her. She is offered an explanation, too, for what is happening to her; she has been chosen for an "experiment." She realizes she has a dangerous knowledge now, not to be revealed to others. Burt, instantaneously, confirms her idea, even though she did not speak it aloud. Despite this glitch in "reality," the scene is one we can enter imaginatively; we can see it in our mind's eye as it unfolds. Any one of us can imagine ourselves in Barbara's position. And the narrator is a logical interlocutor.

> First things first: "What is the nature of the experiment?" Hinton smiled wryly, "Didn't I tell you," he said to Burt, "that it would say that first?" It?... They were reading my mind. I could see it in the ways their eyes focused on my face, the expressions on their faces, as they watched me think. Burt explained: Every thought in the mind of a person like myself was always clear to an Operator who might be tuned in. I considered the situation. Would I, perhaps, be able to think on some sub-cellar level and so reduce this tremendous advantage they had? Nicky grinned broadly and Burt smiled gently. Burt again: No thought of mine on any level could escape them. Operators could penetrate the minds of Things at any level."
>
> (p. 56)

Now the reader is aware that there is malice in these alien presences; they can read the mind of the narrator, and there is no escape from them. In fact, they regard her as no more than a Thing, a thing that they, as Operators, can experiment with in ways that go beyond her knowledge and will. Their designs are the heart of the enigma in this Other. And yet, even as we read this last passage, it is not by any means illogical. Logic and enigma sit side by side. This is one thing that becomes increasingly striking about psychosis—its logic is a logic that can enfold many contraries as though there were no contradictions, a seamless logic that becomes systematic, and then irrefutable.

For some people, the invasion by an alien, enigmatic Other does not involve hearing voices (conversely, hearing voices does not always or even necessarily involve psychosis, a point I'll explain later). In her account, *Father, Have I Kept My Promise?* (1988), Edith Weisskopf-Joelson writes about what she observes of experiences that are strange to her when she is living and working at a Catholic college. The process begins gradually on several fronts and becomes all encompassing. Her account covers many pages, but here I just give glimpses into her experience as it unfolds by tracing what is happening in language and thought around a single word:

> Things have been so strange, as if books were given me or put where I will see them, or incidents related to me containing a message.... I can see a Jewish encyclopedia consisting of many volumes. I feel that the day before it was not there. Have they put it there just for me? To tell me something? The backs of some of the volumes are torn to pieces. Was this done in revenge? Then one

volume catches my eye. The spine reads AARON TO DREYFUS, and the next one reads, DREYFUS TO FREUD. From the moment I see the name Dreyfus, I know I have come closer to the secret of St. Mary and to the strange circumstances which have brought me here.

(p. 81)

What is striking here is that objects are arranged as if the objects *themselves* are meant to carry a message addressed to the narrator. The enigma is to decipher the message, the secret in the objects, and also discover who directs the message. Edith fled the Nazis as a young Jewish woman, but she does not consider that experience in relation to Dreyfus. (The Dreyfus affair in France involved an officer, who was falsely charged with selling secrets to Germans. Alfred Dreyfus, a man of Jewish descent, spent eight years in prison before he was exonerated.) Rather than considering this case and its injustice in relation to her own former status as a Jew in Germany, Edith conjectures that it is the others with whom she is currently living and working who are actively directing her attention to certain clues:

Next I remember the teachers in the faculty house. One evening when I came home they were all walking barefoot. They wanted to make me think of feet so that I would think of Dreyfus; they knew that Fuss was the German word for foot. The name Dreyfus means "three feet." I see so many students walking on crutches. Perhaps they mean to tell me, "Dreyfus, three feet".... And then there is Sister Mary Elizabeth. I said after a conversation the content of which I have forgotten: "I am afraid I have put my foot in a hornets' nest." And she replied, "It is too bad you only have two feet, because we have so many hornet's nests." Only two feet. Did she not say this to make me think of three feet and Dreyfus? How slow I am in comprehending! But if the teachers and students want to tell me something about Dreyfus, why don't they talk to me directly? Why do they disguise their messages? I do not know.

(p. 82)

In this passage, Edith assumes that the associations and connections she makes around the word Dreyfus are not hers, but are imposed on her as a message coming from others around her. She uses a common idiom, "I am afraid I have put my foot in a hornets' nest," but no longer remembers the context of her remark, as she considers Sister Mary Elizabeth's response as another clue about Dreyfus. Edith may be confused about why the messages are disguised, but she does not question that there *are messages* directed to her from all around her. The process leads her more and more deeply into a distinctive logic:

I am sitting in my pew listening to the Litany of the Saints. The priest says, "Holy Mary." The congregation responds, "Pray for us".... The prayer is long. It lulls me into a dreamlike state, but suddenly something strange happens. I sit up in my pew and listen to the voice behind me. The voice does not say, "Pray for us." It says, "Drayfus, which sounds like Pray f' us." Another voice says, "Drayfus." Finally the whole crowd does so: "Drayfus, Drayfus, Drayfus." I realize this is done for my benefit. Some of the sisters to my right and to my left look at me furtively to see if I understand.... As time goes on I feel more and more that God sent me to St. Mary's on a mission, and that it is God's will that I should detect something of great importance. The founder of the order, Mother Guerin, is about to be canonized. She is about to become a saint. Perhaps it is my mission to show that she was involved in the Dreyfus case. It is a difficult task. Captain Dreyfus was sentenced in 1894. Mother Guerin died in 1856. The sisters must have forged the date so no one would know her crime.

(pp. 83, 84)

In this short passage, two things begin to change: the sound of language can slip from one thing to another and can sound like (and become) another message. Edith is not hearing voices, but she is hearing, in voices around her, something Other than what they were saying just moments before. Second, the voices are working to convey something Other to Edith, something outside and beyond herself. Edith now sets herself a task: to uncover something "of great importance." The Other is now a task, or "mission." Although it seems impossible that a nun who died before Dreyfus was tried was actually involved in his case, Edith does not waver in her assessment, "The sisters must have forged the date so that no one would know her crime." Again, we can see contradiction and logic knotted together in a conclusion that seems obvious to the narrator. Ideas that begin as small certainties may, over time, become systems of thought, a kind of knowledge that others have no access to.

But before we enter more deeply into the domain of psychosis as it develops over time, it is useful to ask: how does this experience arise? I do not take the position that psychosis is rooted in solely in genetics, in biology. While there is compelling evidence that schizophrenia occurs in families, families are the crucible of all forms of human subjectivity. There is simply no compelling evidence that schizophrenia has a specific genetic marker.

As I follow the language of psychosis in written accounts, I wonder if it's possible to find traces of the alien Other that invades the mind in childhood experience? Do writers about psychosis refer to any such experiences? It turns out: sometimes they do.

Turning to the accounts of childhood, I am not looking for "causes" or for "reasons" for psychosis. I am interested in precursors in language. I am especially interested in unusual visual, auditory or bodily experiences that echo with the later accounts. I wonder about any confusion concerning what is self and other, imagined sources of intended harm, as well as encounters with spiritual puzzles or enigmatic epiphanies. Do these writers speak of isolation as children, or confusion about the social world, or the inability to lie (as if others could see through them).

These are all questions about existence, about one's place in the social world, and about realms beyond what can be seen, heard and shared with others.

Carol North writes about terrifying experiences in childhood:

> "Pop." Another spark hit the window screen. "There! The fire!" I screamed. Mom pulled me close, so tight I couldn't get away. Dad peered out of the window. "Is that popping noise what's got you upset?" I nodded. Dad looked all blurry through my tears. "Why honey that's just the June bugs hitting against the screen. They're attracted to the light in the house, see?" At first I didn't believe him. In my mind I know he was right.
>
> (pp. 27, 28)

This scene opens up a period of night terrors, as Carol confronts insects that hit her bedroom screen. Soon after, she encounters a voice outside the window: "Where's the fire?" She sees a ghost emerge from her open closet. She also finds herself in danger walking to school.

> Out of the sky came a sparrow, dive-bombing toward my head! I ducked, and leaped under the nearest bush. Several other birds had gathered forces to tear me to pieces. I crouched under the bush for what seemed to me like an eternity, then I jumped to my feet and began running. The birds continued to chase me and zoom past my head....
>
> (p. 37)

As a child, Carol does not distinguish between what she fears and what is actually happening. Birds can form malicious intentions, collectively. We may see this simply as a vivid imagination run wild in a sensitive, anxious child. That may be. But this child is afraid of murderous birds to the extent that, morning after morning, she cannot get to school on time. Around this period, she learns to ride a bike, but as she rides it she quickly gets lost:

> I decided to get on one street and stay on it. Eventually I would have to come to someplace familiar. The street ended in nowhere, dumping me onto another street I didn't recognize.... One of the voices began to give me advice. "Turn right," it said, in a friendly, soothing tone. It didn't scare me at all. In fact, I appreciated the suggestion. I turned right. I stopped crying, even though nothing looked familiar yet. "Do you want a cigar?" the voice said.... "Seven, eight, keep going straight," the voice said in a singsong way. "Turn a corner, Little Jack Horner." This was getting me mixed up.
>
> (p. 49)

Carol finally sees something familiar and realizes she is only six blocks from home. But she wonders, "Could the voices have somehow changed the landscape and stuck a neighborhood street under me? I decided it was possible" (p. 49). Is this childhood schizophrenia? Carol continues to attend school, and though her parents are anxious, they are not alarmed. Carol moves through the world; she navigates learning and language. And she continues to have strange experiences. She hears voices from time to time. She speaks to the dead in a cemetery. She thinks her dog can read her thoughts. She is interested in religion, in speaking in tongues, in accessing Other worlds. But she is also invested in keeping an appearance of normalcy. She explains how she does it:

> I had devised elaborate schemes to check things out to determine whether or not they were real without seeming obvious to others. I had also learned not to talk back to voices when other people were around.... But now with my advancing internal chaos [in adolescence], I would have to strengthen and refine my skills to succeed in the ordinary world.
>
> (p. 67)

Carol's investment in finding a way to succeed in the ordinary world allows her to graduate from high school, ninth in a class of 500. Her persistence and dedication to her studies stand her in good stead through college and through medical school, even as she continues to be overwhelmed and hospitalized repeatedly.

Whitney Robinson was home-schooled, but this scarcely explains the extent of her social isolation. She, too, is very bright. As a child she is interested in religion, she has strange experiences, she wonders about death, and she develops a vivid sense that she is different. Like Carol, Whitney works to appear to fit in with peers. She describes a birthday party:

I smile and eat cake and otherwise try to behave like a normal human being, maybe even one who is happy to see her friends. When everyone has left, I go up to my room and look carefully over my personal effects, particularly the things that are shiny or fragile. I have a feeling that if something were taken, it would be small and useless and of apparent value to me. Nothing is missing, but on everything lingers the ghost of a foreign touch. Something has been here (p. 45).

There is the sense of an alien Other before she is overwhelmed by it. Whitney not only spends a lot of time alone, but she experiences herself as both older and much younger than her peers, especially during adolescence, when she read at the college level and wrote essays on Dante and Emerson, but also went up to the attic to spend hours looking at children's picture books. Throughout childhood and adolescence, she knew that something was terribly wrong, but did not know what it was, and could only refer to strange experiences. Of course, we must wonder how much of childhood is construed in retrospect, highlighted after one has been diagnosed "schizophrenic." And how many adolescents feel, at one point of another, isolated from peers, out of synch with the world? And yet, in account after account, I find a sense of childhood isolation, a vivid sense of being different, set apart, and recalling strange experiences—sometimes hearing voices, and sometimes making frightening attributions.

Edith, like Whitney, thinks about how she is different from others, and she assumes that she will always be a child:

I harbored the notion that I was a child and would remain a child as long as I lived…I accepted this notion, so alien to the ways others understood the nature of human life, a mark of my differentness from others.

(p. 24)

She finds it hard as a child and as an adolescent to situate herself in the world and can't seem to learn anything that isn't in books. She knows others see her as very smart, yet wonders if she is "retarded." The implicit knowledge that children pick up about the wider world escapes her, and common social practices and norms seem foreign to her.

During my early school years, I observed other notions, feelings and experiences that convinced me, little by little, that I was different than others. For example, although I was considered a bright, even brilliant student, I found myself wondering if I were not mentally retarded. I suffered this painful doubt because, while I found it very easy to remember the readings our teacher specifically assigned us, nevertheless I found it very hard to keep up with other children in and out of school. The conversations drifted toward facts that I had not been explicitly assigned to remember. As I moved into adolescence, the problem intensified, and I found it even harder to sustain an interest in, and thus to learn about, the outside world—the world of main streets and side streets, the world of newspapers and books not assigned in school. The world of boys flirting with girls, and girls buying cosmetics and standing in front of the mirror applying lipstick as if they were applying their future. The subject wasn't covered in class, so I didn't know about it…. As time went on, I came to feel more and more like I was from another planet and knew nothing about life on earth.

(pp. 24–26)

But Edith is not without social skills. She earns a Ph.D. in psychology, she meets a man who has also fled the Nazis and marries him (although her marriage does not last). She teaches in a university, then (following tuberculosis) in a Catholic college. She seems to be a bright young woman, perhaps a little awkward socially, but no more. And yet she, too, experiences herself as different and as isolated as a child and adolescent. Like the others who become psychotic, she is interested in religion in an idiosyncratic way, as if seeking personal (not collective) spiritual answers to questions about her existence and purpose. This search happens first in childhood, and again in adulthood as she become increasingly suspicious of others.

When I was nine, ten and eleven, a dream would come back to me night after night. I found myself in the Vienna Woods, and as I walked through a dense forest, I came to a small opening filled with magical objects…. The paintings were loosely fastened to the stems of trees. Behind the scene was a little grotto where the Blessed Virgin held the Christ child. I felt the holy aura that surrounded them... Each time I awoke I felt sure I must have seen a place like this in the real world. I walked in all directions through the Vienna Woods. I asked passersby if they knew of a nearby grotto where souvenirs were sold. I even asked the forest ranger, and he said there was no grotto.

(p. 48)

Edith also recounts going to a Catholic church with a young friend, being called a Jewish brat and expelled. Her family avoided Judaism and arranged for her to have nose surgery so that she would appear less Jewish. All of these events took place during a time when the Nazis were gaining power in Vienna. This was a collective, real menace. Later, Edith began to piece together the paranoid logic of the Dreyfus case in a convent and heard the nuns' voices morph from "Pray for us" during the Litany of the Saints to "Dray-fus" (p. 83).

Edith experienced symbolic and real threats to existence as a child and as a young woman. Her father fought in World War I and become a prisoner. He disappeared and reappeared at the door, disguised as a Jewish beggar. The young Edith did not recognize him and followed her mother's instruction to keep the chain on the door, not to let him in, not to touch his hands. After his death, Edith feels haunted by this scene. Years later, on a train when she is leaving Germany fleeing the Nazis, she is unable to lie to the Nazi Lieutenants who question her about where she is going. She is fortunate; they tell her she does not look Jewish, and they offer money, assistance, none of which she accepts—but she does not think to lie. This is true of others who, as children, feel they have to speak the truth if questioned directly, as though others can see through any lie, no matter the circumstances. I'll return to this point later, and why it is that lying depends on a particular position in language.

Two of the writers, Ken and Barbara, give no accounts of childhood. But each experiences family as radically uninterested and cut off from them.

So far I have offered just a brief glimpse into the bare beginnings of psychosis, that is psychosis as an experienced, vivid, very real imposed Other that is ghostly, ghastly, and enigmatic. But the ways this experience is lived for Ken, Carol, Barbara, Whitney, Edith, and others seem impenetrable, once they are immersed in it.

At least in part, this is due to the fact that *what they experience in language* changes who they are, where they locate themselves in time and space, what the body is (and can become), as well as their ideas about everyone who speaks to them (seen and unseen). They wonder if they will ever again have their own thoughts, purposes, and intentions. They have to navigate language on new terms, and it becomes increasingly difficult to speak across a great divide to be intelligible, to be considered, to be believed.

When I use the pronoun "they" here, I do not exclude myself. I, too, encountered a ghastly Other in adolescence and did not find my way through and back from psychosis for a very long time.

At 13, I had an experience that has stayed with me all my life. Sitting in a chapel by myself I experienced a sudden change in the light—as if everything were glazed with honey—even as the air darkened. The visage of Christ on the cross changed too; his eyes, a livid green, leapt from their sockets and seemed to bear down on me. Faces, contorted with pain, surrounded the altar. I felt myself in the presence of something profoundly evil. Just as suddenly, I heard voices singing an exquisite music, although I could not make out the words. After some time, the world returned to me, and I left the chapel. Confronted by an experience that baffled me and yet was addressed to me, I realized that I must be Joan of Arc, returning to do something I could not escape. Two years later, in high school, I heard voices from a book cabinet—and I *wanted to hear* what they were saying to me, throwing my Latin book to the floor to stop the competing recitation, which had morphed with the voices, in the classroom. I began to hear voices at unexpected moments, sometimes catalyzed by a mechanical noise such a radiator going on or off. I knew, just as suddenly, that I had been elected by a force beyond me to translate these voices, and I began to work on an alphabet and a new language that might speak across all languages and stem the spread of evil throughout the world. I also experienced burning in my arms, and it was clear to me that the cardinals and archbishops had implanted splinters to burn me alive—to stop me as I worked to translate celestial voices. I spoke of these experiences to no one. In high school at one point, I forgot how to move in space without getting lost, and after I attempted to kill myself, ended up spending most of my junior year in a mental ward with schizophrenics. Then, just as suddenly, I had a year's reprieve and did two years of work in one to finish high school with my class. But the reprieve did not last, and I was in and out of hospitals all through college and the start of graduate school—usually twice a year, sometimes for weeks or months—until I was in my early thirties.

Did I experience childhood precursors, as the others have? Yes, I did. My sister Mary, just ten and a half months older, oriented me to the world, introduced me to playmates, and was my companion almost everywhere I went. When I was six, I got lost in my own neighborhood when she was not with me. Streets and houses I saw every day of my life became entirely unfamiliar. Learning to read was a process of sudden recognition for me; I thought my way of grasping words a magical and unique knowledge, and refused to read aloud in school. I did not learn the names of my classmates in the first years of grade school, and by age ten was baffled by their social groupings. With alarming frequency, I arrived back in my body after being "away," as if stolen from my body by some invisible force. I did not know what happened in the intervening time, but learned to cover my disappearances. I believed my stuffed animals were real, that they had thoughts and bodily feelings at age 12. I was an ordinary child in many respects, not so strange as to attract any notice. Sometimes my teachers were puzzled, but not very much; I may have seemed a dreamy, introverted child, and that was the end of it. But by the middle of adolescence, it became clear to others that there was something strange about me. I will take up my story from time to time in this book as I speak about various facets of the experience of psychosis.

I do not stand apart from those who have entered psychosis as an encounter with an enigmatic, terrifying Other. Yet I have had a full life beyond psychosis as madness, taught as a psychologist for over 25 years (alongside a small clinical psychoanalytic practice), and these experiences give me a particular perspective now as I return to explicate, translate, and open up the subjective interior of psychosis, which seems to be both frightening and incomprehensible to those who have not had this unforgettable experience.

It is impossible to grasp how profoundly the Other of language effects every facet of a human being's existence without a careful exegesis of what psychosis is, how it is recognized (and misrecognized), and how baffling it can be to listen to someone in psychosis. I take up these strands in the next chapter.

Note

1 This is excerpted from Chapter 1 of from *Incandescent Alphabets: Psychosis and the Enigma of Language* (London, Karnac, 2016).

References

Covington, Michael, Congzhou He, Cati Brown, Lorina Naci, Jonathan McClain, Bess Sirmon Fjordbak, James Semple, and John Brown. 2005. "Schizophrenia and the Structure of Language." *Schizophrenia Research*, 77, 85–98.

McGhie, Andrew and Chapman, James. 1969. "Perception of Speech in Schizophrenia." *British Journal of Psychiatry*, 110, 377–380.

North, Carol. 2002 [1987]. *Welcome, Silence: My Triumph Over Schizophrenia* (revised edition). Lima, OH: Academic Renewal Press.

O'Brien, Barbara. 2011 [1958]. *Operators and Things: The Inner Life of a Schizophrenic.* Los Angeles, CA: Silver Birch Press.

Robinson, Whitney. 2011. *Demons in the Age of Light: A Memoir of Psychosis and Recovery.* Port Townsend, WA: Process Media.

Steele, Ken and Berman, Claire. 2001. *The Day the Voices Stopped: A Memoir of Madness and Hope.* New York: Basic Books.

Tranströmer. Tomas. 1995. "Memories Look at Me." In *For the Living and the Dead: Poems and a Memoir*. New York: HarperCollins.

Weisskoph-Joelson, Edith. 1988. *Father, Have I Kept my Promise? Madness as Seen from Within*. West Lafayette, IN: Purdue University Press.

Chapter 8

Afterword

Annie G. Rogers

The Erikson Scholar experience in 2014 opened onto rich, vital years of scholarship, art, teaching, and clinical work for me. I continued teaching at Hampshire College and leading its Psychoanalytic Studies Program up until 2020, when I retired. I completed my formation as a Lacanian analyst and found a new home at the Lacanian School of Psychoanalysis in San Francisco as Analyst of the School. My life of printmaking and poetry has become central to my thinking about both the world and psychoanalysis.

But let me return to my stint at Austen Riggs. I was chosen as the Erikson Scholar in Fall, 2014, and I moved to Stockbridge from Amherst, Massachusetts. I taught a seminar on psychosis to interns and senior staff at Austen Riggs, attended clinical cases whenever I could and I offered poetry workshops to patients. But mostly I wrote. I wrote almost all day every day. I had been given an apartment, an office on the corner of the psychoanalytic library, and a stipend to write. What a great gift that was. I chose John Muller as a mentor, and, in this context, I was able to research and write my book, *Incandescent Alphabets: Psychosis and the Enigma of Language*, which was published by Karnac Books in 2016, a premier publisher of psychoanalytic and Lacanian books. My research included close readings of first-person accounts, as well as studying works of art made in psychosis, historic works, and the work of contemporary artists. I found this exploration of art exhilarating, although it was also daunting to learn how to get image permissions, scan professional digital copies, and write all at the same time. I got my final image permission in late July following my Erikson award, and I submitted my manuscript in mid-August. Whenever I speak about this book, I bring copies with me. I have seen that it isn't unusual to meet someone who has experienced psychosis and does not have words to say what has happened and I have a ready gift for that moment.

New commitments soon followed. The following autumn I wrote an article on child analysis for a special issue of French analysis for *Psychoanalytic Review*, the key journal for American psychoanalysts. I was invited to teach at the Chicago Center for Psychoanalysis and to give a paper and lead writing groups at New Directions (a creative writing program for psychoanalysts) in Washington, DC. I was seeing analysands and teaching full time, and also reaching out to colleges and colleagues

DOI: 10.4324/9781003322627-18

about the unique Psychoanalytic Studies Program for undergraduates at Hampshire College. I designed and taught two new courses during 2017: *Reading Freud as Inquiry*, a tutorial course for entering students interested in psychoanalysis, and *A Poetics of the Unconscious*, for advanced students as a sustained engagement with words and images (art, prints, and poetry) understood as constructions of the unconscious.

I was invited as a local poet to sit and write in Emily Dickinson's bedroom when it was under renovation. I wrote some disjointed phrases and was nearly locked in overnight (I was the last poet of the day and lost track of time). However, a poem came to culmination and I joined other poets to read work that was published in a collection of poems from these bedroom sittings. It was one of the highlights of my life.

While these streams of my work (printmaking and poetry) may seem far from psychoanalysis, they are not. They are part of a rich weave of activities that have interested me all my life, and increasingly, they have entered my scholarship and become part of the record of my publications.

My commitments in psychoanalysis continue. I have been an Overseas Member of the Association for Psychoanalysis and Psychotherapy in Ireland, where I attend seminars, teach, give papers, and enjoy lively debates and rigorous clinical thinking about Lacan with my Dublin "tribe." This past year, I co-taught the Wolfman with Lacanian analyst Rik Loose, in a series on Freud's cases hosted by the new Freud/Lacan Institute in Dublin. Finally, I continue to work in the Lacanian School of San Francisco as an Analyst, supervising control cases, participating in talks, events, and seminars, and working with the board as Vice President of the School.

I have returned to the studio at Zea Mays engaged primarily in book making and Maku Hanga printmaking this year. And I write poems between everything else, because I am compelled to do so. Sometimes I publish them, but often I just write them for the sake of writing, for the song singing in my ears.

Psychoanalysis and the Social World

Chapter 9

Guilty Minds[1]

Anne C. Dailey

A criminal confession is a prosecutor's dream. As the Supreme Court tells us, "the defendant's own confession is probably the most probative and damaging evidence that can be admitted against him."[2] Jurors usually give confessions more weight than any other type of evidence (Leo 2015, 3). For some types of crimes, like murder, a confession is the main route to a conviction (2). But confessions present an obvious conundrum: Why would any sane and rational person voluntarily confess to a crime, knowing full well that the state will punish in return? We easily understand why an individual might willingly confess to God, to her loved ones, even to her therapist. Similarly, we readily comprehend why she might confess to the victims of her criminal acts or their families. Confession in the context of these relationships may repair the offender's relationship to others, absolve the offender of guilt, or return the offender to her prior status in the community. Outside of the law, confession repairs and restores. But how do we understand the forces that lead someone to confess, knowing full well that her confessor will punish with little, if any, mercy?

Psychoanalysis gives us a framework for understanding the motive to confess to the punishing authority of the state. Of course, not all criminal confessions require deep-seated explanations. Some suspects might wish to protect an accomplice. Some young, vulnerable, or mentally impaired suspects may confess out of confusion or an unenforceable promise of leniency or simply a desire to go home. Suspects without money to post bond may confess to get out of jail, even temporarily. Others may fear for their physical safety. But in some cases, suspects confess where no such clear explanation exists. The compulsion to confess can transcend circumstances. As Chief Justice Burger once stated, borrowing from the psychoanalyst Theodor Reik, "[t]he human urge to confess wrongdoing is... normal in all save hardened, professional criminals."[3] Freud too famously observed that most people cannot keep themselves from confessing their secrets: "He that has eyes to see and ears to hear may convince himself that no mortal can keep a secret. If his lips are silent, he chatters with his fingertips; betrayal oozes out of him at every pore" (Freud 1953a, 77). A guilty mind, nothing more, may often be the best explanation for a suspect's decision to confess. But is it guilt for the crime under investigation?

DOI: 10.4324/9781003322627-20

The current law of confessions recognizes a guilty mind as a motivating factor in the confessional process. The Supreme Court accepts harsh interrogation practices in part because confession can be said to unburden the accused's sense of guilt. Confession allows the accused to "make a clean breast of things" in the interrogation room.[4] In this regard, confession serves everyone's interests: the interest of law enforcement in catching a criminal, the interest of society in maintaining social order, and the interest of the accused in personal redemption by relieving her guilty conscience. Confession to some extent always engages deep-seated unconscious desires for absolution and atonement, desires long expressed in religious and, later, psychoanalytic confessional models (Brooks 2000, 4, 5; Schmeiser 2007). Yet as we will see, unconscious guilt can be exploited by interrogators to undermine the voluntariness and even the reliability of any ensuring confession.

In our constitutional system, criminal confessions must be voluntary. The Due Process Clause and the Fifth Amendment both ensure that law enforcement does not force confessions from the lips of an accused.[5] The Due Process Clause prohibits confessions that are obtained through methods that override the accused's powers to resist. "The determination 'depends upon a weighing of the circumstances of pressure against the power of resistance of the person confessing.'"[6] This "totality of the circumstances" test has largely been replaced by the Fifth Amendment's requirement that police give *Miranda* warnings to suspects in custody.[7] As long as interrogators read a suspect her *Miranda* rights, courts will generally treat any ensuing confession as the product of free and voluntary choice.[8] In the Supreme Court's words, the warnings ensure that the suspect's will has not been "overborne" and her capacity for self-determination remains intact.[9] The law of confessions offers a prime example of the law's presumption of free will. "[C]ases in which a defendant can make a colorable argument that a self-incriminating statement was 'compelled' despite the fact that the law enforcement authorities adhered to the dictates of *Miranda* are rare."[10] Once the *Miranda* warnings are given, statements by the accused are presumed to be both voluntary and true.

Psychoanalysis opens the door to a fuller understanding of the place of psychological coercion in criminal interrogations. As detailed in this chapter, certain interrogation tactics raise serious questions going to the unconscious dynamics of the interrogation situation. We cannot know for sure in any particular case why an accused has confessed. But psychoanalysis reveals the ways in which certain deceptive and degrading police interrogation tactics shatter law's pretense of a freely confessing subject. We will consider here three interrogation techniques of greatest concern from a psychoanalytic perspective: false sympathy, degradation, and trickery.

We may take it for granted that interrogation tactics aimed at exploiting a guilty conscience are fair game for police interrogators. Unlike the rack and the thumbscrew, such interrogations are, we presume, consistent with the Constitution's prohibition on involuntary or compelled self-incrimination. Yet false sympathy and degradation exploit deep-seated, unconscious desires for absolution and punishment that undermine the voluntariness of a suspect's self-incriminating statements, whether those statements are true or false. Similarly, police trickery can take unfair advantage of a suspect's need to rationalize unconscious guilt for a crime she did not commit. These tactics often work by enlisting unconscious currents of love and aggression that can override an individual's conscious decision-making powers. Given the concerns about voluntariness and reliability that these interrogation tactics raise, *Miranda* should not be the final word on the admissibility of confessions. The interrogation practices discussed here are subjected to close, psychoanalytically informed due process scrutiny as well.

Psychoanalysis is not only a model of the mind relevant to understanding why people confess, but it is itself a confessional practice. Freud learned early on that patients strenuously resist confessing the truth, but he also came to understand that coercive tactics do not effectively overcome that resistance. He abandoned the coercive techniques of suggestion and hypnosis in favor of free association, a method requiring the patient to say anything that comes to mind, uncensored. Psychoanalysis recognizes the core paradox that patients both desire to confess and resist doing so at every turn, as well as other contradictions inherent in the confessional process: that confessions (and the guilt that fuels them) may be true to psychic experience but false in fact; that the relationship between confessor and confessant may engage both loving and aggressive feelings; and that an individual may confess both to absolve himself of guilt and to be punished. Can law accept the psychoanalytic paradoxes surrounding guilt and confession without unseating fundamental ideas of free will and voluntary choice that are the foundation of our criminal justice system?

False Sympathy and Degradation

The most famous case involving interrogation practices aimed at arousing guilt for a crime is *Brewer v. Williams.*[11] An escapee from a psychiatric hospital, Robert Williams, was convicted of murdering ten-year-old Pamela Powers after abducting her from a YMCA in Des Moines, Iowa, where she and her family were attending her brother's wrestling match. Williams surrendered himself to the police in the town of Davenport, about 160 miles from Des Moines, where he was then arrested and advised of his *Miranda* rights. Two Des Moines police detectives then picked Williams up and drove him back to Des Moines. During that long drive, Detective Leaming engaged in a wide-ranging conversation with Williams. Leaming knew that Williams was a former psychiatric patient and deeply religious.

In the course of their conversation, Leaming delivered what is known as the "Christian Burial Speech":

> I want to give you something to think about while we're traveling down the road... Number one, I want you to observe the weather conditions, it's raining, it's sleeting, it's freezing, driving is very treacherous, visibility is poor, it's going to be dark early this evening. They are predicting several inches of snow for tonight, and I feel that you yourself are the only person that knows where

this little girl's body is, that you yourself have only been there once, and if you get a snow on top of it you yourself may be unable to find it. And, since we will be going right past the area on the way into Des Moines, I feel that we could stop and locate the body, that the parents of this little girl should be entitled to a Christian burial for the little girl who was snatched away from them on Christmas [E]ve and murdered. And I feel we should stop and locate it on the way in rather than waiting until morning and trying to come back out after a snow storm and possibly not being able to find it at all.[12]

Soon after, Williams directed the detectives to the body of the girl. At his subsequent trial for murder, Williams argued that Leaming's speech coerced him into confessing in violation of the Due Process Clause. The Court did not reach the question of the voluntariness of the confession, holding instead that the state had failed to meet its burden of showing that Williams had knowingly waived his Sixth Amendment right to counsel. Williams was retried and convicted of first-degree murder.[13]

Leaming's Christian Burial Speech is a classic, if subtle, example of the use of guilt-inducing tactics in police interrogation. In the Supreme Court's words, the interrogators in the case hoped to "prick the conscience" of the accused, Robert Williams.[14] At first blush, there might seem to be nothing particularly objectionable about Detective Leaming's guilt tactics. Had the Supreme Court decided the issue, it would likely have ruled that Williams's confession was voluntarily given. As Justice White argued in dissent, "[m]en usually intend to do what they do, and there is nothing in the record to support the proposition that [Williams's] decision to talk was anything but an exercise of his own free will."[15] Unlike the rack and the lash, the appeal to conscience seems designed to persuade the accused rather than break him. It aims to induce the accused into confessing by stimulating a desire to "come clean."[16] Appeals to the accused's sense of guilt do not appear to "wring a confession out of an accused against his will" in the same way as questioning in the third degree.[17] Under questioning designed to arouse guilt, the suspect remains a freely choosing, autonomous decision maker. Law's presumption of free will stays decidedly intact.

But should it? Psychoanalysis pushes us to inquire more deeply into how certain guilt-inducing interrogation tactics go beyond ordinary acceptable methods of police pressure by creating a particular kind of confessor–confessant relationship undermining free choice. Two guilt-inducing practices in particular deserve our attention: police tactics that use false sympathy for the accused in order to develop a feigned relationship of trust and honesty, and police tactics that amplify a suspect's unconscious self-destructive urges by creating a relationship with sadomasochistic overtones. These interrogation practices may prompt the accused to seek, respectively, absolution from a falsely benevolent confessor or punishment from a dominating confessor, or both (Brooks 2000, 23). Interrogation tactics fuel both the love for the other and the hatred for the self that are the affective core of these two paradigmatic confessional relationships.

False Sympathy. As the facts in *Brewer v. Williams* exemplify, police interrogators often seek to cultivate a false bond of trust and affection with the accused (Leo 2015; Simon Kerr). Through a false alliance, the interrogators hope to stimulate the accused's desire to cooperate with and even please his interrogators. The interrogators "attempt to portray the questioning as a friendly joint problem solving exercise and to convey that they are fundamentally concerned about the suspect's welfare" (Leo 2015, 122, 123). But interrogation tactics that use false sympathy to obtain a confession obscure the indisputably adversarial nature of the encounter. The interrogators deceive the accused into believing that they have the accused's best interests in mind when in fact nothing could be further from the truth. A relationship based on false sympathy thus runs the risk of conscripting the accused unconsciously into seeking absolution from his benevolent confessors for his guilty acts.

The Supreme Court specifically designed the *Miranda* warnings with a concern about false sympathy in mind.

> The warning that anything said can and will be used against the individual in court… may serve to make the individual more acutely aware that he is faced with a phase of the adversary system--that he is not in the presence of persons acting solely in his interest.[18]

The Court openly acknowledged that interrogation environments are created "for no purpose other than to subjugate the individual to the will of his examiner."[19] Indeed, "[t]he entire thrust of police interrogation… [is] to put the defendant in such an emotional state as to impair his capacity for rational judgment."[20] The Court emphasized that "the process of in-custody interrogation contains inherently compelling pressures which work to undermine the individual's will to resist and to compel him to speak where he would not otherwise do so freely."[21] At the time it was decided, the *Miranda* decision aimed to dispel the fiction that police interrogators were truly sympathetic to the plight of the accused by awakening the suspect to the reality of the situation and his right to call a halt to the interrogation.

We might be tempted to presume that any reasonable person brought into custody and read his *Miranda* rights should be aware that he is not in the presence of friends. From this perspective, reading an accused his *Miranda* rights firmly establishes the adversarial frame for the encounter no matter what expressions of compassion or friendship may follow. A reasonable person who read his *Miranda* rights, the Court suggests, should have no difficulty resisting the charms and seductions of his police interrogators. As already noted, the Supreme Court has confirmed that "cases in which a defendant can make a colorable argument that a self-incriminating statement was 'compelled' despite the fact that the law enforcement authorities adhered to the dictates of *Miranda* are rare."[22] In the years since *Miranda* was decided, the Supreme Court has backed away from its emphasis on the inherently coercive nature of custodial interrogation and instead erected *Miranda* as a shield against claims of coercion. Since *Miranda,* the Due Process Clause's prohibition on involuntary confessions has largely dropped from view.

Psychoanalysis helps us to see how false sympathy violates the constitutional injunction against involuntary confessions. From a psychoanalytic perspective, voluntariness can be compromised even after the warnings have been given. Confession always takes place in the context of a relationship: with God, with one's priest, with one's analyst, or with police interrogators. When interrogators deploy false sympathy, they change the terms of the relationship between interrogator and accused. The technique is aimed at cultivating a feigned benevolent relationship between the suspect and her police interrogators. In psychoanalytic terms, we would say that police interrogators use false sympathy to foster a "transference" relationship with the accused, one that amplifies the accused's childlike dependency upon her accusers and her need for their approval. The relationship between confessor and confessant "contains, and activates, elements of dependency, subjugation, fear, the desire for propitiation, the wish to appease and to please" (Brooks 2000, 35). Isolation, fatigue, and fear may heighten the regressive feelings of dependency on the interrogators. The accused may be swept up into a transference storm of emotions that drives her to comply with her quasi-parental interrogators. From a psychoanalytic perspective, false sympathy deploys the transference – the childlike yearnings for approval – to lure the accused into seeking absolution for her sins. The phenomenon of transference explains how some accuseds will be coerced into confessing to police interrogators even after they have been told that any confession will be used against them.

Courts are not blind to transference and its implications for voluntariness. Interrogation-based transference resembles the kind of transference seen in therapy and other contexts in which individuals experience childlike dependence upon an authority figure. In these other confessional relationships, courts recognize that intense transference feelings undermine consent. For example, law restricts sexual choices in the context of the therapist–patient relationship expressly because the transference dynamics between the two parties throw into question any purported "consent" on the part of the patient. Many states ban sexual relationships between clergy and penitents and between family lawyers and their clients for the same reason. Yet despite attention to transference in the sexual realm, law remains doggedly blind to the fact that strong transference feelings similarly operate in the interrogation room. False sympathy does not cultivate an explicitly erotic transference, as it does in therapy or other professional relationships, but rather libidinally charged longings for parental love and approval. The desire is for absolution rather than sex.

When interrogators set out to cultivate a transference relationship that emotionally ensnares the accused, their tactics raise serious questions about the voluntariness of any ensuing confession. Police interrogation that pretends to offer spiritual solace or moral redemption can ignite unconscious transference processes that override rational thinking. It is possible, of course, that false sympathy may lead an accused to deliberate carefully about her options rather than drive her to confess. But from a psychoanalytic perspective, conscious consideration of one's needs for absolution from a more powerful confessor under these circumstances is not likely. In his Christian Burial Speech, Detective Leaming used false sympathy to deepen

Williams's guilt over his role in depriving the parents of a Christian burial for their daughter. By assuming the guise of a benevolent confessor, Leaming was able to enlist Williams, a deeply religious man, in the very process designed to prosecute and convict him. Expressions of false sympathy for the accused risk igniting unconscious needs for acceptance and absolution that may override an individual's capacity to realistically assess whether to talk to the police.

False sympathy almost always plays on guilt. Detective Leaming expressed his desire to help Williams ease his conscience, thus misleading him into thinking that confessing – making a clean breast of things – would be in his best interests. Minimization tactics – "by which interrogators normalize and suggest moral justification for the crime" – comprise another common form of false sympathy (Meissner and Kassin 2004, 86). In *Miller v. Fenton,* the detective's false reassurance that the suspect was "not responsible" appeared to prompt the confession. The following exchange took place: Detective Boyce: "I want to help you, because you are in my mind, you are not responsible. You are not responsible, Frank. Frank, what's the matter?" Frank: "I feel bad."[23] In the *Miranda* case itself, the Supreme Court offered the following example of an interrogator's supplication:

> Joe, you probably didn't go out looking for this fellow with the purpose of shooting him. My guess is, however, that you expected something from him and that's why you carried a gun--for your own protection. You knew him for what he was, no good.[24]

When police follow this line of questioning, essentially asserting: "[m]orally, you are not to be condemned" or "[c]learly you were acting in self-defense," the interrogators mislead the suspect into believing their falsely benevolent intentions.[25]

Police interrogation practices that use false sympathy do not break the accused's will in the same way as the rack and the thumbscrew, but the psychological coercion inherent in these practices is both overpowering and concealed. As Justice Frankfurter observed in the 1961 case *Culombe v. Connecticut*:

> [T]he risk is great that the police will accomplish behind their closed door precisely what the demands of our legal order forbid: make a suspect the unwilling collaborator in establishing his guilt. This they may accomplish not only with ropes and a rubber hose, not only by relay questioning persistently, insistently subjugating a tired mind, but by subtler devices.[26]

In the realm of criminal law, the confessors are not God or loved ones or even the victims, but accusers bent on judging and punishing rather than forgiving. Absolution in other arenas – Catholic confession or psychoanalytic therapy – may bring spiritual or psychological solace. But once a confession is obtained, criminal interrogation quickly reveals its punitive aims.

Psychoanalysis does not require that every expression of friendliness be prohibited. Far from it. But it does raise serious concerns about expressions of false sympathy that go too far in stimulating transference distortions in the interrogation relationship. Good-cop, bad-cop routines may heighten the risk of coercion by enhancing the benign, protective, quasi-parental role of the "good" interrogator. Courts apply the Due Process Clause's voluntariness standard to ascertain whether the interrogators' efforts to create a relationship built upon expressions of sympathy and support have overridden the accused's powers of resistance. This due-process inquiry does not require putting the parties on the couch to explore the subjective terrain of their relationship. Bright lines of behavior can be established to identify when the police cross the line between valid interrogation practices and unconstitutional tactics of false sympathy. Psychoanalysis thus brings the Due Process Clause back into play, supplementing *Miranda*'s Fifth Amendment protections as a vital guarantor of criminal defendants' rights.

Degradation. An accused may not always be taken in by false sympathy. Instead, she may remain fully aware that confession to police brings punishment. Indeed, punishment may be the point. Psychoanalysis teaches us to look for signs that interrogators have developed, not a falsely benevolent relationship with the accused, but one imbued with sadomasochistic impulses and desires. Police practices that trade in degradation run the risk of overriding an accused's powers of reason by activating unconscious self-destructive urges (Reik 1959). As we have seen, the due process inquiry turns on "a weighing of the circumstances of pressure against the power of resistance of the person confessing."[27] Degrading tactics override the suspect's powers of resistance by mobilizing unconscious desires to suffer in atoning for an inner sense of guilt, bringing the voluntariness of the confession into question.

Guilt that precipitates a desire for punishment may be conscious or unconscious. An accused may feel consciously guilty for a crime she in fact committed. But innocent people can feel guilty, too. They may consciously know they did no wrong but feel like criminals nevertheless. As psychoanalysis helps us to see, all of us suffer to some degree from unconscious guilt. Freud believed that unconscious guilt results from a successful resolution of the Oedipus complex, which involves the subordination of powerful incestuous longings and murderous envy to parental authority. For Freud, the internalized parental code against incest and murder consolidates into the morally exigent superego (Freud 1964; Freud 1961b). Constituted by the internalization of parental prohibitions, the superego is the source of our self-critical feelings. "[T]he external restraint is internalized and the superego takes the place of the parental agency and observes, directs and threatens the ego in exactly the same way as earlier the parents did with the child" (Freud 1964, 62). The Freudian superego's self-punitive features are fueled by guilt stemming from the psychic residue of early childhood aggression toward parental figures. Guilt over the original psychic "crime" against the parents can be animated, amplified, and redirected by subsequent wrongdoings, whether they be fantasized or real, a desire to kill or an actual rageful encounter, a fantasy of murder or the crime itself.

Psychoanalysts since Freud have drawn attention to the loving as well as the aggressive elements of the superego (Sandler and Sandler 1987, 333). In this regard, object relations theorists have shifted attention from the Oedipal period of conflict within the family triad to pre-Oedipal attachment feelings within the dyadic caregiver–child relationship. Melanie Klein's work on the pre-Oedipal dynamics of love and guilt in the infant's psychic life located the origins of guilt in the early relationship to a caregiving figure (Klein 2002a). In Klein's work, the development of guilt feelings begins before the triadic drama of the Oedipal period, during an earlier period of infant care when the child struggles with "good" and "bad" fantasies of the caregiver. In her view, learning to integrate opposing feelings for the primary love object is a necessary developmental task leading to the attainment of a more mature integrated state of mind and orientation toward other people. Klein views guilt as a sign of an infant's developing capacity for integration, what she calls achieving the "depressive position," a state in which the child finally attains a fuller, more integrated picture of the caregiver (Klein 2002b; Kernberg 1995, 454). For Klein, "the establishment of the depressive position brings with it a number of fundamental changes to mental life, including... the capacity for guilt and concern" (Auchincloss and Samberg 2012, 130). While some actual oral aggression toward the maternal caregiver takes place, it is the overpowering fantasy of destroying the maternal object that animates the unconscious guilt of the depressive position (Klein 1946). Once achieving a more mature, integrated state, the child must now contend with guilt resulting from the knowledge that destructive fury was directed toward a loving caregiver (Jacobson 1964).

The later psychoanalyst Hans Loewald tied unconscious guilt to the emergence of a sense of an autonomous self. He views the child's Oedipal rage toward the parents as the stimulus for the child becoming an autonomous individual freed from parental control.

> [I]t is no exaggeration to say that the assumption of responsibility for one's own life and its conduct is in psychic reality tantamount to the murder of one's parents, to the crime of parricide, and involves dealing with the guilt incurred thereby.
>
> (Loewald 1979)

For Loewald, the Freudian parricidal wishes constitute the founding moment of autonomous selfhood; unconscious guilt necessarily follows from an individual's murderous assumption of control over her own life. Loewald's theory of unconscious guilt focuses our attention on the close psychic connection between free choice and guilty submission: between the freely choosing autonomous individual voluntarily confessing her sins and the abject, guilt-ridden subject driven to confess her crimes. In Loewald's theory, there is no broad chasm separating these two states of self.

We can learn from psychoanalytic thinkers like Klein and Loewald about the centrality of unconscious guilt in human experience. The structure of psychic life – the superego demands, the depressive ambivalence, the autonomy strivings – rests upon a foundation of unconscious guilt that stays with an individual, with varying degrees of intensity, throughout life. We express unconscious guilt in our everyday lives when we engage in self-criticism, self-denial, and masochistic thoughts and behaviors. When we say someone suffers from a harsh superego, we mean that she engages in excessive forms of self-criticism and self-chastisement for usually exaggerated or even imagined wrongs (Freud 1964, 61). A guilty conscience manifests itself in

> a self-reproaching attitude, a self-accusatory one, a self-attacking one."[28] In his paper on masochism, Freud described "the satisfaction of this unconscious sense of guilt as perhaps the most powerful bastion in the subjects'... gain from illness.
>
> (166)

The degree of self-reproach corresponds to the internal sense of wrongdoing rather than to any external reality.

Unconscious guilt can fuel the desire for self-punishment. An individual may unconsciously look for ways to confirm the belief that he has violated some fundamental moral norm. The fantasy of punishment may thus predate an actual crime. Freud referred to "criminals from a sense of guilt" in describing individuals who go so far as to commit criminal acts in order to obtain the satisfaction of punishment for some earlier crime – real or imagined (Freud 1957, 311). At least one federal appellate court has reversed a criminal conviction on this ground, holding that the defendant acted from "an unconscious desire to be apprehended and punished" ((Schmeiser 2007, 323, quoting Pollard v. United States, 282, F. 2d 450, 460 (6th Cir. 1960)). For purposes of atonement, the present-day offense makes almost no difference. One might plan carefully or avail oneself of circumstances. "In such instances, one form of suffering has been replaced by another, and we see that all that mattered was that it should be possible to maintain a certain amount of suffering" (Freud 1961a, 166). Self-reproach never works to expiate the guilt. "It is hoped that punishment will extinguish guilt, but it does not work for any length of time and more punishment is needed" (Loewald 1979, 242).

Freud wrote regularly on the topic of masochism (Freud 1955). In his work on beating fantasies, for example, Freud described masochism as providing both punishment for forbidden wishes and, simultaneously, libidinal (sexual) gratification (Akhtar 2009; Freud 1955; Glick and Meyers 1988). In "The Economic Problem of Masochism," Freud argued that the need for punishment becomes sexualized, thus turning superego retribution into an instinctual gratification (Akhtar 2009, 184; Freud 1961a, 159). Later analysts have emphasized that masochism can have roots in early abuse, emphasizing "the interpersonal, attachment, and (predominantly preoedipal) object relations aspects of masochism" and locating the origins of masochism in "the need to preserve a tie to an object at whose hands one has suffered in childhood" (Auchincloss and Samberg 2012, 146). In this view, the adult love of suffering has its roots in the child's adaptive response to an abnormal environment

(Berliner 1958). Freud also related masochism to trauma. He described the human need to master a psychic trauma, a process that leads individuals to return to the traumatic event in thoughts, dreams, or repetitive actions (Herman 1997, 40). The repetition compulsion, as Freud called it, represents the individual's wish to redo the traumatic event in an effort to master its overwhelming effects by evoking a sense of agency (Auchincloss and Samberg 2012, 273; Schmeiser 2007, 34 n.22). Masochistic repetition rarely brings relief. To the contrary, masochistic repetition "causes the violent rupture of the self, a profound experience of fragmentation and chaos" (Benjamin 1988).

The law of confessions masks this messy, disruptive reality of unconscious guilt and self-punitive forces behind a veil of free will and voluntary choice. From a psychoanalytic perspective, we should worry about interrogation practices that, through degradation and humiliation, inflame a suspect's unconscious desires for punishment. Unrelenting hostile accusations of guilt "exert psychological pressure on the suspect... They carry out the demand that the suspect stop denying, bend to the will of the interrogator, and confess" (Leo 2015, 135). At some point, such interrogation practices may give rise to an actual sadomasochistic encounter, one at the opposite extreme from the feigned benevolent relationship created by false sympathy. In *Miranda*, the Supreme Court described these interrogation dynamics: "[The interrogator] 'must dominate his subject and overwhelm him with his inexorable will to obtain the truth... with no respite from the atmosphere of domination.'"[29] An interrogation with sadomasochistic overtones might be fostered by degrading statements such as "You are garbage," "Everybody knows you are nothing and your life is nothing," and worse. Such accusations work "to break down the suspect's resistance by silencing him, rendering him passive and ultimately inducing resignation and despair" (138). These tactics may work particularly well when unconscious self-destructive urges already pervade the suspect's psychic life, now ignited by the accusations being hurled at him. Criminal suspects who have suffered from early childhood trauma may be especially vulnerable to the unleashing of ungovernable desires for punishment.

The psychoanalytic perspective on unconscious self-destructive urges can be found in footnote 27 of the *Miranda* opinion itself. In this footnote, Chief Justice Warren notes that "[t]hirteenth century commentators found an analogue to the privilege grounded in the Bible," quoting the preeminent medieval Jewish thinker Moses ben Maimon (Maimonides): "To sum up the matter, the principle that no man is to be declared guilty on his own admission is a divine decree."[30] Jewish law prohibits all confessions, voluntary or not (Levine 2006, 264). Maimonides understood the law's prohibition to rest in part on the insight that self-destructive urges might lead an accused to falsely confess.

The [Court]... is not empowered to inflict the penalty of death or of flagellation on the admission of the accused. For it is possible that he was confused in mind when he made the confession. Perhaps he was one of those who are in misery, bitter in soul, who long for death, thrust the sword into their bellies or cast themselves down from the roofs. Perhaps this was the reason that prompted him to confess to a crime he had not committed, in order that he might be put to death.

(Maimonides 1977)

In Maimonides's view, Jewish law excludes all confessions because they are inherently unreliable.

Chief Justice Warren's footnote 27 does not stop with Maimonides but goes on to cite Norman Lamm's 1956 article "The Fifth Amendment and its Equivalent in the Halakhah" (Lamm 1956). In this article, Lamm argues that Maimonides anticipated "a major achievement of psychoanalysis (56). He contends that "modern psychoanalytic theory supports Maimonides's explanation of the [ancient Jewish] view of self-incrimination, an explanation which relies on the universality of the instinct of self-destruction" (57). A year later, the Supreme Court returned to Freud in *Garrity v. New Jersey*.[31] Justice Douglas, writing for the Court, invoked Maimonides, Lamm, and Freud for the purpose of highlighting the law's "concern for saving man from his own destructive inclinations."[32] Douglas quotes extensively from Lamm's discussion of psychoanalysis, including the following paragraph explaining the connection between Maimonides and Freud:

The Halakhah, then, is obviously concerned with protecting the confessant from his own aberrations which manifest themselves, either as completely fabricated confessions, or as exaggerations of the real facts... While certainly not all, or even most criminal confessions are directly attributable, in whole or in part, to the Death Instinct, the Halakhah is sufficiently concerned with the minority of instances, where such is the case, to disqualify all criminal confessions and to discard confession as a legal instrument. Its function is to ensure the total victory of the Life Instinct over its omnipresent antagonist. Such are the conclusions to be drawn from Maimonides' interpretation of the Halakhah's equivalent of the Fifth Amendment.[33]

While Lamm focuses on Freud's theory of the death drive, contemporary psychoanalysts offer a much stronger rationale for law's concerns about the self-destructive desires that can drive confession.

The Supreme Court's turn to psychoanalysis in the context of confessions was short-lived, but both *Miranda* and *Garrity* draw our attention to police tactics that strategically inflame the accused's self-destructive urges. Accusations that degrade or humiliate the accused may lure her into a sadomasochistic encounter that threatens the voluntariness and truthfulness of any confession to the crime. The danger is not confined to a few masochistic individuals. Understanding the role of unconscious guilt in psychic life opens the door to a more psychologically nuanced understanding of how degrading police tactics can inflame self-destructive urges in a forced sadomasochistic relationship between dominant accusers and an abject, self-punitive accused.

As with feigned sympathy, degrading interrogation tactics that exploit an individual's self-destructive urges should be reviewed with care under the due process test of voluntariness. Careful judicial scrutiny does not mean that every case will require a long, drawn-out inquiry into a defendant's state of mind. No one is suggesting that defendants and interrogators be put on the couch. Objective standards for police conduct can be established over time. But false sympathy and degradation tactics should be evaluated with care to ensure that they have not overpowered an accused's powers of resistance, thus crossing the constitutionally protected line against coerced confessions.

Displacement and Trickery

Psychoanalytic views on unconscious guilt provide an important explanatory framework for the puzzling phenomenon of false confessions. Law presumes that only a truly guilty person would have a guilty conscience for the crime. But clearly not all suspects who confess are actually guilty. DNA exonerations, laboratory studies, and surveys of prisoners and police investigators confirm that false confessions play a significant role in the criminal justice system (Lassiter and Meissner 2010, 42 and 42). Experts speculate that the documented cases only represent "the tip of the iceberg" (Redlich and Meissner 2009). We would not be overstating the problem in concluding that police-induced false confessions constitute one of the most serious causes of criminal injustice (Lassiter and Meissner 2010, 12; Leo and Ofshe 1998, 429).

We have already seen how desire for punishment may be exploited to coerce a suspect into confessing to a crime that she did not commit. Here, we will examine the phenomenon of false confessions more closely. A psychoanalytic inquiry reveals that certain police tactics, most importantly interrogation "trickery," run the risk of displacing guilt from one bad act to another, leading some innocent individuals to confess to crimes. What turns fantasy into reality – what motivates the false confession – is guilt relating to some other wrongful act, real, or imagined (Brooks 2000, 6). Unconscious guilt for prior transgressions may generate the psychological uncertainty that allows police suggestions to take hold. Law thus overlooks the one factor that might best explain the psychology of false confessions: the presence of a guilty conscience but *for something else* (23).

n *Miller* v. *United States*, Chief Judge David Bazelon famously explored the phenomenon of the innocent accused.[34] It was a seemingly innocuous case of pickpocketing. On a summer day in 1961, Cornell Watson took the bus home from work. As he was boarding the bus, he felt a slight jostle and soon discovered that his wallet was missing. Other riders on the bus reported that two men had just exited and fled down the street. Watson immediately followed, entering an alley where he saw four or five men, including Lawrence Miller, looking through a wallet. Watson yelled, "Hey, that's my wallet. Give it back to me." Miller then took flight. Watson chased Miller, who purportedly had possession of the wallet, for several blocks until Miller suddenly stopped and turned back toward Watson, reportedly saying, "Here, man, take this dollar and my ring and I will go back and get your wallet." Watson took the dollar, and about then a police officer arrived and arrested Miller. During the ensuing excitement, an unknown person returned the wallet to Watson. No one either saw Miller pick Watson's pocket or identified him as one of the men on the bus. He was convicted by a jury and received an astonishing two-to-six-year sentence (Schmeiser 2007, 318).[35]

The most damning piece of evidence tying Miller to the crime of pickpocketing involved Miller's flight from the alley. The trial judge had given the jury the following instruction on the significance of flight: "you are entitled to draw from testimony which you accept as credible a conclusion that flight on the part of a defendant was or is evidence of guilt."[36] The court of appeals agreed with Miller that this instruction was wrong, and reversed the conviction, sending the case back to the trial court for a new trial. The opinion was a short *per curiam* statement: "The judgment of the District Court is reversed."[37] But Chief Judge David Bazelon wrote an opinion setting out his individual views on the significance of Miller's flight from the alley. His opinion was long, but the point can be succinctly stated: Bazelon did not believe that flight necessarily indicates actual guilt. He did concede that flight can indicate a guilty conscience. But drawing on psychoanalysis, Bazelon argued that a guilty conscience does not always mean actual guilt for the crime charged. By running, Lawrence Miller may have enacted the equivalent of a false confession to the crime.

Bazelon drew from psychoanalytic theory to explain why an individual might develop a guilty conscience for a crime he did not commit, referencing 39 psychoanalytic sources to make the point. Bazelon noted that, early in his career, Freud had described the phenomenon in a talk given to law students: "You may be led astray... by a neurotic who reacts as though he were guilty even though he is innocent – because a lurking sense of guilt already in him assimilates the accusation made against him on this particular occasion."[38] Freud stressed that unconscious guilt for some earlier transgression underlies the present self-incriminating behavior. The individual *does* have a guilty conscience, just not for the act he is accused of committing. The individual may have confessed his guilt through behavior, but this "confession" – while true at the level of psychic experience – falsely implicates him in a crime he did not commit. We do not know whether Lawrence Miller was innocent or guilty of the pickpocketing when he ran from the alley. Miller might have run for all sorts of reasons, including simply a child-like scramble to avoid getting into trouble. Miller may also have run because he had a "consciousness of guilt" about the wallet in hand. But Bazelon forces us to consider that Miller's guilty conscious might actually have referenced some other act of wrongdoing.

The displacement of guilt reflects the kind of unconscious transference phenomenon common in mental life. Freud used the term "displacement" to describe how the mind disguises the latent meaning of a dream with the seemingly unrelated and often bizarre manifest dream content (Freud 1953b). But the mind's capacity for displacement extends well beyond dreamwork. Displacement operates along a continuum from simple reminiscence to fantasizing to psychosis: at one end, the reactivated feeling states of a prior time – Proust's emotional experience upon smelling the madeleine reminiscent of his childhood, for example – and at the other end, a full-blown, delusional reliving of past relationships and experiences in the present. Transference is a common form of displacement. It captures the idea that beliefs, emotions, and memories can shift in time and space. While highlighted in the analytic relationship, all our important relationships resonate with early child-hood experiences. Our adult lives are enriched and made meaningful by the migration of feelings, perceptions, and wishes from past to present. We view the world and other people through these well-worn psychic pathways. Psychoanalysis is a mode of treatment designed to change these transference patterns when they cause problems or suffering.

Like all emotions, therefore, guilt migrates. It can undergo displacement "such that the individual's experience of guilt about one issue may obscure a more intense guilt about another" (Auchincloss and Samberg 2012, 95). Guilt for the earlier violation – real or fantasized – unconsciously shifts to later acts of wrongdoing leading an individual to behave *as if* he were the truly guilty party. We have already encountered the kind of guilt everyone can feel from riding the strong aggressive currents of childhood. But the migration of guilt can be more immediate. Bazelon quotes Freud for the example of an innocent child accused of some wrongdo-ing, who nevertheless acts like a guilty transgressor because of guilt over some other violation of parental strictures.[39] More examples come easily to mind. One might feel relatively little conscious guilt around the death of a parent, but collapse with self-accusations upon the subsequent death of a beloved pet. One might feel no remorse after abruptly ending a close friendship, only to succumb to violent self-reproach following a minor dispute with another. One might be mysteriously overcome with guilt upon the commission of a trivial offense, unaware of the effect of an earlier, much more serious wrong. The sufferer knows herself to be guilty of something, although the true source of the guilt remains securely locked out of awareness.

The displacement of guilt explains the phenomenon of false confessions, at least in some cases. The displacement from past to present serves two needs simultaneously. The present confessional behavior (the running, the collapsing, and the self-reproach) both rationalizes unconscious guilt and alleviates it by way of the resulting punishment (Auchincloss and Samberg 2012, 95). A false confes-sion rationalizes unconscious guilt by attaching it to some known transgression. This migration of guilt reassures: "Now I understand why I feel so guilty." One's identity as a wrongdoer is externally verified. The accused may have done other bad acts in her life for which she feels she deserves to be punished, or she may suffer from guilt over fantasies dating back to early childhood. A false confes-sion thus has an integrating effect for an individual suffering from unconscious guilt to the extent it brings psychic truth into line with external reality. But false confessions also punish. They gratify the individual's desire to atone for the earlier crime. False confessions both explain the guilty conscience and carry out the sentence (Brooks 2000).

Psychoanalytically, we should be skeptical about interrogation practices that foster the displacement of guilt in other words, that specifically target guilt for behavior other than the crime at hand. Such police tactics include focusing upon an accused's guilt for other bad acts, such as domestic violence or child neglect. Police interrogation that veers off course in this way – that focuses its attention on matters unrelated to the crime – weakens the reliability of any subsequent confession. By confessing, an innocent accused may simply be submitting to the demands of a guilty conscience for punishment. When designed to enhance guilt for other, unrelated bad acts, police tactics may justify the false confession in the mind of the accused, at least in the moment. Law assumes that guilt-inducing tactics aimed at unrelated wrongs merely open the door to a suspect's admission of actual guilt for the crime at hand. But psychoanalysis suggests, to the contrary, that confessions obtained as a result of police interrogation focused on amplifying guilt for other bad acts can exploit the psychic needs of innocents.

Psychoanalytic views on the displacement of unconscious guilt give us insight into the rare but mystifying phenomenon of innocent individuals who come to *believe* that they are guilty of the crime, even momentarily. Internalized false confessions, as they are called, are an empirically documented phenomenon (Horselenberg, Josephs, and Merckelbach 2003, 6; Kassin and Kiechel 1996, 126). Paul Ingram is a well-known example (Wright 1993a; Wright 1993b). Ingram was a police officer living in Olympia, Washington. In November 1988, Ingram's two adult daughters accused him of having sexually assaulted them starting when they were five years old and continuing throughout their childhood. As the days and weeks went by, the daughters' stories became increasingly elaborate. They alleged that Ingram's friends raped them during orgies at their house, that their mother would "prepare" them for the abuse, and that the abuse extended to satanic rituals involving the slaughter of babies. At first, Ingram responded to his daughters' allegations with bewildered self-doubt: "I can't see myself doing this... [but t] here may be a dark side of me that I don't know about" (Wright 1993a, 60). Under police interrogation, he soon began confessing to raping his two daughters. Over the course of the next six months, Ingram admitted to an increasingly implausible series of offenses roughly echoing his daughters' accounts, culminating with descriptions of orgiastic satanic ritual abuse involving scores of people, dead babies, and bestiality. While his daughters' accounts were riddled with contradictions and clear falsehoods, Ingram nevertheless pleaded guilty to six counts of aggravated rape and was sentenced to 20 years in prison.

Paul Ingram's belief that he committed crimes of satanic ritual abuse eludes rational explanation. He began the interrogation believing in his own innocence, but somewhere along the way fantasy took over. How are we to make sense of this strange turn of events? Social psychologists focus on an accused's psychological suggestibility, a trait that, in the view of many, explains an individual's susceptibility to self-doubt about historical truth (Gudjonsson 1999, 105). The study of suggestion has a distinguished history in psychology. The phenomenon was the focus of the renowned European hypnotists of the late nineteenth century, including French neurologist Jean-Martin Charcot, who studied the role of suggestion under hypnosis in curing hysteria. Modern behavioral scientists study how individuals can develop uncertainty about what happened in situations in which police interrogators aggressively "suggest" that the individual committed the crime.

Psychoanalysis gives us some guidance in understanding why certain individuals are more suggestible than others under interrogation. Of course, we are all prone to some level of suggestion. We are influenced, swayed, and persuaded by others in all sorts of situations. Yet not *any* suggestion or accusation exerts a reality-loosening pull on our minds. Some people may be innately more suggestible than others, in the same way that some are more prone to daydream or to dissociate. But psychoanalysis raises the possibility that suggestibility is heightened when an individual feels strong unconscious guilt for some earlier, unrelated transgression. When the suggestion of culpability matches the unconscious guilt – when the outward accusation confirms an inner truth – then the accused may be led to believe it. A false confession answers the question: What have I done to justify the guilt that is causing me so much distress?

Paul Ingram may fall into this category. He expressed guilt for behavior other than the crime of child sexual assault. He felt he had been an abusive and cold father (Wright 1993b, 76). "I have a hard time hugging [my children], or even telling them that I love them, and, uh, I just know that's not normal" (61). His children were likely exposed to some group sexual activity in the house. At one point, he threw an axe at one of his sons in anger (76). The interrogation led him to the point of lamenting, "I wasn't a good father" (76). It also led the police interrogators to exploit this guilt. "I hope you're not going to make these girls go through a trial," was one of their tactics (60). Paul Ingram may in fact have been guilty of sexually abusing his daughters, but the evidence clearly did not support the bizarre allegations of satanic ritual abuse and dead babies. But accounts of the interrogation do indicate strong feelings of guilt for other forms of child abuse: corporal punishment, emotional berating, lack of affection. We do not know why Ingram confessed to the most bizarre crimes of satanic abuse. But we can speculate that his confession may have been a way of expiating overwhelming feelings of unconscious guilt over these *other* transgressions.

These psychoanalytic insights into the migration of guilt also raise concerns about police interrogation that relies on trickery. Interrogators lied to Ingram when they told him that his daughters had accused him of certain acts. The Court currently allows such police deception (White 1979).[40] Police investigators can lie about having videotape evidence that a suspect committed the crime when they do not; they can tell her that she failed a polygraph test when she passed; they can pretend that other people under investigation have named her as the perpetrator when they have not. There may be many reasons to oppose police trickery, including the belief that the state should be prohibited from lying to suspects as a matter of fundamental fairness and human dignity (Simon-Kerr). Justice Brennan said as much: "The deliberate use of deception and manipulation by the police is incompatible 'with a system that presumes innocence and assures that a conviction will not be secured by inquisitorial means.'"[41] But psychoanalysis uncovers another stratum of concern.

Police deception casts doubt on confessions obtained as a result of leading suspects into believing that concrete evidence of their guilt exists when none actually does. "[T]he presentation of false incriminating evidence – an interrogation ploy that is common among the police and sanctioned by many courts – can induce people to internalize blame for outcomes they did not produce" (Kassin and Kiechel 1996, 127; Ofshe and Leo 1997, 1000). Given these tactics, a person under stress, like Paul Ingram, may actually begin to doubt his own mind. Did I in fact commit the crime? Did I repress my memory of the act? Do I have a hidden dark side? Ingram said it himself: "It's almost like I'm making it up, but I'm not" (Wright 1993a, 71). In the mind of the innocent accused, unconscious guilt corroborates the false evidence. Thus for many accuseds, trickery may not ferret out the truth. To the contrary, police deceit may undermine the accused's capacity to keep unconscious guilt from validating the false accusations.

Psychoanalysis works at the boundary between psychic and historical truth. While psychoanalysis "insists on the work of patient and analyst – comparable to confessant and confessor – toward the discovery of the most hidden truths about selfhood," the "truth" arrived at in psychoanalysis is not necessarily truth in the sense of representing some material or historical reality (Brooks 2000, 54). In psychoanalysis, the patient reluctantly divulges the truth about her subjective experience, one that may or may not conform to events or experiences in the real world. As we have seen, confession may be false in fact but true to an individual's subjective experience. When an accused says

> I did it," law interprets these words as a statement about historical reality rather than, possibly, an expression of subjective guilt. Confession "can be the truth of desire, of affect, of that which make sense of things in an emotional register.
> (Kassin et al. 2010)

And when the confession is given to the police – not to a priest or analyst, but to a punishing representative of the state – psychic truth *becomes* historical truth in the form of a guilty verdict. From a psychoanalytic perspective, police interrogation that uses trickery risks transforming psychic guilt into actual guilt, and thus lead a suspect to confess to a crime she did not commit.

Can law absorb psychoanalytic insights into unconscious guilt without unduly compromising the state's ability to elicit confessions from the truly guilty? Psychoanalysis opens our eyes to the ways in which our criminal justice system resorts to the fiction of free will in the face of a much more complicated psychological reality of unconscious desires for forgiveness, self-destructive wishes, and displaced guilt. Obviously, the criminal law cannot be tailored to every irrational nuance in human nature. But the legal fiction of the freely choosing actor simply cannot be squared with the full range of psychologically-coercive tactics of criminal interrogation currently allowed by law.

Given psychoanalytic concerns about false sympathy, degradation, and trickery, courts should be careful to evaluate these methods of interrogation with a close eye for voluntariness and reliability. Justice Frankfurter best described the challenge:

> The line between proper and permissible police conduct and techniques and methods offensive to due process is, at best, a difficult one to draw, particularly in cases such as this where it is necessary to make fine judgments as to the effect of psychologically coercive pressures and inducements on the mind and will of an accused.[42]

Obviously, these methods of interrogation cannot be eliminated entirely, in part because law enforcement legitimately uses less severe forms of them, and in part because eliminating *all* traces of sympathy, degradation, and trickery would be impossible. All human interactions are emotionally colored, to some extent, and all pressure tactics have some element of deceit, however, small. Yet by drawing attention to the risk associated with these methods, psychoanalysis calls for eliminating the most egregious practices from our criminal justice system. Psychoanalytic insights into interrogation tactics will not revolutionize the law or threaten law's general presumption of free will, but it holds law to its own best ideals of fundamental fairness in the interrogation room.

Notes

1 This is excerpted from Chapter 4 of *Law and the Unconscious: A Psychoanalytic Perspective* (New Haven, CT: Yale Press, 2017).
2 Arizona v. Fulminante, 499 U.S. 279, 296 (1991) (quoting Bruton v. United States, 391 U.S. 123, 139–40 (1968) (White, J., dissenting)).
3 Brewer v. Williams, 430 U.S. 387, 420 (1977) (Burger, C.J., dissenting) (citing Theodor Reik, The Compulsion to Confess (1925)).
4 Culombe v. Connecticut, 367 U.S. 568, 616 (1961).
5 *Id.* at 582.
6 Dickerson v. United States, 530 U.S. 428, 434 (2000) (quoting Stein v. New York, 346 U.S. 156, 185 (1953)).
7 See Miranda v. Arizona, 384 U.S. 436 (1966); see also Seidman 1992, 745.
8 See *Dickerson*, 530 U.S. at 444.
9 *Culombe*, 367 U.S. at 602.
10 *Dickerson*, 530 U.S. at 515.
11 Brewer v. Williams, 430 U.S. 387 (1977).
12 *Id.* at 392, 393.
13 See Nix v. Williams, 467 U.S. 431, 440 (1984).
14 *Brewer*, 430 U.S. at 419.
15 *Id.* at 434 (White, J., dissenting).
16 *Culombe*, 367 U.S. at 642 (Harlan, J., dissenting).

17 *Fulminante*, 499 U.S. at 293.
18 *Miranda*, 384 U.S. at 469.
19 *Id*. at 457.
20 *Id*. at 465.
21 *Id*. at 467.
22 *Dickerson*, 530 U.S. at 444.
23 Miller v. Fenton, 474 U.S. 104, 107 n.2 (1985).
24 *Miranda*, 384 U.S. at 451 (quoting Fred E. Inbau et al., Criminal Interrogation and Confessions 40 (1962)).
25 *Id*. at 450.
26 *Culombe*, 367 U.S. at 574, 575.
27 *Stein*, 346 U.S. at 185.
28 Miller v. United States, 320 F.2d 767, 772 n.10 (D.C. Cir. 1963) (quoting Gregory Zilboorg, The Psychology of the Criminal Act and Punishment 50 (1954)).
29 *Miranda*, 384 U.S. at 451 (quoting Charles E. O'Hara & Gregory L. O'Hara, Fundamentals of Criminal Investigation 112 (1956)).
30 *Id*. at 458 n.27.
31 Garrity v. New Jersey, 385 U.S. 493 (1967).
32 *Id*. at 497 n.5 (quoting Norman Lamm, *The Fifth Amendment and Its Equivalent in Jewish Law*, 17 Decalogue 9, 12 (1967)).
33 *Id*.
34 See Miller v. United States, 320 F.2d 767 (D.C. Cir. 1963).
35 *Id*. at 768.
36 *Id*. at 770 n.5.
37 *Id*. at 767.
38 *Id*. at 772 (quoting Sigmund Freud, *Psycho-Analysis and the Establishment of the Facts in Legal Proceedings,* in 9 Standard Edition 97 (1906/1959)).
39 See *Miller*, 320 F.2d at 772.
40 See Frazier v. Cupp, 394 U.S. 731 (1969).
41 Illinois v. Perkins, 496 U.S. 292, 303 (1990) (Brennan, J., concurring) (quoting Miller v. Fenton, 474 U.S. at 116).
42 *Culombe*, 367 U.S. at 575.

References

Akhtar, Salman. 2009. *Comprehensive Dictionary of Psychoanalysis*. London: Karnac Books.

Auchincloss, Elizabeth L. and Eslee Samberg, eds. 2012. *Psychoanalytic Terms and Concepts*. New Haven, CT: Yale University Press.

Benjamin, Jessica. 1988. *The Bonds of Love: Psychoanalysis, Feminism, and the Problem of Domination*. New York: Pantheon Books.

Berliner, Bernhard. 1958. "The Role of Object Relations in Moral Masochism." *Psychoanalytic Quarterly* 27 (1): 38–56.

Brooks, Peter. 2000. *Troubling Confessions: Speaking Guilt in Law and Literature*. Chicago, IL: University of Chicago Press.

Freud, Sigmund. 1953a. "Fragment of an Analysis of a Case of Hysteria." In Vol. 7 of *The Standard Edition of the Complete Psychological Works of Sigmund Freud*, translated and edited by James Strachey, 1–123. London: Hogarth Press, 1953–74.

———. 1953b. "The Interpretation of Dreams." In Vol. 5 of *The Standard Edition of the Complete Psychological Works of Sigmund Freud*, translated and edited by James Strachey, 1–339. London: Hogarth Press, 1953–74.

———. 1955. "'A Child Is Being Beaten': A Contribution to the Study of the Origin of Sexual Perversions." In Vol. 17 of *The Standard Edition of the Complete Psychological Works of Sigmund Freud*, translated and edited by James Strachey, 175–205. London: Hogarth Press, 1953–74.

———. 1957. "Some Character-Types Met with in Psychoanalytic Work." In Vol. 14 of *The Standard Edition of the Complete Psychological Works of Sigmund Freud*, translated and edited by James Strachey, 309–37. London: Hogarth Pres, 1953–74.

———. 1961a. "The Economic Problem of Masochism." In Vol. 19 of *The Standard Edition of the Complete Psychological Works of Sigmund Freud*, translated and edited by James Strachey, 155–73. London: Hogarth Press, 1953–74.

———. 1961b. "The Ego and the Id." In Vol. 19 of *The Standard Edition of the Complete Psychological Works of Sigmund Freud*, translated and edited by James Strachey, 1–60. London: Hogarth Press, 1953–74.

———. 1964. "The Dissection of the Psychical Personality." In Vol. 22 of *The Standard Edition of the Complete Psychological Works of Sigmund Freud*, translated and edited by James Strachey, London: Hogarth Press, 1953–74.

Glick, Robert A. and Donald I. Meyers, eds. 1988. *Masochism: Current Psychoanalytic Perspectives*. Hillsdale, NJ: Analytic Press.

Gudjonsson, Gisli H. 1999. *The Psychology of Interrogations, Confessions and Testimony*. Chichester, NY: Wiley.

Herman, Judith. 1997. *Trauma and Recovery: The Aftermath of Violence--from Domestic Abuse to Political Terror*. New York: Basic Books.

Horselenberg, Robert, Harald Merckelbach, and Sarah Josephs. 2003. "Individual Differences and False Confessions: A Conceptual Replication of Kassin and Kiechel (1996)." *Psychology, Crime & Law* 9, no. 1: 1–8.

Inbau, Fred E., John E. Reid, Joseph P. Buckley, and Brian C. Jayne. 2013. *Essentials of the Reid Technique: Criminal Interrogation and Confessions*. 2nd ed. Burlington, MA: Jones & Bartlett Learning.

Jacobson, Edith. 1964. *The Self and the Object World*. New York: International Universities Press.

Kassin, Saul M. and Katherine L. Kiechel. 1996. "The Social Psychology of False Confessions." *Psychological Science* 7, no. 3 (May): 125–128.

Kassin, Saul M., Steven A. Drizin, Thomas Grisso, Gisli H. Gudjonsson, Richard A. Leo, and Allison D. Redlich. 2010. "Police-Induced Confessions, Risk Factors, and Recommendations: Looking Ahead." *Law and Human Behavior* 34, no. 1 (February): 3–38.

Kernberg, Otto. 1995. "Psychoanalytic Object Relations Theories." In *Psychoanalysis: The Major Concepts*, edited by Burness Moore and Bernard Fines, 450–462. New Haven, CT: Yale University Press.

Klein, Melanie. 1946. "Notes on Some Schizoid Mechanisms." *International Journal of Psychoanalysis* 27: 99–110.

———. 2002a. *Love, Guilt and Reparation and Other Works 1921–1945*. New York: Simon and Schuster.

———. 2002b. *Envy and Gratitude and Other Works 1946–1963*. New York: Free Press.

Lamm, Norman. 1956. "The Fifth Amendment and Its Equivalent in the Halakhah." *Judaism* 5: 53–64.

Lassiter, Daniel and Christian A. Meissner. 2010. *Police Interrogations and False Confessions: Current Research, Practice, and Policy Recommendations*. Washington, DC: American Psychological Association.

Leo, Richard A. 2015. *Police Interrogation and American Justice*. Cambridge, MA: Harvard University Press.

Leo, Richard A. and Richard J. Ofshe. 1998. "The Consequences of False Confessions: Deprivations of Liberty and Miscarriages of Justice in the Age of Psychological Interrogation." *Journal of Criminal Law and Criminology* 88, no. 2 (Winter): 429–496.

Levine, Samuel J. 2006. "An Introduction to Self-Incrimination in Jewish Law, with Application to the American Legal System: A Psychological and Philosophical Analysis." *Loyola of Los Angeles International and Comparative Law Review* 28, no. 2: 257–277.

Loewald, Hans W. 1979. "The Waning of the Oedipus Complex." *Journal of the American Psychoanalytic Association* 27, no. 4 (Fall): 751–775.

Maimonides, Moses. 1977. *The Book of Judges*. Book 14 of *The Code of Maimonides (Mishneh Torah)*, translated by Abraham M Hershman. New Haven, CT: Yale University Press, 1949–2004.

Meissner, Christian A. and Saul M. Kassin. 2004. "'You're Guilty, So Just Confess!': Cognitive and Behavioral Confirmation Biases in the Interrogation Room." In *Interrogations, Confessions, and Entrapment*, edited by G. Daniel Lassiter, 85–106. New York: Springer.

Ofshe, Richard J. and Richard A. Leo. 1997. "The Decision to Confess Falsely: Rational Choice and Irrational Action." *Denver University Law Review* 74, no. 4 (January): 979–1122.

Redlich, Christian and Christian Meissner. 2009. "Technique and Controversies in the Interrogation of Suspects." In *Psychological Science in the Courtroom*, edited by Jennifer L. Skeem, Kevin S. Douglas, and Scott O. Lilienfeld, 124–148. New York: Guildford Press.

Reik, Theodor. 1959. *The Compulsion to Confess: On the Psychoanalysis of Crime and Punishment*. New York: Farrar, Straus and Cudahy.

Sandler, Joseph and Anne-Marie Sandler. 1987. "The Past Unconscious, the Present Unconscious, and the Vicissitudes of Guilt." *International Journal of Psychoanalysis* 68 (3): 331–341.

Schmeiser, Susan R. 2007. "Punishing Guilt." *American Imago* 64, no. 3 (Fall): 317–337.

Seidman, Louis Michael. 1992. "Brown and Miranda." *California Law Review* 80, no. 3 (May): 673–753.

Simon-Ker, Julia. "Legitimacy and Deceptive Interrogations." Unpublished manuscript, on file with author.

White, Welsh S. 1979. "Police Trickery in Inducing Confessions." *University of Pennsylvania Law Review* 127, no. 3: 581–629.

Wright, Lawrence. "Remembering Satan--Part I." *The New Yorker*, May 17, 1993a.

Wright, Lawrence. "Remembering Satan--Part II." *The New Yorker*, May 24, 1993b.

Chapter 9

Afterword

Anne C. Dailey

When I arrived at Austen Riggs in the fall of 2012 for my semester as an Erikson Scholar, I expected that I would be separated off in my office, not having much contact with the day-to-day life of the institution. Instead, I was thrown into this utterly amazing world I didn't know existed – a psychiatric care facility that took seriously the life of the mind, and the deep complexity and richness, difficulties, and resilience of the human psyche.

I felt I had changed universes. The world at Riggs was unspeakably far from the view of the individual that informs and guides the law. I began my book because I had grown weary of trying to reconcile this legal fiction of the reasonable person or rational actor with what I knew about human experience. Assuming that people are rational in all circumstances leads to unjust results in many cases – people who go to jail for deeds they did not commit, or did not intend to commit; people whose children are removed from them when in fact they are devoted parents; people who enter into contracts that are clearly unfair. I turned to psychoanalysis in order to come up with a better account of why people behave the way they do.

And here are some of the "subversive" psychoanalytic ideas that I draw on in the book, ones entirely familiar to everyone connected to Riggs, but worth repeating here: (1) the idea that there is an unconscious and that much of what goes on in our unconscious minds is repressed, (2) that our early relationships determine much about who we are, (3) that people utilize particular defenses, such as denial and projection, (4) that we are conflicted beings who can be self-destructive, want things that hurt us, betray our own deeply held values, and (5) that transference colors most of our intense personal interactions and experiences. The book aims to correct for injustices in the system that arise from the denial of these core aspects of what it means to be a human being.

Yet it is precisely these ideas that lawyers and judges reject because they undermine the fundamental legal principles of free will and rationality. These are truths that the law is not eager to accept. To challenge the fundamental principles of rationality and free will necessarily opens the door to the radical, disruptive implications of psychoanalysis for the settled legal order. The question for law is how to recognize the role of the unconscious in our everyday lives while at the same time holding people responsible for their decisions and behaviors. Psychoanalysis may tell us that people often act from unconscious motivations, but the law still needs

DOI: 10.4324/9781003322627-21

to *judge*, which means the legal system must impose some degree of personal accountability even where it is impossible to say that an individual was fully aware of what she did.

Let me take an example. In the area of criminal law, we assume that a suspect's confession is the strongest evidence of guilt. For why would a rational person confess to a crime that he did not commit? But psychoanalysis confirms what we should already know: that individuals, out of unconscious guilt or other self-destructive forces, might indeed falsely confess to a crime. Drawing on psychoanalytic ideas about transference, guilt, and masochism, I advocate in the book for reforming the rules governing interrogation which allow the police to exploit a suspect's need for approval and unconscious guilt in ways that override the suspect's powers of rational decision making.

The book is my effort to show how it is possible to introduce psychoanalytic ideas into the law while holding onto the basic fundamentals of a legal system that values individual autonomy and personal responsibility. This effort has its parallel in psychoanalysis. This tension between the model of the rational actor and the psychoanalytic idea of the dynamic unconscious mirrors Freud's own ambivalent stance between Enlightenment beliefs in rational thought and inquiry, and his uncovering of a Romantic unconscious realm beset by aggressive, irrational, and often self-destructive impulses and desires. To undergo psychoanalytic treatment is to embrace this ambivalence – to believe in the mind's powers of reason while at the same time acknowledging the hold that unconscious desires and beliefs have on us. We necessarily behave "as if" we are rational, knowing, integrated selves despite knowing full well that much of what we do is beyond our conscious control. We give it names: intuition, gut instinct, déjà vu, the uncanny. We assume an "as if" stance because we need to operate in the world, to engage with others, to rise above brute instinctual forces. As Freud would say, civilization demands it.

And the law demands it, too. In the courtroom, we act "as if" the trial establishes some true historical reality at the same time that we know trials produce a legal narrative that may be only loosely related to historical truth. We act "as if" individual actors are rational when of course we know they're not.

So my project is to make this "as if" status of the law clear. What we see today is a legal regime that is "willfully blind" to the reality of the deeper, more transgressive forces in human nature. When we keep firmly in mind that the autonomous rational legal actor is a legal fiction, one that we embrace with ambivalence, then we find ourselves in a realm of what I call good-enough judging: a style more uncertain and skeptical, less harshly punitive, more open to understanding the people caught up in the legal system and what has brought them there.

Being an Erikson Scholar has been central to my identity as a scholar doing interdisciplinary work. I came to Riggs hoping that I could ground the psychoanalytic ideas that I was using in the clinical work being done here, and that is exactly what happened. More broadly, I was deeply inspired by watching the clinicians at Riggs making the effort to understand their patients in deep and holistic ways. My time at Riggs helped to fortify me in my effort to bring the law into line with the reality of human experience and subjectivity.

Chapter 10

The Hero's Personality[1]

Mark Lipton

Decades after the real era of Mad Men there was Peter Arnell, the legendary advertising impresario who helped shape brands the likes of Pepsi, Samsung, DKNY, and Bank of America, and the boss from hell (Steinhaurer 1997). One former employee, who spoke to me for this book on the condition of anonymity, described Arnell as punishing a personal assistant by making him spend a meeting sitting under a desk. Other employees and clients spoke of Arnell excoriating office workers and provoking tears for mundane tasks or utterances.

"He has this remarkable capacity to be both the most intoxicating character—lovable, brilliant, seductively intellectual—and then turn on a dime and be staggeringly cruel," a former business associate recalled in a *Newsweek* feature on the "brand guru." "He is unencumbered with any sense of morality. Until you experience it firsthand, it's just completely and utterly unfathomable" (Lyons 2009).

Yuck. And the obvious question is how exactly did Peter Arnell get this way? What drove this sick behavior? Arnell's early life story is classic among a certain strand of entrepreneurs: he overcame obstacles through sheer grit and brilliantly invented a new life that left his past far, far behind.

Arnell grew up in Sheepshead Bay in Brooklyn. His maternal grandfather, Nathan Hutt, was a Jewish immigrant from Russia and a fishmonger who raised Peter and his sister, along with his wife, after Arnell's father abandoned the family. As a child, Arnell also had a weight problem. "I was always the fat guy," he said. "And fat guys always did well in school. I did well. That's how I got attention" (Linnett 2022).

Arnell was influenced by Hutt's strong work ethic—sometimes rising before dawn to work with him at Manhattan's Fulton Fish Market. Arnell graduated from Brooklyn Technical High School, studying architecture, and later had the good fortune to hook up with postmodernist architect Michael Graves. He met Graves at a lecture and talked his way into an internship at Graves's offices (Linett 2022).

Peter Arnell was on his way.

He got into advertising after he met a Princeton architecture student, Ted Bickford, and they started a print design shop together in SoHo. Their big break came when the fashion designer Donna Karan asked them to design an ad for her. Later, they designed the iconic DKNY logo, with the Manhattan skyline in

DOI: 10.4324/9781003322627-22

the distance. By the mid-1980s, the Arnell-Bickford agency was on a roll, with clients that included Bank of America, Chanel, Condé Nast, and Tommy Hilfiger. Arnell, still in his late twenties, was driven to succeed—growing the firm to book millions of revenue. And he liked the finer things in life, too, eventually acquiring an 8,000-square-foot penthouse in Tribeca and an estate in tony Katonah, New York.

Yet even as Arnell won more accolades for his work, stories began to circulate about his volatile temper and his misogyny. The harsh reality of working for Arnell would eventually be exposed in detail by a sexual harassment suit brought against him in the 1990s. The suit was novel at the time because it didn't accuse Arnell of making unwanted sexual advances to the plaintiffs, but rather of verbally abusing them during "fits of rage" simply because they were women. "Mr. Arnell constantly degraded and abused me and other female members of my staff in front of other male employees" is how one plaintiff put it. "On numerous occasions, I heard Mr. Arnell say, 'Those women out there are [expletive deleted] useless,'" another former employee detailed in the deposition. And also, "While yelling at me from a distance of approximately one inch from my face, Mr. Arnell asked me how I could be so [expletive deleted] stupid to ask a caller to leave his beeper number" (Steinhaurer 1997).

In responding to the plaintiff's allegations, Arnell's lawyer pointed out his behavior was "not illegal" and claimed his "right to free speech." The essence of Arnell's defense: "As case law demonstrates, words like 'stupid,' 'useless,' 'worthless,' and 'incompetent' constitute nonactionable, protected opinions" (Steinhaurer 1997).

In 2007, when Arnell made Gawker's "Worst Boss of the Year," one employee/ reader gave a complicated review of the ad man, finding the ability to forgive him his considerable faults:

> It's all true. Arnell is a difficult boss as well as a sadist with a lower case, sans serif 's.' He's also a crude bully, a terrible coward and famously insincere. But, in his favor, when he's not pretending to kiss the ass of the insipid rich, famous and powerful, he shows a refreshing contempt for authority and takes an anarchistic delight in creative destruction. His saving grace is that the man is ultimately an aesthete. Of his many fetishes, his love of beauty has compelled him to create some of the most beautiful advertising work in the last twenty years.
>
> (Gould 2007)

(These same rationalizations would later be applied to Steve Jobs.)

Arnell's career would eventually hit major turbulence after controversial design work on the Tropicana and Pepsi brands, and later, through a fallout with Omnicom, the company that bought his advertising firm in 2001 (Arnell 2010, 22).

Arnell's behavior begs two questions: Why would someone so successful be so mean? And what drives a guy like this? The answer can be found in the List of Ten, a group of common characteristics that decades of research strongly suggests entrepreneurial leaders share. We can all think of successful entrepreneurial examples, from the triumphant nerd turned billionaire to the working-class Joe who rose from nothing to command a vast empire. But while the various types of entrepreneurs and the fields they work in are varied, their behavior patterns are not. On first glance, the list might seem overwhelmingly positive in that many of these characteristics would seem to increase an individual's potential. What's wrong with ambition and drive, you might ask? The answer is nothing—in moderation. The trouble comes when an individual is all about the need to achieve and when ambition eclipses empathy. In fact, when too much of one or more of the characteristics on this list is "expressed," to use the psychologists' term, it can lead to diagnosable personality problems.

The List of Ten: Characteristics of an Entrepreneurial Personality

Need for Achievement

You don't climb from a broken home in the depths of Brooklyn to the pinnacle of the advertising world unless you simply must succeed. A deep need for achievement was among the first variables ever associated with entrepreneurs—it's the stalwart anchor of entrepreneurial traits. Arnell has it in spades, as do most of the other men discussed in this book.

The need to achieve was first researched in depth by the psychological theorist David McClelland, who spent most of his career trying to understand what motivates us as human beings. McClelland's question was simple: Why do some of us strive to excel, while others try to skate by? Unconvinced these differences were simply personal idiosyncrasies, McClelland sought to lay out underlying laws of behavior that could explain and even predict individual choices and life trajectories. McClelland viewed human motivation as the result of three basic needs—the need to achieve, the need for power, and the need to affiliate with others (McClelland 1988, 1574–1579). The relative importance each of these holds for an individual determines how strong their drive to succeed will be.

The need to achieve can be boiled down to a strong desire for success and realizing it through challenging situations. It starts developing early, kids picking it up through life experiences and by reading the value signals of our culture. Troubled or stable, healthy or dysfunctional backgrounds can also shape this desire. Individuals who are forced to master problems on their own earlier on in life tend to exhibit a higher need to achieve in adulthood. That certainly jives with Arnell's situation as a boy who was abandoned by his father, and we saw how a rough upbringing shaped Aaron as well. We'll see similar backgrounds in other entrepreneurs later in this book.

McClelland's findings have largely stood the test of time. In 2004, a group of psychologists confirmed that the need for achievement is closely associated with the choice of an entrepreneurial occupation and with success in entrepreneurship (Collins, Hanges, and Locke 2004, 95–117).

It's not hard to imagine how this trait can take a wrong turn. The desire can be so powerful that high achievers see others as mere tools rather than people. Individuals might feel they are above the rules, given the grand importance of what they are doing. The most published organizational psychologist in the history of the field, Edwin Locke, sees the need for achievement as nothing less than the moral authority to do what you must to satisfy your personal needs (Locke and Baum 2007, 93–112). In short, the individual has a moral obligation, or passion, to achieve his dreams. Locke (standing on Ayn Rand's shoulders) implies that one's own happiness is the highest moral purpose. This obliges entrepreneurs to put their work before other priorities because acting in their own interest is conflated with what is right. Whether the entrepreneur is in business or politics or another sector, they come to see their life's work and mission as so important that all else must be secondary.

Drive

Needing to achieve—and achieve big—is one thing, but doing so is quite another. That's why drive is such an all-important factor for entrepreneurs. At its root, drive is composed of three elements: proactivity, ambition, and energy. Entrepreneurs are not ivory-tower intellectuals, content to sit and dream. They're action oriented, with a compelling need to make things happen and to make their vision real. Proactive rather than passive, they become impatient for results. Entrepreneurial ambition focuses on the operational challenges and on outlining the specific steps needed to move toward a high-level goal.

Energy is the third essential ingredient of drive. Any person trying to propel themselves to the height of their field needs to have a high level of raw endurance. They need to be able to work long hours, tolerate physical discomfort, and stay focused with no sleep, little food, and zero downtime. Bringing organizations from idea to working reality—often referred to as "standing up" a firm—takes enormous amounts of effort. Drive, including high energy and stamina, is critical to managing these demands. Those with drive go further in life and work. But a determination to make things happen, and now, can lead these types to rush forward with such intensity that they dismiss the feelings of others, intrude on their turf, ignore the potential contributions of others, or just shove them out of the picture altogether.

In fact, drive, particularly for entrepreneurial personalities, is embodied by a strong desire for mastery and can mask underlying insecurity. Karen Horney, the prominent twentieth-century psychologist who developed an essential theory of neurosis, first showed how the incessant drive to be the best is closely related to doubt (Horney 1991). Raging drive, in some cases, owes something to the fear of amounting to nothing. Simply put, some ambitious people are neurotically obsessed with impressing others. In many of these cases, while they appear confident, they lack independence and self-esteem. Their drive to succeed is simply about trying to look good in other people's eyes.

Autonomy

A familiar reason people strike out on their own is that they can't stand working for others or depending on a team for results. If you create your own company or make it as a star athlete, you may feel accountable only to yourself. It's common to hear stories of highly successful people who are incapable of sharing responsibility and want to make everything happen themselves.

Autonomy, in other words, is a key entrepreneurial trait. Those craving autonomy not only are drawn to careers where they don't have to follow the normal rules, but they also tend to prefer working on their own without direct oversight from others (Brandstätter 1997, 157–177; Cromie 2000, 7–30).

Nobody succeeds entirely on their own, of course, but there are various spheres where the individual, not the group, may seem to be the central player: politics; medicine; sports; the creative arts like music, acting, or directing; and business entrepreneurship. In fact, while the history of technology start-ups looks like a parade of partnerships—Steve Jobs and Steve Wozniak (Apple), Bill Gates and Paul Allen (Microsoft), Larry Ellison and Robert N. Miner (Oracle), and Mark Zuckerberg and Dustin Moskovitz (Facebook)—none of those "partners" stayed together.

It's a phenomenon not only with business entrepreneurs, of course. We can see prescient examples in politics. Shortly after the election of New York City Mayor Bill de Blasio, the two most powerful Democratic politicians in New York State—de Blasio and Governor Andrew Cuomo—diverged to stake out extreme positions. Instead of working together, the two started a public "war of independence," and their tension and one-upmanship hurt the same voters who had put them there. While neither man may make the cut as "mean," they are both clearly entrepreneurial actors where party affiliation is outweighed by their strong needs for autonomy.

And there's the rub with entrepreneurs: they deeply desire autonomy and work in fields that reward individual initiative, yet they ultimately need others to bring their success to scale. Any enterprise that is likely to generate major wealth, political power, or fame is just as likely to entail constant interaction with others. Entrepreneurs need to hire, organize, and inspire a collection of people with diverse points of view. Particularly key is recruiting others with complementary skills and then trusting them to do their jobs. Successful entrepreneurs are able to call up collaborative skills and behaviors to a point, and many can create their own organizations and sustain them—sometimes for years. But being a brilliant creator is not enough. The entrepreneur also needs to be a savvy politician, a charismatic speaker, an inspiring coach, a bit of a technical expert, and an efficient administrator. Building a company, winning the Super Bowl, and passing new laws all require nurturing a set of interdependent relationships and interaction. Positive interaction. But the prevailing need for autonomy can get in the way. The emphasis on rugged individualism is so prevalent in Western culture in general, and in the United States in particular, that working with others is often diminished as an important entrepreneurial characteristic.

Need for Control

In addition to a high need for achievement, the best organizational builders also exhibit a strong need for power. That power takes different forms: personal power to direct others and socialized power to organize a team toward a larger goal. Research holds that those individuals who possess a high need for both achievement and power and who exhibit a high degree of self-control are the most successful entrepreneurs in society, so long as their need for power is directed toward positive social outcomes.

But many entrepreneurs are preoccupied with the need for power over others. This affects their ability to take direction or to give it properly, which in turn alters their aptitude for getting along with others. Some have what I call "authority ambivalence." They are filled with fantasies of grandiosity, power, influence, and authority, but they simultaneously feel helpless. As their fantasies become real, they develop a painful fear that their continued desires for "more" and "better" will spiral and put them ultimately at the mercy of others—the very people they are often intent on controlling.

Control issues are deeply embedded. Strong managers can identify in positive and constructive ways with authority figures, even looking to them as role models. Many entrepreneurs are less adaptable. Those with high needs for control are suspicious about authority and often lack finesse when confronted by themes of dominance and submission. For them, structure can be stifling. They can work with others in structured situations only if they both design and run the game. It's no wonder that successful entrepreneurs sometimes get forced out by investors, that star athletes often have conflicts with coaches and teammates, or that little gets done when the politicians in the US Congress are unable to collaborate. If there's any doubt the world of politics can mimic the characteristics and compulsions of corporate entrepreneurs, we need look no further than Michael Grimm.

Dogged by a potentially devastating tax fraud and campaign finance investigation near the end of his first term, the New York City congressman was accustomed to high levels of control when he was an entrepreneurial businessman. His 2014 reelection campaign tested him, with the charges causing an increasing degradation of his credibility, and the local press was all over him. On January 28, 2014, Grimm lost it with a local TV reporter who asked him about the charges. On camera, Grimm threatened to both break the reporter in half and throw him off the balcony on which they were standing. Though Grimm won the election, he later pled guilty to federal tax evasion. Going into his second term as a convicted felon, he refused to resign, but the party finally persuaded him to quit in early January 2015.

The dark side of an overwhelming need for control is obvious. Pejorative terms such as "control freak" and "micromanager" have long been part of our lexicon, and nobody likes to work for, or with, these kinds of people, though we'll often dismiss obsessive control in the face of perceived "genius" or talent. Trust, too, is a factor here, since for any act of delegation in a relationship, the decision to keep a tight grasp on control is really about trust—or, more accurately, distrust of others. Delegation is always, at its core, an act of trust.

Internal Locus of Control

Believing deeply in their destiny and future is crucial for entrepreneurs, as is believing in their own ability to influence the world around them. This internal sense of self-determination makes success seem more likely and increases motivation. A strong need for control, combined with an internal locus of control, can shape an entrepreneur's domineering style. They may enjoy the power to direct and even intimidate, to evoke obedience if not respect. Tough and unsentimental, they may see themselves as effective leaders because they coerce performance from subordinates. They get stuff done.

But the threat of external control can preoccupy many entrepreneurs. The fear of someone dominating them or infringing on their will often create a sense of impotence. Unfortunately, the conflict does not remain internalized. Those deeply concerned about being in control don't admire or tolerate autonomy in others; they want people who will do their bidding.

Impulsivity

In a fast-moving, competitive world, being quick on the draw can translate into a decisive edge. But impulsivity is also dangerous. The absence of careful planning and an inability to delegate can introduce a serious threat to any venture—whether a company, a campaign, or the building of a celebrity brand. Impulsive entrepreneurs may find it difficult, if not painful, to differentiate between day-to-day operational decision making and more strategic actions. His penchant for relying on "hunches" makes for a time horizon that is biased to the short term.

Impulsivity for the entrepreneur reflects a shortsighted fixation on immediate gratification that reaps collateral damage. High levels of impulsivity may make someone more likely to cleverly manipulate or deceive others for personal gain. At the extreme, those with impulse drives may act out toward others or may have compulsive needs for gambling, shopping, or sex.

Suspicion of Others

Entrepreneurs have a disproportionate tendency over the general population to distrust those in the world around them, and this can easily extend to those who work for them. They fear becoming victims, and in reaction, they develop their own means for monitoring their environment, keeping watch for signs that confirm their suspicions. Suspicion of others is closely related not only to impulsivity but also to the desire for autonomy and the need for control we've already discussed.

Distrust, and the simultaneous monitoring for threat, can serve the powerful entrepreneur as it may relate to some business needs—competitor moves, supplier manipulation, radical changes in customer preferences, for example. Intel's tough former CEO and idol of Steve Jobs, Andy Grove, made this argument in his book *Only the Paranoid Survive,* and his huge success suggests that maybe there was something to the idea (Grove 2010). But the picture looks darker to the extent that distrust of others isn't motivated at its core by business needs but by the need for self-protection and a fear of being victimized by someone else. In the face of ongoing suspicion, the people around the entrepreneur suffer deteriorating morale as his need for control trumps the imperative of organizational effectiveness and wounds the enterprise. In order to alleviate the entrepreneur's ever-present suspicion, those around him become sycophants, the last people someone in power needs giving them advice.

Biographers and journalists have long noted Rupert Murdoch's nearly obsessive control needs and suspicious nature. James Murdoch may have been easy for his father to control, but if the senior Murdoch had put in place a more independent, seasoned executive, he or she may well have steered News Corp clear of the massive wiretapping scandal of 2011. But in 2014, Murdoch the father transferred "future leadership of two publicly held firms worth a combined $80 billion to his two sons, almost as casually as if they were the keys to the family station wagon" (Carr 2014). The message was self-evident: the family legacy was to remain intact, regardless of what might have been best for public shareholders.

A ranking executive at the firm subsequently told the New York Times, "How did you think it was going to turn out?" (Carr 2014)

Finally, in June 2015, 84-year-old Rupert announced his diminishing role by solidifying his sons' authority, with both sons expected to take over the most important executive roles in the company. These moves may not have been the best for the long-term growth of a $78 billion worldwide monolith but, for better or worse, he retains the control he's had for the past 60 years.

Predisposition to Take Risks

Richard Cantillon, the eighteenth-century Irish French economist, laid claim to the term "entrepreneur" by defining it as a "bearer of risk" (Surowiecki 2014b). And risk-taking was one of the first characteristics ever investigated in relation to entrepreneurs, as economists theorized that it was the primary differentiator between entrepreneurs and non-business-owning managers (Knight 1921). If everyone had the same comfort with risk, many more people might be their own boss. There is now a large and nuanced literature about risk-taking and entrepreneurship, but one thing is clear: those who strike out on their own, and aim high, tend to have a reasonably strong appetite for risk. What's tricky, though, is having the right level of appetite. Some successful entrepreneurs get as far as they do because of their willingness to put everything on the line (and refusal to take credit for failure). Yet this same risk-seeking can lead to their undoing where a more measured taking of account would prevent high-stakes losses.

Self-confidence

To get ahead, entrepreneurs must believe they can deal with the world, meet life's challenges, overcome obstacles, and achieve the goals they set for themselves. All this boils down to good old-fashioned self-confidence, typically developed from early childhood experiences in which one undertakes independent projects, masters difficulties, and succeeds. Yet the line between self-confidence and arrogance is famously thin.

As far back as 1921, the economist Frank Knight argued that the function of entrepreneurs was to "specialize in risk-taking" (Knight 1921). But studies of entrepreneurs find that, in general, they're as risk-averse as everyone else. However, when it comes to starting a business, they are daring. Does this contradict the rule that came before about their predisposition to take risks? It is very much consistent because self-confidence influences entrepreneurs' behavior so powerfully. A study in the *Journal of Business Venturing* found entrepreneurs to be overconfident about their ability to prevent bad outcomes and also overconfident about the prospects of their business. The examination of approximately 3,000 entrepreneurs found that 81 percent thought their businesses had at least a 75 percent chance of success, and one-third thought there was no chance they would fail, data that bear no relation to reality (Cassar and Craig 2009).

Marked overconfidence is a genuine psychological hazard. And whether it's due to ignorance or to some psychological disorder that denies real risks, overconfidence indicates that an entrepreneur may not be in touch with reality. Overconfidence also tips easily into arrogance, which usually combines excess self-confidence with a gross underestimation of risk, including of one's competitors.

In today's start-up culture, this tendency for false, self-focused optimism is intensified by other factors. Developing new products and finding seed funding often gives early stage positive feedback to entrepreneurs—possibly false feedback that underestimates the risk. Amplifying this is the "fail fast, fail often" mind-set that gives many entrepreneurs gold stars for trying to develop the Next Big Thing. But two comprehensive studies show that practice does not make perfect. One study found that around 80 percent of entrepreneurs with unsuccessful businesses would go on to fail again. The other, a study of German entrepreneurial ventures, concluded past failures made entrepreneurs more likely to fail than those trying their hand for the first time (Cassar and Craig 2009, 149–164).

Not surprisingly, we also hold these con(fidence) artists in some esteem; there are parts of them, alluring parts, that we admire and even wish to emulate. They are independent and usually self-made. The same men who are willing to risk everything and, in truth, do have outsized talents can prove to be horrendous bosses and partners. Now a philanthropic hero, Bill Gates in his earlier CEO years rarely let his employees forget that he was smarter than they were, while Steve Jobs was inclined to let an underling know what a "stupid shithead" the employee was for not living up to Jobs's expectations. Then there is the oft-told joke about Oracle's Larry Ellison: "Question: What's the difference between God and Larry Ellison? Answer: God doesn't think he's Larry Ellison."

Need for Approval

Given the nine characteristics noted already, the need for approval may seem counterintuitive. These guys, you may think, probably don't care what others think of them. But entrepreneurs often reveal a great need for admiration and applause and an overriding concern about being heard and recognized. Entrepreneurs don't seek direct approval so much as they search for more oblique approval. Alex Preda, a behavioral finance scholar at King's College, writes that "talent for persuasion is key: after all, the public must be convinced to part with their money on the basis of the simple promise that an idea will yield profit in the future" (Surowiecki 2014a). Influencing others to give them something, whether it's investment capital, accolades, or votes, is the entrepreneur's way of reaffirming his self-esteem. Raising money to start a business or fund a nonprofit requires selling an imagined future—you have to influence others to buy into your dream. Running a successful campaign requires getting voters to buy the vision, which must embody the personification of the candidate.

"Some entrepreneurs I have known hear an inner voice that tells them they will never amount to anything," notes leadership scholar and psychoanalyst Manfred Kets de Vries.

> But regardless of who put this idea into their minds, these people are not retiring types who take such rebuke passively; they are the defiant ones who deal with it creatively through action… They will ride to the top in spite of all the dangers; they will get the applause; they will find a way to master their fears.
>
> (Kets de Vries 1985)

An entrepreneur's need for applause fights their inner feeling that they might be insignificant, nothing.

Ten + T: The Amplifying Effect of Testosterone

In some ways, entrepreneurial leaders are almost superhuman—more driven, more confident, more independent—than most of us mere ordinary mortals. It's no wonder that these people play such a profound role in shaping society and get so much media attention. They are the real-life action figures of our time. It's also no wonder that so many of them are male, given how testosterone amplifies many of the traits we've been discussing.

As a steroid hormone, it affects much of the neurology and physiology of both genders (from aggressiveness to bone mass). However, genders do not produce testosterone in equal amounts and hence are not influenced equally by the hormone. Levels are typically seven to eight times greater in adult males than in females, and men produce far more of it—on average 20 times the daily amount—than women.

Research has found a close relationship among testosterone, certain personality traits, and occupation. Known simply as "T" among endocrinologists, testosterone is associated not only with physical characteristics such as strength and size, but also with psychological tendencies such as aggressiveness, risk-taking, and persistence. Testosterone amplifies most of the characteristics on the List of Ten.

One exception is its effect to mitigate or help regulate the need for approval and to keep it in check. What's more, evidence links T with antisocial behaviors like violence and aggression, as well as with less socially toxic behaviors such as assertiveness and fearlessness. Actions related to dominance- and status-seeking have been associated with testosterone in both men and women. A drive to dominate seems to be associated with the need for achievement and esteem from others—needs that we already correlate strongly with entrepreneurship. High T is closely associated with the need for independence, greater self-centeredness, and being more action oriented, restless, and nondeferential.

Researchers at the University of Western Ontario have gone the furthest in declaring an empirical association between key behaviors related to entrepreneurship and those affected by T. Simply put: men with higher levels of testosterone are more likely to behave entrepreneurially, and they have a higher propensity to have had an entrepreneurial experience (White, Thornhill, and Hampson 2006, 21–34).

The Rough Road to the List of Ten

Before condensing my findings into a neat numbered list, I was still at Austen Riggs with two research goals in mind. First, I needed to dig deep into the literature on the entrepreneurial personality. Piece of cake. The second goal was to learn as much as possible about psychopathology from the ever-helpful Riggs clinicians. I was both annoyed and surprised when I got bogged down on that first goal. It turned out that analyzing the available research on entrepreneurial personalities was no easy task.

The annoyance: By that time, most psychologists studying the entrepreneurial personality had been hammered by a strongly leveled critique of their work by one William Gartner, a professor of entrepreneurship at Clemson University. Gartner, among others, was reacting to the approach researchers had taken to create the most accurate personality profile. In essence, scholars had found a startling number of traits and characteristics attributed to entrepreneurs. When you put them all together, they portrayed a person full of contradictions. In effect, there was enough shoddy and uncoordinated research that the end result described a generic "Everyman," not the archetypal entrepreneur.

One cause of the problem was that researchers never agreed on the fundamental definition of "entrepreneur." When you're measuring something, everyone needs to be on board with precisely the same understanding of what the "it" is that's being measured. Makes sense, right? Added to this uncertainty was biting criticism of the research designs and analysis of the data emerging from these ambitious studies. Years later, a new crop of highly skilled researchers entered the field, but they too persisted in focusing their research such that they missed the whole. "Something gets lost," Gartner noted, "when the focus of research on entrepreneurship sticks too closely to the 'esoteric knowledge' of a narrow disciplinary perspective. A finding can be right and interesting to a scholar within a specific theoretical perspective, but, wrong or obvious" to the public (Gartner 2016).

Gartner's words struck a deep chord with me. I was coming at this with my experiences of mean entrepreneurs and looking for some rationale to contextualize my understanding. But then an article by Mark Singer in the New Yorker put me back on the path. Singer chronicles the method used by Michael Zinman to build a fine collection of books... okay, not mean men, but no matter. The advice holds. "You don't start off with a concrete theory about what you're trying to do," says book dealer William Reese. "You build a big pile. Once you get a big enough pile together—the critical mess—you're able to draw conclusions about it. You see patterns...." (Singer 2001).

And so I broadened the scope of my work, staying open to ways to understand the mean men. I went for the "critical mess." This was when I expanded my view of "entrepreneurs" beyond only business founders. There were other professions where the entrepreneurial personality flourishes.

My experience at Austen Riggs gave me two critical insights, first of which was that few disordered personalities are disordered in only one way. The second aha was the List of Ten and the startling place to which it led. Psychopathology was the topic of my conversations daily with psychiatrists and psychologists. As we will see in the next chapter, any overblown personality characteristic can start creating problems when combined with certain others. The epiphany was that this unique and specific collection of personality characteristics, the List of Ten, had the potential for defining one particular personality disorder that could explain it all. Before we go further, let me be clear that this book is not meant to "diagnose" any of the public figures or disguised fact-based cases. Not only is this practice frowned upon by both the American Psychiatric Association and the American Psychological Association, but in a time when facts have come to have less meaning than ever before, I have no desire to contribute through armchair diagnoses[2] (Kahney 2009). While *Mean Men* stops short of pinning a psychiatric disorder on any one person, to you, the reader, I say this: study the self-made men you know and certain entrepreneurial figures in the public eye and compare their behaviors, motivations, and actions to the List of Ten. Because whether someone is tagged with a clinical diagnosis is really not the point. The List of Ten is important because we must recognize the abnormal extremes of these otherwise common personality traits in order to combat the behaviors they engender, and tear down these false heroes before they establish a new normal from which there is no return.

Every Mean Man Needs Someone to Abuse ...And Some of us Need *Him*

Identifying mean men and understanding the roots of their behavior is critical for all of us, whether we are part of the corporate world, work in the nonprofit sphere, or simply exist in modern society—its own type of organizational environment. That's because too many of us fall victim to their mind games and abuse. While he was alive, critics cavalierly compared Jobs to a sociopath in trying to explain his lack of empathy or compassion. Apple workers were his human objects, mere tools to get things done. But for every critic, there is often a disciple. To explain why employees and coworkers put up with him, some of these critics invoked Stockholm syndrome, saying his employees were captives who had fallen in love with their captor (Arthur 2005).

"Those who know anything much about his management style know he work[ed] by winnowing out the chaff—defined as those both not smart enough and not psychologically strong enough to bear repeated demands to produce something impossible (such as a music player where you can access any piece of music within three clicks) and then be told that their solution is 'shit.' And then hear it suggested back to them a few days later," the British technology analyst and historical commentator Charles Arthur remarked in the Register. "That's not how most people like to work, or be treated. In truth, Steve Jobs wasn't an icon to any managers, apart from sociopathic ones" (Arthur 2005).

Were all the people who stuck with Jobs at Apple really sociopaths? Of course not. But these employees, like others who endure the abuse of mean men, probably had characteristics that amplified their vulnerability to manipulation and control. (Truthfully, the stock options probably didn't hurt either.)

What kinds of people, exactly? For starters, individuals with psychological scarring or high levels of stress are particularly liable to fall under the spell of mean men. They're also most likely to stick with these individuals over time. Meanwhile, people who feel alienated and marginalized can be powerfully drawn to the grand sense of purpose conveyed by "leaders" such as these. Many felt the 2016 election gave proof to this idea, with a highly energized, economically disenfranchised group of voters powerfully drawn to "make America great again" as defined by Donald Trump. But the psychological underpinnings of this common dynamic explain why many of us continue to embrace mean.

Dancing a Psychological Tango

Psychoanalyst Hans Kohut (1978) asserted that some individuals have what are known as mirror-hungry personalities, in that their narcissism hungers for reactions from others. Our mean man needs that feedback to tell him he is not only accepted but admired, and he sees validation in the "mirror" reflection of other peoples' responses to him.

But no matter how positive the response, his own sense of worthlessness means he cannot be satisfied, so he continues to seek new audiences who will give him the attention and recognition he craves.

To become attractive to more and more people, our mean man works to convey a sense of grandeur, omnipotence, and strength, and in doing so becomes attractive to those seeking this idealized source of strength. The mean man carries a sense of conviction and certainty that is manna to those who are plagued by doubt.

It is in the follower's reaction that we recognize a complementary theory that explores how these men attract what are called ideal-hungry followers. It may explain why so many of us are not only willing but eager to follow and idealize the mean man.

He comes to the psychological rescue of his followers, taking the form of whoever the followers need him to be. In serving as their hero, he protects them from confronting themselves and their fundamental inadequacies and alienation. Marc Galanter of New York University conducted systematic studies of "charismatic religious groups" (aka cults). He found that psychologically wounded individuals are particularly attracted to charismatic leader–follower relationships. The lonelier and more isolated the individuals were before joining, the more committed they would be to the movement and the recruitment process. Instead of relying on their individual judgment, they tended to follow without question the dictates of the leader (Galanter 1978, 588–591; Galanter et al. 1979, 165–170; Galanter 1980, 1574–1579; Galanter 1983, 1197).

If this makes, the followers sound like they are under a spell, that's not quite accurate. Nor would the organizations, sports leagues, or political groups these men rule be deemed "cults" in any way. But understanding the average person's willingness to tolerate and endure such treatment is essential if we are to understand the potential long-term impact these men may have.

Conflict- Averse—To a Fault

Mean men draw most of their power of attraction and fascination from the emotional dependence of their followers. Driven by their need for the mean man to fit their ideal, the followers establish what psychologists call a fusional relationship, in which at least one individual avoids conflict at virtually any cost because they see the relationship as utterly conditional. We know that won't be the mean man.

Most of us instead go through a process of differentiation. You and the other person in the pair each take responsibility for knowing what you want and how to get it. You know how to negotiate with each other about what you are both able and willing to provide. But when the relationship is fused, there is a dependency that precludes raising disagreements or expressing needs. You're walking on eggshells.

Recall that one overriding need of our mean man is to be in control. If he can develop and maintain undifferentiated relationships with others, the odds of his staying in control improve. If he is successful in this strategy, his entourage will be stocked with these desirables, sustained by their inability to break the connection once their dependency has been established.

It's a Family Thing

Psychoanalyst and Columbia University medical school professor Ethel Person looked to the Freudian theory known as seduction of the aggressor to explain our attraction to mean men (Spector Person 1986). According to Person, masochism could be the result for the small percentage of the population with unresolved childhood development issues in adulthood. And the mean man becomes the trigger for their masochism.

Putting Freud aside, what might this look like? Some people with parental scarring will attach themselves to people they actually fear, then try to overcome this fear by "taking" their abuse. An employee may "need" the experience of an abusive boss to show that they will not be fazed by the harsh treatment. While it may seem that the mean man is the "seducer," he is in fact sensitive to the particular needs of these followers. He doles out abuse, and the trigger gets pulled for the abused to want to satisfy him.

But even those of us with a healthy developmental scorecard—loving parents, a happy childhood, healthy boundaries, and comfort in our own skin—will still often put up with mean. As mean becomes normalized in organizations and in society, our tolerance increases. (Google "normalization Trump" and see how many articles pop up.) "That didn't take very long," writes Tom Toles in the Washington Post. "The specter of Donald Trump moving into the central position of American power seemed troublesome for a minute there, but it is amazing how adaptable people are!" (Toles 2016). We stop calling these mean men or their behaviors to account. And this is what must change.

Notes

1 Excerpted from Chapter 2 of *Mean Men: The Perversion of America's Self-Made Man* (New York: Voussoir, 2017).
2 It should be noted, the behavior of at least one man included in these pages, President Donald J. Trump, prompted a group of mental health workers to break the 1973 "Goldwater Rule," which cautions professionals against profiling the mental health of public figures. In a February 2017 letter to the New York Times, a retired Harvard psychiatry professor and a former research committee chair of the International Psychoanalytic Association, along with 35 other psychiatrists, psychologists, and social workers, call him unfit for office, citing among other reasons the fact that his "speech and actions demonstrate an inability to tolerate views different from his own, leading to rage reactions" and that "his words and behavior suggest a profound inability to empathize." See Dodes, L. and Schacter, J. "Mental Health Professionals Warn About Trump." *New York Times*, February 13, 2017, https://www.nytimes.com/2017/02/13/opinion/mental-health-professionals-warn-about-trump.html?_r=0.

References

Arnell, Peter. 2010. *Shift: How to Reinvent Your Business, Your Career, and Your Personal Brand*. New York: Crown Business.

Arthur, Charles. 2005. "Steve Jobs: Smoke and Mirrors or ICon?" *The Register*, May 20, 2005. http://www.theregister.co.uk/2005/05/20/jobs_biography/.

Brandstätter, Herrmann. 1997. "Becoming an Entrepreneur—A Question of Personality Structure?" *Journal of Economic Psychology*, February, 157–177.

Carr, David. 2014. "In Media Moguls' Rarefied Realm, It's Like Father, Like Son." *The New York TImes*, March 30, 2014. http://www.nytimes.com/2014/03/31/business/media/in-media-moguls-rarefied-realm-its-like-father-like-son.html?_r=0.

Cassar, Gavin and Justin Craig. 2009. "An Investigation of Hindsight Bias in Nascent Venture Activity." *Journal of Business Venturing* 24, no. 2: 149–164. https://doi.org/10.1016/j.jbusvent.2008.02.003.

Collins, Christopher, Paul Hanges, and Edwin Locke. 2004. "The Relationship of Achievement Motivation to Entrepreneurial Behavior: A Meta-Analysis." *Human Performance* 17, no. 1: 95–117.

Cromie, Stanley. 2000. "Assessing Entrepreneurial Inclinations: Some Approaches and Empirical Evidence." *European Journal of Work and Organizational Psychology* 9, no. 1: 7–30. https://doi.org/10.1080/135943200398030.

Galanter, Marc. 1978. "The 'Relief Effect': A Sociobiological Model for Neurotic Distress and Large-Group Therapy." *American Journal of Psychiatry* 135, no. 5: 588–591. https://doi.org/10.1176/ajp.135.5.588.

———. 1980. "Psychological Induction into the Large Group: Findings from a Modern Religious Sect." *American Journal of Psychiatry* 137, no. 12: 1574–1579. https://doi.org/10.1176/ajp.137.12.1574.

———. 1983. "Engaged Members of the Unification Church: Impact of a Charismatic Large Group on Adaptation and Behavior." *Archives of General Psychiatry* 40, no. 11: 1197. https://doi.org/10.1001/archpsyc.1983.01790100043006.

Galanter, Marc, Richard Rabkin, Judith Rabkin, and Alexander Deutsch. 1979. "The 'Moonies': A Psychological Study of Conversion and Membership in a Contemporary Religious Sect." *American Journal of Psychiatry* 136, no. 2: 165–170. https://doi.org/10.1176/ajp.136.2.165.

Gartner, William. 2016. *Entrepreneurship as Organizing*. Cheltenham: Edward Elgar Publishing. https://doi.org/10.4337/9781783476947.

Gould, Emily. 2007. "New York's Worst Bosses: Peter Arnell." Gawker. March 15, 2007. https://www.gawker.com/244608/new-yorks-worst-bosses-peter-arnell.

Grove, Andrew S. 1999. *Only the Paranoid Survive: How to Exploit the Crisis Points That Challenge Every Company*. Currency Book. New York: Doubleday.

Horney, Karen. 1991. *Neurosis and Human Growth: The Struggle toward Self-Realization*. New York: Norton.

Kahney, Leander. 2009. *Inside Steve's Brain*. New York: Penguin Group.

Kets de Vries, Manfred F. R. 1985. "The Dark Side of Entrepreneurship." *Harvard Business Review*, November 1, 1985. https://hbr.org/1985/11/the-dark-side-of-entrepreneurship.

Knight, Frank H. 1921. *Risk, Uncertainty and Profit*. Boston, MA: Houghton Mifflin.

Kohut, Heinz, and Paul H. Ornstein. 1978. *The Search for the Self: Selected Writings of Heinz Kohut, 1950-1978*. London: International Universities Press.

Linnett, Richard. 2002. "The Gospel of Peter: Arnell on a Mission." *Advertising Age*, November 18, 2002. http://adage.com/article/news/gospel-peter-arnell-a-mission/50827/.

Locke, Edwin, and J. Robert Baum. 2007. "Entrepreneurial Motivation." In *The Psychology of Entrepreneurship*, 93–112. Mahwah, NJ: Lawrence Erlbaum Associates Publishers.

Lyons, Daniel. 2009. "The Crazy Genius of Brand Guru Peter Arnell." Newsweek. March 27, 2009. https://www.newsweek.com/crazy-genius-brand-guru-peter-arnell-76137.

McClelland, David C. 1988. *Human Motivation*. Cambridge: Cambridge University Press. https://doi.org/10.1017/CBO9781139878289.

Singer, Mark. 2001. "The Book Eater." *The New Yorker*, February 5, 2001.

Spector Person, Ethel. 1986. "Manipulativeness in Entrepreneurs and Psychopaths." In *Unmasking the Psychopath: Antisocial Personality and Related Symptoms*, 256. New York: W. W. Norton & Company.

Steinhaurer, Jennifer. 1997. "Testing a Wider Concept of Sexual Harassment." *The New York Times*, March 27, 1997, sec. Business. http://www.nytimes.com/1997/03/27/business/testing-a-wider-concept-of-sexual-harassment.html.

Surowiecki, James. 2014a. "Do the Hustle." *The New Yorker*, January 13, 2014. http://www.newyorker.com/magazine/2014/01/13/do-the-hustle.

———. 2014b. "Epic Fails of the Startup World." *The New Yorker*, May 12, 2014. https://www.newyorker.com/magazine/2014/05/19/epic-fails-of-the-startup-world.

Toles, Tom. 2016. "The 'Normalization' of Donald Trump Is Already Complete." *The Washington Post*, December 20, 2016. https://www.washingtonpost.com/news/opinions/wp/2016/12/20/the-normalization-of-donald-trump-is-already-complete/?utm_term=.aa1490f617dc.

White, Roderick E., Stewart Thornhill, and Elizabeth Hampson. 2006. "Entrepreneurs and Evolutionary Biology: The Relationship between Testosterone and New Venture Creation." *Organizational Behavior and Human Decision Processes* 100, no. 1: 21–34. https://doi.org/10.1016/j.obhdp.2005.11.001.

Chapter 10

Afterword

Mark Lipton

By 2007, I was gliding into the thirtieth year of my day job as a Graduate Professor of Management at Parsons School of Design and The New School in New York. I also ran a laser-focused consulting practice for CEO leadership development, providing services chiefly through intensive and intimate executive coaching sessions. Little did I know that 2007 would represent the start of a transformational pivot in my life.

Until about 2005—during and after the epic dot-com crash—my consulting clients were disproportionately tech entrepreneurs. Before the bubble burst in 2000, these CEOs were the era's golden boys (along with a few women). They could capitalize on new businesses with nothing more solid than a well-sold vision. Investors, employees, and others were attracted to this new generation of business founders by their quirky awkwardness, infectious enthusiasm, and a magician's ability to poke holes in any skepticism. It was still the late 1990s, and these were, after all, good times. From the late 1990s until after the bubble burst, I began my journey into "mean men."

I wondered: Was there a dark side to entrepreneurship? Did the role of entrepreneur attract a particular personality or personality *disorder*? Why did many of these men, who initially seemed emotionally mature and charismatic, come to turn on those they were close to, the people they said they trusted?

By 2005, with a prior book about organization vision in the market for more than three years, I was still intrigued to understand this new breed of entrepreneur better. I was ready for new research and a writing project. However, I acknowledged that my interest in "mean men" was a mile wide, but my intellectual background for understanding them was about two feet deep. My experience in psychology, or psychopathology, in particular, was far too thin.

One day, feeling somewhat glum by the apparent reality of this disconnect, I saw an announcement from The Austen Riggs Center soliciting applications to the Erikson Scholar program. So how would I, an academic in management and an organizational consultant, fit into the world of a psychiatric hospital for six months? Jane Tillman, the search committee's chair, assured me this was a transdisciplinary role, and that my relative lack of experience or academic achievement in psychology or psychiatry would not be problematic. Instead, they would focus

DOI: 10.4324/9781003322627-23

their review process more on the problem for which I was in search of answers. They ultimately awarded me the position, and I moved onto the Austen Riggs campus in January 2009.

It may sound peculiar, but it doesn't get much better for a transdisciplinary researcher like me. The offer from Riggs was a singular opportunity to learn about psychopathology, dig into two decades of research about the inner drama that gets played out in so many entrepreneurs' heads, and determine if there is an untold story lurking in the data. At Riggs, I was provided full access to the wickedly smart staff, clinical privileges to read case workups before patient case conferences, and an open invitation to attend all patient case conferences. It was an extraordinary opportunity to see firsthand some of the most complex psychiatric disorders and learn how to map their potential origins.

On my first day, I asked Dr. Gerard Fromm, then director of Riggs's research and professional development division, the Erikson Institute, why the committee chose me over others as the Erikson scholar-in-residence. "We have a good measure of self-interest in what you're probing, Mark," he told me.

> Because some of the patients who come to us for help are from very high-achieving families, often with driven fathers whose stress plays itself out in their relationships with their spouses and children. The more you can answer your questions and understand what's behind their behavior, the better we may understand the parental influence that perhaps helped to shape these patients and what they are now struggling with.

That first day at Riggs already had yielded an "a-ha moment."

As obvious as it may seem, I honestly never considered the effect of these mean entrepreneurial men as fathers. Instead, my focus until that moment was on the collateral damage to employees. I had heard plenty of carping from venture capitalists and angel investors about "the crazy SOB we sunk our money into." But I walked out of Jerry Fromm's office wondering about the broader impact these grown men were making way beyond their employees and investors, permeating their families and leaking out to affect us all. This was the moment *Mean Men* truly began to take shape.

My involvement with The Austen Riggs Center did not end when my Erikson Scholar position terminated, and the relationships I made in 2009 continue, primarily, to this day. In addition, the Riggs experience kindled some new ways of thinking, a fondness for psychodynamic theory, and an award-winning book that would never have seen the light of day without the interest, support, and critiques from Riggs colleagues. Were it not for Riggs' emphasis on psychodynamic theory, for example, I may never have been so intrigued by a variable common to so many mean men rarely ever noted in the literature: The absence of a father in their lives during crucial developmental years.

Chapter 11

Wooden Ships

Cultural Cohesion and Continuity in Freud and Erikson[1]

Daniel Burston

What holds cultural communities together, especially in times of crisis? And what causes them to fragment sometimes, even when they enjoy material prosperity? These are not idle questions. In *The Future of An Illusion* (Freud, 1927) and *Civilization and Its Discontents* (Freud, 1930), Freud drew attention to the forces that disrupt or destroy cultural cohesion, including our supposedly innate propensities to incest and homicide, our natural disinclination for work, and our eagerness to enslave or objectify others. According to Freud, the intrapsychic forces that normally prevent these impulses from surfacing or being acted on are anchored in a kind of social contract, in which participants yield a significant portion of their freedom to follow their spontaneous inclinations and desires in exchange for guarantees of security and freedom from violence in turn (Freud, 1930).

This collective renunciation of aggressive instincts is supported, said Freud, by a "cultural super-ego" that intervenes to punish transgressions and enforce the laws impersonally, ostensibly for everyone's benefit (Freud, 1927), and by the secondary transformation of our raw, instinctual desires via sublimation and "aim-inhibited" Eros, resulting in strong interpersonal and institutional bonds, the glue or cement that presumably holds a family and a culture together, and holds the individual's aggressive drives in check (Freud, 1930). Though no fan of democracy himself, Freud nevertheless allowed that the social stability engendered by these "civilizing" trends is endangered by stark economic inequalities, which afford the ruling elite far more opportunities for instinctual satisfaction and the sublimation of the drives than commoners enjoy. Indeed, when the level of instinctual renunciation the masses must endure exceeds a certain threshold, warned Freud, it profoundly intensifies our innate and enduring "hostility to culture."

Without denying or minimizing the role of Eros, aggression, and the superego in fostering (or eroding) social cohesion, Erik Erikson added another dimension to the discussion that merits continuing reflection – intergenerational identification, or the ability of one generation to identify with the experiences and attitudes of their elders, and to inspire a similar sense of identification in their own offspring, as well. Absent a strong degree of intergenerational identification, adolescents and young adults identify far more with one another than with their elders, the usual social barriers of race and class may become attenuated, or even drop away

DOI: 10.4324/9781003322627-24

entirely. That's the good news. While we'll explore the negative consequences of the decline of intergenerational identification momentarily, the point is that these are different issues than the ones Freud addressed, because they involve conflict or tension between children and their elders, rather than between an individual's instinctual endowment and the requirements of civic order, or between the elites and the masses respective claims on the available wealth.

While born of clinical experience, of course, Erikson's ideas were also grounded in firsthand experience. After all, he witnessed or participated in two movements and moments in history where intergenerational ties were profoundly eroded, and where an element of cynicism and mistrust toward one's elders colored most adolescents' and young adults' search for identity and self-definition. The first time was as an itinerant youth in the *Wandervögel* movement between WWI and WWII. Young Erik Homberger spent many months wandering the fields and forests of Weimar trying to "find himself" and to settle on a vocation. And as he noted in *Young Man Luther* (Erikson, 1957), he and his fellow wanderers often shared a profound mistrust of their elders, and above all, of their fathers (Burston, 2007).

Then, in late middle age, Erik (Homberger) Erikson was teaching at Harvard at the height of the so-called "generation gap", when young people felt that their elders had abdicated their ethical responsibilities, embracing a deadening complacency, or a mind-numbing conformity that robbed them of the capacity to inspire trust and respect. In other words, they had "sold out."

Though they seldom said so explicitly, it was evident from their music that despite their disenchantment with their parents, young people of that era still yearned for a sense of connection with elders whom they could trust and emulate. Illustrations of this abound. For example, for a raw, unvarnished expression of their collective disappointment, take the song "My Generation", a rock anthem from the British invasion, sung by Rodger Daltrey of *The Who*, released in 1964. This was one aspect of the phenomenon. On the other end of the spectrum (though still in the United Kingdom), we find *The Moody Blues'* memorable album of 1970, *To Our Children's Children's Children*. The title alone expressed a yearning for intergenerational connection and the hope that the experiences and sensibilities of young adults living in those turbulent times would still have resonance for their distant progeny three generations hence. Here in the United States, a similar sort of ambivalence – a conflict between anger and disappointment, on the one hand, and a deep desire for connection, on the other hand – was vividly expressed in Crosby, Stills, Nash, and Young in their iconic album, *Déja Vu.*

The song "Wooden Ships" contained a plaintive and undisguised reproach to their elders– a very vivid and direct reference to what Erikson termed the "missed mutuality" that underscores so much psychopathology. And yet, in striking contrast to this reproach, Graham Nash's moving melody "Teach Your Children" stresses the possibility that a degree of reconciliation, even of mutual respect and love, is actually attainable, once youth grasp the struggles and deprivations that their elders endured and embrace the dreams that they dreamt, but never achieved for themselves, and still cherish for them.

Songs like these are quite rare, nowadays, but there were many other songs like this in the 60s and 70s. Consider "Conquistador," by *Procol Harum*, a smash hit in 1967, or the song "Father and Son" on Cat Stevens' album *Tea for the Tillerman* in 1970. On the surface, they appear quite different. "Conquistador" was electric, fast paced, and narrates the thoughts and impressions of a young man who is deeply disenchanted with an older role model. By contrast, "Father and Son" is lyrical, folksy and slow paced. It narrates a father's well-meaning admonitions to his son to seek safety and stability, and the son's internal dialogue, as he wrestles with the difficulty of explaining his frustration with the "status quo", and his decision to leave home, take risks, and to live his life authentically. But the core similarity between the two songs is that in neither one is there any genuine *dialogue* between the two generations. In "Father and Son", the father holds forth while the son listens, while in "Conquistador" the younger man addresses his older counterpart in a monologue suggestive of conversation, but with the older party remaining silent. Different songs, different styles, different artists – but the underlying message is the same.

So artists like *the Who, Procol Harum, the Moody Blues, Crosby Still and Nash,* and Cat Stevens all expressed varying degrees of optimism or despair about our ability to remedy the intergenerational malaise they experienced, which was commonly referred to as "alienation." And as Erikson's pre-eminent biographer, Lawrence Freidman points out, when Erikson taught at Harvard, he sought to assure students that people can grow older without losing their moral or spiritual compass, whilst cautioning them that if *they* remained stuck in bitterness and estrangement, their youthful cynicism would breed despair in middle and old age, which in turn, would harm their own children, and erode the hopefulness and wholesomeness of the next generation (Friedman, 1999). Indeed, Erikson's eloquence on this score was integral to his immense popularity as a teacher.

Nevertheless, while he was wildly popular with students, Erikson worried that most baby-boomers would never achieve the stage he termed generativity, being arrested, as he thought, in a prolonged adolescence. And later, as evidence of this socially patterned defect, Erikson cited our looming ecological crisis, cautioning us repeatedly that our collective unwillingness or inability to protect the biosphere and avert the climate catastrophes which threaten all life on this planet, are symptomatic of arrested development, a lack of foresight, and a mind-boggling indifference to the toxic and hostile environment that will greet our children's children's children as the result of our collective shortsightedness (Burston, 2007). In effect, by our actions (and collective inaction on climate change), we are saying to future generations: "Aprés nous, le déluge."

If developmental arrest at a cultural or collective level gives rise to a decline of generativity, as Erikson feared, it is abetted by the concurrent decline of tradition. Let's not forget that the crises and conflicts between adolescence and middle age, which Erikson described so persuasively, take place in between the two overarching transitions of the human life cycle; birth and death. One of the hallmarks of tradition, as Erikson pointed out, is that we rely on it to endow these existential transitions with a numinous significance through ritual (Erikson, 1966).

But tradition does much more than that. Unlike many other species, we have relatively little deeply wired instinctual programming and are therefore "generalists", said Erikson, capable of adapting to almost any ecology on the planet. But our lack of instinctual programming means even in the most natural of settings, our instincts, such as they are, are too diffuse to provide us with immediate and obvious answers to urgent questions that normally confront teens and young adults, like: "What can I eat, how do I acquire food, or cope with scarcity. How do I find or build shelter? How do I find a mate, rear my young, greet strangers, fight my enemies, etc."

Our instincts don't provide us with self-evident answers to urgent questions like these, and so different cultures generate a multitude of responses to them. Why? Because there is no single instinctual or hereditary pattern for us to follow, and the basic repertoire of knowledge and skill required to address these needs and contingencies varies widely according to a society's language, customs, history, climate, geography, and the overall level of technological development.

Despite the dazzling diversity of culture patterns across the globe, for most of human history, tradition has provided our kind with authoritative and uncontroversial answers to basic, existential questions. And while skeptics and sophisticates may scoff at it, if they wish, one clear advantage to this state of affairs is that it is fairly stable, and entails a very low degree of identity confusion. In traditional societies, people know who they are, what to expect of others, and what is expected of them in turn. This all changed drastically in the wake of the industrial revolution. The global reach of capitalism displaced large populations and provided powerful incentives for immigration, bringing very disparate cultural sensibilities and norms into close and frequent contact with one another.

Moreover, it is instructive to note that in bygone eras, tradition modulated the pace of technological change and the changes in social and political structures that inevitably followed in their wake. Nowadays, however, competition drives the relentless pursuit of technological innovation, which in turn drives the market (and creates large-scale unemployment, which is a separate issue). And finally, don't forget that the free market is such a fickle and a-moral entity that looking to precedent, or to the experiences and perspectives of our elders for guidance, yields less and less of the "competitive edge" young people need to thrive in our brave new world.

In such circumstances, the idea that tradition – *any* tradition – can provide clear cut and authoritative answers to basic questions of how to live seems quaint or faintly ridiculous to many people. Why? Because the more rapid the rate of technological innovation, the less capable the younger generation are of empathizing and identifying with the older generation's typical attitudes, experiences, and skills. No one understood this better than Erikson's friend (and former graduate assistant) Kenneth Keniston, who said:

A man born in the beginning of this (20th) century has seen in his lifetime changes in the quality of life which no one in his youth could have anticipated or prepared him for. Changes that once took centuries... now take less than a generation. Technological changes that were the science fiction of our parents are the commonplaces of their children ...

The human capacity to assimilate to such innovations is limited. Men can of course adjust to rapid change - that is, make an accommodation to it and go on living - but truly to assimilate it involves retaining some sense of connection with the past, understanding the relationship of one's position to one's origins and one's destination, maintaining a sense of control over one's life in a comprehensible universe undergoing intelligible transformations. This assimilation becomes increasingly difficult in times like our own. Whatever is radically different from the present inevitably tends to lose its relevance.

(Keniston, 1974, 25)

What Keniston said then, in 1974, is even more true today. And if, as Keniston implied, the capacity for intergenerational identification declines in proportion to the speed of technological and social change, we are in deep trouble. Why? Technological developments move at such blinding speed nowadays (Kurzweil, 1999) that the vast majority of people haven't the faintest idea of what they entail or portend for the future, and cannot engage in a rational or democratic debate about their potential uses and abuses (Fukuyama, 2002).

In some ways, Erikson anticipated our present predicament in "Identity and Uprootedness in Our Time", where he wrote that:

...somewhere between the exploitation of nature and the self- exploitation of mercantile and mechanized man a gigantic transformation has taken place which was first the subject of Marx's passionate attention: it is the creation of middle men between man and nature. And it dawns on us that the *techno-logical* world of today is about to create kinds of alienation too strange to be imagined.

(1964, 104, 105)

Why so strange? Because we are the *only* species capable of driving a wedge, as it were, between sex and reproduction – of becoming "middle men", as Erikson put it, between ourselves and nature. This distinctive ability makes us the only species capable of stepping completely outside the evolutionary framework of natural selection that has governed the destiny of *all* species on this planet until now. Who knows where this could lead?

In 1932, Aldous Huxley published a dystopian novel called *Brave New World*, which anticipated a society where sex and reproduction had been entirely divorced from one another. In this technologically savvy consumer paradise, sex is never more than a novelty or a past-time. Like the "hook up" culture that has replaced dating in the last few decades, the sexual landscape in Huxley's world did not entail a search for lasting commitments or emotional attachments between adults, much less to children, whose entry into the world is managed in industrial "hatcheries" run by scientists who tinker with the human genome to create different strains of human beings – the Alphas, who are extremely intelligent, and generally run the show, the Betas who are less intelligent, but necessary, and generally obliging, while less intelligent strains were confined to purely menial tasks. In short, a new caste system of well-adjusted conformists, run on eugenic lines.

Up until recently, Huxley's nightmare was the stuff of science fiction. Now, however, it is an objective possibility, given the advent of CRISPR, an extremely precise and efficient gene editing technology that makes these kinds of interventions into the human gene pool entirely possible within the next few years. Some scientists imagine that the use of CRISPR on human genes can be limited to averting serious, life threatening, and debilitating diseases, somehow. But others caution that once we start down this road, there is no turning back. We've been told that cloning humans is off limits, too. Possibly so. But we are already hearing about scientists cultivating chimeras – or animal-human hybrids of various kinds – and very soon, perhaps designer babies, including some who are not the product of in vitro fertilization, but bona fide "test tube babies," whose genetic material may come from three or more donors.

Meanwhile Ray Kurzweil and his friends at Google predict that with the help of nano-technology and other kinds of "enhancements", we will soon produce human-machine hybrids that are in constant rapport with myriad other computerized systems, and that these will vastly exceed our species in intelligence, physical strength, speed, sensory range, and acuity, and last, but not least, longevity.

In *Civilization and Its Discontents*, Freud remarked that science has conferred powers of perception, communication, and destruction on human beings that would have appeared god-like to our ancient forbears. In his words, modern technology had made us all "prosthetic gods." But a prosthesis is an artificial limb or body part, and Freud was merely talking about telegraphs and telephones, telescopes and microscopes, balloons, and biplanes – all of them "prostheses", in that they can be turned on or off, attached or detached at will.

Post-humanists are not talking about "prostheses" in this sense, but of radical biological interventions that have irreversible consequences: electronic implants in our brains and bodily organs, modifications to our DNA, RNA, mitochondria, and so on, through genetic engineering and nanotechnology – modifications that are not detachable, and cannot be "switched off" at will. On the contrary, their effects will be irreversible. A lot of capital is already invested in pursuit of technologies that promise to enhance or augment our basic biological capabilities, because they promise to alter the molecular and atomic structure of our DNA, RNA, and neural networks so that we become even more exquisitely receptive and responsive to information and "feeds" emanating from machines, which will modify our experience and behavior drastically. (They are piloting this research on rats already!)

What is at stake here is an effort to transcend the built-in biological limits and constraints that have shaped our evolution as a species to date. Many researchers greet these developments as the next stage in human evolution – though strictly speaking, they bypass the normal evolutionary mechanisms of impregnation, gestation, childbirth, and attachment and have nothing to do with natural selection. Sadly, however, few (if any) of the scientists involved in these efforts pause to reflect on what effect these technologies will have on our collective mental health; to wonder whether clones, chimeras, and human–machine hybrids, who are manufactured, rather than born, and divorced from the experience of early attachment and acculturation, will really identify deeply with *any* of their "progenitors" – if that is even the right word. If Erikson is right, we are probably paving the way for a new, more intense, more bizarre, and more dangerous kind of "generation gap" than anything we've experienced in the past – a technological nightmare then blends the worst features of Nietzsche's "übermensch" with Mary Shelley's *Frankenstein*.

While we cannot anticipate precisely what new, enhanced, and/or hybrid entities will emerge in the decades ahead, we know one thing for sure. They won't be the product of human sexual activity, will not be subject to natural selection, and may very well lack many of the nurturing and restraining features that promote the growth of mature, judicious human beings. And if it ever came to a contest between us and them – well, I am not a betting man, but my money is on the hybrids and the cyborgs.

So, our collective efforts to transcend the hitherto insurmountable limits of aging and death, and the vagaries of natural (and sexual) selection, have placed us on a very slippery slope. While some approach this new threshold with naïve enthusiasm (Firestone, 1970; Harraway, 1991; Kurzweil, 1999), the sense of unease and foreboding that grips many more reflective science watchers nowadays reflects the fact that events "on the ground" are rapidly outpacing public awareness, and society's ability to regulate technological developments in the public interest (Fukuyama, 2002; Rubin, 2014).

Another worrisome dimension to this issue is that the "benefits" of the emerging biotechnologies will doubtless be showered disproportionately on the wealthy, and those who serve and protect their interests. If wealthy people can buy the enhancements that enable them to live significantly longer lives – 200, 300 years, or longer – they will have a longer time to accumulate capital and power. In short, the new biotechnologies, ostensibly designed for the ill and elderly, will likely benefit the wealthy far more than the average person, deepening existing inequalities.

So yes, the emerging bio-technologies will empower us to do god-like things in medicine, communications, and warfare. But they will also lead to new forms of alienation and depravity. Why? Because since the dawn of recorded history, human societies have had markets in flesh – flesh for rent, and flesh for sale. Only now, it will be "designer flesh," and not quite human, but built to our prior specifications. And the market, as we know, is an inherently a-moral mechanism. And for that very reason, the newer forms of alienation that await our kind will be more subtle and pervasive than they are now, and inscribed, enforced, and legitimated by the powerful technocratic elites that own and manage the new means of reproduction.

And what is the solution to this emerging problem? Perhaps there is no single, simple, or straightforward solution. It is difficult to impossible to put the genie back in the bottle once it is out, and for every new experiment or breakthrough that is reported in the popular press, there are probably a dozen or more that are performed discretely in the shadows to push these technologies further ahead. But if we take Erikson's work seriously, we must try to raise public awareness about these issues, to insure that the public is informed, and able to develop creative responses to contain and minimize the dangers that lie ahead. Erikson would expect no less from us.

Granted, Erikson's reflections on the human life cycle and his developmental schemata are dated, in need of revision, and not always suited perfectly to this purpose. Because of the ways technology rapidly transforms the "average expectable life world" of teens and young adults today, changing our definitions of (and expectations for) children, teens, and adults, they need to be constantly updated to reflect the changing worlds that we and our children inhabit. But his reflections on intergenerational identification, and the role it plays in insuring cultural vitality and continuity, remain valid in any case. Let us hope that our children's children, and their children's children, still get the message when we have all returned to dust.

Note

1 This chapter is based on an essay first published in *Free Associations: Psychoanalysis and Culture, Media, Groups, Politics* (2017).

References

Burston, Daniel. 2007. *Erik Erikson and the American Psyche: Ego, Ethics and Evolution.* Lanham, MD: Jason Aronson.

Erikson, Erik. 1957. *Young Man Luther.* New York: W.W. Norton.

———. 1964. "Identity and Uprootedness in Our Time." In *Insight & Responsibility.* New York: W.W. Norton.

———. 1966. "The Ontogeny of Ritualization." In *Psychoanalysis – a General Psychology. Essays in Honor of Heinz Hartmann*, edited by R. Lowestenin, L, Newman, M. Schur, and A. Solnit. New York: International Universities Press.

Freud, Sigmund. 1927. *The Future of An Illusion.* Standard Edition, vol. 21, London: Hogarth.

———. 1930. *Civilization and Its Discontents.* Standard Edition, vol. 23, London: Hogarth.

Friedman, Lawrence, J. 1999. *Identity's Architect: A Biography of Erik H. Erikson.* New York: Scribner.

Firestone, Shulamit. 1970. *The Dialectic of Sex. The Case for Feminist Revolution.* New York: William Morrow.

Fukuyama, Francis. 2002. *Our Posthuman Future: Consequences of the Biotechnology Revolution.* New York: Picador.

Haraway, Donna. 1991. *Simians, Cyborgs and Women.* New York: Routledge.

Huxley, Aldous. 1932. *Brave New World.* New York: Perennial Modern Classics, Harper Collins, reprint, 2006.

Keniston, Kenneth. 1974. "Psychological Development and Historical Change." In *Explorations in Psychohistory: The Wellfleet Papers*, edited by R. Lifton and E. Olson. New York: Simon and Schuster.

Kurzweil, Robert. 1999. *The Age of Spiritual Machines. When Computers Exceed Human Intelligence.* New York: Penguin.

Rubin, Charles. 2014. *The Eclipse of Man: Human Extinction and the Meaning of Progress.* New York: New Atlantis Books.

Chapter 11

Afterword

Daniel Burston

I applied for an Erik Erikson fellowship after deciding to write a book about Erikson in 1998. My desire to write an intellectual biography of Erikson stemmed from my belief that there were important elements of his life and work that had been over-looked, oversimplified, or dismissed too harshly by Paul Roazen, whose book *Erik Erikson: The Power and Limits of a Vision* appeared in 1976, and to a lesser extent, by Erikson's biographer, Lawrence Friedman, whose book *Identity's Architect: A Biography of Erik Erikson,* appeared shortly before my arrival at Riggs. Much as I learned from Roazen and Friedman, I believed that these issues and ideas, which are alluded to below, needed closer scrutiny to get Erikson's life and legacy in proper perspective. To that end, I spent August of 1999 and July of 2000 at Austen Riggs together with my wife and children, studying in the library, attending clinical case conferences, learning about the culture, and interviewing former friends and students of Erikson who work there.

Another topic I wished to explore was Erikson's relationship to the psychohistory movement that he launched with the help of psychiatrist Robert J. Lifton, historians Frank Manuel, Peter Gay, and John Demos and his former student Kenneth Keniston. More than his clinical contributions, and more than *Childhood and Society*, his first best-selling book, Erikson's psychohistorical musings contributed a great deal to his growing fame as a public intellectual, and no doubt, to his teaching appointment at Harvard. I found his biographies of Luther and Gandhi and his psychobiographical reflections on William James, Sigmund Freud, Albert Einstein, and George Bernard Shaw, which are scattered among several different papers, to be intriguing. Much as I appreciated these efforts to extend psychoanalysis beyond the clinic, however, I became somewhat skeptical of Erikson's tendency to idealize many of the figures he studied.

Riggs is a residential treatment facility unlike any other I've encountered before or since. On arriving there, I was agreeably surprised to discover the diversity of viewpoints among clinicians there – ego psychology, object relations, Lacanian psychoanalysis, Sylvan Tomkins' personality, affect and script theories, etc. But with that said, I was studying Erikson's case histories and papers on theory and technique at the time and was therefore somewhat puzzled by the paucity

DOI: 10.4324/9781003322627-25

of references to Erikson's own approach to clinical work in the clinical case conferences I attended, particularly with respect to his concepts of identity and intergenerational identification. It also struck me that the theory and practice of dream interpretation – which was so important to earlier generations of analytic clinicians – was seldom (if ever) mentioned during my time there. (This did not deter me from devoting a chapter on Erikson's reading of Freud's "Irma dream "in my own book, however.)

My immersion in Erikson's work lasted through the early 2000s and eventually resulted in a book entitled *Erik Erikson and the American Psyche: Ego, Ethics and Evolution,* which was published in 2007. During this (post-Riggs) period of research, I became alarmed by the bourgeoning post-humanism/trans-humanism movements and attempted to salvage insights from Erikson's work on alienation and the role of rapid technological change in disrupting intergenerational identification to critique these emerging trends. Similar concerns animate my contribution to the present volume, which builds upon my earlier reflections, with a few new twists.

My work on Erik Erikson also had a significant impact on my next book, entitled *A Forgotten Freudian: The Life and Work of Karl Stern,* which appeared in 2016. Like Erikson, Stern was raised in an assimilated German/Jewish family and struggled with his Jewish identity as an adolescent and young adult. Having fled the Nazis in 1937, he landed in London, then Montreal in 1938, where he worked as a (psychoanalytically oriented) psychiatrist at the Allen Memorial Institute. After a prolonged period of indecision, he finally decided to convert to Catholicism in 1943 and was shunned and vilified by Montreal's Jewish community as a result. Nevertheless, Stern became famous in 1951 for his memoir *The Pillar of Fire,* which was hailed as a literary masterpiece in many quarters, and went on to apply psychoanalytic theory to the study of religion in *The Third Revolution* (1954) and philosophy in *The Flight from Woman* (1965). Erikson's theories of identity formation and intergenerational identification helped me to discern and to thematize several psychological processes that preceded and accompanied Stern's fateful decision to convert, and his lingering misgivings over that decision later in life.

I will always be grateful for my time at Austen Riggs. I learned a great deal from my stay there and will never forget the long and intimate conversations I had with several of the clinical faculty there about their experience of Erikson as a clinician and a teacher.

Chapter 12

Psychoanalytic Reflections on Limitation

Aging, Dying, Generativity, and Renewal[1]

Nancy McWilliams

When I was asked what I wanted to talk about in this keynote, mortality was on my mind. I was about to turn three score and ten, and I was going through a health crisis. A tiny spot on my right cheek had been diagnosed as Merkel carcinoma, a rare, aggressive skin cancer with a bad prognosis. Mercifully, it had been caught early enough that my own prognosis was deemed excellent, provided I had immediate surgery and then a long course of daily facial radiation. I was lucky. I had a good dermatologist, a fiancé (now husband) who pushed me to see the doctor sooner than I had intended, and a pathologist who knew enough to check for the unusual Merkel tumor. Because my face was visibly damaged by the surgery and then by the radiation, my health issues immediately invaded my clinical work, ready or not. Just as when I was diagnosed with an aggressive (and also ultimately treatable) breast cancer 22 years ago, I was shaken by this cameo appearance of the Grim Reaper. I had virtually no risk factors, and I was assuming my good health habits were somehow protecting me.

My patients were upset, too. Several of them, even those in my age range who had been with me for years, had not thought much about my inevitable decline and death. Or their own – at least not in a realistic, clear-eyed way. Although I am optimistic about recovering this time around, I can now see my funerary writings on the wall, and so can they. Thinking about mortality at 70 is different from thinking about it at three, when I first learned about death and greeted the new knowledge literally kicking and screaming, or at nine, when I lost my mother, or at 35 (the year John Updike referenced as our "Midpoint"), or when I reached the respective ages at which my parents had died, or when I lost my husband of 40 years. And no doubt different still from thinking about it at 80 or 95.

A different kind of experience also went into my deciding to talk about this topic. A couple of years ago, a student in my graduate school supervision group directed a general question to her 20 and 30 something classmates, asking advice from any of them who had worked with geriatric populations. What had they learned about doing psychotherapy with the elderly? Several students engaged in discussion. I began to notice that they were giving me furtive glances as they pooled their knowledge, and I asked if they were feeling self-conscious about talking about the aged with an aged professor.

DOI: 10.4324/9781003322627-26

With some embarrassment, they nodded. I began talking about both the up- and the down-sides of the years past 65, the point Erikson (1950) stated more than once that if he were *then* writing his developmental theory, he would have subdivided the years after 65 rather than lumping together the psychology of 95-year-olds with that of 65-year-olds. Accordingly, in 1997, Joan Erikson added material to their book *The Life Cycle Completed*, addressing the stage of the "old-old" and the concept of "gerotranscendence." And in 2001, Marcia Spira and Barbara Berger, in yet another needed correction of the historic masculine tilt of psychoanalytic theories, and a protest against the cultural consignment of post-menopausal women to the developmental dustbin, postulated a "penultimate" phase in women between 55 and 70 in which generativity predominates.

Some weeks after our discussion in the supervision group, my students told me it was eye-opening to learn of the positive aspects of getting old – the increased self-acceptance and acceptance of others, the relief in not being pushed around so much by hormones, the loosening of the grip of vanity, the easing of competitiveness, the pleasures of grandchildren, the enjoyment of age-mates with shared memories, the serenity, the sense of proportion. I told them about Hedda Bolgar, who, at 103, commented on how nice it was to have nothing to prove now, to be more deeply comfortable with herself and more tolerant of other people. Contemporary Western culture had given my students very little in the way of a vision of late-life gratifications. No one had ever talked to them about a positive side of aging.

And finally, another event in the past decade, one I found quite amusing at the time, prompted me to think and speak today about mortality and limitation in general. In 2007, just after Stanley Greenspan published the first edition of the *Psychodynamic Diagnostic Manual* (2006), he and the leaders of the project's committees asked readers for feedback, both about anything they found useful in the PDM and also about what seemed wrong or lacking. One of the first responses was an email from a geriatric psychiatrist in Los Angeles, Daniel Plotkin, who queried, "You frame this as a biopsychosocial, developmentally sensitive document, and you cover issues of infancy, childhood, and adulthood. What about the elderly?" The main architects of the PDM turned to one another in clueless surprise, as if to say, "The elderly? What elderly?!" Not an uncommon reaction to such an omission, given how little attention there has been in *any* taxonomical system to those who are well along in years, but a particularly arresting one in this case, given that the modal age of the people involved in leading the PDM effort was, by my calculation, about 75, and several were pushing 90. We were a study in denial.

Mortality, Limitation, and Psychoanalysis

At this age, as I hear the waterfall in the distance, the shortness of time frames all my plans and expectations in new ways. As you can imagine from hearing a bit about my childhood, I have thought about mortality and its ramifications for a very long time. Now I have a large cohort of psychoanalytic age-mates who, whatever their early histories, are also thinking about it, and in perhaps similarly new ways. It occurred to me that as psychoanalytic professionals, we should be talking together, as analysts traditionally do, about topics that are hard to keep in consciousness and that are not welcomed by our social conventions. And we should be talking in the presence of colleagues of all ages – about getting old, dying, and other unalterable realities.

Increasingly, I notice that we are doing so. I see no evidence, though, that psychoanalysts as a group are any more comfortable with the reality of death than anyone else, as is evident in the anecdote about the PDM. Still, it is a core part of our professional ego ideal to get our minds around the implications of all disturbing human experiences. Several decades ago, Ernest Becker (1973) took Freud to task for not fully engaging with the consequences of the human terror of no longer existing – a reality that Freud, probably rightly, believed was not comprehensible to the vast unconscious part of the mind. I remember Erik Erikson once commenting on what he called the "ego chill" by which one is afflicted when one tries to put aside other thoughts and think specifically about not going on being. Try it: It's terrifying.

In the early 1980s, considerably before there was much psychoanalytic literature about serious illness in the analyst (e.g., Pizer 1997), my colleague Peggy van Raalte (1984) wrote a doctoral dissertation on what happens to people whose analysts die during their treatment. One of her most arresting findings was that in cases of an analyst's long and eventually terminal illness, those bereaved clients who had noticed a change in their analyst and whose questions been answered honestly tended to do better after the loss. Those whose analysts had tried to continue as usual, without addressing their health issues with the patient, tended to have difficulty trusting any therapist after their analyst's death and were also more likely to struggle with self-blame for the loss ("If only I had been more interesting …"). In the case of sudden demise of the analyst, some went afterwards to another professional, whom several then devalued and left (perhaps out of identification with the aggressor, abandoning that therapist as their analyst had abandoned them); most of these settled more or less comfortably with a third person, who helped them with their grief. Overall, the analysands who did the best after the loss were those to whom an "intermediary person" had reached out to offer a consultation in the wake of their bereavement.

Such findings have important clinical implications. Psychoanalysis establishes a powerful attachment. We need that power in the therapeutic relationship in order to help people free themselves from profoundly overdetermined suffering. But the relational power necessary for healing has just as much potential to do harm. Given that our death risks traumatizing those who have depended upon us, I was particularly interested in an ancillary set of conversations that Van Raalte (1984) had with several very elderly analysts, whom she interviewed about their attitudes toward their mortality. Most of them emphasized that they didn't have to worry about that yet; they were healthy, they ate well, they exercised, etc.

So it is pretty evident that a central way that all of us, analysts and non-analysts alike, deal with death is by dissociating any self-state in which it is visible.

Additional evidence for this avoidance may be seen in our reluctance, which I can see in myself and numerous colleagues who have admitted a similar procrastination, to make plans for our patients if we should die or become unable to work with them. Periodically, we all hear from APA that we should have a professional will. "A very good idea," I always find myself thinking, as I keep transferring that task from one to-do list to another.

Another way human beings historically have dealt intellectually with the certainty of their eventual demise is to claim that our knowledge that we will die is a distinctively human insight and curse. One example, among many, of that assumption is a statement that my friend George Atwood is fond of making, attributing it to Pascal: "Man is the most magnificent creature in the universe because he is the only one who perceives his own wretched destiny to be extinguished." Such beliefs offer the consoling conceit of human exceptionalism. Our species has a long history of trying to find "*the* way" in which we differ qualitatively from other animals – it seems to be important to our species narcissism to protest our uniqueness. Many qualitative differences have been suggested – use of tools, use of language, use of symbols, capacity for abstraction, theory of mind – all of which have been eventually shown to be differences of degree, not differences of kind, from at least some other creatures. Are we the only ones who have a concept of death, of the inevitability that we all die? I doubt it. Elephants clearly grieve, and crows take turns sitting with a mortally ill bird in their flock until the bitter end. We will have to look for other consolations.

Aging

Putting aside temporarily an explicit focus on dying, what about the aging process? It may begin at birth, but it certainly becomes harder to ignore at my time of life. The physical decline is a nuisance, but it is the mental part I find most distressing. I somehow never expected not to be able to depend on my own mind. I could not have imagined this loss at a younger age – my mind is "me" and feels ongoing. For me, it is names that I can't always depend on surfacing, nor can I count on retrieving nouns in general. I have "senior moments." I lose my watch, my glasses, my car keys. I forget whether I have turned down the heat or sent a thank-you note. I can't recall why I came upstairs. I have to ask my students if I've already told them a favorite story or joke. When I see at this meeting people I've known and liked for years, their names sometimes make a terrifying pause before percolating from my underground storage tank to my tongue (thank God for nametags). Only a young Freud could have ascribed all forgetting to unconscious conflict.

I used to remember the patient that a supervisee presented a week or two ago, but now I have to ask for a nutshell recap before the descriptors of the client kick in and activate the constellation of knowledge, images, and associations that were starting to make sense in my mind of his or her suffering and how it was appearing in the intersubjective space of therapist and patient. I wonder how many years I have before these small, accumulating deficits become a qualitative detriment in my capacity to do effective psychotherapy, teaching, and supervising. (Already I try not to schedule patients at 3:00 p.m. because I need a nap.) And yet at the same time, I see ongoing evidence of the usefulness of my knowledge base to the people with whom I consult.

I am reminded of a supervisor I had in the mid-seventies who was disturbed by a colleague's mental deterioration, probably from Alzheimer's, and alarmed by her insistence on continuing to practice. He entreated his students to let him know when he should be put out to pasture. We felt dismayed by that request; we idealized him and couldn't envision him as mentally deteriorating. But we learned something valuable in his anticipating both an eventual loss of function and his probable loss of judgment about its most painful implications. He is still practicing, by the way, at 90, and like many analysts we have all known, is still able to make brilliant, intuitive, therapeutic connections despite whatever mental limitations he is managing.

The idea that wisdom is somehow the consolation prize for getting older, and that it compensates for the less benevolent effects of aging, is not entirely a wishful fantasy; neuroscientists are beginning to describe for us in biological and chemical terms the specifics of that trade-off. We are unusually fortunate in our field in that, unlike most professions in a rapidly changing global technological culture, analysts are generally considered by their colleagues to be more rather than less useful as they get older. And, on average, analysts (at least male analysts – females have not been studied) live longer than other people, including other professionals (Jeffrey 2001). Not all loss of function equates with total loss, and some loss may even leave room for newer capacities. And yet I think we should be talking together about late-in-life practice issues such as whether and when and for what reasons to retire, or cut down, or continue working with minor adaptations to our infirmities – all individual decisions with individual plusses and minuses that nevertheless can profit from some communal attention.

Limitation is an old emphasis for psychoanalysts, going back at least to Freud's framing of maturation in terms of giving up the pleasure principle for the reality principle, the ultimate prototype of which is the reality of death. His attention to limits is consistent with a temperate, cautious, mature European intellectual perspective very much at odds with more adolescent American sensibilities that can include, as we have seen all too clearly in the current election season, a sense of exceptionalism, invincibility, and baseless optimism about how everything will come out okay if only we apply a can-do attitude.

As George Makari (2015) is only the most recent scholar to argue, the United States was founded on a radical Lockean metapsychology that assumed unlimited resources, boundless potentials, the inevitability of progress, and a confidence that all problems can be solved with common sense and individual ingenuity (and, one might add, with denial about the genocides necessary to support that mythology). We Americans burden our children with the psychotically omnipotent message that they can be anything they want to be, can accomplish anything they set their minds to do – a setup for depression when the reality of one's limits becomes clear.

Another way of depicting our cultural surround, and noting the divergence of psychoanalysis from the mainstream, is that most Americans subscribe to a version of the comic rather than the tragic vision of human life, the pursuit of happiness rather than the coming to terms with inevitable pain. Many of you know Messer and Winokur's (1984) helpful distinction in comic-versus-tragic terms between the mindset of psychologists from the American behavioral tradition, on the one hand, and that of European-influenced psychoanalytic thinkers, on the other. In the comic narrative, limits are challenged and overcome, complex difficulties resolve themselves in the end, and people live happily ever after. Give us a symptom, and we'll apply a technique that will fix it. Problem solved. Steven Reisner (2016) has memorably called this phenomenon the "commodification of the symptom" and noted how it obliterates the possibility of seeing any larger meanings in suffering. Not exactly the vision of the ancient Greeks, who venerated the constraints of time, fate, and acts of the gods, and ascribed the most painful life outcomes to hubris, the human tendency to deny limitation. Temperamentally, most analysts are skeptical about comic visions and prefer either the tragic sensibility, or, as Frank Summers (2011) has articulated, the romantic view, which has also emphasized limitation.

All of this is intimately connected with our cultural attitudes about mortality. If we have scant shared language for our essential limitation, and we also surround dying and death with practices that embody various versions of denial (as Jessica Mitford [1963] and many others since have noted), there is not much room for appreciating what our limitedness might *offer* us psychologically, or what space the ultimate closing off of life might open up. It occurs to me that part of our problem is that we have no lived experience of a contrast class or "control group" to mortality. We have no emotional sense of what we would be in a world in which we lived forever. But I suspect that James Grotstein (quoted in K. Gentile 2016) was right in speaking of the "agonizing sense of the infinite." Immortality just might be unbearable. And we do occasionally get a glimpse of the idea of death as deliverance. When one gets sufficiently old, or tired, or in pain, death may be greeted as a blessing. I am told that when the playwright Arthur Miller was asked, in his advanced years, if he would like to live forever, he replied in the negative, saying that eternity would give him "nothing by which to measure my life."

The individualistic ethos that pervades American mythology is a problem for our relationship to mortality. In cultures whose members venerate ancestors, or keep the tribe's oral traditions alive generation after generation, or have more geographical stability than our restless, rootless civilization, there is presumably some sense of the continuity of the larger human group when particular selves exit the scene. In contrast, in a society that organizes its politics according to individual rights and offers little language about communal obligations, much less about sacrificing for the common good, people tend to think of themselves as isolated, entitled units. The prospect of death is consequently the loss of everything valuable.

The consumerism that has dominated American economic life since the middle of the twentieth century has exploited our tendency to think in terms of unlimited gratifications. Public discourse is replete with the implication that getting what one wants –what one is "entitled to," what one "deserves" – equates with life satisfaction. This appeal to our allegedly insatiable drive and limitless narcissism, which is especially striking in commercial ads and other efforts to get us to buy things, has been fed by both behaviorist assumptions and psychoanalytic ones. John Watson (1930), after losing his academic position at Johns Hopkins because of a personal scandal, became an executive in the J. Walter Thompson ad agency, where he participated enthusiastically in efforts to shape the preferences of the American consumer via conditioning. Freud's nephew Edward Bernays (1928), often called the Father of Public Relations, was the original advocate of selling products via their implicit promise of more and better sex. As a contrast with this American consumerist pathology, consider the Japanese adage that true happiness is not getting what you want, but coming to want what you have – not a naturally resonant observation to most Westerners, but not an unfamiliar concept to most analysts, given what we witness again and again in our offices.

Implications for Psychoanalytic Professionals

How do these musings bear on our functioning as psychoanalytic therapists, supervisors, consultants, scientists, teachers? Although many contemporary researchers in psychotherapy define progress in terms of measurable behavioral changes, analytic therapists are distinctively interested in helping people to accept what *cannot* be changed. While the American positive psychology movement puts most of its emphasis on attaining happiness, psychoanalysts believe that a critical element of psychological health is the capacity to bear suffering. Freud was not joking when he defined psychoanalytic healing as the replacement of neurotic misery with ordinary human unhappiness. Surrender to what is larger than we are is, as Emmanuel Ghent (1990) elegantly elaborated, a necessity of human life that is not entirely devoid of satisfaction.

This appreciation runs across all the major psychoanalytic orientations, from Freud's recurrent reminders that our mortality stimulates our creativity, through Kernberg's work (2008) on how the healing of disabling narcissistic pathology involves the acceptance of death and the finiteness of time, through Lacan's (1989) concept of the "name" or "no" of the father (punning "*nom*" and "*non*"), to the concept of the "third" that interferes with the doer-done to polarity and opens a transformative space (Benjamin 2004), to Lichtenberg's and Wolf's (1997) self-psychology manifesto, whose first principle connects a strengthened sense of self, the development of creativity, and the acceptance of mortality. Carlo Strenger's (2009) writing on mid-life similarly relates creativity to the acceptance of death and limit. So does Spyros Orfanos's (2006) exploration of the Prometheus myth. And Leanh Nguyen's (2007) reflections on victims of trauma and torture who have obliterated mortality and the creativity that goes with it. We find this sensibility in collected writings of diverse psychodynamic authors, such as in the 2007 book edited by Brent Willock, Lori Bohm, and Rebecca Curtis, *On Death and Endings*.

Analytic therapists understand the process of accepting what cannot be changed as involving the creation of a relationship in which we can name our desires, rage about the gratifications we may have deserved but did not get, and go through a grief process that culminates in moving on to satisfactions that *are* possible – rather than staying frozen in either resentment or chronic victimhood. When our patients respond to adversity with the complaint "Why me?," we may be sympathetic, but we also tend to convey "Why *not* you? Bad things happen to us all." Freud (1917) is the first writer I know of who framed mourning as "work" – to my mind one of his most brilliant insights. The "mourning labor" is a kind of toil that we both resist and seek out when we engage in the process he called "working through."

Martha Stark (1994) and others have gone so far as to say that psychoanalytic therapy itself is an extended process of grieving. In an earlier era, Hendrik Ruitenbeek (1983) talked about the task in analysis of mourning one's own eventual death – bringing that issue out of the unconscious where he believed it blocks one's emotional maturity. We therapists may foster acceptance of limitation in trivial ways, such as via off-hand comments to patients like, "Yes, I suspect your husband is never going be very good at picking up after himself" and also in dramatically consequential ways, such as the frank admission to a multiply traumatized man that although he can look toward having a good-enough life, he will never again be the self he was before the disasters.

And we now seem to agree that, in contrast to beliefs suffused with the comic mentality to the effect that mourning is "resolved," or that people facing loss come to "closure," mourning never ends. Peter Shabad (2001) has made this point, as has Marilyn McCabe (2003) and many other analytic writers. Unless we stay persistently in the paranoid-schizoid position, sadness about limits stalks every developmental accomplishment. Instead of coming to an eventual halt, mourning becomes the background of the capacities for gratitude, empathy, and generativity. Rupture generates possible repair.

Creativity and Generativity

The great spiritual and religious wisdom traditions have emphasized the gains that come out of loss, the appreciation for what *is* that results from the mourning of what *is not*, the serenity that comes with not striving after what *cannot be*, and the ways that creative phoenixes can arise from the ashes of devastation. Acceptance of limitation, via the grief process, seems to be the best cure we have for narcissistic fantasies of omnipotence and boundlessness. We are probably doing even our most talented children no favors when we emphasize their unlimited potential. Limitlessness is too vast a frame for structuring a meaningful life.

In very practical clinical ways, disappointment can benefit people. This is not an easy lesson to learn for those of us with big hearts who hate to disappoint our patients. As I grew as a therapist, I had to learn to get comfortable with confronting patients with limits and tolerating their rage and grief. Initially, I tended to see neurotically unhappy or traumatized people more as hungry children needing to be adequately fed than as angry, aggressive ones needing to react to realistic limitations with pained protest that had to be accepted and even embraced – especially when I was the target of their enraged protestations.

Parenthood helped me with what the CBT therapists call a "cognitive reframe." For example, when one daughter was about seven, I told her she'd have to clean up her room by the end of the day. She flounced angrily out of the house into the backyard, yelling that she hated me. I called after her, "You can hate me, but you still have to clean up your room." She came back to the kitchen door, stuck her head in, and announced, "And what's more, I've *never* liked you!" And slammed the door behind her. But she did clean up her room. More importantly, she seemed to feel a new pride in how she decided to organize her belongings.

I was also helped in my maturation toward more comfort in setting realistic limits by psychoanalytic writing, perhaps especially Winnicott's (1968) idea that young children need to "destroy" the mother and then to absorb emotionally the fact that she survives their destructiveness – one of his most vivid depictions of the relationship between limits and maturation. The growth that comes with giving up the fantasy that one can have everything, including mutually exclusive things, is precious.

Michael Balint (1979) believed that the area of creation is essentially object-less, and hence, because it cannot be studied in the context of the transference is more mysterious than either the oedipal area or the area of the basic fault, which presents themselves directly in the clinical interpersonal space. I agree about the mystery, but I'm not sure that Balint was right about that objectlessness. If my own sojourns in the area of creation are typical, they involve a clear, ongoing relationship with an internalized object, my idealized dead mother, whose "mission" I am carrying on, a process characteristic of normal mourning described in depth by Otto Kernberg (2010) in a touching paper written after the death of his wife Paulina. The limit of death created a space for something reparative and ongoing.

There are empirical grounds as well for inferring a connection between early experiences of the reality of death and later creative activity. My former student Annalisa Erba, who wrote her doctoral dissertation (2003) on the relationship between childhood parental loss and creative activity, discovered an *American Psychologist* article (Eisenstadt 1978) and a later coauthored book (Eisenstadt, Haynal, Rentchnick, and De Senarclens 1989), in which J. M. Eisenstadt reviewed massive evidence that childhood bereavement correlates with creativity in the older years. In this context, by the way, I recommend also the book by Phyllis Cohen, Mark Sossin, and Richard Ruth (2014): *Healing after Parent Loss in Childhood.*

In losing a major love object at any age, survival guilt kicks in, and one carries on, on behalf of the dead person as well as the self. Undoing guilt is certainly part of why bereavement can foster vital activity. If a child believes that his or her hostile fantasies have somehow killed a love object, there would be some need to atone by compensatory good deeds. This effort at atonement is perhaps especially true when there is realistic as well as unconscious omnipotent, neurotic guilt. Adlai

Stevenson was once prevailed upon to comfort a boy who had accidentally shot and killed a young friend. He had been asked to do so because he had had a similar experience: Stevenson, at the age of 12, accidentally shot and killed a 16-year-old friend of his sister at a party at his home with a gun that was thought not to be loaded. His comment to the mother of a boy with a similar story was to tell her devastated son, "He must live for two" (McKeever 1991).

And there is also the simple fact that without a living parent, one has to sort of "make it up" – a very practical kind of creativity necessitated by the absence of a model for one's life. My own generation, now living, on average, an unprecedentedly long and healthy life, finds itself having to "make it up" in a comparable way. There are enough of us charting this new territory of health and vitality beyond 70 that we may find we have something to say about what the good life looks like in the advanced years.

But I think that the largest contributor to the creative mobilization of resources in response to loss and limit is the indelible lesson that life is capricious, that anything can happen to anybody at any age. Live now, for tomorrow, quite literally, you may die. Death of beloved friends and relatives may cause some survivors to feel that life is meaningless – we often see such depressed people in treatment – and yet it seems to impel others to conclude that one had better live fully in the truncated time one has. And when we can work with the more deadened survivors of what feels to them like unbearable loss, the mourning process may restore them to vitality.

In a similar phenomenon, individuals diagnosed with terminal illnesses often say that they now enjoy life with a heightened sense of its preciousness. Or they have a burst of creativity like the one we recently witnessed from David Bowie. Eric Fair, the NSA intelligence officer who just published a searing memoir, *Consequence* (2016), about his involvement with torture in Iraq, has a serious heart problem from which he almost died, and a consequent heart transplant that extended his life but probably at most for a couple of decades. The looming sense that "the clock is ticking" created in him a deep urgency to get his book done in the time he had.

One wonders what have been the complex psychological consequences for people in our era of, for the first time in human history, not living in a world with high mortality for women bearing children, or with the predictable loss of offspring to childhood illness, or with the much shorter lifespans of the pre-penicillin generation. One consequence is a sense of relief and safety, but is there also possibly more ennui, sense of existential despair, and lack of a sense of urgency to live life to the fullest? None of us would likely trade our long average lifespan for the mortality rates of a previous era, and yet few changes are entirely without some loss.

Most of us have treated patients who may not have obviously suffered in crippling ways but who get stuck psychologically and seem to feel an odd absence of pressure to get on with their lives. They may passively wait for us to tell them how to do so, or spend their sessions complaining about the unfairness of life, or get lost in questions of "What if?" rather than "What *is*, and what options are possible, given that reality?" They wait for something external to change. They destroy time. They drag on in therapies that sap both parties of their vitality, in the hope that the gratifications they should have had at a younger age will spontane-ously come about in treatment, and they experience us as hostile, depriving, and/or incompetent when we tactfully suggest that this is not going to happen. Despite the fact that time may be the only nonrenewable resource we have, they seem to have no sense of time as passing.

Until such clients get some kind of wake-up call – until they "bottom out" in some way, or suffer an unexpected illness, or become inspired by a different narra-tive from the standard American version of getting and spending as salvation – they seem to be very hard to help. In contrast, some patients with calamitous histories and disabling limitations can use therapy in the service of remarkable progress in adapting to their considerable challenges. Our depressed patients often say to us, "What does it matter? We're all going to die anyway." And yet it may be precisely the fact that we are all here on borrowed time that gives our lives meaning.

Implications for the Division of Psychoanalysis

The modal age of members of Division 39 is, as we have noted with worry at several Board meetings, continuing to increase. As in many areas, the population bulge of post-World War II babies has dominated our era; those who follow are less numerous and also less inclined to fall in line with various boomer initiatives. In the past decade, we in the immediate post-war cohort have lost many of our cherished elders, both members of the Division and other seminal analysts, including, among others: Ann Appelbaum, Martin Bergmann, Sidney Blatt, Hedda Bolgar, Norbert Freedman, James Grotstein, Harold Searles, Gerald Steckler, Hans Strupp, Johanna Tabin, Robert Wallerstein, and Elisabeth Young-Breuhl. Not to mention that poster-child for the value of long-term treatment (as in, 50 years in psychoanalysis, with a brilliant career and graceful life well lived to show for it), Oliver Sacks (2015). To my knowledge, there is no one left who knew Freud as a real person, at least as an adult. A big piece of the lived history of psychoanalysis has become the ghost that we now need to turn into an ancestor.

In 2000, when Stephen Mitchell was suddenly taken from us, we tended to see it as a freakish calamity. He was only 54, my age also at the time. Now, mortality seems a lot less jarring. The generation of analysts with whom I identify is starting to face the ultimate limitation. Muriel Dimen left us this year. Several notable colleagues are coping with severe chronic and/or terminal illnesses. At a recent dinner party of seven analysts, we realized that only one of us had not had cancer. My close friend and age-mate Sandra Bem, in her later years a psychodynamic therapist, systematically pursued and carried out a suicide two years ago rather than "stop being Sandy" when her Alzheimer's was beginning to destroying her sense of self-continuity.

It is a time-honored task for elders to try to pass on their wisdom to their successors. I find myself thinking about what my own cohort of analysts in this Division has contributed, and about the ways in which we are now generative, in that newer way of fostering the capacities of the next generation. Many of our own accomplishments began in a context of limitation: As psychologist–analysts, we were originally not acceptable to the reigning powers in organized psychoanalysis. Instead of licking our wounds, we founded our own creative spaces, and ultimately, we opened psychoanalysis up beyond an insular, self-reinforcing medical community.

In addition, Division 39 was the original home of what became the "relational turn." Our members normalized countertransference, called for a new appreciation of the intersubjective, democratized the tone of analytic treatment, and attested to the inevitability of enactment. They challenged the pathologizing of sexual differences and opened up new ways of thinking about gender, desire, and sexuality. They critiqued the logical positivist bias of academic psychology and looked at psychoanalysis from new angles of vision: phenomenology, hermeneutics, postmodernism, fallibilism, constructivism, general systems theory, field theory, neuroscience, and numerous philosophical perspectives. They rejected a metapsychology that excludes the arts, literature, and humanities from the legitimate sources of our knowledge and practice.

Even by a narrow definition of science, we have accomplished a lot. Psychoanalytically impelled investigations into attachment have had a significant impact on academic thinking about both development and psychotherapy and ultimately on our general cultural understanding of what young children need. We have created, tested, and improved short-term psychodynamic models of treatment, and we are empirically testing long-term models of therapy for personality disorders. And it has been preponderantly our members who have relentlessly attacked organized Psychology's latest descent into the narcissistic attractions of colluding with the powerful at the expense of the weak. We have insisted that APA acknowledge crimes committed in the name of psychology, and we continue to try to hold their feet to the fire.

We have kept alive the moral vision of analysts who have insisted that psychotic patients deserve sensitive therapy, not just medication for their "chemical imbalance." We have developed services for the poor, the disenfranchised, the addicted, the homeless, trauma survivors, veterans and their families, those in foster care. We have integrated Buddhism and other Eastern disciplines with Western psychoanalysis. Although we have a long way to go in this area, our meetings look a lot more diverse than those of most other psychoanalytic bodies, or, for that matter, of our Division at its inception, which was overwhelmingly dominated by white, putatively heterosexual, older, urban, Jewish males.

All of the above notwithstanding, it is only fair, I think, to cop to some ways in which we have failed the next generation. We have not sufficiently preserved a psychoanalytic presence in academia, agency practice, counseling centers, hospitals, accrediting procedures, and the differentiation of professional ethics from risk management, as Stephen Soldz (2016) has eloquently noted. We have been blind to many dimensions of majority privilege. We have preferred to talk to one another and to fight with one another, over talking to the wider world and fighting for the value of an overall psychoanalytic sensibility. We have sometimes behaved with the smugness about our superiority as psychologists that we used to resent when psychiatrists treated us with similar arrogance. Boomer narcissism has been indulged and fed for decades by companies trying to sell us things, from records in the 1950s to Botox more recently. We like to see *ourselves* as the creative generation – after all, we're the ones who "invented" sex, drugs, and rock 'n roll. People who see themselves as perpetually young may pay insufficient attention to the needs of those who follow.

It is my fervent hope, though, that despite our failings, my generation has passed on to the next era of psychoanalytic psychologists the fire in the belly that ignited all the areas of creativity of which we can be legitimately proud. Analysts have been legitimately accused of being highly individualistic, like the culture in which we have grown up. But we are *also* part of a community, a set of social links, a historical movement, and from that larger perspective, not everything about us dies when we die as individuals. Let me don the mantle of my own psychoanalytic era for a final moment and address those who are coming of age in this weird profession where it takes forever to be an elder – or sometimes even to be seen as a grown-up – but where the individual and communal satisfactions of becoming experienced and seasoned are far from insignificant.

Your younger colleagues face a tougher professional world than we did at your professional age. You will have different fights from the battles of which we are veterans. And you "get" things about the contemporary world that we do not. Don't wait to start working creatively on the basis of your knowledge and your own psychoanalytic experience. Launch peer supervision groups, study groups, new sections of the Division, and new political efforts. And please write. You don't have to have mastered the whole vast psychoanalytic canon before contributing to it. How psychoanalysis looks 40 years from now will doubtless be a lot different from how it looks now, but its core focus on the power of unconscious processes and its viscerally shared sense of limitation and relational good-enough-ness can provide the basis for numerous new and vital metaphors and integrations. That is all you have to have to begin a journey whose end will be unknown but certain, and whose paths can be inspiring beyond our limited imagination

Note

1 This chapter is based on a talk given at the 2016 Spring Meeting of Division 39 of the APA, later published in *Psychoanalytic Psychology* (2017).

References

Balint, Michael. 1979. *The Basic Fault: Therapeutic Aspects of Regression*. London: Tavistock.

Becker, Ernest.1973. *The Denial of Death*. New York: The Free Press.

Benjamin, Jessica. 2004. "Beyond Doer and Done to: An Intersubjective View of Thirdness." *Psychoanalytic Quarterly* 73: 5–46.

Bernays, Edward. 1928. *Propaganda*. New York: H. Liveright.

Cohen, Phyllis, Mark Sossin, and Richard Ruth. 2014. *Healing After Parent Loss in Childhood: Therapeutic Implications and Theoretical Considerations.* Lanham, MD: Rowman & Littlefield.

Eisenstadt, Marvin J. 1978. "Parental Loss and Genius." *American Psychologist* 33, no. 3: 211–223.

Eisenstadt, Marvin J., André Haynal, Pierre Rentchnick, and Pierre De Senarclens. 1989. *Parental Loss and Achievement.* Madison, CT: International Universities Press.

Erba, Annalisa. 2003. *Paradise lost: Potential long-term sequelae of early maternal death in two exceptionally creative people in history.* Unpublished doctoral dissertation, Rutgers University Graduate School of Applied & Professional Psychology.

Erikson, Erik. 1950. *Childhood and Society.* New York: Norton.

Erikson, Erik and Joan Erikson. 1997. *The Life Cycle Completed: Extended Version with New Chapters on the Ninth Stage of Development.* New York: Norton.

Fair, Eric. 2016. *Consequence: A Memoir.* New York: Henry Holt & Co.

Freud, Sigmund. 1917. "Mourning and Melancholia." *Standard Edition of the Complete Works of Sigmund Freud* 14: 243–258.

Gentile, Katie. 2016. "Generating Subjectivity Through the Creation of Time." *Psychoanalytic Psychology* 33, no. 2: 264–283.

Ghent, Emmanuel. 1990. "Masochism, Submission, Surrender – Masochism as a Perversion of Surrender." *Contemporary Psychoanalysis* 26, no. 1: 108–136.

Jeffrey, Edward H. 2001. "The Mortality of Psychoanalysts." *Journal of the American Psychoanalytic Association* 49, no. 1 (2001): 103–111.

Kernberg, Otto F. 2008. "The Destruction of Time in Pathological Narcissism." *International Journal of Psycho-Analysis* 89, no. 32: 299–312.

Kernberg, Otto F. 2010. "Some Observations on the Process of Mourning." *International Journal of Psycho-analysis* 91, no. 3: 601–619.

Lacan, Jacques. 1989. *Ecrits.* London: Routledge.

Lichtenberg, Joseph D. and Ernest Wolf. 1997. "General Principles of Self Psychology: A Position Statement." *Journal of the American Psychoanalytic Association* 45, no. 2: 531–543.

Makari, George. 2015. *Soul Machine: The Invention of the Modern Mind.* New York: Norton.

McCabe, Marilyn. 2003. *The Paradox of Loss: Toward a Relational Theory of Grief.* Santa Barbara, CA: Praeger.

McKeever, Porter. 1991. *Adlai Stevenson: His Life and Legacy.* Columbus, GA: Quill (Harper).

Messer, Stanley B. and Meir Winokur. 1984. "Ways of Knowing and Visions of Reality in Psychoanalytic Theory and Behavior Therapy." In *Psychoanalytic Therapy and Behavior Therapy: Is Integration Possible?*, edited by Hal Arkowitz and Stanley P. Messer, 63–100. New York: Plenum Press.

Mitford, Jessica. *The American Way of Death.* New York: Simon and Schuster, 1963.

Nguyen, Leanh. 2007. "The Question of Survival: The Death of Desire and the Weight of Life." *American Journal of Psychoanalysis* 67, no. 1: 53–67.

Orfanos, Spyros. 2006. "Mythos and Logos." *Psychoanalytic Dialogues* 16, no. 4: 481–499.

PDM Task Force. 2006. *Psychodynamic Diagnostic Manual.* Silver Spring, MD: Alliance of Psychoanalytic Organizations, 2006.

Pizer, Barbara. 1997. "When the Analyst is Ill: Dimensions of Self-disclosure." *Psychoanalytic Quarterly* 66, no. 3: 450–469.

Reisner, Steven. 2016. "How the APA Became the Sorcerer's Apprentice." Unpublished panel talk: Spring meeting, Division of Psychoanalysis (39), APA, Atlanta, GA.

Ruitenbeek, Hendrik M. (Ed.). 1983. *The Interpretation of Death*. New York: Jason Aronson.

Sacks, Oliver. 2015. *On the Move: A Life*. New York: Vintage.

Shabad, Peter. 2001. *Despair and the Return of Hope: Echoes of Mourning in Psychother-apy*. Northvale, NJ: Jason Aronson.

Soldz, Stephen. 2016. "How the APA Became the Sorcerer's Apprentice." Unpublished panel talk, Spring meeting, Division of Psychoanalysis (39), APA, Atlanta, GA.

Spira, Marcia and Barbara Berger. 2001. "The Penultimate: Understanding Women Beyond Menopause." *Psychoanalytic Social Work* 8, no. 1: 27–42.

Stark, Martha. 1994. *Working with Resistance*. Northvale, NJ: Jason Aronson.

Strenger, Carlo. 2009. "Paring Down Life to the Essentials: An Epicurean Psychoanalysis of Midlife Change." *Psychoanalytic Psychology* 26, no. 3: 246–258.

Summers, Frank. 2011. "Psychoanalysis: Romantic, Not Wild." *Psychoanalytic Psychology* 28, no. 1: 13–32.

Van Raalte, Peggy. 1984. "The impact of death of the psychoanalyst on the patient: Theoretical considerations and clinical implications." Unpublished doctoral dissertation, Rutgers Graduate School of Applied & Professional Psychology.

Watson, John. 1930. *Behaviorism*. New York: Norton.

Willock, Brent, Bohm, Lori C. and Curtis, Rebecca C. 2007. *On Death and Endings: Psychoanalysts' Reflections on Finality, Transformations and New Beginnings*, edited by Brent Willock, Lori C. Brohm, and Rebecca Curtis. London: Routledge.

Winnicott, D. W. 1968. "The Use of an Object and Relating Through Cross Identifications." In *Playing and Reality*, 86–94. New York: Basic Books.

Chapter 12

Afterword

Nancy McWilliams

I was invited to be an Erikson Scholar at the Austen Riggs Center because of my work in individual differences and their relevance to psychotherapy – a concern central to the hospital's mission. The invitation was irresistible. In 50 years of practice, I have watched meaningful, effective psychotherapy driven to near extinction by the interests of insurance companies, Big Pharma, and academics with scant clinical experience. In addition to seeing Riggs as a precious and endangered species, a caring epicenter for serious treatment of seriously suffering people, I love its location. I grew up in Western Massachusetts; every summer from age 9 to 18, as my family suffered painful losses and dislocations, I found continuity at a Girl Scout camp in East Otis. I feel at home in the Berkshires.

At Oberlin College, I fell in love with psychoanalytic thinking and studied Erik Erikson's work. Later, as a psychologist, I attended conferences at Riggs, initially when Erikson was still participating in them. The prospect of spending a summer in beautiful Stockbridge, among like-minded therapists, with access to an extensive psychoanalytic library, was my idea of heaven. The community welcomed me and my husband, Michael Garrett, a psychoanalyst with extensive experience in public psychiatry. The Erikson Scholarship struck me as a brilliant way to keep nourishing an unusually stable professional community with new input, while simultaneously, in a world of increasingly siloed disciplines, maintaining psychoanalytic connections with developments in the arts, humanities, social sciences, and natural sciences.

What I most value about Austen Riggs is its commitment to understanding and empowering each patient. To me, the archetypal expression of that commitment is the individual case presentation, scheduled when a patient has been there for six weeks. After receiving extensive written documents, staff members gather for a two-hour meeting. The first 30 minutes involve reports: from nurses and others with daily patient contact, from a social worker summarizing family dynamics, from the medicating psychiatrist, from psychological assessors. In the second half hour, the patient's therapist describes the course of individual treatment, often requesting help with particular challenges. In the next half hour, the patient is invited in, interviewed respectfully, and asked about reactions, concerns, needs, criticisms. In the final half hour, participants pool their knowledge, trying to reach

DOI: 10.4324/9781003322627-27

a shared therapeutic perspective. At the first such meeting my husband attended, he teared up, exclaiming, "Do you know what most case conferences are like in most hospitals? *This is the third admission for this 57-year-old woman who stopped taking her medication. Plan: encourage medication compliance.*"

I spent June through August of 2016 working on two projects: the revised edition of the *Psychodynamic Dynamic Manual (PDM-2)* (Lingiardi & McWilliams, 2017), on which I was doing final edits, and a book on overall mental health that I was intending for a general audience. The former compiles for practitioners an accessible knowledge base of psychoanalytic clinical experience and research – information that is much more relevant to their work than the DSM's "disorder" categories. It has been published and is now in translation in several languages. The latter project eventually underwent a major overhaul; I integrated that material into a book on psychoanalytic supervision (Guilford Press, 2021) that was much influenced by the kinds of clinical consultation I witnessed at Riggs.

While there, I participated in hospital events as fully as I could while preserving valuable writing time. I gave a talk to patients on the history and problems of psychiatric diagnosis, co-taught with my husband a seminar on paranoia, and conferred with staff members on their patients or research projects. Just having lunch with the remarkable employees of the Center – whether newer Fellows or seasoned old-timers – was stimulating.

I eventually explored the possibility of joining the Austen Riggs Board of Trustees, which has welcomed me, and where I have enjoyed maintaining my connection with the Center and the Erikson Institute. Although Riggs is hardly immune to the kinds of stresses and problems that beset any organization composed of human beings, my new insider knowledge has only strengthened my admiration for the community's determination to live by its core values. My husband feels similarly. Following up on initiatives from our summer there, he funded Riggs's 2021 fall conference and continues to collaborate with Jeremy Ridenour, Associate Director of Admissions, on a Riggs-based program to train front-line clinicians throughout the world in psychotherapy for psychosis. I attend as many of the Erikson Institute's webinars as I can; they nourish my interdisciplinary interests. In these ways and others, my summer as an Erikson Scholar keeps on giving.

Index

Note: Page numbers followed by "n" denote endnotes.

For Product Safety Concerns and Information please contact our EU
representative GPSR@taylorandfrancis.com
Taylor & Francis Verlag GmbH, Kaufingerstraße 24, 80331 München, Germany

www.ingramcontent.com/pod-product-compliance
Lightning Source LLC
Chambersburg PA
CBHW050635280326
41932CB00015B/2655

*9 7 8 1 0 3 2 3 4 5 2 8 4 *